D1480954

THE ABDICATION OF PHILOSOPHY:

PHILOSOPHY AND THE PUBLIC GOOD

Open Court Publishing Company
The Publishers of

The Library of Living Philosophers
The Carus Lectures
The Monist
The Monist Library of Philosophy
The Open Court Paperbacks in Philosophy

ESSAYS IN HONOR OF
PAUL ARTHUR SCHILPP

THE ABDICATION
OF PHILOSOPHY:

PHILOSOPHY
AND THE PUBLIC GOOD

EDITED BY EUGENE FREEMAN

OPEN COURT LA SALLE, ILLINOIS

THE ABDICATION OF PHILOSOPHY:
PHILOSOPHY AND THE PUBLIC GOOD

© 1976 by Open Court Publishing Company
FIRST EDITION

Library of Congress Cataloging in Publication Data

Main entry under title:

The Abdication of philosophy.

Essays in honor of Paul Arthur Schilpp.
CONTENTS: Olds, G.A. Introduction: the good man and the good.—Russell, B. The duty of a philosopher in this age.—Popper, K. The myth of the framework; etc.—Bibliography (p.
1. Philosophy—Addresses, essays, lectures. 2. Schilpp, Paul Arthur, 1897-   I. Freeman, Eugene, 1906-   ed. II. Schilpp, Paul Arthur, 1897-
B29.A17   100   72-93357
ISBN 0-87548-274-0

CONTENTS

PREFACE

Philosophers are famous as sharpeners of the tools of the intellect. Sometimes they sharpen tools for others, and sometimes it is their own tools that they sharpen. And some philosophers become so fascinated with sharpening tools that they act out Santayana's definition of fanaticism by continuing to sharpen them with redoubled effort long after they have forgotten why they were doing what they were doing. But as Paul Arthur Schilpp pointed out in 1959, in his memorable presidential address entitled "The Abdication of Philosophy," philosophers have a responsibility which they cannot abdicate, to stop merely sharpening their tools and start using them to solve the *human* problems which confront us at a time of world crisis.

And it is this challenge which unites and sets the theme for the essays of this volume—essays in which the sharpened tools of philosophic research are put to work. They are turned to problems that deal with the good for man, ranging from the awesome problem of survival in the face of the threat of atomic holocaust, to some of the particular practical and theoretical problems of the day which deal with the public good, such as conscience or compromise in political affairs; abortion; the laws of war; paternalism; our debt to future generations; justice and The Black Manifesto; etc. Many of our contributors are united by close personal ties to Schilpp, as colleagues, students, and friends, but some are tied to him only by their shared conviction that philosophy should be concerned with the public good. Thus in each case, the principle of selection of the essays in this volume has been primarily the relevance and importance of what the writer has had to say on our theme, whether or not he was bound by some personal tie to Schilpp.

Not all of those invited to contribute to this volume agreed with Schilpp that philosophers have a special competence or a special role in dealing with the practical problems confronting man at a time of world crisis. Bertrand Russell, for example, in the essay which he wrote for this volume, does not believe that a philosopher has any more responsibility or any more competence than any other plain man in coping with the problems of human crisis. Wayne Leys independently expresses the same view. And C. D. Broad, in response to the Editor's invitation to contribute an essay to this volume on the role of the philosopher in a time of crisis created by the threat of an atomic holocaust, replied that he did not think that he, or any other philosopher, had anything interesting or important to say on this subject. But since I think that his very disclaimer is itself an interesting and important contribution to our discussion, I quote his words in full from a letter he sent to me during the early days of the planning of the present volume:

From Professor C. D. Broad

Trinity College, Cambridge
March 13th., 1964

Mr. Eugene Freeman,
Editor of THE MONIST

Dear Mr. Freeman,

Schilpp Festschrift

Referring to our previous correspondence, and in particular to your letter of October 24th, and November 7th., 1963, I have recently been reflecting fairly carefully on the question whether Philosophy has or has not anything to contribute toward a satisfactory solution of the practical problems raised by the recent acquirement of means to release atomic energy on a possibly devastating scale.

The more I reflect on it the less do I find to say of the slightest interest or importance. It is not merely that *this particular philosopher* finds himself with no advice to offer except the platitude: 'Be particularly careful; don't lose your temper even under extreme provocation; and try never to put yourself or your opponents into positions from which they can't retire without too serious loss of face!' Most ordinary men are as well aware as I, in their cooler moments, that this is sensible advice; but, in moments of excitement, would be just as likely to ignore it whether I or a thousand other philosophers had or had not tendered it to them. I say that it is *not merely* my own inability to offer any sensible and non-platitudinous advice that deters me from writing on the topic. Still more depressing is the fact that I find myself with nothing of interest to say on the more general question whether 'Philosophy' (whatever that may mean in the present context) has or has not anything to contribute toward a satisfactory solution of these problems.

All that I can contribute here are the two platitudes: (1) It might not unreasonably be hoped that the special training and professional pursuits of a philosopher would help him to take a synoptic view of the relevant factors, and would help him to estimate dispassionately their relative importance. But he will have to rely mainly on experts in other subjects, e.g., physicists, biologists, psychologists, sociologists, anthropologists, etc., for detailed information about those factors. (2) On the other hand, it is most unlikely that the conclusions of any one philosopher, or of philosophers as a class (on the extremely unlikely hypothesis that they would be in substantial agreement in their conclusions) would have any appreciable influence on the individuals or the organizations which most directly influence the course of national and international events.

Since, after careful reflexion, I thus find myself with nothing of the slightest interest or importance to contribute, I must, with great regret, withdraw my offer (made in reply to your letter of October 24th., 1963) to contribute to the Festschrift. I do most sincerely apologize for thus letting you down, but *'ich kann nicht anders'*.

Yours very truly

C. D. Broad*

The *Schilpp Festschrift* has been many years in the making. During these years, its scope has broadened, as it became increasingly evident to the Editor that significantly fewer philosophers were abdicating their human responsibilities to wander fruitlessly in the labyrinths of analytic philosophy, in which too many philosophers have been lost for almost three decades. Instead, just as Schilpp and Bertrand Russell and Karl Popper and Brand Blanshard had been urging them to do, more and more philosophers were devoting their lives and their talents to the philosophical analysis of human problems, and were *using* their tools instead of just sharpening and resharpening them.

This volume of essays on *Philosophy and the Public Good* is testimony to the fact that the battle in which Schilpp was one of the earliest leaders is in the process of being won, and philosophy is now once again a human enterprise.

---

* By permission of the estate of C. D. Broad.

It is accordingly with regret for the long delays, but with deep personal satisfaction, that the Editor joins with the Contributors in dedicating this volume to his friend, Paul Arthur Schilpp.

Russell's essay, which was written, of course, expressly for this volume, is here published for the first time. Broad's letter to me, in which he succinctly states his views on the role of the philosopher in times of crisis, has also not been previously published.

It is also my sad duty to report the untimely deaths of two other contributors, Robert S. Hartman, who died in Mexico City on September 21, 1973, and Wayne A. R. Leys, who died in Carbondale, Illinois, on March 7, 1973.

EUGENE FREEMAN

SAN JOSE STATE UNIVERSITY

GLENN A. OLDS

INTRODUCTION: THE GOOD MAN AND THE GOOD

In June of 1963, it was my privilege as the president of Springfield College (Mass.) to present Paul Arthur Schilpp, former teacher, colleague, and friend of half a lifetime, for an honorary degree, in the following terms:

> Tireless teacher extraordinary, innovator of ideas, eternal seeker for Truth who speaks with fearless tongue and clear conscience, Socratic gadfly of classroom and community, you represent the best in the professor as an awakener and leader of youth and shaper of tomorrow. For nearly 40 years you have opened new frontiers in philosophy, religion, ethics, and international understanding. As founder, editor and president of the Library of Living Philosophers, you have brought new perceptions of the profound and perplexing problems of life to millions who seek understanding while the great are still alive to speak; as lecturer, you have delighted and disturbed, prodded and provoked countless students and colleagues to think and act in the largest sense of the distinctly human. Through your writing, teaching and lecturing, you have made philosophy speak a relevant word to the vital issues of our time. Courageous advocate of the conditions that make for peace, the rational and moral links that bind man to man, you have exposed the folly of naked power, the violence of unenlightened self-interest, the peril of ignorance and indolence, and charted in contrast the open adventure of a liberated and dedicated human spirit.

> In honor of your years of distinguished service as University Professor, minister, and friend of youth, in recognition of your scholarly contributions, in appreciation of your unfailing sense of Justice, Dignity and Honor, the faculty and Trustees of Springfield College recommend you for the degree Doctor of Humane Letters, *honoris causa.*

It was poor prose to honor one so prophetic. It could only serve as a footnote to an extraordinary life. Yet it mirrored in miniature, snapshots of a "philosopher in action", at the cutting edge of history, multiplying in meaning and outreach, philosophy's distinctive role, as incisive and inclusive, personal and planetary, "to see life steadily and whole" in a deeply divided world. Indeed, the honor symbolized this deeper truth, that a good man wraps up in his person, critical clues to the good, its private and public nature, its form and fertility.

This circularity between the good man and the good, recognized by Aristotle, and most moral traditions of living cultures, East or West, provides the *apologia* for my brief remarks.

For, to know the man Paul Arthur Schilpp is to discern, however dimly, the profile of the good he seeks, of which he speaks, and the philosophy he *teaches, is,* and *does!* It is to capture the contagion of a catalytic spirit, a philosopher who "bakes bread", a midwife of the self, a herald of a more humane tomorrow.

Nor is this view narrowly personal and appreciative. It reflects critically, the nature of moral philosophy, its prophetic grasp of the inescapable integrity which links knowledge of the good and its nature, conception, and character, into a single, reciprocal whole. Professor Schilpp's insistence on the moral imperative of moral judgment, the rational relation between knowing and doing the good, is at the heart of the compelling sense of urgency of his teaching, the authenticity of the dialogue of his distinctive "Library of *Living* Philosophers", and the purchase on moral reform and social change of his public speaking and writing. The radical (getting at the root!) impact of his total life style roots in this inner connection of knowledge and virtue, wisdom and justice, that testifies to the answered prayer of Socrates in the Phaedrus, "Make the outer and the inner man fast friends". It is with Schilpp!

This wedding of intention, idea, and action in the life and work of Professor Schilpp makes both, at once, more transparent and more complex. It is a clue to his discerning eye for hypocrisy, his fearless fostering of intellectual honesty, his unrelenting quest for realism in thought and life, his passionate commitment to act on the best we know. It makes him impatient with procrastination, suspicious of diversions or abstractions, delighting in the innocence and surprise of moral discernment and development. It gives relevance and responsibility to his classroom, bite to his analyses, and brilliance to his grasp of a more humane public good in the architecture of the future.

His conviction that the nature of the good is in some sense natural to man and his world, rooted in the "nature of things", elemental and planetary, particular yet relevantly and relatively universal, bears witness to this inner life and logic, and is reflected in his earliest writings. It suggests his interest in Kant's precritical ethics, the choice of Dewey as the first of his living library, and the contemporary ring of all his writing. It lives in the bold note of affirmation, the robust confidence with which he addresses the human condition, and the manner in which his "examined life" is eminently worth living.

For Professor Schilpp, the good life is at once rational and human, responsibly free and ordered, lawful but not legalistic, sophisticated yet spontaneous, realistic yet ideal. Built into the universality of change is a dependable natural and human order, open to reason, amenable to action, susceptible to moral transformation. Always a realist, he sees neither nature nor God as sentimental. They play no favorites, offer no cosmic life insurance cheaply; make few exceptions. Though generous in spawning life, they are tough in testing it. And, the moral artistry of life, turns on discerning the direction and dimensions of the deeper moral and rational imperative at work in both the real and ideal world, mediated so fitfully yet fittingly by human nature itself. This adventure of discovery and transformation is the joy of learning, and comprises the context and expectation of Schilpp's classroom, which was conterminous with his life.

Small wonder, Schilpp's students were so stimulated and responsive. Sometimes shocked, always challenged, frequently tormented at exposure of moral nakedness between intent and deed, they recognized the realism of their teacher. This was the context for the *good,* the appropriate setting for its discernment, discussion, and doing.

As provocateur and catalyst of the maturing mind of others, his influence was contagious. He started one on a lifetime of clarification and embodiment of the good. He would not wish to claim the influence, or the shape of the insight, but may draw deep satisfaction from prodding the start of the journey. My own has woven in and out of public life. It has persuaded me of a handful of homemade assumptions about philosophy, persons, education, and the public good, hammered out as he would have insisted on the anvil of my own reflection. These in turn illuminate some current myths describing the direction of the public good, and finally the substance of a new realism adapted to a form of world federalism, model in simplicity of the structure of a good world.

Assumptions

1. Wonder is the beginning of wisdom. Curiosity is the catalyst of creativity. Openness to the world, ourselves, and the future is the prime condition of all learning. It is crippled by fear, force, or arbitrary authority.

2. New worlds are the natural and essential part of the human environment, counterpart of his wonder and curiosity, and should be anticipated in reverence, and nurtured in respect.

3. The human person is finite, fragile, and unique, and a central feature in all learning, to be tended with care, taught with integrity, and enlisted in the partnership of education with joy.

4. Only persons can be educated. Animals can be trained, and gods worshipped. Education requires personal participation and transformation. It cannot be given to anyone; it must be inwardly appropriated.

5. Persons and their worlds are many-splendored things—and proceed multidimensional and multidirectional simultaneously. Education must respect and respond to this organic wholeness.

6. Learners and teachers must be "giftfully" as well as "gainfully" employed. They must work at the cutting edge of their interest and talent.

7. Educational innovation requires flexibility, a climate of expectation and support, a relevance and relationship with a living community.

8. A University is not a place. It is an objective and a process, "to make one". A parochial University is a contradiction in terms; the whole world, and the whole person is its proper orientation, their understanding, integration, and integrity its common life.

9. When one enrolls in the University of the universe, there is no graduation.

10. The sciences of value constitute the exciting intellectual frontiers and challenge for the future which the sciences of fact have had over the past.

The Myths

Rational realism reveals the weakness in popular myths concerning certain public "goods".

1. Security and survival are principally a matter of military power.

This is a half-truth which perverts the whole, which recognizes that economic, social, and human considerations inform the right balance of any prospects for real security and/or human survival.

2. Governments are the principal instruments of international order and justice.

This is a veiled abstraction. In the end, all forms of government rest on the people. Present restlessness, all over the world with governments, betrays the presence of the primacy of persons contending with the power of structures and strictures which must be finally judged by the manner in which they enable and enoble persons to be fully human.

3. The critical economic problem is scarcity.

In spite of shrinking resources, famine, and scarcity, economic problems root solidly in poor production, distribution, mismanagement and sharing, and life styles rooted in economics of waste, obsolescence, and designed disuse. Synergetic systems, producing more with less, oriented to human ends and an ecological ethic are the economies of the future.

4. Domestic and foreign problems can be sharply separated, and we must master the domestic first.

This concept is counterproductive. It is scientifically untrue, politically impossible, and morally wrong. Our problems are human, radically interdependent, and rationally universal.

5. The United Nations is principally a debating society, relatively impotent, and generally irrelevant to the real, work-a-day world.

Its major role in liberating peoples and nations to a status of independence, forging the form of economic, social, scientific and human interdependence, and complementing nationalism with a second and transcending international loyalty gives the lie to this myth.

Middle Axioms Suggesting the Direction of the Public Good

1. Law and the State demand what neither can supply—a proper motive and a sense of personal responsibility.

2. Law is a floor, not a ceiling; prescriptive but not exhaustive of the minimal requirements of a community of power.

3. Rights and responsibilities are reciprocally related and rise or fall together in any lawful community.

4. "All men desire peace, but few men desire the things that make for peace."

5. The universal intention of law must be self-evident or self-legislative: law by coercion or force declares its impotence to legislate over responsible human community; coercion of the recalcitrant is different from coercion of the majority.

6. Minimal shared values, and dependable methods of conflict resolution are basic requirements of any effective system of law.

7. Absolute authority for any law(s) historically conditioned, is a chief source of human idolatry, and a major cause of violence in human affairs.

8. In a world of some powers passing beyond nationhood while others are just coming into nationhood, the concept and function of law must be adjusted to each end of this spectrum—continuum in scope and depth.

9. In protest or disobedience of the law, in the name of a higher order of

law or loyalty, care must be taken not to destroy the fabric of law and community which makes possible the protest and the protester.

10. Ends and means are inextricably related: one may subvert the end by manipulation of means, or transform the means by altered ends. Law must attend to both.

11. The technology of modern warfare renders total war totally obsolete as an instrument of national policy.

12. The power to enforce law must be commensurate with the universal scope of its applicability.

The Substance of a New Realism

The shape of the emerging world and "Public Good" has a simplicity of structure and a dialectical movement. It is rooted in a new realism about man and his world. It rejects the false dichotomies at the root of our paradoxes, and the false polarization implicit in our myths. It recognizes that man's hunger for freedom and justice makes government possible; but that man's appetite for power and its perversion makes it necessary!

The substance of this new sense, lies in the exposure of the false idolatry of absolute freedom and independence, which slips into anarchy, laissez-faire license, and eventual insulation, isolation, and impotence. It turns equally on dispelling those forms of absolute dependence, offering security and order through the surrender of individual liberty, which end in tyranny and monolithic power. It grasps the inescapability of interdependence at the heart of nature, human nature, and community as the viable and vital form for orchestrating freedom and order in a distinctly human society.

This structure and function is the form of federalism at work in all orders of existence. Its analogy in the human body and the forms and functions of ecological systems is a fit symbol of the framework for *World Federalists,* a form of world government as their central symbol and enduring strategy.

It weds the contemporary political poles: by affirming the rightness of the "right" in its emphasis on individual initiative and personal responsibility, whether of man or nations; related integrally to the rightness of the left in its emphasis on minimal order and law insuring the continuities of elemental economic, political, and human justice.

It weds the contemporary international poles by affirming the integrity of national autonomy within a wider order of international law, enforcing power, and genuinely universal human rights and channels of dependable and legislating justice.

It weds the realism of the contemporary worlds' divisions to the idealism of its interlocking human needs, resources, and aspirations.

It carries the logic of a limited and national federalism, at work in the variety of economic, social, and political systems in the world, to its appropriate planetary conclusion.

The Strategy and Form of the Public Good

The paradox and polarity in structure and function of human society carries an implicit logic for an appropriate strategy looking toward World Government. It roots in the "peace paradox"; the diplomatic version of the hedonic paradox which observes that if you pursue pleasure as an end, you miss it! The same is true for "peace" and World Federalism. For peace, and its condition in creative world federalism, like most of man's value experience, is consequential. That is, it follows from the achievement of other ends. It comes indirectly, and not by direct design. Pursued directly, it consolidates conflict, entrenches power, erodes confidence, squanders resources, and thwarts and frustrates the best intentions of men and government. For federalism lives best in the natural disposition to celebrate the values of local, particular people, cultures, and nations, while conceding the necessity for overriding restraints of law and order which secures that freedom, guards against arbitrary breaches of power, and enables and ennobles the human disposition toward justice which is universal, or it is nothing; human or it's demonic; and individual or it is empty.

It is this emerging logic at work in the world which grounds the conditions of peace and world federalism.

Our ecological interdependence transcends, judges, and corrects the arbitrariness and irrelevance of noisy nationalisms reflecting historic accident, arbitrary choice, and fortuitous and precarious arrangements of power. Global concern with the rational use of our resources, conservation and recreation of reliable, nonpolluting sources of energy, and humanizing man's settlements and conditions of life, create conditions of international federation.

Our economic interdependence, reflected in trade, aid, and international development, underlies and undergirds emerging regionalism transcending the sovereignty of nations, and the inescapable necessity for a more dependable international currency, framework of finance, sharing of rich and poor, in production, industrialization, and international economic monitoring, and control. New adaptations of international cooperations in computer coordination, interlocking management systems, adaptation of research and development, give promise of creating, indirectly, conditions of optimal interdependence beyond political and idealogical boundaries.

Our scientific and technical interdependence forges swiftly the conditions of a universal language, an incomparable media of universal intelligibility and cooperation, and inescapable human and cultural links prerequisite to the shared power of a global federalism.

Our human interdependence, reflected in the inescapable continuities of concern for elemental justice, for life, liberty, work, family, association, and the rich forms of human freedom that illustrate the uniquely personal features of life, spills over the narrow loyalties of birth, clan, and community. They condition and create those cultural forms that environ and enlarge the nation-state toward a more universal community.

Our human fragility and vulnerability increasingly focused on this small spinning space ship with limited resources, precarious life supports, and compulsive and sometimes mad men, tempers with realism, our recognition of the need for restraints on power, and powerful restraints on man, the role of authority matched by enforceable law, and lawful enforcement, weighted and shared responsibility. The detente of mutual terror gives way to the strategy of legitimate fear, and subordination of interest to the larger rationale of human survival.

All these contrive and converge to underscore the strategy to move from the law of force to the force of law, from the jungle to justice, from sovereignty to survival, from nation to planet, from governments to global order.

The principle ingredients of the strategy are to *humanize* (the primacy of persons), *universalize* (the force of rational law), *individualize* (the nurture of individual initiative and responsibility), and *federalize* (the orchestration of freedom and order) our human resources and community.

Practically, it will entail (1) a new form of World Development; (2) international exploration and development of the frontiers of space, the seas, and the self; (3) a new form of international currency rooted in a reserve unit of credit sustained by real and potential natural and human resources; (4) a new system of international science and technology linked to human development; (5) a new form of international peacemaking and peace-keeping sustained by new forms of national training and commitment under international authorities and control, and international adaptation of forms of arbitration and conciliation developed in labor, management, and domestic matters; (6) development of natural resources and new forms of synergistic, nonpolluting, renewable sources of energy; (7) generation of new and independent sources of revenue for a strengthened and changed United Nations, with new and weighted forms of representation, voting, administration, and enforceable power; (8) universally developed, acceptable, and enforceable individual bill of human rights; and (9) development of new forms of international, federalist education of leadership, research, and service aimed at producing a new kind of man, a new form of international cooperation, and a new organ of order and freedom appropriate to our emerging world.

In completed circle, we return to our starting point, tribute to a moral man, enmeshed in our time, yet transcending it, with a vision of the good at once personal and public, unique and universal. Professor Schilpp would be the first to eschew any semblance of the Messianic to his message or his life. Yet, those of us, now in the thousands, who have been challenged by his disclosure of our cheap and shabby substitutes for a more compelling public good, know somehow, deep in our bones, it is the integrity of the man, quite as much as the clarity of his thought, that gives us a grip on the good.

We know with Thoreau, this man, singularly out of step with the crowd, does "march to a distant drummer", whose beat he has sometimes helped us hear. But more, we know the words Maxwell Anderson puts in the mouth of his prophetic teacher, "He has called you to torment the earth, and exalt it!", as they apply to this man, his meaning and message, the good he sees, and has done, and to which he has invited us.

GLENN A. OLDS

PRESIDENT
KENT STATE UNIVERSITY
OCTOBER, 1972

BERTRAND RUSSELL

THE DUTY OF A PHILOSOPHER IN THIS AGE

It was with great pleasure that I learned of the forthcoming *Festschrift* in honour of Professor Schilpp, and with still greater pleasure that I accepted the invitation to contribute to the work. His "Library of Living Philosophers" has long commanded my admiration, and deserves the fullest commendation from academic philosophers. On the theme to which my remarks in this contribution will be dedicated, he has expressed opinions with which I am in complete agreement, and this must be my excuse if much of what I shall have to say merely repeats what he has already said. This applies particularly to his article, "The Task of Philosophy in an Age of Crisis." It is my profound conviction that this cannot be said too often or in too many ways.

One of the difficulties in discussing the duty of a philosopher is to find some difference between his duty and that of every other human being. If a philosophy professor were walking on a beach by the sea and saw a child in danger of drowning, he would endeavour to bring the child to safety and, for the moment, would forget his duty to his classes. He would do exactly what any decent human being would do, and the fact that he was a philosopher would not come into the matter. The present situation of the world is similar to that of the drowning child, but multiplied by many millions. Everybody who has studied nuclear warfare with any care knows, first, that a nuclear war is not improbable, and, second, that it may cause the death of all human beings, or, at any rate, of so large a proportion that the miserable survivors will be incapable of any ordered social life. It is the plain duty of all who appreciate these facts to do what they can to make them known. If they do not fulfil this duty, they are accomplices in mass murder. In all this there is nothing to distinguish a philosopher from other men. The only way in which a philosopher can be considered to have a special duty is through the persuasiveness that he may derive from his knowledge and his preoccupations and from such respect as he may command.

There are, in fact, people other than philosophers who are better able to predict the disasters of a nuclear war. There are the atomic scientists. There are medical men. There are meteorologists. There are ecologists. All of these, through their special knowledge, are better able than the philosopher to predict the outcome of a nuclear war. Unfortunately, few of them are active in this direction, and those who are, often fail to rouse general attention. A certain traditional respect attaches to those who are called philosophers, and this respect alone, whether deserved or undeserved, gives a special place in the work of dissuasion to men who are so honoured in public opinion.

The word "philosopher" has a different meaning for the general public from that which it has for those who are professionally engaged in teaching the subject. The popular meaning of the word is exemplified by Shakespeare's remark, "There was never yet philosopher that could endure the toothache patiently." This usage is derived from the Stoics. A man who suffers a misfortune may be advised to bear it "philosophically." The characteristic of a philosopher, in this sense, is courage under suffering, but it is not for courage under suffering that university teachers of philosophy are chosen. If it were, the candidates for a Chair of Philosophy would have their teeth pulled out one-by-one without anaesthetics, and the one who made least fuss would get the professorship. Academic Philosophy is something very different from this. It consists mainly of knowing what other philosophers have said, to which its more lively adherents may, if they choose, add some speculations of their own on subjects similar to those treated by previous philosophers. There is no reason why people subjected to this discipline should be specially wise or specially noble. Nor is their work, as a rule, of any specially great importance. There is no reason to expect, from the majority of teachers of philosophy, a higher standard of wisdom or of courage than is to be expected from teachers of other subjects.

Nor have the admittedly great philosophers of the past shown any special aptitude in regard to public affairs. Thales, the father of philosophy, rested his reputation on the statement that "all is water," which was no great help in government. Plato was virtually a Fascist. Descartes, the founder of modern philosophy, took very little interest in political questions. Hobbes thought obedience to the Government constituted the whole of virtue in an ordinary citizen. Hume had only two maxims in politics: that a Scotsman is better than an Englishman; and a Tory is better than a Whig. Hegel believed in absolute monarchy. None of these great men offered us any thought which is useful in the present day. A modern philosopher faced with the problems of the present day will find little to help him in the dicta of his predecessors.

There is, however, one exception among great philosophers of the past, namely, Locke. Locke came at the end of a period of unrest in England and of civil war brought about by the rivalry of fanatics. This caused him to seek a temper of mind which would make it possible for men to live together in peace. The temper of mind that he recommended was one of tolerance, and tolerance was recommended by him on the ground that all opinions in social matters are questionable. His teaching was so successful that there has never again been civil strife in England. Unfortunately, his disciples in France did not adopt this part of his philosophy.

What, then, can a modern philosopher preach? I think, perhaps, the first thing that he should teach is that everything good is bound up with life and that in a lifeless universe there would be neither good nor bad. Good and bad, alike, are confined, so far as our experience goes, to man and the higher animals. I do not know which of them is preponderant. Philosophers, who are bookish and unusual people, are apt to emphasize forms of good and evil which are unusual and rare and to underestimate the common everyday pleasures and pains which make up the lives of the majority of mankind. This leads to an overemphasis on creeds, and thence to fanaticism. Fanaticism leads to hatred and hatred leads to war. Those who are willing to risk a nuclear war are willing that life, or at any rate the higher forms of life, should disappear from the earth, destroyed, not by some natural cataclysm, but by the fury of human beings. The only way in which such an outlook could be welcomed, is the way of utter pessimism. You may say, like Schopenhauer, that life is essentially evil and that wherever there is life there is a preponderance of pain, but I think that only a morbid despair could adopt such a view. Schopenhauer's sincerity is questionable, since he spent his time consulting doctors as to how to remain alive. There are men who look forward to the extinction of the human species as preferable to any probable alternative. There are men whose hatred and fear of Communism is such as to cause them to reject all compromise and to prefer a world without human beings to one containing Communists. I cannot but regard such men as invalids who need the attention of a medical man rather than a philosopher.

The duty in the present day of a philosopher or of any person of academic capacity is, to my mind, completely clear. He must, first, himself study the probable effects of a nuclear war. He must, then, devote himself, by whatever means are open to him, to persuading other people to agree with him as to these effects and to joining him in whatever protest shows the most chance of success. He will find himself, if he does this, opposed to his Government and to the majority public opinion of his neighbours. He will have to be sceptical of government pronouncements, most of which have for their object the dissemination not of truth but of a belief that, whatever may happen elsewhere, his own country will emerge victorious from the ordeal. Take, for example, the question of civil defence. Public authorities in America and in Britain pretend that large underground shelters will save the lives of most people in an area subjected to nuclear bombs. This is a complete delusion. In a nuclear war, it is to be expected that the first half hour will obliterate Moscow, Leningrad, London, New York and Washington, and will transform the sites of these cities into raging tornadoes of fire storms. Those who, relying upon the advice of their Governments, have sought refuge in shelters will be roasted by the heat and will be no better off than those who die of blast or fallout in the open. The fire storms are likely to spread through large regions many miles distant from their place of origin. They will kill many millions immediately. Those who survive the first onslaught will be left without food, without medical attention and without hope in a black countryside where they will die of the effects of fallout if not of hunger. Animals, vegetables, soil and water would all be poisoned, and nothing could be eaten without risk of disease and death. Those who are remote from the places where bombs fall will be at the mercy of the winds, which will disseminate atomic poisons gradually over the surface of the globe. It may be that some will survive, especially in the Southern Hemisphere, but they will be few. They will be diseased and incapable of producing healthy offspring. This miserable remnant will gradually dwindle. If the last to die belongs to the West, he may die proclaiming a Western victory. If he belongs to a Communist country, he may, with his last breath, proclaim the worldwide victory of Communism. This is what is to be expected of a nuclear war.

There is, perhaps, one duty which falls specially within the province of philosophy, and that is to persuade mankind that human life is worth preserving and that an opposite view is only open to fanatics. That human life is worth preserving would have seemed at most times a truism, but in our day it is possible to doubt it. I think, however, that such doubt springs from a partial and biased survey. Most ordinary people prefer to be alive. Those whose happiness or unhappiness is bound up with a creed are exceptional. Moreover, man has potentialities which go immeasurably beyond what has hitherto been actual. Exceptional men such as poets, composers, painters, architects, and scientific discoverers have shown what man could be. It may be that in time the ordinary population will resemble such exceptional men, and that the great men of that day will stand above the great men of the past as much as the great men of the past exceeded their less gifted contemporaries. So long as there are men, there is hope that they will advance in the future as much as they have done in the past. This thought alone should make the prospect of the end of man intolerable except to blinded fanatics.

Fanaticism is a peculiar form of madness to which individuals and groups of men have always been liable. In the West, the most notable examples have been the Crusades and the Wars of Religion between Protestants and Catholics. Both these were futile and, in time, gave place to toleration. The weapons of war employed in these contests were not very deadly and could be employed without fatal consequences to either party. This has now ceased to be the case. A large-scale nuclear war can destroy everybody. Victory, in the old-fashioned sense, is no longer possible. Even those who remain neutral are likely to be destroyed. These are new facts and require new maxims of statecraft. At the moment, the chief conflict is between Communists and their opponents, but man is a quarrelsome animal and, if the present source of conflict were resolved, he might soon find some other equally futile basis for war. The only long-term cure for this situation is the creation of a World Government strong enough to defeat any hostile combination and able to substitute law for lawless force in deciding disputes among nations. This is, at present, a distant prospect. I do not know whether man has sufficient wisdom to bring it about before his quarrels have brought him to extinction.

It has been a common belief that the human race is divided into groups, each with its own self-interest and each necessarily hostile to some other group or groups by which its welfare is threatened. This belief was never true, but has now become disastrous. It is now necessary to proclaim that the interests of all men are identical. Consider the present condition of armaments on the two sides of the Iron Curtain. Each side continually invents newer and more expensive weapons which keep half the world hungry. If the two sides were tolerant of each other, they could disarm and the useless apparatus of mutual slaughter could be abolished. Similar considerations apply to trade, which could with advantage be free between all nations. Quarrels leading to war can no longer be tolerated. But if those who hope for peace are to succeed, they must appeal to hope rather than to fear. They must point out that we have now only the choice between mutual destruction and mutual happiness. Science, which is at the moment the cause of our fears, is capable of being the very reverse. It has provided the world with means of putting an end to many ancient evils. Poverty could be universally abolished tomorrow if nations could overcome the wish to kill each other. Illness could be enormously diminished. Labour could be reduced to a few hours a day, and the leisure thus gained could be devoted to making life splendid and happy. Those who preach peace should not confine themselves to speaking of the horrors of war, but should build also a picture of what men could achieve if wars were abolished.

Man has existed for about a million years and, during that period, has climbed gradually from the status of a frightened, hunted creature to that of lord of the world. He suffers no longer from fear of wild beasts. He has no need to suffer from famine. He lives secure, except from himself. If he could overcome this last enemy, he could swiftly proceed to new triumphs in art and science and private happiness. Nothing stands in the way except the human passions of pride, envy and hatred. These remain to be overcome. It is the duty of the philosopher to do what he can to bring about this last triumph.

How, in our modern world, should a philosopher live? Some of the lessons of philosophy are ancient and timeless. He should endeavour to view the world, as far as he is able, without a bias of space and time, without more emphasis upon the here and now than upon other places and other times. When he considers the world in which he has to live, he must approach it as if he were a stranger imported from another planet. Such impartiality is a part of the duty of the philosopher at all times. It is only its application to the present day that distinguishes the duty of a philosopher from his duty at other times. Let us consider the probable biography of a philosopher, now young, who has imbibed the timeless lesson of philosophy and wishes to apply this lesson in his own life. Let us, first, look upon the gloomy view. I shall suppose that, until his education was finished, he was too much absorbed in the technicalities of modern philosophy to concern himself with the political problems of his own time. I shall suppose that these problems come to him with an impact of novelty at a time when he is seeking a post as teacher of philosophy. He will find that there is grave danger of the destruction of the human species and that any pupils whom he is likely to teach will probably perish before they have had time to profit by his instruction. He will find that the same thing applies to everything else, both good and bad, that is taught in schools and universities. He will be overcome by the futility of an existence devoted to fitting men for a life which they will not have time to live. The contemplation of a lifeless world will make his hitherto preoccupations seem futile. His duty will be clear. He must devote himself before all else to combatting the danger of human extinction.

But he will soon become aware of the obstacles which ignorant and powerful men place in the way of such a life. The F.B.I. or Scotland Yard will discover that he had an uncle who was a Communist and that at this man's house he had frequently discussed human destiny with Communists. On this ground, he will be blacklisted and, if he is not already world-famous, an academic career will be closed to him.

When this becomes clear to him, he may take to the writing of books or to political agitation. If he takes to books, he may point out the futility of regarding large groups of men as specially wicked. He may point out that Genghis Khan inspired horror in his contemporaries, but that his grandson, Kublai Khan, inspired no such horror and was a wise and just ruler. He may endeavour to persuade his fellowmen that wickedness is not a geographical phenomenon and that armed conflict has usually intensified all the evils on both sides. He may endeavour to produce a mood of mutual tolerance in which armed conflict is viewed as the evil thing it is. He may suggest that education should encourage this point of view, that Russians and Americans should cease to think of each other as only worthy of extermination. He may, by such writings, if he is eloquent and learned, convert a small percentage of mankind to his views, but the effect of his writings will soon be obliterated by rival Establishments. Schools will still teach a nationalist morality and will turn out pupils whose minds are closed against reason and whose hearts have been taught to be deaf to humane feeling. If his writings are of less value than to produce this result, he will achieve only persecution, perhaps prison, perhaps only poverty. If, at last, he survives the first half hour of the nuclear war, other maddened survivors will put him to death on the ground that he has been an obstacle to victory.

If he rejects this dismal prospect, he can restrain his advocacy within a technical framework. He can suggest this or that minor measure which seems calculated to diminish the likelihood of nuclear war. He can proclaim that the enemies of his nation are also human beings and have the same grounds for hating his country as his country has for hating theirs. By the exercise of a certain degree of prudence, he can avoid the worst consequences of his heresy. He can make compromises with his conscience which will gradually grow wider and wider until, if he survives long enough, he is ready to enroll himself in the ranks of patriots. Some few men escape these tragic consequences by achieving technical fame before embarking upon political controversy. Of these, the most notable hitherto has been Einstein, who was world-famous before he began to denounce the policy of universal suicide. But such men, by their nature, are rare, and they are rendered powerless by the attitude of practical men, which is like that of the Roman magistrate who said to St. Paul, "Much learning doth make thee mad" (Acts 26:24).

There is, however, another possibility of a more cheerful kind. It is possible that a band of philosophers may grow up devoted heart and soul to the preservation of Man. It is possible that, by their eloquence, their knowledge, and their grasp of what might be done, they will succeed, before it is too late, in persuading large groups of men to allow themselves to go on living. It is possible that they may be able to paint a glorious and a peaceful world so vividly that men will see more value in their own survival than in the extermination of those whom they have hitherto regarded as enemies. It may be that, on the verge of a disastrous conflict, the folly of such a contest may become overwhelmingly evident and former enemies may unite in a song of joy. Something of the feeling which might lead to such a reconciliation is already not uncommon among the young, who do not wish to be exterminated before they have had a chance to live a complete life. If disaster can be averted long enough, those young people who now desire peace may acquire positions of power and may create a world happier than any that has hitherto existed. Mankind is engaged in a race in which the brutal and stupid are on one side, while, on the other side, are those who are capable of human sympathy and of imagining a world without armed strife. Philosophers should belong to this second group. If they do, their lives may be useful, infinitely useful, since they will open infinite possibilities of a splendid existence. During the struggle, their life will be arduous and painful, but illumined always by a hope as ardent as the Christian hope of heaven. Given time, this hope may be realized. Will the present rulers of the world allow the necessary time? I do not know.

BERTRAND RUSSELL

PENRHYNDEUDRAETH, WALES
AUGUST, 1964

KARL POPPER

THE MYTH
OF THE FRAMEWORK*

"Those who believe this, and those
who do not, have no common ground
of discussion, but in view of their
opinions they must of necessity
scorn each other."

PLATO

I

One of the more disturbing features of intellectual life at the present time
is the way in which irrationalism is so widely advocated, and irrationalist doctrines taken for granted. In my view, one of the main components of modern
irrationalism is relativism (the doctrine that truth is relative to our intellectual background or framework: that it may change from one framework to
another), and, in particular, the doctrine of the impossibility of mutual understanding between different cultures, generations, or historical periods. In
this paper I discuss the problem of relativism. It is my claim that behind it lies
what I call 'The Myth of the Framework'. I explain and criticize this myth,
and comment also on arguments due to Quine, Kuhn, and Whorf which have
been used in its defence.

* Based on a paper which I first prepared in 1965. I am indebted to Arne Petersen and
Jeremy Shearmur for various suggestions and corrections. The motto is from Plato's *Crito,* 49D.

The proponents of relativism put before us standards of mutual understanding which are unrealistically high; and when we fail to meet those standards, they claim that understanding is impossible. Against this, I argue that if common goodwill and a lot of effort are put into it, then very far-reaching understanding is possible. Furthermore, the effort is amply rewarded by what we learn in the process about our own views, as well as about those we are setting out to understand.

This paper sets out to challenge relativism in its widest sense. It is important to present such a challenge. For today, the increasing escalation in the production of weapons has made survival almost identical with understanding.

II

Although I am an admirer of tradition I am, at the same time, an almost orthodox adherent of unorthodoxy: I hold that orthodoxy is the death of knowledge, since the growth of knowledge depends entirely on the existence of disagreement. Admittedly, disagreement *may* lead to strife, and even to violence; and this, I think, is very bad indeed, for I abhor violence. Yet disagreement may also lead to discussion, to argument—to mutual criticism—and this, I think, is of paramount importance. I suggest that the greatest step towards a better and more peaceful world was taken when the war of swords began to be supported, and sometimes even to be replaced, by a war of words. This is why my topic is of practical significance.

But let me first explain what my topic is, and what I mean by my title, 'The Myth of the Framework'. I will discuss, and argue against, a myth—a false story that is widely accepted, especially in Germany. From there it invaded America where it became almost all-pervasive. So I fear that the majority of my present readers may believe in it, either consciously or unconsciously. The myth of the framework can be stated in one sentence, as follows:

A rational and fruitful discussion is impossible unless the participants share a common framework of basic assumptions or, at least, unless they have agreed on such a framework for the purpose of the discussion.

This is the myth I am going to criticize.

As I have formulated it, the myth sounds like a sober statement, or like a sensible warning to which we ought to pay attention in order to further rational discussion. Some people even think that it is a logical principle, or based on a logical principle. On the contrary, I think that it is not only a false statement but also a vicious statement which, if widely believed, must undermine the unity of mankind, and must greatly increase the likelihood of violence and of war. This is the main reason why I want to combat it, and to refute it.

Let me say at once that the myth contains a kernel of truth. Although I contend that it is a vast exaggeration to say that a fruitful discussion is *impossible* unless the participants share a common framework, I am very ready to admit that a discussion among participants who do not share a common framework may be *difficult*. A discussion will also be difficult if the frameworks have little in common, and it will be the easier the greater the overlap between the frameworks. Indeed, if the participants agree on all points, it will often turn out to be the easiest and smoothest discussion possible—though it is likely to be a little boring.

But what about fruitfulness? In the formulation I gave of the myth, it is a *fruitful* discussion which is declared impossible. Against this I shall defend the thesis that a discussion between people who share many views is unlikely to be fruitful, even though they may regard it as pleasant and highly satisfactory, while a discussion between vastly different frameworks can be extremely fruitful even though it will usually be difficult and *perhaps* not quite so pleasant (though we may learn to enjoy it).

I think that we may say of a discussion that it was the more fruitful the more its participants learned from it. And this means: the more interesting questions and difficult questions they were asked; the more new answers they were induced to think of; the more they were shaken in their opinions; and the more they could see things differently after the discussion; in short, the more their intellectual horizon was extended.

Fruitfulness in this sense will almost always depend on the original gap between the opinions of the participants in the discussion. The greater the gap, the more fruitful *can* the discussion be—always provided of course that such a discussion is not altogether *impossible,* as the myth of the framework asserts.

III

But is it impossible? Let us take an extreme case. Herodotus tells a very interesting though somewhat gruesome story of the Persian King Darius the First who wanted to teach a lesson to the Greek residents in his country, whose custom it was to burn their dead. He 'summoned', we read in Herodotus, 'the Greeks living in his land, and asked them for what payment they would consent to eat up their fathers when they died. They answered that nothing on earth would induce them to do so. Then Darius summoned the . . . Callatians, who do eat their fathers, and asked them in the presence of the Greeks, who had the help of an interpreter, for what payment they would consent to burn the bodies of their fathers when they died. And they cried out aloud and implored him not to mention such an abomination.'[1]

Darius, I suspect, wanted to demonstrate the truth of the myth of the framework. Indeed, we are given to understand that a discussion between the two parties would have been impossible even with the help of the interpreter. It was an extreme case of a *'confrontation'*—to use a word much in vogue with believers in the truth of the myth, and a word they like to use when they wish to draw our attention to the fact that a confrontation rarely results in a fruitful discussion.

But assuming that this confrontation staged by King Darius did take place, was it really fruitless? I deny it. There can be little doubt that both parties were deeply shaken by the experience. I myself find the idea of cannibalism just as revolting as did the Greeks at the court of King Darius, and I suppose my readers will feel the same. But these feelings should make us all the more perceptive and the more appreciative of the admirable lesson which Herodotus wishes to draw from the story. Alluding to Pindar's distinction between nature and convention,[2] Herodotus suggests that we should look with tolerance and even with respect upon customs or conventional laws that differ from our own conventions. If this particular confrontation ever took place, some of the participants may well have reacted to it in the enlightened way in which Herodotus wishes us to react to his story.

This shows that there is a possibility of a fruitful confrontation, even without a discussion, of people deeply committed to different frameworks. Of course, *we must not expect too much:* we must *not* expect that a confrontation, or even a prolonged discussion, will end with the participants reaching *agreement.*

But is an agreement *always* desirable? Let us assume that there is a discussion and that the issue at stake is the truth or falsity of some theory or hypothesis. We—that is, the rational witnesses or judges of the discussion—would of course like the discussion to end with all parties agreeing that the theory is true if in fact it is true, or that the theory is false if in fact it is false: we should like the discussion to reach, if possible, a true verdict. But we should dislike the idea that agreement was reached on the truth of the theory if the theory was in fact false; and even if it was true, we prefer that no agreement is reached on its truth if the arguments supporting the theory were far too weak to bear out the conclusion. In such a case we prefer that no agreement is reached. And in such a case we should say that the discussion was fruitful when the clash of opinion led the participants to produce new and interesting arguments, even though these arguments were inconclusive. For conclusive arguments are very rare in all but the most trivial issues, even though arguments against a theory may sometimes be pretty strong.

Looking back at Herodotus's story of a confrontation, we can now see that even in this extreme case where no agreement was in sight the confrontation may have been useful and that, given time and patience—which Herodotus seems to have had at his disposal—it did bear fruit, at least in Herodotus's own mind.

IV

Now I wish to suggest that, in a way, we ourselves and our attitudes are the results of confrontations and of inconclusive discussions of this kind.

What I mean can be summed up by the thesis that our Western civilization is the result of the clash, or the confrontation, of different cultures, and therefore of the confrontation of frameworks.

It is widely admitted that our civilization—which at its best may be described, somewhat eulogistically, as a rationalist civilization—is very largely the result of Greco-Roman civilization. It acquired many of its features, such as the alphabet, and Christianity, not only through the clashes between the Romans and the Greeks, but also through its clashes with the Jewish, the Phoenician, and other Middle Eastern civilizations, and also through clashes due to Germanic and Islamic invasions.

But what of the original Greek miracle—the rise of Greek poetry, art, philosophy, and science; the real origin of Western rationalism? I have for many years asserted that the Greek miracle, *insofar as it can be explained,* was also largely due to culture clash. It seems to me that this is indeed one of the lessons which Herodotus wants to teach us in his *History.*

Let us look for a moment at the origin of Greek philosophy. It all began in the Greek colonies in Asia Minor, in Southern Italy, and in Sicily; places, that is, where, in the East, the Greek colonists were confronted with the great oriental civilizations, and clashed with them, or where, in the West, they met Sicilians, Carthaginians, and Italians such as the Tuscans. The impact of culture clash on Greek philosophy is very obvious from the earliest reports on Thales. It is unmistakable in Heraclitus. But the way in which it leads men to think critically comes out most forcefully in Xenophanes, the wandering bard. Although I have quoted some of his verses on other occasions, I will do so again, because they illustrate my point so beautifully.[3]

> The Ethiops say that their gods are flat-nosed and black
> While the Thracians say that theirs have blue eyes and red hair.
> Yet if cattle or horses or lions had hands and could draw
> And could sculpture like men, then the horses would draw their gods
> Like horses, and cattle like cattle, and each would then shape
> Bodies of gods in the likeness, each kind, of its own.
>
> The gods did not reveal, from the beginning,

> All things to us; but in the course of time,
> Through seeking we may learn, and know things better. . . .
>
> These things are, we conjecture, like the truth.
> But as for certain truth, no man has known it,
> Nor will he know it; neither of the gods,
> Nor yet of all the things of which I speak.
> And even if by chance he were to utter
> The final truth, he would himself not know it:
> For all is but a woven web of guesses.

Although Burnet and others have denied it, I think that Parmenides, perhaps the greatest of these early thinkers, stood under Xenophanes' influence.[4] He takes up Xenophanes' distinction between the one final truth which is not subject to human convention, and the guesses or opinions, and the conventions, of the mortals. There are always many conflicting opinions and conventions concerning any one problem or subject matter (such as the gods), which shows that they are not all true, for if they conflict then, at best, only one of them can be true.[5] Thus it appears that Parmenides (a contemporary of Pindar to whom Plato attributes the distinction between nature and convention) was the first to distinguish clearly between truth or reality on the one hand, and convention or conventional opinion—hearsay, plausible myth—on the other; a lesson which, we may say, he derived from Xenophanes and from culture clash. It led him to one of the boldest theories ever conceived.

The role played by culture clash in the rise of Greek science— mathematics and astronomy—is well known, and one can even specify the way in which the various clashes bore fruit. And our ideas of freedom, of democracy, of toleration, and also the ideas of knowledge, of science, of rationality, can all be traced back to these beginnings.

Of all these ideas the idea of rationality seems to me the most fundamental.

So far as we know from the sources, the invention of rational or critical discussion seems to be contemporaneous with some of these clashes, and discussion became traditional with the rise of the earliest Ionian democracies.

V

In its application to the problem of understanding our world, and thus to the rise of science, rationality has two components which are of about equal importance.

The first is poetic inventiveness, that is, storytelling or mythmaking: the invention of stories which explain the world. These are, to begin with, often or perhaps always polytheistic. Men feel that they are in the hands of unknown powers, and they try to understand and to explain the world, and human life and death, by inventing stories or myths about these powers.

This first component, which may be perhaps as old as human language itself, is all-important and seems universal: all tribes, all peoples, have such explanatory stories, often in the form of fairy tales. It seems that the invention of explanations and explanatory stories is one of the basic functions of the human language.

The second component is of comparatively recent date. It seems to be specifically Greek and to have arisen after the establishment of writing in Greece. It arose, it seems, with Anaximander, the second Ionian philosopher. It is the invention of criticism, of the critical discussion of the various explanatory myths, with the aim of consciously improving upon them.

The main Greek example of explanatory mythmaking on an elaborate scale is, of course, Hesiod's *Theogony*. This is a wild story of the origin, the deeds, and the misdeeds, of the Greek gods. One would hardly feel inclined to look to the *Theogony* to provide a suggestion which can be used in the development of a scientific explanation of the world. Yet I have proposed the historical conjecture that a passage in Hesiod's *Theogony*[6] which was foreshadowed by another in Homer's *Iliad*[7] was so used by Anaximander, the first critical cosmologist.

I will explain my conjecture. According to tradition Thales, the teacher and kinsman of Anaximander, and the founder of the Ionian school of cosmologists, taught that 'the earth is supported by water on which it rides like a ship'. Anaximander, the pupil, kinsman, and successor of Thales, turned away from this somewhat naive myth (intended by Thales to explain earthquakes). Anaximander's new departure was of a truly revolutionary character, for he taught, we are told, the following: 'There is no thing at all that is holding up the earth. Instead, the earth remains stationary owing to the fact that it is equally far away from all other things. Its shape is like that of a drum. We walk on one of its flat surfaces while the other is on the opposite side.'

This bold idea made possible the ideas of Aristarchus and Copernicus, and it even contains an anticipation of Newton's forces. How did it arise? I have proposed the conjecture[8] that it arose out of a purely logical criticism of Thales' myth. The criticism is simple: if we solve the problem of explaining the position and stability of the earth in the universe by saying that it is supported by the ocean, like a ship that is supported by water, are we not then bound, the critic asks, to raise a new problem, that of explaining the position and the stability of the ocean? But this would mean finding some support for the ocean, and then some further support for this support. Obviously, this leads to an infinite regress. How can we avoid it?

In looking round for a way out of this frightful impasse which, it appeared, no alternative explanation was able to avoid, Anaximander remembered, I conjecture, a passage in which Hesiod develops an idea from the *Iliad* where we are told that Tartarus is exactly as far beneath the earth as Uranus, or heaven, is above it.

The passage reads: 'For nine days and nights will a brazen anvil fall from the heavens, and on the tenth it will reach the earth. And for nine days and nights will a brazen anvil fall from the earth, and on the tenth it will reach Tartarus.'9 This passage may have suggested to Anaximander that we can draw a diagram of the world, with the earth in the middle, and the vault of the heavens like a hemisphere above it. Symmetry then suggests that we interpret Tartarus as being the lower half of the vault. In this way we arrive at Anaximander's construction as it is transmitted to us; a construction that breaks through the deadlock of the infinite regress.

There is I think a need for such a conjectural explanation of the tremendous step that carried Anaximander beyond his teacher Thales. My conjecture, it seems to me, makes the step more understandable and, at the same time, even more impressive; for it is now seen as a rational solution of a very difficult problem—the problem of the support and the stability of the earth.

Yet Anaximander's criticism of Thales and his critical construction of a new myth would have led to nothing had these not been followed up. How can we explain the fact that they *were* followed up? Why was a new myth offered in each generation after Thales? I have tried to explain this by the further conjecture that Thales and Anaximander together founded a new school tradition—*the critical tradition.*

My attempt to explain the phenomenon of Greek rationalism and of the Greek critical tradition by a school tradition is again, of course, completely conjectural. In fact, it is itself a kind of myth. Yet it does explain a unique phenomenon—the Ionian school. This school, for at least four or five generations, produced in each new generation an ingenious revision of the teachings of the preceding generation. In the end it established what we may call the scientific tradition: a tradition of criticism which survived for at least five hundred years, and which survived some serious onslaughts before it succumbed.

The critical tradition is constituted by the adoption of the method of criticizing a received story or explanation and then proceeding to a new, improved, imaginative story which in turn is submitted to criticism. This method, I assert, is the method of science. It seems to have been invented only once in human history. It died in the West when the schools in Athens were suppressed by a victorious and intolerant Christianity, though it lingered on in the East. It was mourned during the Middle Ages. And it was not so much reinvented as reimported in the Renaissance, together with the rediscovery of Greek philosophy and Greek science.

The uniqueness of this second component—the method of critical discussion—will be realized if we consider the old-established function of schools, especially of religious and semireligious schools. Their function is, and has always been, the preservation of the purity of the teaching of the founder of the school. Accordingly, changes in doctrine are rare and are often due to mistakes or misunderstandings. When they are consciously made they are as a rule made surreptitiously; for otherwise changes lead to splits, to schisms.

But here, in the Ionian school, we find a school tradition which carefully preserved the teaching of each of its masters while deviating from it afresh in each new generation.

My conjectural explanation of this unique phenomenon is that Thales, the founder, encouraged Anaximander, his kinsman, pupil, and later his successor, to see whether he could produce a better explanation of the support of the earth than he himself had been able to offer.

However this may have been, the invention of the critical method could hardly have happened without the impact of culture clash. It had the most tremendous consequences. Within four or five generations the Greeks discovered that the earth, the moon, and the sun, were spheres; that the moon moved round the earth, while always 'wistfully' looking at the sun; and that this could be explained by the assumption that she borrowed her light from the sun.[10] A little later they conjectured that the earth rotated, and that the earth moved round the sun. But these later hypotheses, due to the Platonic school and especially to Aristarchus, were soon forgotten.

These cosmological or astronomical findings became the basis of all future science. Human science started from a bold and hopeful attempt to understand critically the world we live in. This ancient dream found fulfillment in Newton. We can say that only since Newton has humanity become fully conscious—conscious of its position in the universe.

All this, it can be shown, is the result of applying the method of critical discussion to mythmaking—to our attempts to understand and to explain our world.

VI

If we look back on this development, then we can understand better why we must not expect any critical discussion of a serious issue, any 'confrontation', to yield quick and final results. Truth is hard to come by. It needs both ingenuity in criticizing old theories, and ingenuity in the imaginative invention of new theories. This is so not only in the sciences, but in all fields.

Serious critical discussions are always difficult. Nonrational human elements always enter. Many participants in a rational, that is, a critical, discussion find it particularly difficult that they have to unlearn what everybody is taught in a debating society, for they have to learn that victory in a debate is nothing, while even the slightest clarification of one's problem, even the smallest contribution made towards a clearer understanding of one's own position or that of one's opponent, is a great success. A discussion which you win but which fails to help you to change or to clarify your mind at least a little should be regarded by you as a sheer loss. For this very reason no change in one's position should be made surreptitiously, but it should always be stressed, and its consequences explored.

Rational discussion in this sense is rare. But it is an important ideal, and we may learn to enjoy it. It does not aim at conversion, and it is modest in its expectations: it is enough, more than enough, if we feel that we can see things in a new light, or that we have got even a little nearer to the truth.

VII

But let me now return to the myth of the framework. There are many tendencies which may contribute to the fact that this myth is often taken for an almost self-evident truth.

One of these tendencies I have already mentioned. It results from an overoptimistic expectation concerning the outcome of a discussion; the expectation that every fruitful discussion should lead to a decisive and deserved intellectual victory of the truth, represented by one party, over falsity, represented by the other. When it is found that this is not what a discussion usually achieves, disappointment turns an overoptimistic expectation into a general pessimism concerning the value of discussions.

A second tendency which deserves careful scrutiny is connected with historical or cultural relativism, a view whose beginnings may perhaps be discerned in Herodotus, the father of history.

Herodotus seems to have been one of those somewhat uncommon people whose mind was broadened by travel. At first he was no doubt shocked by the many strange customs and institutions which he encountered in the East. But he learned to respect them, and to look on some of them critically, on others as the results of historical accidents: he learned to be tolerant, and he even acquired the ability to see the customs and institutions of his own country through the eyes of his barbarian hosts.

This is a healthy state of affairs. But it may lead to relativism, that is, to the view that there is no absolute or objective truth, but rather one truth for the Greeks, and another for the Egyptians, and still another for the Syrians, and so on.

I do not think that Herodotus fell into this trap. But many have done so since—perhaps inspired by an admirable feeling of tolerance which they have combined with very dubious logic.

There is one version of the idea of cultural relativism which is obviously correct. In England, Australia, and New Zealand we drive on the left-hand side of the road, while in America and in most other countries we drive on the right-hand side. What is needed is *some* such rule of the road, but which of the two—the right or the left—is obviously arbitrary and conventional. There are many similar rules of greater or lesser importance which are purely conventional or customary. Among these are the different rules for pronouncing and spelling the English language in America and in England. Even two quite different vocabularies may be related in a conventional way closely resembling the two different rules of the road, provided the grammatical structures of the two languages are very similar. We may regard such vocabularies, or such rules, as differing in a purely conventional way: there is really nothing to choose between them—nothing of importance.

As long as we consider only conventional rules and customs such as these, there is no chance for the myth of the framework to be taken seriously; for a discussion between an American and an Englishman about the rule of the road is likely to lead to an agreement. Both are likely to regret the fact that their rules do not coincide. Both will agree that in principle there is nothing to choose between the two rules, and that it would be unreasonable to expect the United States to adopt the left-hand rule in order to achieve conformity with Britain; and both are likely to agree that Britain cannot at present make a change which may be desirable but which would be extremely costly. After agreement has thus been reached on all points, both participants are likely to part with the feeling that they have not learned anything from the discussion.

The situation changes when we consider other institutions, laws, or customs—those for example which are connected with the administration of justice. Different laws and customs in this field may make all the difference for those living under them. Some customs can be very cruel, while others provide for mutual help and the relief of suffering. Some countries and their laws respect freedom while others do so less, or not at all.

It is my opinion that a critical discussion of these important matters is not only possible, but most urgently needed. It is often made difficult by propaganda and by a neglect of factual information. But these difficulties are not insuperable. Thus it is possible to combat propaganda by information, and information, if available, is not always ignored; though admittedly it often is ignored.

In spite of all this there are some people who uphold the myth that frameworks of laws and customs cannot be rationally discussed. They assert that morality is identical with legality or custom or usage, and that it is therefore impossible to judge, or discuss, whether one system of customs is morally better than another, since the existing system of laws and customs is the only possible standard of morality.

This view has been stated by Hegel with the help of the formulae: 'What is real is reasonable' and 'What is reasonable is real'. Here 'what is' or 'what is real' means the world, including its man-made laws and customs. That these are man-made is denied by Hegel who asserts that the World Spirit or Reason made them, and that those who seem to have made them—the great men, the makers of history—are merely the executors of reason, their passions being the most sensitive instrument of reason; they are the detectors of the Spirit of their Time, and ultimately of the Absolute Spirit, that is of God Himself.

This is just one of those many cases in which philosophers use God for their own private purposes; that is, as a prop for some of their tottering arguments.

Hegel was both a relativist and an absolutist: as always, he had it at least both ways, and if two ways were not enough, he had it in three ways. And he was the first of a long chain of post-Kantian, that is, postcritical or postrationalist philosophers—mainly German philosophers—who upheld the myth of the framework.

According to Hegel, truth itself was both relative and absolute. It was relative to each historical and cultural framework: there could thus be no rational discussion between the frameworks since each of them had a different standard of truth. But his doctrine that all truth was relative to the various frameworks was absolutely true, since it was part of Hegel's own relativistic philosophy.

VIII

Hegel's claim to have discovered absolute truth does not now appear to attract many people. But his doctrine of relative truth and his myth of the framework still attracts them. What makes it so attractive is that they confuse relativism with the true insight that all men are fallible. This doctrine of fallibility has played an important role in the history of philosophy from its earliest days on—from Xenophanes and Socrates to Charles Sanders Peirce—and I think that it is of the utmost importance. But I do *not* think that it can be used to support relativism with respect to truth.

Of course, the doctrine of human fallibility can be validly used to argue against that kind of philosophical absolutism which claims to *possess* the absolute truth, or at least a criterion of absolute truth, such as the Cartesian criterion of clarity and distinctness, or some other intuitive criterion. But there exists a very different doctrine of absolute truth, in fact a fallibilist doctrine, which asserts that mistakes we make can be absolute mistakes, in the sense that our theories can be absolutely false, that they can fall short of the truth. Thus the notion of truth, and that of falling short of the truth, can represent absolute standards for the fallibilist. These notions are a great help in critical discussions.

This theory of absolute or objective truth has been revived by Alfred Tarski who also proved that there can be no universal criterion of truth. There is no clash whatever between Tarski's theory of absolute or objective truth and the doctrine of fallibility.[11]

But is not Tarski's notion of truth a relative notion? Is it not relative to the language to which the statement belongs whose truth is being discussed?

The answer to this question is 'no'. Tarski's theory says that a statement of some language, say English, is true if and only if it corresponds to the facts; and Tarski's theory implies that whenever there is another language, say French, in which we can describe the same fact, then the French statement which describes this fact will be true if and only if the corresponding English statement is true. Thus it is impossible, according to Tarski's theory, that of two statements which are translations of each other, one can be true and the other false. Truth, according to Tarski's theory, is therefore *not* dependent on language, or relative to language. Reference to the language is made only because of the unlikely but trivial possibility that the same sounds or symbols may occur in two different languages and may then perhaps describe two totally different facts.

However, it may easily happen that a statement of one language is untranslatable into another, or in other words that a fact, or a state of affairs, which can be described in one language cannot be described in another.

Anybody who can speak more than one language knows, of course, that perfect translations from one language into another are very rare, if they exist at all. But this difficulty, well-known to all translators, should be clearly distinguished from the situation here discussed—that is, the impossibility of describing in one language a state of affairs which can be described in some other language. The ordinary and well-known difficulty consists of something quite different, namely this. A crisp, simple, and easily understandable statement in French or English may need a highly complex and awkward rendering in, say, German, and a rendering which is even difficult to understand in German. In other words, the ordinary difficulty known to every translator is that an aesthetically adequate translation may be impossible, not that *any* translation of the statement in question is impossible. (I am speaking here of a factual statement, not of a poem or an aphorism or bon mot, or of a statement which is subtly ironical or which expresses a sentiment of the speaker.)

There can be no doubt, however, that a more radical impossibility may arise; for example, we can construct artificial languages which contain only one-termed predicates, so that we can say in these languages 'Paul is tall' and 'Peter is short', but not 'Paul is taller than Peter'.

More interesting than such artificial languages are some living languages. Here we can learn much from Benjamin Lee Whorf.[12] Whorf was perhaps the first to draw attention to the significance of certain tenses of the Hopi language. These tenses are experienced by a Hopi speaker as describing some part of the state of affairs which he tries to describe in his statement. They cannot be adequately rendered into English, for we can explain them only in a roundabout way, by referring to certain expectations of the speaker rather than aspects of the objective states of affairs.

Whorf gives the following example. There are two tenses in Hopi which might inadequately be rendered in English by the two statements

'Fred began chopping wood', and
'Fred began to chop wood'.

The first would be used by the Hopi speaker if he expects Fred to *go on* chopping for some time. If the speaker does *not* expect Fred to go on chopping, then he will *not* say, in Hopi, 'Fred began chopping'; he will use that other tense rendered by 'Fred began to chop'. But the real point is that the Hopi speaker does not wish by the use of his tenses merely to express his different expectations. He rather wishes to describe two different states of affairs—two different objective situations, two different states of the objective world. The one tense may be said to describe the beginning of a continuing *state* or of a somewhat repetitive *process,* while the other describes the beginning of an *event* of short duration. Thus the Hopi speaker may try to translate Hopi into English by saying: 'Fred began sleeping', in contradistinction to 'Fred began to sleep', because sleeping is a process rather than an event.

All this is very much simplified: a full restatement of Whorf 's description of the complex linguistic situation could easily take up a whole paper.

The main consequence for my topic which seems to emerge from the situations described by Whorf and more recently discussed by Quine is this. Although there cannot be any linguistic relativity concerning the *truth* of any statement, there is the possibility that a statement may be untranslatable into some other language. For the two languages may have built into their very grammar two different views of the stuff the world is made of, or of the world's basic structural characteristics. In the terminology of Quine this may be called the 'ontological relativity' of language.[13]

The possibility that some statements are untranslatable is, I assert, about the most radical consequence we can draw from what Quine calls 'ontological relativity'. Yet in actual fact most human languages seem to be intertranslatable. We may say that they are mostly *badly* intertranslatable, mainly because of ontological relativity, although of course for other reasons too. For example, appeals to our sense of humour, or comparisons with a well-known local or historical event which has become typical may be completely untranslatable.

IX

It is obvious that this situation must make rational discussion very difficult if the participants are brought up in different parts of the world, and speak different languages. But I have found that these difficulties can often be surmounted. I have had students in the London School of Economics from various parts of Africa, the Middle East, India, Southeast Asia, China, and Japan, and I have found that the difficulties could usually be conquered with a little patience on both sides. Whenever there was a major obstacle to overcome, it was as a rule the result of indoctrination with Western ideas. Dogmatic, uncritical teaching in bad Westernized schools and universities, and especially training in Western verbosity and in Western ideologies were, in my experience, much graver obstacles to rational discussion than any cultural or linguistic gap.

My experiences suggested to me that culture clash may lose some of its value if one of the clashing cultures regards itself as universally superior, and even more so if it is so regarded by the other: this destroys the major value of culture clash, for the greatest value of culture clash lies in the fact that it can evoke a critical attitude. More especially, if one of the parties becomes convinced of his inferiority, then the critical attitude of learning from the other will be replaced by a kind of blind acceptance, a blind leap into a new magic circle, or a conversion, as it is so often described by fideists and existentialists.

I believe that ontological relativity, though an obstacle to easy communication, can prove of immense value in all the more important cases of culture clash if it can be overcome slowly. For it means that the partners in the clash may liberate themselves from prejudices of which they are unconscious—from taking theories unconsciously for granted which, for example, may be embedded in the logical structure of their language. Such a liberation may be the result of *criticism* stimulated by culture clash.

What happens in such cases? We compare and contrast the new language with our own, or with some others we know well. In the comparative study of these languages we use, as a rule, our own language as a metalanguage—that is, as the language in which we speak about, and compare, the other languages which are the objects under investigation, including our own language. The languages under investigation are the object languages. In carrying out the investigation, we are forced to look upon our own language—say English—in a critical way, as a set of rules and usages which may be somewhat narrow since they are unable completely to capture, or to describe, the kinds of entities which the other languages assume to exist. But this description of the limitations of English as an object language is carried out in English as a metalanguage. Thus we are forced, by this comparative study, to transcend precisely those limitations which we are studying. And the interesting point is that we succeed in this. The means of transcending our language is *criticism.*

Whorf himself, and some of his followers, have suggested that we live in a kind of intellectual prison, a prison formed by the structural rules of our language. I am prepared to accept this metaphor, though I have to add to it that it is an odd prison insofar as we are normally unaware of it. We become aware of it through culture clash. But then, this very awareness allows us to break out of the prison if we wish to: we can transcend our prison by studying the new language and comparing it with our own.

The result will be a new prison. But it will be a much larger and wider prison; and again, we will not suffer from it; or rather, whenever we do, we are free to examine it critically, and thus to break out again, into a still wider prison.

The prisons are the frameworks. And those who do not like prisons will be opposed to the myth of the framework. They will welcome a discussion with a partner who comes from another world, from another framework, for it gives them an opportunity to discover their so far unfelt chains, to break them, and thus to transcend themselves. This breaking out of one's prison is, of course, not a matter of routine:[13a] it can only be the result of a critical effort—of a creative effort.

X

In the remainder of this paper I will try to apply this brief analysis to some problems which have arisen in a field in which I am greatly interested—the philosophy of science.

It is now fifty years since I arrived at a view very similar to the myth of the framework; and I not only arrived at it but at once went beyond it. It was during the great and heated discussions after the First World War that I found out how difficult it was to get anywhere with people living in a closed framework; I mean people like the Marxists, the Freudians, and the Adlerians. None of them could ever be shaken in his adopted view of the world. Every argument against their framework was by them so interpreted as to fit into it; and if this turned out to be difficult, then it was always possible to psychoanalyse or socioanalyse the arguer: criticism of Marxian ideas was due to class prejudice, criticism of Freudian ideas was due to repression, and criticism of Adlerian ideas was due to the urge to prove your superiority, an urge which was due to an attempt to compensate for a feeling of inferiority.

I found the stereotyped pattern of these attitudes depressing and repelling, the more so as I could find nothing of the kind in the debates of the physicists about Einstein's General Theory, although it too was hotly debated at the time.

The lesson I derived from these experiences was this. Theories are important and indispensible because without them we could not orientate ourselves in the world—we could not live. Even our observations are interpreted with their help. The Marxist literally sees class struggle everywhere; thus he believes that only those who deliberately shut their eyes can fail to see it. The Freudian sees everywhere repression and sublimation; the Adlerian sees how feelings of inferiority express themselves in every action and every utterance, whether it is an utterance of inferiority or superiority.

This shows that our need for theories is immense, and so is the power of theories. Thus it is all the more important to guard against becoming addicted to any particular theory: we must not let ourselves be caught in a mental prison. I did not know of the theory of culture clash at the time, but I certainly made use of my clashes with the addicts of the various frameworks in order to impress upon my mind the ideal of liberating oneself from the intellectual prison of a theory in which one might get stuck unconsciously, at any moment of one's life.

It is only too obvious that this ideal of self-liberation, of breaking out of one's prison of the moment, might in its turn become part of a framework or a prison—or in other words, that we can never be absolutely free. But we can widen our prison, and at least we can leave behind the narrowness of one who is addicted to his fetters.

Thus our view of the world is at any moment necessarily theory impregnated. But this does not prevent us from progressing to better theories. How do we do it? The essential step is the linguistic formulation of our beliefs. This objectivizes them; and this makes it possible for them to become targets of criticism. Thus our beliefs are replaced by competing theories, by competing conjectures. And through the critical discussion of these theories we can progress.

In this way we must demand of any better theory, that is, of any theory which may be regarded as progressing beyond some less good theory, that it can be compared with the latter. In other words, that the two theories are *not* 'incommensurable', to use a now fashionable term, introduced in this context by Thomas Kuhn.

(Note that two logically incompatible theories will be, in general, 'commensurable'. *Incommensurability* is intended to be much more radical than *incompatibility:* while incompatibility is a logical relation and thus appeals to one logical framework, incommensurability suggests the non-existence of a common logical framework.)

For example, Ptolemy's astronomy is far from incommensurable with that of Aristarchus and Copernicus. No doubt, the Copernican system allows us to see the world in a totally different way; no doubt there is, psychologically, a *Gestalt* switch, as Kuhn calls it. This is psychologically very important. But we *can* compare the two systems logically. In fact, it was one of Copernicus's main arguments that all astronomical observations which can be fitted into a geocentric system can, by a simple translation method, always be fitted into a heliocentric one. There is no doubt all the difference in the world between these two views of the universe, and the magnitude of the gulf between the two views may well make us tremble. But there is no difficulty in comparing them. For example, we may point out the colossal velocities which the rotating sphere of the fixed stars must give to the stars which are near to its equator, while the rotation of the earth, which in Copernicus's system replaces that of the fixed stars, involves very much smaller velocities. This, together with some practical acquaintance with centrifugal forces, may well have served as an important point of comparison for those who had to choose between the two systems.

I assert that this kind of comparison between systems is always possible. Theories which offer solutions of the same or closely related problems are as a rule comparable, I assert, and discussions between them are always possible and fruitful; and not only are they possible, but they actually take place.

XI

Some people do not think that these assertions are correct, and this results in a view of science and its history very different from mine. Let me briefly outline such a view of science.

The proponents[14] of such a view can observe that scientists are, normally, engaged in close cooperation and discussion; and the proponents argue that this situation is made possible by the fact that scientists normally operate within a common framework to which they have committed themselves. (Frameworks of this kind seem to me to be closely related to what Karl Mannheim used to call 'Total Ideologies'.[15]) The periods during which scientists remain committed to a framework are regarded as typical; they are periods of 'normal science', and scientists who work in this way are regarded as 'normal scientists'.

Science in this sense is then contrasted with science in a period of crisis or revolution. These are periods in which the theoretical framework begins to crack, and in the end breaks. It is then replaced by a new one. The transition from an old framework to a new one is regarded as a process which must be studied not from a logical point of view (for it is, essentially, not wholly, or even mainly, rational) but from a psychological and sociological point of view. There is, perhaps, something like 'progress' in the transition to a new theoretical framework. But this is not a progress which consists of getting nearer to the truth, and the transition is not guided by a rational discussion of the relative merits of the competing theories. *It cannot be so guided since a genuinely rational discussion is thought to be impossible without an established framework.* Without a framework it is not even thought to be possible to agree what constitutes a point of 'merit' in a theory. (Some protagonists of this view even think that we can speak of truth only relative to a framework.) Rational discussion is thus impossible if it is the framework which is being challenged. And this is why the two frameworks—the old and the new—have sometimes been described as *incommensurable.*

An additional reason why frameworks are sometimes said to be incommensurable seems to be this. A framework can be thought of as consisting not only of a 'dominant theory', but also as being, in part, a psychological and sociological entity. It consists of a dominant theory *together* with what one might call *a way of viewing things in tune with the dominant theory,* including sometimes even a way of viewing the world and a way of life. Accordingly, such a framework constitutes a social bond between its devotees: it binds them together, very much as a church does, or a political or artistic creed, or an ideology.

This is a further explanation of the asserted incommensurability: it is understandable that *two ways of life and two ways of looking at the world* are incommensurable. Yet I want to stress that *two theories* which try to solve the same family of problems, including their offspring (their problem children), need *not* be incommensurable, and that in science, as opposed to religion, it is the *theories* that are paramount. I do not wish to deny that there is such a thing as a 'scientific approach', or a scientific 'way of life'; that is, the way of life of those men devoted to science. On the contrary, I assert that the scientific way of life involves a burning interest in objective scientific theories—in the theories in themselves, and in the problem of their truth, or their nearness to truth. And this interest is a *critical* interest, an *argumentative* interest. Thus it does not, like some other creeds, produce anything like the described 'incommensurability'.

It seems to me that many counterexamples exist to the theory of the history of science that I have just discussed. There are, first, counterexamples that show that the existence of a 'framework', and of work going on within it, does not characterize science. Philosophy during the scholastic period, astrology, and theology, are such counterexamples. Secondly, there are counterexamples that show that there may be several dominant theories struggling for supremacy in a science, and there may even be fruitful discussions between them. My main counterexample under this heading is the theory of the constitution of matter, in which atomism and continuity theories were, fruitfully, at war from the Pythagoreans and Parmenides, Democritus and Plato, to Heisenberg and Schrödinger. I do not think that this war can be described as falling into the prehistory of science, or into the history of prescience. Another counterexample of this second kind is constituted by the theories of heat. Even after Black we have fluidum theories[16] of heat warring with kinetic and phenomenological theories; and the clash between Ernst Mach and Max Planck[17] was neither characteristic of a crisis nor did it occur within one framework, nor, indeed, could it be described as prescientific. Another example is the clash between Cantor and his critics (especially Kronecker) which was later continued in the form of exchanges between Russell and Poincaré, Hilbert and Brouwer. By 1925 there were at least three sharply opposed frameworks involved, divided by chasms far too wide for bridging. But the discussions continued, and they slowly changed their character. By now not only have fruitful discussions occurred but so many syntheses that the animadversions of the past are almost forgotten. Thirdly, there are counterexamples that show that fruitful rational discussions may continue between devotees of a newly established dominant theory and unconvinced sceptics. Such is Galileo's *Two Principal Systems;* such are some of Einstein's 'popular' writings, or the important criticism of

Einstein's principle of covariance voiced by E. Kretschmann (1917), or the criticism of Einstein's General Theory recently voiced by Dicke; and such are Einstein's famous discussions with Bohr. It would be quite incorrect to say that the latter were not fruitful, for not only did Bohr claim that they much improved his understanding of quantum mechanics, but they led to the famous paper of Einstein, Podolsky, and Rosen which has produced a whole literature of considerable significance, and may yet lead to more:[18] no paper which is discussed by recognized experts for thirty-five years can be denied its scientific status and significance, but this paper was, surely, criticizing (from the outside) the whole framework which had been established by the revolution of 1925-26. Opposition to this framework—the Copenhagen framework—is continued by a minority to which for example de Broglie, Bohm, Landé, and Vigier belong—apart from those names mentioned in the preceding footnote.[19]

Thus discussions may go on all the time; and although there are always attempts to transform the society of scientists into a closed society, these attempts have not succeeded. In my opinion they would be fatal for science.

The proponents of the view of the myth of the framework distinguish sharply between rational periods of science conducted within a framework (which can be described as periods of closed or authoritarian science) and periods of crisis and revolution, which can be described as the almost irrational leap (comparable to a religious conversion) from one framework to another.

No doubt there are such irrational leaps, such conversions, as described. No doubt there are even scientists who just follow the lead of others, or give way to social pressure, and accept a new theory as a new faith because the experts, the authorities, have accepted it. I admit, regretfully, that there are fashions in science, and that there is also social pressure.

I even admit that the day may come when the social community of scientists will consist mainly or exclusively of scientists who uncritically accept a ruling dogma. They will normally be swayed by fashions; they will accept a theory because it is the latest cry, and because they fear to be regarded as laggards.

I assert, however, that this will be the end of science as we know it—the end of the tradition created by Thales and Anaximander and rediscovered by Galileo. As long as science is the search for truth it will be the rational, critical discussion between competing theories, and the rational critical discussion of the revolutionary theory. This discussion decides whether or not the new theory is to be regarded as better than the old theory: that is, whether or not it is to be regarded as a step towards the truth.

XII

Almost forty years ago I stressed that even observations, and reports of observations, are under the sway of theories or, if you like, under the sway of a framework. Indeed, there is no such thing as an uninterpreted observation, an observation which is not theory-impregnated. In fact, our very eyes and ears are the result of evolutionary adaptations—that is, of the method of trial and error corresponding to the method of conjectures and refutations. Both methods are adjustments to environmental regularities. A simple example will show that ordinary visual experiences have a pre-Parmenidian absolute sense of up and down built into them—a sense which is no doubt genetically based. The example is this. A square standing on one of its sides looks to all of us a different figure from a square standing on one of its corners. There is a real *Gestalt* switch in moving from one figure to the other.

But I assert that the fact that observations are theory-impregnated does not lead to incommensurability between either observations or theories. For the old observations can be consciously reinterpreted: we can learn that the two squares are different positions of the same square. This is made even easier just because of the genetically based interpretations: no doubt we understand each other so well partly because we share so many physiological mechanisms which are built into our genetic system.

Yet I assert that it is possible for us to transcend even our genetically based physiology. This we do by the critical method. We can understand even a bit of the language of the bees. Admittedly, this understanding is conjectural and rudimentary. But almost all understanding is conjectural, and the deciphering of a new language is always rudimentary to start with.

It is the method of science, the method of critical discussion, which makes it possible for us to transcend not only our culturally acquired but even our inborn frameworks. This method has made us transcend not only our senses but also our partly innate tendency to regard the world as a universe of identifiable things and their properties. Ever since Heraclitus there have been revolutionaries who have told us that the world consists of processes, and that things are things only in appearance: in reality they are processes. This shows how critical thought can challenge and transcend a framework even if it is rooted not only in our conventional language but in our genetics—in what may be called human nature itself. Yet even this revolution does not produce a theory incommensurable with its predecessor: the very task of the revolution was to explain the old category of thing-hood by a theory of greater depth.

XIII

I may perhaps also mention that there is a very special form of the myth of the framework which is particularly widespread. It is the view that, before discussion, we should agree on our vocabulary—perhaps by 'defining our terms'.

I have criticized this view on various occasions and I do not have space to do so again.[20] I only wish to make clear that there are the strongest possible reasons against this view; all definitions, so-called 'operational definitions' included, can only shift the problem of the meaning of the term in question to the defining terms; thus the demand for definitions leads to an infinite regress unless we admit so-called 'primitive' terms, that is, *undefined* terms. But these are as a rule no less problematic than most of the defined terms.

XIV

In the last section of this paper I will briefly discuss the myth of the framework from a logical point of view: I will attempt something like a logical diagnosis of the malaise.[21]

The myth of the framework is clearly the same as the doctrine that one cannot rationally discuss anything that is *fundamental;* or that a rational discussion of *principles* is impossible.

This doctrine is, logically, an outcome of the mistaken view that all rational discussion must start from some *principles* or, as they are often called, *axioms,* which in their turn must be accepted dogmatically if we wish to avoid an infinite regress—a regress due to the alleged fact that when rationally discussing the validity of our principles or axioms we must again appeal to principles or axioms.

Usually those who have seen this situation either insist dogmatically upon the truth of a framework of principles or axioms, or they become relativists: they say that there are different frameworks and that there is no rational discussion possible between them, and thus no rational choice.

But all this is mistaken; for behind it there is the tacit assumption that a rational discussion must have the character of a justification, or of a proof or a demonstration, or of a logical derivation from admitted premises. But the kind of discussion which is going on in the natural sciences might have taught our philosophers that there is also another kind of rational discussion: a critical discussion which does not seek to prove or to justify or to establish a theory, least of all by deriving it from some higher premises, but which tries to test the theory under discussion by finding out whether its *logical conse-*

quences are all acceptable, or whether it has, perhaps, some undesirable consequences.

We thus can logically distinguish between *a mistaken method of criticizing* and *a correct method of criticizing*. The *mistaken method* starts from the question: how can we establish or justify our thesis or our theory? It thereby leads either to dogmatism; or to an infinite regress; or to the relativistic doctrine of rationally incommensurable frameworks. By contrast, the *correct method* of critical discussion starts from the question: what are the *consequences* of our thesis or our theory? Are they all acceptable to us?

Thus it consists in comparing the consequences of different theories (or, if you like, of different frameworks) and tries to find out which of the competing theories or frameworks has consequences that seem preferable to us. It is thus conscious of the fallibility of all our methods, and it tries to replace all our theories by better ones. This is, admittedly, a difficult task, but by no means an impossible one.

To sum up. Frameworks, like languages, may be barriers; but a foreign framework, just like a foreign language, is no absolute barrier. And just as breaking through a language barrier is difficult but very much worth our while, and likely to repay our efforts not only by widening our intellectual horizon but also by offering us much enjoyment, so it is with breaking through the barrier of a framework. A breakthrough of this kind is a discovery for us, and it may be one for science.

KARL POPPER

PENN, BUCKINGHAMSHIRE
ENGLAND
OCTOBER, 1972

NOTES

¹ Herodotus, III, 38. I refer to this passage in n. 3 to Chap. 5 of my *Open Society and Its Enemies* (London: George Routledge & Sons, 1945; Princeton: Princeton University Press, 5th rev. ed., 1966), Vol. I.

² The distinction between nature and convention is discussed in my *Open Society,* Vol. I, Chap. 5, where I refer to Pindar, Herodotus, Protagoras, Antiphon, Archelaus, and especially to Plato's *Laws* (cp. nn. 3, 7, 10, 11, and 28 to Chap. 5 and text). Although I mention (p. 60) the significance of 'the realization that taboos are different in various tribes', and although I (just) mention Xenophanes (n. 7) and his profession as a 'wandering bard' (n. 9 to Chap. 10), I did not then fully realize the part played by culture clash in the evolution of critical thought, as witnessed by the contribution made by Xenophanes, Heraclitus, and Parmenides (see esp. n. 11 to the *Open Society,* Chap. 5) to the problem of nature or reality or truth versus convention or opinion. See also my *Conjectures and Refutations: The Growth of Scientific Knowledge* (New York: Basic Books, 1963; London: Routledge & Kegan Paul, 4th rev. ed., 1972), passim.

³ Cp. my *Conjectures and Refutations,* 4th rev. ed., pp. 152 f. The first two lines of my text are fragment B 16 and the next four fragment B 15. The remaining three fragments are B 18, 35,

and 34 (according to Diels-Kranz, *Fragmente der Vorsokratiker,* 5th ed.). The translations are mine. Note, in the last quoted two lines, the contrast between the one final truth and the many guesses, or opinions, or conjectures.

⁴ Parmenides used Xenophanes' terminology; see *Conjectures and Refutations,* 4th rev. ed., e.g., pp. 11, 17, 145, 400, 410. See also my *Open Society,* Vol. I, n. 56, section (8), to Chap. 10, p. 312.

⁵ See Parmenides' remark (in fragment B 6) on the muddled horde of erring mortals, always in two minds about things, in contrast with the one 'well rounded truth'. Cp. *Conjectures and Refutations,* pp. 11, 164 f.

⁶ *Theogony,* 720-25.

⁷ *Iliad,* VIII, 13-16; cp. *Aeneid* VI, 577.

⁸ See my *Conjectures and Refutations,* 4th rev. ed., pp. 126 ff., 138 f., 150 f., 413.

⁹ *Theogony,* 720-25.

¹⁰ The discovery is, it appears, due to Parmenides; see fragments B 14-15:
      Bright'ning the night she glides round the earth with a light that is borrowed;
      Always she wistfully looks round for the rays of the sun.

¹¹ See Alfred Tarski, *Logic, Semantics, Metamathematics,* trans. by J. H. Woodger (New York: Oxford University Press, 1956). I have expounded it in various places; see, for example, my *Conjectures and Refutations,* pp. 223-25.

¹² See Benjamin Lee Whorf, *Language, Thought, and Reality,* ed. by John B. Carroll (Cambridge, Mass.: MIT Press, 1956).

¹³ See W.V. Quine, *Word and Object* (Cambridge, Mass.: MIT Press, 1960); and *Ontological Relativity and Other Essays* (New York: Columbia University Press, 1969).

¹³ᵃ Cp. p. 232 of T. S. Kuhn, 'Reflections on my Critics', in *Criticism and the Growth of Knowledge,* ed. by Imre Lakatos and Alan Musgrave (London: Cambridge University Press, 1970), pp. 231-78.

¹⁴ When writing this section, I had originally Thomas Kuhn in mind, and his book *The Structure of Scientific Revolutions* (Chicago: Chicago University Press, 1962, 1970). (See also my contribution, 'Normal Science and its Dangers', to *Criticism and the Growth of Knowledge,* ed. by Imre Lakatos and Alan Musgrave [London: Cambridge University Press, 1970], pp. 51-58.) However, as Kuhn points out, this interpretation was based on a misunderstanding of his views (see his 'Reflections on my Critics', in *Criticism and the Growth of Knowledge,* pp. 231-78; and his 'Postscript 1969' to the 2d ed. of *The Structure of Scientific Revolutions*), and I am very ready to accept his correction. Nevertheless, I regard the view here discussed as influential.

¹⁵ For a Criticism of Karl Mannheim, see Chaps. 23 and 24 of my *Open Society,* Vol. II.

¹⁶ Few people seem to realize that by his equation $E = mc^2$, Einstein resurrected the fluidum theory of heat (caloric) for which the question whether heat has any weight was regarded as crucial. According to Einstein's theory, heat *has* weight—only it weighs very little.

¹⁷ Cp. the discussion between Planck and Mach, especially Planck's paper 'Zur Machschen Theorie der physikalischen Erkenntnis', *Physikalische Zeitschrift,* **11** (1910), 1186-90.

¹⁸ See, for example, J. S. Bell, 'On the Einstein Podolsky Rosen Paradox', *Physics,* **1** (1964), 195-200; J. S. Bell, 'On the Problem of Hidden Variables in Quantum Mechanics', *Reviews of Modern Physics,* **38** (1966), 447-52; John F. Clauser, Michael A. Horne, Abner Shimony, and Richard A. Holt, 'Proposed Experiment to Test Local Hidden Variable Theories', *Physical Review Letters,* October 13, 1969. An extension or strengthening of the EPR paradox

described in my *Logic of Scientific Discovery* (New York: Basic Books, 1959, 1972), pp. 446-48, seems to me to involve a decisive refutation of the Copenhagen interpretation since the two simultaneous measurements together would allow simultaneous 'reductions' of the two wave packets which cannot be carried out within the theory. See also the recent paper by James Park and Henry Margenau, 'Simultaneous Measurability in Quantum Theory', *International Journal of Theoretical Physics,* **1** (1968), 211-83.

[19] See my paper 'Quantum Mechanics Without "The Observer" ', in *Studies in the Foundations, Methodology and Philosophy of Science,* Vol. 2: *Quantum Theory and Reality,* ed. by Mario Bunge (New York: Springer-Verlag, 1967).

[20] See my *Open Society,* Vol. II, Chap. 11, Sec. II; or my paper 'Quantum Mechanics Without "The Observer" ', esp. pp. 11-15; or my *Conjectures and Refutations,* pp. 19, 28, section (9), and pp. 279, 402.

[21] I am greatly indebted to my friend Alan Musgrave for reminding me to include in this paper the logical diagnosis contained in the present section.

BRAND BLANSHARD

PRACTICAL REASON: REASON AND FEELING IN 20TH-CENTURY ETHICS

To the rest of the world the United States is a moral paradox. We have the most wealth, the highest standard of living, the most universities and colleges, the most church members, of any country in the world. We also have the highest crime rate. According to the National Commission on Violence, our rate for homicide is more than four times that of our neighbor Canada, and between eight and nine times that of Britain; the incidence of rape is three times that of Canada and twelve times that of Britain; our robbery rate is twice that of Canada and nine times that of Britain; our rate of aggravated assault is eighteen times that of Canada and double that of Britain. The Commission added to its report some sinister notes: there were probably twice as many crimes as were officially reported and the majority of those apprehended for their crimes were under twenty-one.

Much of this misconduct is no doubt due to special American circumstances—our conglomerate of races, the decay of our inner cities, the rise of narcotics addiction. Such facts explain much of the license that obtains at the lower levels of our society. But they will hardly explain the rash of corruption in high places. There has been tragic exposure in recent years of moral insensitivity at the highest levels of government. It has also come to light in Congress and even in candidates for the Supreme Court, and in the heads of large companies and powerful unions, who have not only indulged in shady practices, but have defended them as if the lines between right and wrong had been blurred or obliterated in their minds. James Reston has written that in spite of the differences between hawks and doves, blacks and whites, Republicans and Democrats, they are all united on one thing, "that something is wrong, that there is now no common code of conduct in the United States that unites the nation and guides the people about what is right and what is wrong."

I wish I were in a position to ferret out the causes of this confusion and to make useful suggestions for clearing it up. But on questions of public policy, as Bertrand Russell has argued elsewhere in this volume, philosophers can hardly set up as prophets; what is needed is special knowledge of social cause and effect, which they seldom have. One kind of special knowledge, however, they do or should have, namely knowledge of ethical theory. And this knowledge has bearing at the present time because the same uncertainty and conflict that exists at the lowest levels of practice unhappily exists also at the highest levels of theory. The most competent doctors of the schools disagree as to what makes an experience good or bad, what makes an act right or wrong, and what in us pronounces judgment on either question. They are poles apart even as to whether there is such a thing as moral knowledge at all. It is this last division among them that I want to discuss. Are moral convictions matters of insight or matters of taste? May a moral "judgment" be an expression of knowledge or is it an expression of feeling? That is the great question of our time in ethics, and it has split the community of moral philosophers down the middle. I should like to state the problem, to compare some contemporary answers to it, and to suggest an answer of my own. And I hope the reader will be charitable if he finds that in trying to answer it, I have been forced into the outline of an ethical system as a whole.

I think it is clear enough where most of us stand on this issue. When we say, for example, that stealing is wrong or that Albert Schweitzer was a good man, we suppose that we are saying something true, and that any reasonable mind can see it to be true. On the other hand, philosophers of great ability and influence have recently been telling us that in this we are mistaken, that a moral statement expresses not knowledge but feeling. And likes and dislikes are obviously neither true nor false, neither provable nor refutable. It follows that morality is not a rational affair, and that there is and can be no such thing as a rational standard of conduct.

Now this cleavage in the theory of morals is not just a passing conflict. It reflects a rift at the heart of our western ethical tradition. That tradition has two main sources, Athens and Jerusalem. The three great Greeks were rationalists in ethics. Socrates established the Greek tradition by arguing that to see what was right was an exercise of reason; for him the first essential of the good life was wisdom, an understanding of how a proposed act was related to one's own good, to the good of the community, and ultimately to the good of the world. Indeed the real difficulty in doing what was right was intellectual, for if we only saw clearly what we ought to do, we should do it automatically. His philosophic son and grandson, Plato and Aristotle, with some footnotes of their own, took the same view.

In the other main strand of our ethical tradition, this emphasis on reason almost wholly disappears. The stress of the Hebrew-Christian ethics is not on a clear head but on a clean heart. When the call came to condense the law and the prophets into a single word, that word was not knowledge but love—love of God and love of man. Out of the heart of man good or evil proceeded; if the inside of the cup was cleansed, the outside would take care of itself. The kind of wisdom prized by the Greeks, St. Paul thought a stumbling block. "Where is the wise? Where is the scribe? Where is the disputer of this world? Hath not God made foolish the wisdom of this world?" Babes and sucklings as regards such wisdom were farther than the philosophers in the knowledge of good and evil if their hearts were pure. Not that wisdom in every sense was depreciated; faith had its own kind of wisdom; but this was a divine gift and neither an achievement of natural reason nor, if recent theologians are to be followed, even continuous with or necessarily consistent with it.

This ancient conflict between reason and feeling as the guide and judge of conduct has plagued the whole later development of ethics, though in different times it has taken different forms. It has broken out anew in each of the last three centuries. In the early eighteenth century, it erupted in the debate between Clarke and Shaftesbury. Clarke held that the duties of being just and benevolent had the same sort of clearness and necessity as attached to propositions in geometry. Shaftesbury held on the contrary that insight in moral matters was not a function of reason at all; it was a kind of taste, like the sense of beauty. Later in the eighteenth century the conflict broke out again between two of the giants of philosophy, Hume and Kant. For Hume moral approval was a feeling. To be sure, reason might be at work in moral judgment in the sense of spinning out for us the consequences of an action, but the approval accorded in the light of these consequences was a response of pure feeling. Moral appraisal, therefore, was not a rational affair; goodness is neither more nor less rational than wickedness; "it is not contrary to reason," said Hume, "to prefer the destruction of the whole world to the scratching of my finger." To Kant such teaching was anathema. The perception that an action was right was an activity of reason alone. When in doubt about a proposed action, what you were to do was first to see what it was in essence or in principle, for example a lie or a breach of promise; and you were then to ask whether you could will consistently that this principle should be adopted by everyone. If you could, the action was right; if not, wrong. The stress was on conceiving the act correctly and grasping the consistency of the principle—intellectual operations both. The pendulum had swung to the opposite extreme from Hume.

The conflict broke out again in the nineteenth century. Among the moralists of that century the greatest, I think, was Henry Sidgwick. Like Kant he was a rationalist, but he seems to me a more clearheaded one. He held that on moral matters we have self-evident rational insights at many points. "I undoubtedly seem to perceive," he wrote, "as clearly and certainly as I see any axiom in Arithmetic or Geometry, that it is 'right' and 'reasonable' for me . . . to do what I believe to be ultimately conducive to universal Good or Happiness." He thought it self-evident to reason that happiness was good and the only good, that I should prefer my greater good to my lesser, that I should prefer your greater to my own lesser good, that I should treat people equally unless I could adduce some ground for treating them differently, that experience A was intrinsically better or more worth having than experience B. If persons and peoples differed as widely as they did on moral issues, that was because their intelligence differed natively, or had been repressed or distorted by circumstances. In Sidgwick "the fundamental precepts of morality are essentially reasonable."

One day there appeared in Sidgwick's study a young man from Finland named Edward Westermarck, who discussed this point with the master and seems to have gone away shaking his head. The differences in ethical judgment were far greater, he thought, than could be accounted for by differences in intelligence; indeed some of the very propositions Sidgwick took as self-evident were denied by other moralists of the highest standing. There was only one course, Westermarck believed, that would do justice to these differences, and that was to identify approval with a more capricious and variable element in our emotions. He went beyond even Hume, for though he still made approval a matter of feeling, he interpreted the judgment "that is wrong" to mean not, as Hume did, "most people have a feeling of disapproval for it," but "*I* have such a feeling." The massive volumes of his *Origin and Development of the Moral Ideas* he regarded as a single sustained inductive argument for this position.

There were many who thought that with this debate between Sidgwick and Westermarck the cleft between reason and feeling in ethics had reached its nadir; it could hardly go deeper. The twentieth century has shown, in the conflict between deontologists and emotivists, that it can go deeper still. The deontologists were the new rationalists. Sir David Ross put their position flatly: "That an act, *qua* fulfilling a promise, or *qua* effecting a just distribution of good . . . is *prima facie* right, is self-evident. . . . It is self-evident just as a mathematical axiom, or the validity of a form of inference, is self-evident. In our confidence that these propositions are true there is involved the same trust in our reason that is involved in our confidence in mathematics; and we should have no justification for trusting it in the latter sphere and distrusting it in the former." Ross did not hold, with Kant, the strange doctrine of once-right-always-right; it was only the prima facie rightness of promise-keeping, for example, that was self-evident, not its rightness in a particular case, where he admitted that good consequences might justify breach of promise. But whether these consequences were themselves good or evil, and whether the duty to produce them outweighed the duty to keep a promise, were themselves matters of intellectual apprehension. By his masterly defense of these positions, Ross kept the rationalist tradition vigorously alive.

His defense, however, was promptly and bluntly challenged. Eminent moralists were soon saying that even Westermarck had admitted too large an intellectual element into moral appraisal. After all, he agreed with the rationalists in saying that "X is right" is an assertion, even though it only asserts that I have a feeling. The emotivists and imperativists, however, would deny that it is an assertion at all. For the emotivists it is an exclamation expressing attraction or repugnance; for the imperativists it is a veiled command to do X. In neither case is one saying anything that could be assented to or denied. If someone says "Hurrah!" one can hardly answer "Nay, not so"; if he says "Turn out the light," one cannot sensibly answer "I think so too." The same holds of moral statements; they are utterances that assert nothing; their value terms refer to nothing. They do not ascribe characters to any object; they express the attitudes of the subject.

It may be that between the party of reason and the party of feeling an even deeper cleavage will develop, but I confess that I do not see how it could. The difference here is flat, uncompromising, and ultimate. Ross held that when you say "promise-keeping is right," you are asserting as true something you see to be as necessarily true as that two straight lines cannot enclose a space. The party of feeling holds that, far from seeing anything to be necessary, you are not even seeing anything to be true. You are of course conceiving or contemplating a kind of act, promise-keeping, but, contemplating this object, you are saying something like "Cheers!" or "Please do act in conformity with it."

The parties in this ethical debate have now drawn so far apart that they have left the center of the stage invitingly open for anyone else who wants to make an entrance. One cannot take sides with both parties, and for my own part I cannot take sides with either. Indeed the real choice in recent ethics seems to me to lie between three ways of thinking. First there is what I have called the party of feeling, who deny that moral judgments express knowledge at all, a view that has been held in somewhat different forms by Ayer, Hare, Russell, Carnap, Reichenbach and Stevenson. Secondly, there are the deontologists who revived rationalism in a new form, and who have been led by a brilliant quartet of thinkers—H. A. Prichard, E. F. Carritt, and Sir David Ross of Oxford, and—some would add—C. D. Broad of Cambridge. Between these extremes lies another school, with a longer tradition than either, which insists that in deciding what we ought to do there is one factor that is always decisive, namely the value of the consequences. The leading member of this school in the twentieth century was G. E. Moore, though Hastings Rashdall, now largely forgotten, was also an able proponent of it. I have had the rare privilege of knowing all these men and of having had a fair number of them as teachers and friends. If we now look briefly at the two extremes, it may help us to see why many persons, including myself, have felt compelled to draw back from both.

First, then, as to the weaker of the two extremes, emotivism. I do not think that emotivists are always clear what they are trying to do. When they tell us what "X is right" means, are they trying to give us (1) what the plain man means, or (2) what the self-critical and reflective man means, or (3) what we ought to mean, whether in fact anyone does mean it or not? If it is number (1), what the plain man means, that they are offering us, we may dismiss it at once. For the plain man certainly thinks he is saying something true, and I see no reason for holding that he is in the dark about this intention of his. If it is account number (3) that we are being given, namely what people ought to mean, this must signify for an emotivist either a usage that happens to arouse in him favoring emotion, and then if one does not feel in the same way it would be pointless to say one ought to adopt it, or else what reflective and self-critical people mean, and then we have sense number (2). Is it true, then, that self-critical people intend when they judge morally to express attitudes only, as distinct from saying anything true or false?

Surely not. To put such an intention in their mouths would make it impossible for them to say many things that they plainly want to say. For example, they could not in consistency say that anyone had ever been good or bad in the past, or any act right or wrong, or any experience valuable or disvaluable, or that any would ever be so in the future. If they used language that seemed to say this, they would find that they were only expressing how they felt now about something in the past or future, not reporting any character that people or actions had when they existed. They are ascribing no badness to Judas, no goodness to St. Francis, no wrongness to Booth's act of assassination, no evil to that future atomic destruction that we are nevertheless somehow afraid of. In speaking of past or future evil, they are expressing nothing that could not be removed by merely thinking of something else. No crime is a crime until it is discovered, and it remains a crime only so long as we have a feeling about it. To offer evidence that an act is wrong, or to try to justify it by reasoning, is inept, for an exclamation can be neither proved nor disproved. In short, emotivism can be accepted only by someone who is ready to renounce the clear intentions of both plain and reflective men and substitute a meaning of his own.

Many people now think of emotivism as an old-fashioned theory that went out with logical positivism, of which it was indeed one thesis, and that the new methods of linguistic analysis have gone on to something more sound and subtle. There is no doubt that these methods have made us aware of shades of meaning and attitude not clearly distinguished before. But on the issue we are considering, the place of reason in moral judgment, the linguistic philosophers seem to me to stand where the emotivists stood. Mr. Toulmin thinks he is going beyond them when he interprets "X is right" as meaning "there are valid reasons for taking X to be right." But then taking X to be right still seems in his account to be not a judgment, but the having of a feeling or attitude, and how a feeling or attitude can be validated by reasons he does not make clear. Mr. Hare thinks he goes beyond the emotivists both in his analysis of moral approval and in his way of supporting it. His improvement in respect to analysis is to make "X is wrong," into a command, "don't do X," rather than the expression of a feeling. But to argue that when we say "Judas's betrayal was wrong" we mean "Judas, don't do it," seems even less convincing than to take it as an expression of revolted feeling. As for the support of a moral utterance, Mr. Hare holds that we can defend a command rationally by showing that it is implied in a system of commands required by our way of life as a whole. A Communist could thus support by reasons his restriction of free speech, and a Christian his rule of forgiveness. This is true, and so far as it goes, is an advance over emotivism. But how is the Christian or Communist to show that his way of life is better than its rival? Here, so far as I can see, Mr. Hare comes out where the emotivists did. The statement that one way of life is better than another is not, for him, a statement at all, but a sort of Kierkegaardian commitment, made for no reasons and defensible by none. Between two ways of life there is no possibility of rational appraisal or choice. And to me it seems clear that even when we say "Christianity is better than communism," we mean to say what at least *may* be true and defensible. All the arguments against emotivism can here be applied again.

We must leave emotivism and its more pallid linguistic legatees behind us and go on to a view that will admit reason to a larger part in ethics. We certainly find that in the deontologists. Sir David Ross wanted no part of emotivism; he was clear that in saying "X is right" he was thinking or asserting something, and not merely indulging in a private emotional or imperative explosion. What part, if any, does rational insight play in such a judgment? It plays a very important part; and we shall do well to see what this is in the sort of case Ross liked to take.

Suppose I have borrowed money from a man of means and have promised to return it on a certain day. On that day I set out with it to his house, but on the way I see a Salvation Army lass tinkling her bell appealingly and collecting for the relief of the down and out. I pause and reflect. What if I should break my promise and give the money for such relief? My creditor will not miss it; he might not even notice my default; while if I gave to relief instead, it would alleviate real need. Which should I do? According to a great tradition in ethics, supported by such names as Mill and Moore, I should always try to produce the greatest good. That would seem to suggest that I should give the money to the Salvation Army lass, and go home with a light purse and a light heart. Now, says Ross, that is an impossible suggestion; none of us really thinks that way or acts that way. It probably would not even occur to us to ask whether breaking our promise would produce better results than keeping it; that is not the point. The point is that we have made a promise, and we can see that we ought to keep it, even at times if it entails worse consequences. If we stopped to think at all, we should probably say to ourselves: "I certainly do have an obligation to concern myself about people in need. I certainly also have obligations to pay my debts and keep my promises. In this case it seems clear that these latter obligations outweigh the former one. I am *more* obligated to repay the loan as promised than to bestow a bounty elsewhere."

We must surely agree with Ross that this is the way we actually think in such situations. When the time comes to repay a debt or keep a promise, we do not resort to calculations of private or even public profit before deciding what we should do; we seem to see our duty in advance of any such calculations; here the deontologists are faithful to the facts. But they go on to explain this duty in a puzzling way. They say that the duty to keep a promise or pay a debt arises wholly out of the character of the act itself; it is not based on any good that may lie either in the action or in its results; strictly speaking it is obligatory for no reason at all.

Here I cannot follow. I agree that we can recognize the duty of keeping a promise without any actual reference to the good involved; what I find it harder to admit is that when we come, on reflection, to justify this obligation, we still dispense with good. With his characteristic fairness, Ross concedes that if the evils entailed by breaking a promise grow great enough, the promise should be broken; no one except possibly Kant in a darker moment would say that if a man's keeping his promise would make it impossible for him to buy medicines needed to save his child's life, he should keep his word and let the child go. It is therefore possible to weigh our obligation to cling to principle and keep a promise against the obligation to produce good. But there is a strange difference between the two obligations. When we are considering only the duty to produce good, the obligation rises and falls with the good involved. On the other hand, the obligation to keep promises may rise and fall without any regard to such good. And when we weigh the two types of obligation against each other, the procedure is curious. The good in one pan rises and falls, while that in the other remains steady at zero. Yet the pan in which there is no good may keep increasing in weight till it far outweighs the other. Now there is nothing self-contradictory in such a view. It may be that there are different kinds of reason for actions' being obligatory, or that some duties have reasons and others not. I can only say that this seems to me less likely than the view that all our duties have grounds, that these grounds will be found in all cases to be what deontologists admit to be the ground in many or most cases, namely the good involved, and that when we weigh our duties against each other, it is on this single scale that we do so.

One knows what the deontologists will reply. It is their main point that we ought at times to take one course rather than another, even when no greater good seems to be involved, and that the greatest good must therefore be abandoned as the test of rightness. Here I think they are wrong. But they can be shown to be wrong only by the development of a new type of teleological ethics, which breaks sharply with Mill, Sidgwick, and even Moore. These thinkers made the rightness of an act depend on the consequences of this act when taken alone, that is, apart from the framework of further practices that it implies. And on that basis, the teleologist is bound to lose his case. It seems mere sophistry to argue that the receipt by a wealthy man of money that he would not miss involves a greater good than the relief of pressing need. Is there any further good, unnoted by the traditional calculations, that is involved in repaying the debt?

Surely there is. If the plain man who refuses to lie or break a promise were asked why he refuses, his first response might well be one of bewilderment, and his second some such remark as, "if people were to lie and break their promises at will, society would go to pieces." This is vague, but suggestive. What is suggestive is the sense that his keeping a promise or repaying a debt is a duty that does not stand alone, and that its fall would carry much else with it. There is enough reason stirring in him to show that he cannot throw over these practices himself without granting a like privilege to others; the real question, as Kant saw, is whether he can approve people generally acting as he does. And the setting of his act is even wider. His keeping a promise or repaying a debt is part of a network of duties that make up his pattern of life. A challenge to any one of them he feels as a challenge to this way of life as a whole; that is why his flouting of one obligation is felt to have such widespread repercussions. If he is really free to throw off a debt, then he is free to break a promise; if he is free to break promises, he is free to deceive people; if he is free to disregard their interests in this way, there is no reason why he should not do so in other ways, to take their property, for example. But if he may do that, he is free to dodge his grocery bills, to cheat the government out of his taxes, to pocket the spoons of his host, to lie out of military service; and if he thinks, he sees that he must in consistency grant these privileges to everyone else. But to do that would be to surrender his whole way of life. He can no more drop one duty without affecting other duties than he can drop an eye or leg without affecting his organism as a whole.

To accept this is to accept a broadened ethics of consequences. H. W. B. Joseph in England and John Rawls in this country have reminded us that the consequences to which utilitarians in the past have appealed have been too narrow, those of the isolated act rather than of the fabric of actions with which this one is bound up. Professor Rawls uses, more happily perhaps than Wittgenstein, the analogy of playing a game. When Casey goes to the bat, he is not free to take four strikes or to gather daisies; by going to the plate, he has committed himself to the game as a whole, with all its rules; if he insists on four strikes just this once, or a pause between bases to gather daisies, the coach and umpire may display imperfect sympathies. If he is to play the game, he cannot pick and choose among its rules. In the same way, the keeping of promises and the paying of debts are rules of a game of honor which we and our fellows are playing with each other, and if each person were free to suspend a rule when he felt like it, the result would not be a minor inconvenience merely; the game as a whole would be wrecked. For the keeping of particular rules, then, there is a very strong rational ground. That ground is that this rule belongs to a network of rules which must be obeyed as a whole if our way of life is to be maintained.

But clearly this is not the end of the road. Why should one way of life be maintained rather than another? Mr. Hare thinks this an unanswerable question. If that is true, practical reason is doomed to defeat, for if the defense of a particular duty turns on the way of life to which it belongs, and this in turn is indefensible by reason, then the particular duty is itself in the end indefensible. Those who believe with Kierkegaard that the good life has no rational foundation will accept this serenely enough, but those of us who have been brought up to believe that the right is the reasonable will not be expected to acquiesce in it unless we have to. And do we have to? I think not. When we objected to the utilitarian, it was not on the ground of his appeal to consequences; indeed in saying that the objective rightness of acts depends on their conduciveness to good, we believe he has the true view. The only rational defense of a way of life—of asceticism or epicureanism or Christianity—lies in showing that it produces the most good. To that major point we resolutely adhere.

But now what does one mean by "good"? That is the next point and it is an all-important one.

We must creep up warily on this notoriously treacherous term. It is easier to illustrate "goods" than to define "good." Among the goods of life we should include happiness, health, books and music, an education, an ample income, and friends. That is a miscellaneous lot, which needs inspection. Some of these things, books and an income for example, are plainly instrumental goods, valued as means to others that are intrinsic, so we may confine ourselves to these latter. But then what is an intrinsic good? Music we should call such; we certainly value it for itself and not merely as a means to something else. But when we speak so, we do not refer to the music scored on a page, or sound waves in a hall; we mean a musical experience. And I think we shall find on reflection that everything about which we are clear that it is intrinsically good is also an experience. Happiness is a kind of experience. The health that we call good is either a state of the body, which is an instrumental good, or else, if it is intrinsically good, is the state of mind subserved by a healthy body. When we speak of an education as good, we mean again the knowledge and wisdom that it should bring. The good of friendship lies in the experience of knowing friends. All good belongs in experience.

But granting that only experiences are intrinsically good, what is it about an experience that makes it so? Some have said, the pleasure in it and only that. Most of us are not inclined to take this very seriously; I sometimes think that the main argument for hedonism is that it was accepted by Henry Sidgwick, an argument of weight indeed, though somewhat less than decisive. The reason for rejecting hedonism is very simple; it is that between two experiences which, in point of mere pleasure, we could not appraise as first and

second—for example that of a drunken spree and that of at last under
standing *Process and Reality* or *Finnegan's Wake,* we do often find it easy to
choose. That is not as it should be if pleasure alone counts.

Nevertheless, on two points I find it impossible to disagree with the
hedonist. The first is the obvious point that pleasure is a good and an intrinsic
good. The second is more disputable, but perhaps more important. It is that
every experience that is intrinsically good brings with it some degree of
pleasure. The exceptions that leap at once to mind—experiences of pain
bravely borne, of the fortitude of fireman or surgeon or Ph.D. candidate—are
cases of instrumental goods; anyone who sought out these experiences for
their own sakes would be an eccentric. And as for the experience of tragedy,
of hard work, mental or physical, of the strenuous effort of sport, there is
much genuine pleasure in them along with elements that, taken alone, would
be evil. But if a man finds no pleasure at all in what he is experiencing, then it
has no value for him. Suppose that the understanding of Whitehead or Joyce
gave you not the slightest wisp of satisfaction, that it were a function of pure
unaffective intelligence in which you took not the slightest interest, would the
experience be valued as intrinsically worth having? Mill went through such an
experience in his famous breakdown at twenty, and he has left it on record
that life without the power to enjoy was only a sapless cactus. Here he seems
to me right. Pleasure, though not *the* good, is a component of all goods.

But it is plainly not the only component. What more is involved in intrin
sically good experiences? According to G. E. Moore what is essential in all
such experiences is just goodness itself. Take the experience of a luxurious
dinner, of rest after labor, of a round of golf when one is fresh, of the Fifth
Symphony, of seeing an old friend, of the relief in getting a difficult letter
written. When we call these experiences good, do we mean the same thing in
each case? Moore held that we do, that the goodness of all these things is the
same, and that it consists of a quality so simple that we cannot analyze or
define it, though if we look carefully we can isolate it from the other qualities
with which it comes. It is a peculiar kind of quality; we might not even think
of including it if we were to offer a description of anything good. Hume im
agines a geometer exclaiming about one of his figures, say a perfect circle,
that it is beautiful, and then going on to describe to you its properties of hav
ing all its points equidistant from its center, and so on. You then say to him
"Yes, yes, I see all these properties, but now point out to me the beauty that
you were speaking of." Could he do it? Of course, not; beauty is not that sort
of character. This is what Moore is saying about goodness. It is not a descrip
tive or natural quality at all. But the conclusions drawn from this insight by
Hume and Moore were very different. Whereas Hume concluded that

goodness, not being a natural quality, could not be a quality at all and must therefore lie in our feelings, Moore concluded that it was still a quality, but a nonnatural quality, apprehended by intelligence but unobservable, based on natural qualities and following from them with a synthetic necessity, but not itself a member of the order of nature. Under the attacks of the neo-Humians, Moore himself wavered for a time, but he never quite gave in to them. It was my privilege to have Moore as a guest for a period of some months in the early days of the war. He admitted at that time as strong an inclination to the view that "good" is only an expression of feeling as to the view that it denotes an objective quality. But when I saw him in Cambridge after the war, and asked whether he felt the same way, his response was, "Oh, no: I now feel more strongly drawn to my original view." When I saw him for the last time in 1955, I asked the same question again. He was more emphatic still that his earlier view was the right one.

That Moore was indeed right against the emotivists I do not question. He was talking, of course, not about moral goodness, the goodness of the habitually dutiful man, but of the intrinsic goodness of experiences. He saw that we do intend to assert something when we say that an experience is good, and he was too clear in this insight to be dislodged from it. But is he equally correct about the character we mean to assert? When we use the word "good" of a satisfying dinner, of a golf game, of the Fifth Symphony, is the character we are asserting really an identical nonsensible nonnatural simple? Many moralists have professed themselves unable to find any such quality and have doubted whether it exists, and I must confess to being one of them. I would go further and say not only that it is doubtful whether this character is in fact present, but that another and more likely candidate is ready to hand. This other character is that of fulfilling impulse. The dinner is good because it quenches the elemental demands of hunger and thirst; the golf is good because it fulfils at once our competitive interest in winning, our interest and pride in physical prowess, and probably our interest in being abroad in an attractive countryside. The Fifth Symphony, which E. M. Forster has called "the most sublime noise that ever penetrated the ear of man," is good because it fulfils an aesthetic need and impulse that in some people is among the most imperative demands of their nature. Without such interests or impulses, the experience would cease to be good. A dinner to a man already satiated has no goodness in it. There are many executives, engrossed in other interests, to whom the chasing of a little white ball about the countryside would seem mere lunacy; and to persons like Macaulay and Charles Lamb, Dean Inge and Prime Minister Asquith, who conspicuously lacked ears, the Fifth Symphony would have been martyrdom. William James has speculated on the values that the gorgeous art on the walls of the Vatican Gallery would have for a dog lost in its halls. The answer, of course, is None, and the reason is that there is nothing in its humble bosom to which they can speak; it is apparently unstirred by aesthetic impulses or needs. Some need, some natural demand which an experience may fulfil, is the condition of that experience's being found good.

I hold, then, that what makes an experience good is its possession of two components, the fulfilment of impulse and the feeling of satisfaction that normally attends such fulfilment. No doubt I shall here be charged with the naturalistic fallacy, the fallacy of confusing the *conditions* of goodness, "good-making characteristics," with the meaning of goodness itself. Moore would pretty certainly make this charge. If anyone professed, he would say, to define goodness in terms of fulfilment and satisfaction, you could always show that he was committing this fallacy by pointing out that you could meaningfully ask whether being fulfilling and satisfying was really good. If it was identical with being good, one would be asking the meaningless question whether good is good, whereas the question is an open and significant one. My answer is of course to deny that the question is an open and significant one; indeed to say that this definition commits the naturalistic fallacy is itself the fallacy of begging the question. If a person says that he means by "good" fulfilling and satisfying, anyone who tells him that he can meaningfully ask whether these things are good is assuming that what he says is not true. I am suggesting that the joint fulfilment and satisfaction provided by an experience are not merely the conditions of goodness, or characters from which its goodness may be deduced; they *are* the goodness; their presence is what being good means.

Of course I do not expect this to go unprotested. There is an obvious objection to it. This is that when one calls the golf game or the Fifth Symphony good, and then looks into one's mind for any explicit reference to its being fulfilling or satisfying, one simply does not find it. I admit this. But the objection is less important than it seems. For it assumes that we cannot mean anything by our words that we cannot readily make explicit. If that is true much of what has passed as philosophy has been curiously pointless. Socrates tried through ten books of the *Republic* to run down what he meant by justice, and there are those who think that he barely got his hands on it in the end. What a waste of energy if the meaning really lay on the surface, ready to be picked up! Whatever we may think of the linguistic analysts, we must surely admit their contention that the great little words of our language, such words as "true," "know," "life," "can," "ought," though they give us no trouble if we ask no questions, are full of mystery and bafflement if we do. Now "good" is one of these words. It is on our lips every day, and no one looks puzzled when we use it. We should never think of looking it up in a dictionary, and if we did, we should probably be quite content with the Oxford Dictionary's offering: "a term of general or indefinite commendation." But if this is all there is to the meaning, how did it become a battleground, with such clear heads as Hume and Moore on opposite sides?

The fact is that the term, like the others just mentioned, has more than one kind of meaning. It has a common or current meaning that is definite enough for all ordinary purposes, but not for ethics. It also carries a penumbra of implicit meaning which ethics must try to crystallize. When we say that a "good" experience means one that is fulfilling and satisfying, we are not suggesting that the plain man would come out with this as what he obviously meant; he would all too probably repudiate it. What we are contending is that if he hung on to his search in Socratic fashion till it yielded a meaning that covered consistently his applications of the term, which gave the intension required by its extension, he would find that only this would do. It is not his first meaning, but his last.

Whatever you may think of this view, it would clear up with grateful ease the old disputes about the objectivity of values and of value judgments. Some influential writers—Dean Inge and Nicolai Hartmann, for example—have held that values are eternal, that like the multiplication table they loom over against all human apprehension of them as independent and timeless essences. This view of course we cannot accept. Values are relative and dependent on the minds whose needs and impulses they fulfil. If some comet were to switch its tail of noxious gases over our planet tonight and asphyxiate all life upon it, would there be any value in the world tomorrow? I think not, unless indeed in some corner of the universe there are other creatures with needs and impulses that are in some measure fulfilled. To say, as some Aristotelians and Thomists do, that value lies in the achievement of form by matter and that a rock on a lifeless planet has value to the extent that it realizes its rockness conveys no meaning to me. When there is no consciousness there is no value. Values in that sense are subjective.

But it is confusion to argue from this that value judgments are not objectively true. They are as true or false as any judgments in physics. If the golf game or the symphony does fulfil and satisfy the person who experiences it, then his experience is good, and the goodness of that experience is a fact as objective, as little dependent on any judge's thinking or feeling about it, as Gibraltar. The relativity of values to experience is wholly consistent with their independence of value judgments.

There are people whose patience will be taxed by this account of goodness because it seems to violate a first principle of theirs. They will say, "The drift of all this is painfully clear. You are really reducing the 'ought' to the 'is,' and we know the end of all such schemes. There may be some plausibility in defining the right action as the one productive of most good, and even in defining the good as experience that is fulfilling and satisfying, but what can you make of duty on such a theory? When we say that a man *ought* to do something, we are not referring to any fact; we are plainly not describing anything that is. There is something in that 'ought' that eludes, and is bound to elude, every kind of naturalism."

Now it is true that I am proposing one kind of naturalism, and am ready to apply it to the ought as well as to the good. Just as I find it hard to verify Moore's nonnatural goodness, so I find it hard to verify Kant's nonnatural ought, that tremendous ukase issued by a transcendantal self, permitting of no exceptions, and carrying with it the guarantee of God, freedom, and immortality; nonnatural ethics is usually also unnatural ethics. When one turns from Kant's categorical to Emil Brunner's Divine Imperative, discontinuous with our psychology, logic and ethics, one feels as if ethics had exalted itself right out of the world of merely reasonable men. And as for Kierkegaard, with his "teleological suspension of the ethical" in the interest of what more benighted moralists would call murder, one can only recall gratefully W. K. Clifford's "still small voice that murmurs 'Fiddlesticks.' " Duty is a high and serious matter, too serious to be left in the hands of prophets of the irrational. That is why I should like to see it naturalized and made intelligible. We can still believe with Christians that duty is of the first moment while also believing with the Greeks that every ideal has its natural basis and every impulse its ideal fulfilment.

"Education is good"; we have seen what "good" means. But "I ought to educate myself"; what does that "ought" mean? Its meaning is appointed, I suggest, by the facts of human nature. A man is a bundle of drives or impulses, impulses to know, to love, to create, to fight, to laugh. These make him what he is; their fulfilment in himself and others is the whole and only point of his existence. As he fulfils them he becomes more fully himself; as he represses them, he commits partial or total suicide. He can do that, of course, if he chooses; he can elect to shrivel his being nearer and nearer to zero. But if he does, something in him protests. The voice he hears protesting is the voice not of what is, but of what might be, of the unborn possibilities he has elected to kill, of ends that the race itself lives to realize. This "ought" is not a hypothetical imperative of the form "*if* you want *x,* do *y.*" The ends are unavoidable ends because prescribed for him by nature, and they can be rejected only at the cost of throttling his own soul. To say that I ought to educate myself is not of course to say that I must do so; it is to say, first, that it is better to do so, and then to add that by failing to do so I shall deny that inner demand whose partial fulfilment has made me what I am and whose further fulfilment is the point of living at all. I do not think that this makes duty trivial. It is still a categorical imperative—not now the descent of "skyey influences" into the human scene, but rather the coming to flower of a deeply rooted natural growth. By such a naturalism duty is domesticated and rendered rational.

With this rationalization of duty, what we set out to do is done. To the question whether moral judgment is primarily a matter of reason or of feeling, we have answered that it is a matter of reason, though feeling is deeply involved in the values on which reason must pass its judgment. The three chief terms of the moral life are "right," "good," and "ought," and to use any of them in a case of choice is to say something objectively true or false. To ask about an action whether it is right is to ask whether it, or more strictly the network of actions implied in it, would or would not produce the greatest good; and reason is involved, though in somewhat different senses, both in forecasting the consequences and in weighing them against each other. To ask whether an experience is good is again to ask a question answerable only by a reason which can take account of two independent variables, the fulfilment by the experience of a natural impulse or need, and the satisfaction which normally accompanies such fulfilment. The comparison and balancing are clearly functions of reason. But the contents that are compared depend on feeling, if impulse and satisfaction may be allowed to fall under that head. Finally, to recognize that we ought to do something is to see not only that it is right, as productive of good, but that it is so linked with the ends of the self and the race that we cannot evade it without abandoning both.

Or if a historical summary is preferred, one may put the matter thus: Kant and his modern followers were right in insisting that reason is still reason when it turns to practical life. Aristotle and the self-realizationists were right that the range of what we find good depends on the wants and needs of human nature. And though Sidgwick and the hedonists were wrong in holding that pleasure *is* the good, they were right in holding that it is an indispensable component of the good.

BRAND BLANSHARD

NEW HAVEN, CONNECTICUT
MAY, 1972

CARL J. FRIEDRICH

SOME REFLEXIONS ON THE POLITICS OF THE PUBLIC GOOD

In contemporary American political science the notion of a Public Good, often spoken of as the public interest, has been seriously questioned. It has been asserted at length that these terms lack specific content. The implicit scepticism, or even cynicism, has not always been realized by the authors of such views.[1] The proposition is more readily arguable regarding the public interest; for an interest is often understood as something separate, distinct and hence necessarily plural.

It is of course true that in the rhetoric of practical politics the public good is frequently a facade claimed by special interest groups who wish themselves to be identified with the public good. In fact, there usually is a basis in fact for such claims; for in a well-ordered society the well-being of each component group or element is "in the public interest." But that is not as a rule the political issue. That issue is rather whether a particular interest conflicts with other particular interests, and whether and how all these interests might be adjusted to each other and balanced with each other. In a rather telling German way of putting it one may say that the public good *(oeffentliche Wohl) ist uns nicht gegeben, sondern aufgegeben.* It is an *Aufgabe,* a task and not a given that could serve as a premise.

Without pursuing this line of argument further, let us at this point ask: what are public goods? and how can they be secured? Among the many possible public goods, let us select peace; for it is surely by most men acknowledged to be a good which is good for most men most of the time.

Revolutionaries and conquerors—two aggressors who seek change by violence—are the obvious exceptions. If one reviews the classical writings which justify war and revolution he finds that the argument, whether in St. Augustine or Hegel, is based upon the assertion that some other public good is greater, is a more valuable good, than peace. It might be the spread of Christianity, or the promotion of communism—it is usually a gospel, a *Heilslehre,* which is involved. It is the recurrent dialectic of such gospels that the cost of violence appears too high in retrospect, that is to say: the public good of peace appears greater than the new society or faith, at least to those who are not converts.

The last remark leads to the question: whose good is the public good, *or,* to put it in personal terms: who is the public that is meant when the public good is exorcised. In our democratic way of looking at politics the answer seems obvious: the people. The public good is the people's good. *Res publica est res populi.* Cicero formulated the basic tenets, and they have remained the core of republicanism. If one looks farther afield, he finds that the public good is closely linked to the particular political order; in a monarchy the public good is what is good for the prince, in an aristocracy what is good for the nobles, in a theocracy what is good for the priests and their church and so forth. Empirically speaking, the person or persons who are meant by *public* depends upon who is seen as the ruler of the community. If one were to generalize, he could say that the public good is the good of the political order.

This conclusion demonstrates the vacuity of the outlook of our political scientists as referred to above. For it is certainly meaningful to speak of and to search for what is good for such a particular group of persons as princes, noblemen, priests, or members of a party. When a Hitler rants about the public good *(Gemeinwohl geht vor Eigennutz),* he is referring to his partisans, the so-called Aryans who believe in a Nordic race whose interest, whose well-being must be admitted as providing the ultimate standard for the Public Good. Such a "thought" may seem utterly ludicrous to others, but it is meaningful and legitimate within Hitler's own frame of reference. To shift to contemporary America, when it is insisted that, e.g., the Vietnam War is not in the public interest, that is to say that no public good is being pursued in fighting it, it is evident that the sharp disagreement on such a statement turns upon a disagreement over who is the public whose good should be taken as paramount. When the president talks about "peace with honor" he assumes that for America "honor" is a paramount good, and that no peace without honor is worth having. These conflicts over what constitutes the paramount public good are recurrent and of the essence of politics, as they are of human existence. And when at the time of grave threat from the Soviet Union people in Europe began to say: I'd rather be dead than red, they were convinced that a non-Communist society was more valuable, was a public good more worthy of pursuit than peace. This sentiment is so strong in some parts of the United States today that it has found its way upon automobile license plates. In the State of New Hampshire one reads: live free or die. An inquiry among persons sporting these plates (inevitably, if they want to drive a car, like the writer) reveals that quite a few prefer life to freedom, if a choice has to be made. Fortunately the consensus in America is so strong on freedom that this alternative is not admitted by most ordinary folk.

The issue of freedom is one in which public and private good become considerably mixed. In the struggle of formerly colonial populations the issue arose in an acute form. For the colonial masters, notably the British, the French, and the Belgians claimed that individual liberty would suffer, if the government were turned over to natives. And surely in many of the new states it has turned out that way. Without citing particular cases, it is fair to say that quite a few of these states are not exemplars of civil liberty protection. Even in a relatively advanced state, such as Puerto Rico, civil liberties are far from secure.[2] Still, it would be maintained by many that the liberation was a *public good,* that freedom gained. A well-known British political philosopher, Isaiah Berlin, has sought to escape from this dilemma by insisting that the collective freedom of peoples seeking liberation is not truly freedom at all. In a striking sentence, he recalled that "the French Revolution, like all great revolutions, was, at least in its Jacobin form, just such an eruption of the desire for 'positive' freedom of collective self-direction on the part of a large body of Frenchmen who felt liberated as a nation, even though the result was, for a good many of them, a severe restriction of individual freedoms."[3] Such national aspirations, he felt, constitute a search for status rather than for freedom; freedom he held, is meaningful only for individuals. Extended to our topic, it would follow that "good" and "interest" are only meaningful for individuals and the concept of a "public good" is meaningless, because there is no collective freedom which would seek to realize such a good, such an interest.

The Greeks, by contrast, saw freedom primarily as the public freedom of participating in decision-making. Their deep concern with the public good, so marked in Plato, led many of them into "democratic" paths. I put the quotation mark, because the meaning of that word in Greek writings is noticeably different from our own. The Greeks, when talking about freedom, when calling themselves *hoi eleutheroi,* the free, were thinking largely in terms of such participating in the community's decisions. These decisions were seen as choices involving the *public good.* The Greek polis knew little of the rights of private persons; private and public good were seen as interdependent—indeed it has been argued that there was no private sphere. In the words of the great Fustel de Coulanges the Ancients "did not believe that there could exist any rights as against the city and its gods."[4] Hence, in the protracted discussions about happiness, it was the public good that was seen as the necessary condition of it. Plato, Aristotle, and many others argued thus. The Romans, and more especially Cicero saw *res publica,* the public good, as the *res populi*—the people's thing. At this point, the terminology of the public good becomes interchangeably interwoven with thoughts on the form of government. The *res publica* in Cicero's treatment suggests what is the central thought on the public good in political perspective: the public good is what the public thinks it is (or ought to think it is—an echo of earlier philosophical speculations on the public good). This thinking of the public is governed by the "law of nature." In Book III, Chapter 22, of his *De Republica,* as reported by Lactantius, he claimed that "the true law is the reason of nature." This ratio is constant, eternal and "distributed among all."[5] We cannot here pursue further the complex issues involved in this crucial category of political thought, except for pointing out that for many a political thinker, including Cicero, the law of nature is the basis for discerning the public good. The public are believed to be guided by this standard, and therefore are seen as the source of public good. "Law, according to Cicero, is not based upon opinion, but upon the very nature of man."[6] Thus natural law provides the basis for a belief in democracy: the belief in man, the common man in American political parlance, justifies the belief that the public good will be realized by the public. Not the speculation of philosophers seeking the stone of wisdom but the common sense of the majority of free citizens will discern the public good. Hence the public good is what such a majority of a free community says it is.

Such a statement may, however, lead to fatal error, if it is understood in a relativistic or sceptical way. Rosenstock Huessy once wrote: "Not the thoughts of the clever or wise, but the talk of the people create the law. . . . Thus a genuine necessary right will be called for and implored, until it becomes law."[7] I later commented: "This process of creating law is the task of the community in its wholeness and strength, its manifold forms as well as its unity; the process results from the interaction and cooperation of all the vital elements of such a community."[8] The law in these passages incorporates the Public Good, it manifests it, and it suggests that what constitutes the public good cannot be understood as something apart from the public, nor can it be understood as something absolute and unalterable. As Rousseau exclaimed when discussing public opinion as "the veritable constitution of the

state": "It takes on every day new powers, when other laws decay or die out
. . . ."⁹ Rousseau mistakenly believed that this veritable constitution is "a
power unknown to political thinkers." As we suggested, it on the contrary
forms the core of political thought since the Ancients. The words may differ,
but the public good, however named, is the core and focal point of political
philosophy, as well as of jurisprudence and law. It cannot be defined or
specified as to content, but only procedurally circumscribed. *Salus publicum
suprema lex esto,* the Romans said. We might translate it as "the public good
should be the highest norm." A shallower age corrupted this proposition into
an existential one. Falsely, it held that *salus publicum suprema lex est,* a
statement which is true only in a *res publica,* a community of free men.
Another Roman principle may, therefore, conclude these rambling reflexions: *Videant consules ne res publica detrimentum capiat!* Let those in charge
see to it that the public thing do not take damage! The public good presupposes an effective government of the people, by the people, for the people.
These familiar words say what needs to be said on the politics of the public
good.

To Saint Augustine we owe the transformation of these universal principles. He did it by transforming or reinterpreting the pagan concept of the
legal community as found in Cicero in a Christian sense. Such a community
is not merely an agreement on law, not merely a mutuality of interests, nor a
compromise on such interests and their integration into a public interest, but
a shared love or cherishing of values and beliefs which identify the public
good. Whether there be a highest value or not, as Plato maintained and
Hobbes denied,¹⁰ there are common values which determine the public good.
Augustine sees the community of law as transcended by the community of
love. Such community of love is the foundation of a *res publica* and its public
good.

By way of a conclusion and in the light of the foregoing reflexions it may
be said that in the political perspective the public good is a standard of
evaluation for public policies. Often a facade for nonpublic interests, it will be
appealed to as indicating what a majority believes to be of benefit to the community at large. Peace, prosperity and other similar generalities serve as abbreviations for what the people desire. In certain respects it resembles the
general will to which Rousseau attributed infallibility.¹¹ The *public good* is,
however, a category of reason and not of will—unless the will is narrowly
defined in rational terms. In normative terms, it may be asserted that the
public good is that policy or act which a rational collective would choose, if it
were acquainted with all the relevant facts. Empirical politics knows of no
such rational collectives; some myth like that of Plato's cave is the only way

to make concrete the existential basis of the public good. Whether this kind of public interest theory is worthy of the name or not, it seems to me worthy of the attention of political philosophers.

CARL J. FRIEDRICH

HARVARD UNIVERSITY

OCTOBER, 1972

NOTES

[1] *The Public Interest—Nomos V,* yearbook of the American Society For Legal And Political Philosophy, ed. by Carl J. Friedrich (New York: Atherton Press, 1962), and therein especially Glendon Schubert, "Is There a Public Interest Theory?" pp. 162 ff. Cf. also the papers by C. W. Casinelli, W. Friedmann, Frank J. Sorauf, and Schubert's volume *The Public Interest,* 1960; he concludes that "there is no public interest theory worthy of the name" (p. 223).

[2] See *Informe al Honorable Gobernador de Estado Libre asociado de Puerto Rico,* a report prepared by the Comite del Gobernador para el Estudio de los Derechos Civiles en Puerto Rico (San Juan: Government of Puerto Rico, 1959). The issue is briefly discussed in my *Puerto Rico—Middle Road to Freedom—Fuero Fundamental* (New York: Rinehart, 1959), and in Henry Wells's *The Modernization of Puerto Rico—A Political Study of Changing Values* (Cambridge: Harvard University Press, 1969), pp. 307-9.

[3] (Sir) Isaiah Berlin, *Two Concepts of Liberty* (New York: Oxford University Press, 1958), pp. 156, 157; reprinted in *Four Essays on Liberty* (New York: Oxford University Press, 1949), pp. 118 ff.

[4] See my *Man and His Government* (New York: McGraw-Hill, 1963), p. 355; and Fustel de Coulanges, *The Ancient City,* 7th ed. (Boston: Lee and Shephard, 1889), p. 298.

[5] See for Cicero's *De Republica,* the splendid critical translation by George H. Sabine and Stanley Barney Smith (Columbus, Ohio: Ohio State University Press, 1929), p. 215.

[6] Ibid.

[7] Eugen Rosenstock (Huessy), *Der ewige Prozess des Rechts gegen den Staat* (Leipzig: Felix Meiner, 1919), p. 20.

[8] See my *The Philosophy of Law in Historical Perspective* (Chicago: Chicago University Press, 1958), p. 199.

[9] Jean-Jacques Rousseau, *Contrat Social,* Book II, Chap. XII.

[10] In the *Leviathan,* Hobbes makes an emphatic point of this position, as it indeed is crucial to his approach; cf. Chap. XI, and my comments in *Man and His Government,* pp. 55 f.

[11] *Contrat Social,* Book II, Chap. III; Book IV, Chaps. I, II; Book II, Chap. VI; cf. for this my *Inevitable Peace* (Cambridge: Harvard University Press, 1948), Chap. VI, esp. pp. 172-73, and the discussion on the rational will and the categorical imperative in their bearing upon this position.

HERBERT FEIGL

THE OUTLOOK
OF SCIENTIFIC HUMANISM

"Scientific Humanism" (or "Naturalistic Humanism") is the philosophy that is appropriate for our age of science. It attempts to combine consistently an intellectual view of man's place in the universe with a moral outlook of man's obligations, ideals and aspirations.

What sort of philosophy appeals to a person depends largely on his temperament, education and cultural environment. Modern psychology is beginning to understand why different personalities favor different views of the world and of life. It is unlikely that men will ever agree in these matters of basic outlook and attitude. (And perhaps one may ask whether it is even desirable that they should agree.)

Statistical evidence shows that among scientists, physicists and astronomers are much more disposed toward religious orthodoxy (of one sort or another) than are psychologists, anthropologists or sociologists. Very likely this is because psychologists and social scientists are much more fully aware of the self-deceptions engendered by wishful thinking.

The very fact that both religious *and* irreligious attitudes are intelligible on scientific (psychological) grounds, and can thus be accounted for scientifically in a much more simple and reliable way than on theological grounds, in itself speaks favorably, though of course not conclusively for the scientific outlook.

The craving for the ultimate truth of a world view, and for absolute, unshakable moral principles is readily understandable from a psychological point of view. The quest for certainty and the wish for security reflect man's precarious situation in a world he never made.

This desire for absolute foundations and indubitable first principles and the deep yearning to be taken care of by a friendly providence or a benevolent (even if severely watchful) God—though entirely understandable—is however in conflict not only with the (tentative) conclusions of science, but especially with the very spirit of scientific method. The most essential lesson modern science can teach us is that of the value of a policy of the *open mind*.

The scientific method of the modern age has produced its momentous results primarily by offering theories which are open to revision, and whose truth is held only "until further notice." A theory is not scientific if it could not conceivably be refuted by contrary evidence. The history of modern science is a sequence of modifications, often of thorough alterations; it is a search for ever new frames of knowledge. Nevertheless, the progress of science is far from chaotic. Usually there is a central core in the older theories which remains valid, as a special case or in restricted domains, within the more embracing new theories.

Philosophers throughout the ages have often displayed a peculiar attitude toward the advance of science. New theories are first declared *taboo* or *anathema* because they do not fit in with the prejudices of the current philosophical outlook. But after the success of the new theories becomes so striking as to be undeniable, the philosophers hug these theories so much to their bosom that they are turned into philosophical *dogmas*. (Some philosophers have tried to demonstrate scientific theories as truths based on pure reason!) But such is the tragicomedy of wisdom, that science, impelled by newly found evidence, meanwhile has moved on to a new stage—and the philosopher's dogma has turned into *superstition!* (I owe these formulations to Philipp Frank.)

Some scientifically oriented thinkers hence have come to regard philosophy as well as theology as self-deceptions and have advocated the complete liquidation of these questionable enterprises. There is however—and to some extent there has always been—another strand in philosophical thought. This strand does not pursue the quest for certainty but adopts the policy of the open mind. As I see it, this is fruitful only if it steers a sane middle course between the extremes of dogmatism and skepticism. The dogmatist, if ever his mind was open at all, has swallowed something that he took for "The Truth" and then shut his mind forever. The extreme skeptic on the other hand, has—as it were—his mind "open at both ends." Everything floats through it, and nothing sticks. The golden mean is of course the *critical attitude* which works with the judgments confirmed by experience thus far, but holds even the best confirmed views in principle ready for modification or even for complete replacement.

More generally and fundamentally, the middle course pursued by the open mind is gradually leading to a new *philosophy of enlightenment*. There are two kinds of fallacies which this philosophy endeavors to avoid. These fallacies are usually expressions of what William James, the great psychologist and philosopher, called the tough-minded and the tender-minded temperaments. The tender-minded always look for the *"something more"*—beyond that which objective evidence can warrant. And the tough-minded tend to restrict knowledge-claims to only the most strongly confirmed judgments, and thus are constantly in danger of reducing the world to *"nothing but"* material things or processes. The new enlightenment proposes instead a philosophy of the *"what is what"!* A truly mature philosophy can avoid the *reductive fallacies* of materialism as well as the *seductive fallacies* of spiritualistic metaphysics.

The new philosophical enlightenment pursued by scientific humanists utilizes as one of its most helpful tools the *logical analysis of language and meaning*. Language, the instrument of human communication, serves many functions. And although these various functions are often most intimately intertwined and fused, it is indispensable, for the sake of clarity (while granting the *fusions*) to distinguish these different functions (and types of significance) and thus to prevent or eliminate *confusions*. It is imperative to distinguish *cognitive significance* from *emotive significance*. Cognitive meanings attach to information (true or false) regarding matters of fact; emotive significance consists in the capacity of language to express or to elicit mental images, emotions, attitudes or actions. Both types of significance are of tremendous importance. But mistaking one for the other is logically disastrous. It is one thing to use words for the communication of knowledge-claims (information); it is another thing to use words in order to convey edification, fortification or consolation.

This is poignantly illustrated in the case of such words as "belief" or "faith." The word "belief" may stand for the sort of assent we give to judgments which are capable of confirmation (or disconfirmation) by empirical evidence. But "belief" (or "faith") is also used for the religious, theological or metaphysical creeds. Here, the believers themselves usually emphasize that beliefs of this kind are not susceptible to confirmation or disconfirmation by the evidence of experience. Thus the suspicion arises that beliefs of this sort are not cognitive at all, but are *emotive* in character, thus expressing an attitude toward life or a basic commitment to certain values or ideals.

The so-called "warfare between science and religion" may be more helpfully viewed, and perhaps even brought to a peaceful conclusion, if the parties to the dispute come to realize fully in just what sense they use the word *"belief."* If it is cognitive, empirical belief, then there is much in the scriptures and dogmas of many historical religions which (if literally interpreted) is incompatible with the best confirmed truths of modern science. Fundamentalism and Literalism are therefore impossible to defend in our age of science. But if theologians start to "demythologize," one must wonder where can they stop, and what will remain as a cognitive core of their "beliefs" or "faiths."

If fundamentalism is abandoned and demythologization carried out completely, perhaps all that is left of theology is its moral appeal and religion will be reinterpreted as a way of life, deeply committed to such ideals as peace, the brotherhood of man, universal kindness and justice, and the self-perfection of man in the arts of living, knowing and creative *doing* (as in literature, music, the arts—and indeed in the wise application of science toward the betterment of mankind). This is precisely the outlook of scientific humanism held by many scientists and philosophers today. (It is also represented, or at least approximated, by the Unitarian Church, especially in the Western United States.)

Many objections to, and criticisms of, scientific humanism rest on misunderstandings. Humanism is often accused of holding a "crass materialism." This is sheer slander. There are many humanist philosophers who take *mind* or some mindlike substance or qualities or events as the inner and fundamental reality of the universe. And no humanist is a "materialist" in the sense that he considers human values and ideals as sheer illusions, or that he recognizes only the needs of the animal in man. (This would indeed be a regrettable "reductive" fallacy.) But it is true that humanists do not look for, or rely upon, indubitable overarching principles of explanation (concerning the universe) or for an absolutistic foundation of morality.

Humanists interpret the facts of human existence along naturalistic but not along materialistic lines. They are not perplexed by the torments of the problem of evil which has notoriously and perennially plagued theologians in the Judeo-Christian tradition. In the last resort the theologians have to admit absolute and unsolvable mysteries: How could an omniscient, omnipotent and benevolent God create a world which contains so much misery, cruelty, injustice, disease and catastrophes? Their answer is ultimately that we human beings are in no position to judge the ways of God. While this may be an expression of praiseworthy humility, the idea of *Deus absconditus,* of a hidden and inscrutable God clearly removes theology from the domain of empirically testable beliefs. Philosophers by now know (or should know) that this is the typical escape for beliefs held on emotional grounds but jeopardized by contrary evidence. Any belief, no matter how fantastic, can be made proof against disproof by the device of "inscrutability." Many modern religionists have therefore abandoned all attempts at proof (even of only very indirect and inconclusive arguments) for the existence of God. But then, does not intellectual honesty demand that the "act of faith," the "leap of belief" be interpreted as a deep moral commitment rather than as a knowledge-claim?

Scientific humanists have no need to admit *unsolvable mysteries*. But they concede (or should concede) that there are many unsolved problems in science and many serious unresolved shortcomings in the life of individuals and of the nations. Those theologians who still fix their attention upon the unsolved problems of science, do more harm than good to the cause of religion. This search for "the chinks in the armor of science," is doomed to end in frustration. Surely, there are unanswered questions in all fields of science. We do not yet know all about atoms and galaxies, about the origin and evolution of life, about the workings of the human mind, etc., nor is it likely that we ever shall. But it is a virtue of scientific humanism to be able to live with an unfinished world view. Advancing science, the endless quest, has solved many a formidably difficult problem and may well be expected to solve many more in the future. And it is another virtue of humanism to be actively interested and engaged in the improvement of the condition of man in his earthly life, rather than to consider this earthly life as a mere preparation for a wishfully hoped for existence in the hereafter.

To the scientifically oriented thinker it is truly strange (but not really astonishing) to observe the strong interest of many religious people in *psychic phenomena, occultism* and *spiritism*. There seems to be now a fair amount of evidence for the occurrence of mental telepathy and clairvoyance. It is not likely that all this evidence can be explained away as due to experimental errors, statistical miscalculations, or to outright fraud or hoax. We have indeed no reliable or even plausible hypothesis or theory which would explain these alleged facts and relate them satisfactorily to the bulk of our established scientific knowledge. Further research is urgently needed in this controversial field. But any theological conclusions seem to me, to put it mildly, entirely premature. Not premature but hopelessly confused is the observation used by some theologians that according to modern physics matter is now to be conceived as much more "spiritual" than it used to be according to the mechanistic-materialistic philosophies of an earlier epoch. This does not even help much with the puzzles of the notorious mind-body problem, but it does not help at all in any argument for the existence of God.

There is one theological argument, however, that deserves a little more careful scrutiny: the argument from religious experience (and especially from mystical experience). No open-minded person can or should deny that many people have religious experiences, and that at least some people have mystical experiences. The question is only what to make of these experiences, how to interpret them. If they are taken to be self-authenticating, i.e. to make self-evident (to the believer) the existence of God, then of course people who have no such experiences will have to trust others who have them. But the scientific temper of our time will not tolerate such a purely subjective and esoteric approach. We shall want to know for what good reason those experiences are to be accepted as *indications* of a supernatural power. And we shall not pay much attention to these reasons if the facts of religious (and mystical) experience can be accounted for in a perfectly naturalistic way. There is indeed a very plausible psychological explanation of these experiences: The reason why so many people, in such varied cultural situations have the experience of a personal God, is that they all were helpless infants and children at one time, surrounded by comparatively all-powerful adults on whom they depended, at first for their physical survival and sustenance, and later on—very significantly—for moral guidance, encouragement and discouragement. No wonder then, that once emancipated from their natural parents, people need a substitute and tend to erect the idea of God in their father's (or mother's) image.

At this point I am usually told that the tables may well be turned on the naturalistic atheist: His refusal to believe, his lack of religious experience, can equally well be explained on psychological or psychoanalytic grounds. His aversion to "father figures" of any sort may well be due to a strong Oedipus complex. To this I reply that if our psychology is to be adequate at all, it had better be able to account for the atheist's attitude just as much as for the attitude of the theist (and, *mutatis mutandis,* for the metaphysician's belief in Absolutes, as well as for the positivist's militant repudiation of Absolutes). But this is exactly as it should be. From a scientific point of view both sorts of attitudes should be explainable on the basis of the same type of psychological premises. The argument which attempted to "turn the tables" on the naturalist is beside the point; it does not concern the issue under dispute. The question was: can the features of religious experience be explained without theological hypotheses? And to this question I have sketched an affirmative reply.

It is often said that the scientists' world view also rests on faith and that it could not possibly be established without an "inductive leap." The reply to this is simply that if theologians could formulate testable hypotheses, then no matter how large the inductive leap, theology would differ from science only in degree of, but not in the kind of method used for, confirmation. But at crucial points, the theologians withdraw to the nontestability (inscrutability) position already discussed before. The inductive beliefs of science are all in principle objectively testable, even if practically-technically there are often serious difficulties in testing them.

Finally, there is the contention that life can have no meaning, and morality no firm foundation unless a religious point of view is adopted. If by "religion" is meant a commitment to certain ideals of life, then humanists are religious people. But the word "religion" like so many another emotionally charged word is open to persuasive definition. "Religion" may mean a way of life either *with* a theological creed or *without*. I have no axe to grind on this terminological issue, although my own preference is to label the outlook of scientific humanism a *philosophy,* rather than a religion. In the Western world of the Jewish-Christian traditions, the word "religion" almost always connotes a creed involving belief in a personal God. It is therefore misleading for scientific humanists to call their outlook a religion.

Does life have meaning without a transcendent creed? Of course it does. The aspirations of individuals and of communities toward a better condition of mankind are directed toward a universal goal. The joys of work and leisure, the happiness of love and friendship, the deep satisfactions that come with unselfish, kindly acts, the appreciation or creation of works of art—all this and much more—give life a very full meaning. The trouble with most of us is that we are such egregious blunderers in the art of living. Here, scientifically enlightened education and politics could help enormously.

That there is a tragic aspect to life only very superficial humanists would deny. But the mature humanist will face the evil and the tragedies of life and try to *do* something about it instead of bemoaning the basic sinfulness of man, or giving way to a philosophy of despair.

Human values and ideals are indeed the product of natural biological, psychological and social evolution. They have, in this way, a firm foundation in human nature as it exists in the social context. But neither human knowledge nor human values can be regarded as absolutely infallible or unalterable. Social evolution may carry us to greater heights than purely biological evolution could ever attain.

Herbert Feigl

University of Minnesota
November, 1971

ARTURO FALLICO

PHILOSOPHY AND HUMAN COMMITMENT

The fundamental business of the philosopher, according to one long tradition that begins with Socrates, is to make sure that good and wise men are not ruled by evil men, by usurpers, or political ignoramuses. This has been the central premise of the European tradition in philosophy, which from the start has been ethnically and politically oriented. Around the turn of the century, however, with the rise of the new positivists and language analysts, philosophers in this very influential movement renounced their concern with human affairs. They relinquished the ancient role of the philosopher as an educator dedicated to making men more civilized, and in doing so, as Paul Schilpp has eloquently pointed out, abdicated their very duty toward humanity. And this at a time when the affairs of mankind were increasingly headed for a crisis, as we were warned by thinkers like Burkhardt, Spengler, Sorokin, Schweitzer, Tolstoy, Thoreau, Marx, Tawney, Mayieux, Durkheim, Tannenbaum, Huxley, and Einstein. The crisis which these men saw in prospect can be put in terms of four paradoxes.

The first is that the more man's knowledge of himself as a physical object in a physical world increased, and the more his knowledge of that physical world increased, the less he seemed to know about himself as a human being. So that today man's most pressing question is himself—his own being.

The second paradox is that as the demand upon man to make far-reaching value judgments and value decisions and choices has increased, man's confidence and very ability in the making of such value judgments and decisions has decreased. And I think that this deterioration in the field of values and value-deciding is in part due to the direction that education has taken: education which has in late years been directed by fear of what one's enemies are going to do rather than by the Socratic aim of helping men make their rules compatible, so that men can coexist in the same world.

Third, to the extent that our institutions have, with the help of science and technology, become more effective in dealing with quantities of men, and to the extent that these same efficient institutions have become more mechanical and impersonal in their operation, the significance, importance, and value of the individual, of the person taken as the very center and in-itiator of free choice in decisions, has waned to an extreme where the only decisions left to individuals in any country, under any regime, including our own democratic regime, threatens to be limited merely to the area of trivial and banal decisions; all other decisions being made no longer by men, but by computers or gangs of men, anonymous committees hidden in the cellars of the Pentagon building or of a state capital, men who because they are anonymous and impersonal in their decisions, do not have to give account of their deeds and actions that affect the millions upon millions of their fellow men.

A fourth paradox of crisis: in proportion as the technological, in-strumental means for communicating have increased, man's ability to com-municate anything significant, anything that determines value-decisions among men, has decreased. So that we have the spectacle of fast-moving vehicles that transport the written word from one place to another, the spec-tacle of instant transmission by radio and television on the one hand and the gradual impoverishment of human expression, the reduction of human com-munication to a contentless performance that only transforms and—I should say transports—meaningless jargon, deceptive, smoggy double-talk from one conference to another, from one nation to another. Generally, man's ability to exercise the kind of intelligence which clarifies ends and purposes has decreased in proportion as has increased the kind of intelligence that per-mits him to devise the mere means and techniques by which he can affect ends. And so this situation, this paradox, reminds me of the sense of a little song that I found popular in America when I first came here. I think the title of it was "I Don't Know Where I'm Going, But I'm On My Way." Einstein once put it to a graduating class in the East: "Why is it that the more civilized we become, the more unhappy we become?" Why is it that the more we learn about human communication, the more curtains—Iron Curtains, Bamboo Curtains, double-talk curtains, gold curtains—come between men so that communication itself becomes arrested? Yet the element of this crisis which is most important, the one that is best seen by all reasonable men, is the absolute absurdity and madness of a world divided and poised against itself in mortal threat at the very time when at least the potential for eliminating poverty, sickness, and disease from the populations of the world is in sight.

Now the state of philosophy in our day mirrors these paradoxes, mirrors this same crisis. The history of philosophy taken in its entirety seems to me like a creeping skepticism with respect to human knowledge and eventually with respect to human values, only occasionally interrupted by luminous beacons of light, the great philosophers, each one of whom, however, has then appeared in retrospect as a mere mirage, as a delusion, something to be replaced by some other system, some other man, some other school. Between these luminaries the trend has always been toward skepticism. This trend reached its culmination in our day in the Anglo-American school of philosophizing. This school goes under many names, but generally it represents some form of positivism, and what is called "language-analysis" covers the main title of the many variations of this theme. But metaphysics itself, which was the oldest concern of philosophers, was declared to be nonsense, something that should be thrown out of philosophizing; and insofar as any philosopher considers his main concern to be the quest after being, the elucidation of being, just so far, these philosophers maintain that man ought to be informed that he is, if not crazy altogether, then surely in need of some therapy that will help him to get rid of philosophy, that will help him to cure himself of his disease.

The territory of philosophy is, like Caesar's Gaul, divided in three parts: continental European philosophy; Soviet Marxism; and Anglo-American philosophy. But unlike Caesar's Gaul there is virtually no communication between these three territories. Analogous to the situation on the political and economic levels where the various kinds of curtains make sure that communication between humans, particularly on the important question of human values, comes to a stop, philosophers have been even more ingenious in impeding communication with one another, depending on the region of philosophical exploration that we're talking about. They have devised a method of preventing communication which consists simply in declaring that your philosophical opponent has nothing to say, even before he speaks, to insure that when he does open his mouth he has said nothing. Any one of us can, by even a cursory glance at the literature of philosophy in the form of journals and books nowadays or by attending some of our national and international philosophical conventions, be treated to the most fascinating spectacle. You will find in our profession the finest epithets, the most genteel profanity, the most subtle forms of defamation of character, and the most professionally executed mayhem that can ever be imagined. The impression that one gets is that most professional philosophers think that most other professional philosophers do not know what they are talking about.

Now of course my threefold division here of the region and territory of philosophy is something of an oversimplification, for in addition to continental philosophy which means existential phenomenology or phenomenological existentialism, and Soviet philosophy, and Anglo-American positivism and language analysis, there are still around the remnants of all of the ancient schools, the Neo-Scholastics, the Neo-Kantians, and the Neo-Hegelians, and it wouldn't surprise me that some school of the Neo-Neons will be developed one of these days.

My divisions are directed to serving one purpose, even at the cost of oversimplification. They indicate a division of philosophical interest in two major camps where the differences go deep. They are radical differences, I think, despite the fact that many of us who are concerned about this division occasionally try to explore the possibilities of rapprochement, with and without success. On the one hand we have a kind of philosophizing which has stayed with the main trend of Western civilization in being true to the fundamental and original commitments of a value kind. That goes for existentialism, it goes for phenomenology, it goes for Marxism. And, on the other hand, we have a type of philosophizing which, beginning with David Hume—although I think here the great master was misrepresented if any would use him as a justification for what they have done to that kind of philosophy—expressed utter and complete skepticism about human knowledge and gradually disowned the ancient questions of metaphysics and also the ancient questions with respect to the management of our values on earth.

I was very much fascinated by a recent perusal of a volume in the "Library of Living Philosophers" on the most influential positivist in America, and in the world as a matter of fact, a man by the name of Carnap. There is included in this volume a short autobiography written by Mr. Carnap, and he tells us about the beginnings of contemporary positivism in the so-called Vienna Circle in Austria. He takes a kind of pride in informing the reader that here was a school that deliberately stayed away from political concerns, quite deliberately and in the name of scholarship avoided getting involved in problems of value, and I could not help but put the book down at that point and consider my dates and the men involved in this movement. For you see all this was happening while the Nazis were marching millions of humans into fiery ovens. What has happened to philosophy when philosophers take pride in having abandoned their fellow men, having abandoned the most important concerns that any man can have in this world?

Paul Arthur Schilpp, the editor and founder of the "Library of Living Philosophers" has this to say: "Where then do values fall," he asks, "if both the natural and social sciences wash their hands of having any truck with value theory? Who is going to work in this field if philosophers, too, refuse to be concerned with it?" Is it really the case that philosophy can concern itself only with what is not valuable? Or if our so-called philosophers claim that their work of analysis, semantics, and linguistics is valuable, how do they know that it is valuable so long as they will have nothing to do with any realm of normative value theory?

These are serious questions, but the Anglo-American school of philosophy has other characteristics that are worthy of note, worthy of being contrasted with the more traditional philosophical trend represented by all three of the other schools. For one thing, in an attempt to become scientifically respectable, in an attempt to acquire for themselves the name of objective thinkers, the Anglo-American school of philosophy has impoverished first the very language of philosophy by attempting to reduce it, to expurgate it of every sense of expression, by attempting to approximate it to something like mathematics, or of symbolic discourse that can function only in logic where you are never talking about anything and you never know what you are talking about, but you most certainly can set relations that obtain their proper place between all of these fictions. Not only is the very language of philosophy impoverished by these philosophers, but the problems themselves are finally reduced to minutiae. The courageous attempt on the part of the traditional philosophers to have big views, to paint the big perspectives, to be synoptic in their thinking, is totally disregarded by this school of thought.

All in all this impoverishment has meant that a whole movement in philosophy has deprived itself of the human content of philosophy. It has deprived itself of that rich heritage that comes to philosophy and to every other human being from history, from literature, from poetry, from art. What is art, taken in this general and comprehensive sense, but the expression of what is human? Who is the artist and the writer but the man who gives the thinker the stuff by which he can think and help himself to shed light on this perilous road that we call human existence?

Now on the other side, beginning long before the Second World War but particularly accentuating their activity during that war, we find a school of young and vigorous philosophers who became reacquainted with the Socratic Agora. They began to philosophize in the thick of battle. Their philosophizing came as a result of their involvement, their engagement with life, their concern about despots and despotism. These are men who recaptured the ancient ideal of philosophy: the stance which holds that a philosopher must be committed, otherwise there is no purpose to philosophizing. The brand of sterile philosophizing, previously discussed, in my opinion, can be called philosophy without commitment. And in this sense, philosophy that has relinquished its ancient role, the kind of commitment that existentialism and phenomenology together and Marxism have represented in the modern field of philosophical thinking is a commitment. I repeat, that comes from firsthand experience with the problems that mankind has been facing, the kind of thinking that comes from barricades, from the underground movements, from the agony of having to stay alive, but even more from the agony and the despair of having to give meaning to an existence which is becoming more and more meaningless, even if more and more spectacular by the technological display and fireworks that are accumulating around us. This is the kind of philosophizing in which young men while trying to get rid of despotism in human societies discovered anew the human being—what it means to exist not as a thing that is looked upon by an observer as if his own being were not involved in the exploration that he's undertaking, but the kind of being that peculiarly belongs to a man, and that's what existentialism is all about. It's basically about that form of being that is our own; a form of being that includes mortality; a form of being that includes a desperate, responsible assumption of freedom; a form of being that is aware of the fearful responsibility that we bear to ourselves and to others. Says Jean-Paul Sartre, "We Frenchmen were never so free as when we were under the heel of the Nazis." What does he mean? He certainly is not talking about the question of freedom as it is discussed academically by the traditional philosophers. This is not an academic question. The kind of freedom that he's talking about is the freedom that a man discovers suddenly when finding himself, let's say, captured by an enemy to whom he can betray his friends and country; or who can die by being true to what he believes. And there's no one save himself about to condemn him, to force him, to reward him, for the decision that he makes. This is the kind of freedom that Jean-Paul Sartre is talking about.

But earlier his great teacher, Martin Heidegger, made a very great discovery based on the things that his teacher, Edmund Husserl, and others had said. Heidegger decided that what was needed most in the confusion of modern philosophy was a return to the fundamental question of being that Western philosophy had raised in the beginning. He thought that the question had been lost, had been diluted. Philosophers not only were no longer interested in the question, but when they seemed to be asking the question of being—"What is it to be?"—they really were asking the question about beings, what is it to be this, that, or the other thing, rather than what is it to be. And so he set out not to answer the question, not to raise the question, but to discover how the question can be asked. He felt that man had forgotten how to ask this question. And along the way of this search after the question of being he made a very interesting discovery. Let me put it in my words. When a man seriously asks what is it to be, he ought to realize that that question is, in the first place, addressed not to the world, the beings that are, but to himself and to his manner of being. When I ask what is it to be, I might as well put the question by saying "What is *my* form of being? Of this being who is capable of asking the question about being?" And so he wrote a book called *Sein und Zeit* which is a phenomenological account of what existing being, human being, is like. This book has been a source of inspiration for many modern philosophers and I predict that it will be as influential a book for the future as it has been for our time.

But let me conclude a paper that is and must remain incomplete. We have this schism, this seemingly unbridgeable gulf between philosophies of commitment, philosophies that grapple with ethics and with value problems on the one hand, and on the other philosophies that are basically scientistic—that is, they still stand in awe before the undeniable success of the natural sciences and of mathematics and are still hopeful that the philosopher can come out with a truth that resembles the truth of the sciences. In this endeavor they have eliminated value concerns; they're not interested in the development of a theory of man, and there seems to be very little interest among them in political philosophy and in ethics except to declare on occasion that ethics or ethical judgments are matters of wish expression or emotional expression. Can there be any rapprochement between these schools? Surely not until philosophers stop aping the sciences of nature which have their own justification in the historical advance of human knowledge. Not until philosophers make it their business to work on the doctrine of man which is sadly needed in our time, a philosophy of man, a philosophy of the subject man as the chooser and maker of values. For the existence of modern man is without supports now, without recourse to the dead deities of past ages. The principal problem of man in our time is man himself, this same man of flesh and bone we see alienated, desperate, living his brief moment between fratricidal wars, legislated hatred and death.

ARTURO FALLICO

SAN JOSE STATE UNIVERSITY
JULY, 1972

HERBERT W. SCHNEIDER

DECLARATION, THEORY, AND EXISTENCE OF HUMAN RIGHTS

The Declaration of Human Rights drafted by leaders of the United Nations and adopted on December 10, 1948, by its General Assembly was not a "universal declaration," though it conceived human rights as universal. It was a very practical document created in response to a crisis in human history, and in view of the demands and expectations confronted by the United Nations for a concrete program of action. This practical urgency induced the drafters of the Declaration not to engage in a discussion of the theory of "universal human rights" since such discussion might be endless and inconclusive. The proclamation is made "as a standard of achievement for all peoples," and these rights were frankly called "goals." But the first sentence of Article 1 is a dogmatic statement of theory: "All human beings are born free and equal in dignity and rights. They are endowed with reason and conscience." The theorists of human nature and social sciences had long ago discarded this traditional doctrine as myth. It was reasserted here not as scientific fact or moral theory, but as the mythical sanction or ground for the remainder of the sentence: "and should act towards one another in a spirit of brotherhood." This "spirit" is stated as a moral obligation; the myth of universal brotherhood is not asserted as dogmatically as the myths of the first part of the sentence. The "goal" of this first article is evidently to transform the spirit of fraternity, which the French Revolution had nationalized, into an international spirit for all peoples.

The theoretical distinctions between rights, goals, and freedoms are not even suggested; the terms are used as synonyms. The first twenty-one articles formulate the substance of "civil liberties," extended somewhat to include the "New Freedom" of Woodrow Wilson and the "Freedoms" of Franklin D. Roosevelt. Articles 22 to 25 have come to be called by interpreters "economic rights" and Articles 26 to 29 "cultural rights." I have no intention to discuss these particular "rights," but I shall try to suggest theoretical problems of analysis which have haunted increasingly this loose use of terms when the concrete realization of "goals" has been attempted.

First, what is the relation between "natural endowments" and dignified goals? The frequent reference in popular literature and political appeals to man's "inherent" freedom and dignity do not express adequately what the rhetoric of "endowed by the creator" has been intended to express. "Reason" and "conscience" are not inherent in human nature or innate. The natural ability to learn to be reasonable and conscientious, provided the appropriate means of learning are available in the culture, is, to be sure, born into normal, healthy human beings. This ability to learn can be called metaphorically an "endowment," but there is nothing inherent in man to guarantee that he will learn. Learning to be reasonable and conscientious is a complicated art, promoted differently in different cultures. These facts have been recognized as elementary for both theory and practice. Similarly, on the basis of man's biological equipment or endowment, human beings, given the appropriate cultural environments, can achieve in addition to "reason and conscience" freedom and dignity. Such achievements are well referred to as "standards" for a spirit of community.

What the preambles to the Declaration might proclaim, then, is: We believe that we have learned enough reason and conscience to regard the following standards as universal and necessary in order to achieve the general human goals of peace, freedom, and dignity. It is significant theoretically, though not practically, that the Declaration is explicitly addressed to "peoples" rather than to governments or international organizations. However, the language of the Declaration is not that of asserting desirable standards for achieving the goals that reason and conscience have set; it is the language of rights which all men have, the language of what all men are "entitled" to. Such language requires examination.

If a man is entitled to something, he can reasonably ask who does the entitling and to whom he must go to get his due. To tell a person he naturally and actually *has* a right or title to something without telling him to whom he can make his claim and who is responsible for responding to the claim is to deceive him. If a right really exists, it must exist responsibly; it must be somehow established. Otherwise, to declare or proclaim that a right exists means no more than: You ought to demand from someone who will pay attention to your claim that a right *should be* recognized and established. To assert that a person has rights as if he had appropriated property is not true. No man can appropriate a right; it must be admitted by someone as due to him because this "someone" recognizes a duty toward him. Making claims in the universal void does not imply that a right actually exists. In short, rights may be declared to all peoples, but they do not exist until there are agencies to deal with them responsively and responsibly.

The first score of declared rights has some existence or establishment in law and government as "civil liberties." They are not "goals" but recognized standards of good policy and law. By this time it is reasonable to expect governments to respect civil rights because they exist in good governments and in legal procedure.

But to whom shall the claimants of one of the other rights, numbered 22 to 29, turn for recognition? They are not universally recognized even as goals, to say nothing of not being established publicly as rights. "Full employment" is a recognized goal of policy, but that does not establish a right to labor. (The government of the United States of America has insisted on this point.) Similarly, the other declared economic and cultural goals are generally admitted by whatever agencies of production, education, art, or science are engaged in their achievement, but this is far from making them "universal human rights" either in theory or practice. The Declaration is a work of moral leadership in the face of universal needs (natural, political, economic, and cultural). It attempts to formulate what needs to be achieved by peoples, but its language, in the declarative mood, asserts supposedly existing rights.

I am reminded of the effort of Thomas Hobbes, who in a similar desperate situation declared that he had discovered the science of "natural justice" (*ius naturale*). By this he meant that he had formulated about ten "universal principles of peace" or natural laws and commandments, which must be observed universally if men wish to establish peace on earth. He based them on human experience, attempting to prove empirically that their violation leads inevitably and historically to conflict. These contemporary "universal declarations" might well be defended as universally necessary obligations for peace. But, like Hobbes, they go well beyond anything that the law could accept as "natural justice."

Going beyond law and "natural justice" is, of course, necessary in any culture. Legal procedure, for all its precision and generality, cannot cope with all human goals. No reasonable government should claim that its policy of "public welfare" means making all men happy. A universal declaration of human rights is a Western way of repeating the Oriental prayer: "May all men be happy." Happiness is a reasonable general goal for theoretical moralists and practical reformers; the goal should be taught and preached and observed. But rights are by their nature or essence public, not necessarily political; they imply some kind of social establishment or responsible recognition. The claims or demands men make upon each other are the circumstance that makes morality and government, both personal and public, a necessary human need. To go "beyond" morality and responsibility is folly, a well-established folly. But every generation, in order to gain experience and peace, is tempted to experiment with this folly. Moral education, even in school, is learned "the hard way." This fact is, to be sure, discouraging for any "rational animal," but it is prudent to accept it and to deal with it, too, as best we can on the basis of sad experience, with reasonable hope for the future, but without too much declamation.

HERBERT W. SCHNEIDER

CLAREMONT GRADUATE SCHOOL
MARCH, 1972

WAYNE A. R. LEYS

POLITICAL AND MORAL PLURALISM

An essay on the merits of pluralism is, I trust, a fitting way to show my respect for the philosophical and civic labors of Professor Paul Schilpp. Unlike many peace seekers and war resisters, Schilpp has not tried to explain away the facts of plurality. He follows Kant's lead in recognizing that a peaceful world order is neither desirable if it has to be a *Pax Romana* nor feasible if it must be a *City of God.* Kant believed that war could be abolished, not by destroying the many existing governments but by securing agreements among those governments. Federalism of some sort was the basis of his hope for peace with freedom, a pioneering proposal which Professor Schilpp has endorsed on many occasions.

Schilpp has gone beyond Kant in accepting pluralism as the condition under which peace must be sought. Unlike Kant, he has frankly admitted that he is a moral relativist. Schilpp finds in the existing moral will of humanity as inadequate a basis for peace as Kant found in men's satisfaction-seeking desires. By "moral relativism" Schilpp refers not only to the fact that various groups now disagree in their value judgments ("cultural or descriptive relativism"), but to the probability that many of these value differences will not be overcome ("metaethical relativism").

The combination of political pluralism and moral relativism seems to me to be a correct diagnosis of the nature of the war problem. I realize that such a diagnosis will strike many thoughtful readers as an acceptance of the inevitability of war, either as a permanent condition or inevitable as the means of establishing peace by military conquest. There is now, as there was in earlier times, a widely held belief that social order must be grounded either in a moral consensus or a monopoly of coercive power. This belief was not the only reason for trying to "refute" relativism, but it was at least one consideration in Plato's attack upon Protagoras and Thrasymachus, in Cudworth's objections to Hobbes, and in the antirelativist arguments of many others. It is this "Either One Moral Right or One Sovereign Might" thesis that I wish to combat with evidence for a counterthesis, as follows: It is the absence of a monopoly of power that justifies hope and work for peace among nations and classes that have diverse moral commitments.

The "Refutations" of Moral Relativism

Before disputing the political implications of relativism we should examine the "refutations" of relativism, to make sure that the theory has not lost its plausibility, and also to learn how clashing wits may have sharpened the theory.

Plato's strategy in opposing the relativists was to treat moral assertions as statements that are either true of false. He then represented his opponents as falling into logical self-contradictions. This strategy has been followed by many other philosophers who made the strong claim that relativism is simply false. Cudworth, for example, argued that the objects of moral judgment must be what they are; either they are good or they are not good; either they are just or unjust. What these objects are cannot be changed by the will of God or man. From this appeal to the law of identity, it would follow that contradictory assertions about these moral objects cannot both be true.

The Platonic strategy has been one factor (but not the only factor), goading latter-day relativists to abandon the (metaethical) theory that moral assertions are a kind of knowledge. Although not usually denying that there are cognitive components in moral judgments, relativists do not now talk about evaluations as being "true for me and false for you." Nor do they accept the contention of Cudworth, Richard Price, G. E. Moore, et al, that, if two men disagree about such a moral right as the right to be a conscientious objector, one of them (at least) must be in error. There is no contradiction between the propositions: "A believes X has that right" and "B believes X does not have that right."

An attack, less direct than that of the Platonists, is one that was first mounted against the ancient sceptics. Moral relativism is in this view identified as a theory which throws doubt on moral judgments by explaining how people come to accept various moral opinions. If two groups differ on the rightness of usury, their difference is explained, not by the nature of usury, but by indoctrination, temperament, status or something else that is not an inherent characteristic of usury. The critics of relativism then ask whether the theory of relativism is not subject to the same sort of doubt. Thus, it is said that Protagoras could not properly claim to be expressing more than a prejudice of his cultural community. So, also, Freud may have been rationalizing his own drives, when he theorized that ideas rationalize drives. And the Marxists may be expressing the ideology of an economic class when they insist that the material conditions of production create classes with ideologies that blind them to what seems reasonable to other classes.

The extensive literature on "the sociology of knowledge" now aids (or hinders) anyone who wants to untangle the confused contexts of this controversy. Curiously enough, the antirelativists worked out a rejoinder which is as helpful to the relativists as it is to their adversaries. That rejoinder is that "the origin of a theory is not necessarily an index of its truth," just as the value of a practice does not depend upon its genesis. The debate over the self-refuting character of relativism is, thus, inconclusive, although it can be said that the debate was instructive: the debate has made us aware of many kinds of moral disagreements.

More indirect and cautious than the antirelativism of either the Platonists or the antisceptics is the criticism offered by Brandt, Frankena and Stevenson. Although these three rather analytic philosophers disagree on other matters, they seem to agree that the theory of relativism by itself fails to justify any particular attitude toward moral disagreements. Frankena uses the label "metaethical relativism" for the theory that there is no rational way of settling some moral disputes. He labels as "normative relativism" the judgment that we should tolerate alien practices, tolerance being justified by saying, "what is right for us is wrong for them." Even if metaethical relativism is true, each party to a moral disagreement presumably can and will decide what he should do about the disagreement in the light of his own moral commitments.[1]

The distinguishing of metaethical and normative relativisms is an enlightening contribution to the subject. It separates an empirical question (Do some moral disagreements persist in spite of all known methods of resolving moral disputes?) from an action question (What should be done about these disagreements?). Later in this essay I shall make use of this clarification. I cannot leave the "refutations" of relativism, however, without one more observation. Brandt and Frankena, in the same essays where they disentangle metaethical and normative relativisms, also take a poke at metaethical relativism. Frankena notices, for instance, that the persistence of cultural and class differences does not prove the *impossibility* of overcoming such disagreements by rational means. If this is a prudential advice to keep on trying, I have no objection to it. But if it is offered as freeing our normative deliberations from the burdens imposed by the presence of a lot of disagreeing neighbors, I find it as irrelevant to our political problems as the older and bolder "refutations" of metaethical relativism. At the present time metaethical relativism seems to be a true theory about the conditions under which we live.

It is difficult to understand how the logical and epistemological arguments against metaethical relativism could ever have thrown much light on political problems. Possibly, teachers and preachers were misled by their successes with immature, captive, and like-minded audiences; maybe, they imagined that alien and hostile communities would sit through long lectures and be overwhelmed by clever arguments. If that was the rationalists' hope, it should by now be dashed by the staggering cost of getting the attention of mass audiences focussed on anything and the even greater costs of eliciting the simplest responses. Most of the human race is preoccupied with personal and local matters. It is difficult to detect progress toward any common orientation. The relativity that is important politically is not the relativity that might remain after a long Platonic dialogue, but the diversity that confronts anyone who makes a move to change a national or international policy.

Common Morality and Coercion as Supposed Alternatives

Turning to the political objections that are directed against relativism, we find a good many contemporary writers who see metaethical relativism (or moral pluralism) as a pernicious influence. Moral pluralism is alleged to tempt political leaders to resort to violence and coercion. It is alleged to dispose other men to acquiesce in a reign of terror. Disbelief regarding a common, true morality is said to be pragmatically bad.

A much-discussed proponent of this view was Gustav Radbruch, a professor of law who had been a relativist and positivist prior to 1933. Radbruch was horrified by the barbarity of the Nazi regime. In 1945, as soon as he could speak out, he urged his students and the public to insist upon conformity to common moral standards, regardless of the power situation.[2] He contended that the value-relativism prevalent among educated Germans had predisposed them to go along with the increasingly outrageous Nazi practices of the 1930s.

This opposition to metaethical relativism is shared by theorists who make no claim to an intuitive or revealed knowledge of the true, common morality. Professor Melvin Rader, for example, writes:

As opposed to a pluralistic relativism, we must uphold the ideal of universality. The very possibility of an enduring peace depends upon the organization of an international community upon the basis of a common humanity and a common justice. Such universalism, however, must avoid the rigid and unempirical doctrines of a monistic absolutism.[3]

Professor Brand Blanshard also denounces relativism and noncognitivism as destroyers of decent politics:

I have suggested that if you adopt this theory in ethics, you may as well give up in political theory. Why? Because the major fact in the modern world is that cultures are in conflict, with enormous powers of destruction on each side, and this theory affords no rational way of dealing with that conflict.[4]

It is this alleged necessity of a choice between a common morality and sheer coercion that I wish to dispute. I believe that metaethical relativism is a true theory, and I also believe that it does not commit me to brutal political action or, for that matter, to an acquiescence in whatever others approve of.

I grant that Machiavelli and Hobbes and many other political theorists have encouraged this "Might versus Right" talk by the ways in which they tried to convince us that governments no longer coincided with the boundaries of folk cultures and tribal moralities. Picking one such theorist almost at random, John Austin was trying to show law students that their own personal judgment of what was right and fair in a given case might be very different from the legal system's disposition of the case. Britain was no longer a tribal community. Austin then defined law as the command of the sovereign. Although he qualified his definition, it was easy for critics to quote this slogan as evidence that Austin viewed law as no different from the orders of a gunman; law was simply a command backed by the threat of punishment.

Another relativist who gave antirelativists a lot of useful ammunition was Justice Oliver Wendell Holmes, Jr. Holmes talked about the obligatory force of a lawful order as being derived ultimately from physical force. He expressed this idea in memorable wisecracks in his public speeches and in his letters, many of which were published, for instance:

Every society is founded on the death of men. . . . Our morality seems to me only a check on the ultimate domination of force, just as our politeness is a check on the impulse of every pig to put his feet in the trough. When the Germans in the late war disregarded what we call the rules of the game, I don't see there was anything to be said except: we don't like it and shall kill you if we can. So when it comes to the development of a *corpus juris* the ultimate question is what do the dominant forces of the community want and do they want it hard enough to disregard whatever inhibitions may stand in the way?[5]

Holmes seemed to be conceding the Might-vs.-Right theory of the Christian

Platonists, differing from them only in his faith that arbitrary power provided a basis for peace that was not short-lived. Accordingly, Justice Douglas attacked Holmes's faith in durable power, when Douglas began his Tagore Lectures at the University of Calcutta in 1955. He recalled Holmes's letter to Laski: " . . . when men differ in taste as to the kind of world they want, the only thing to do is to go to work killing. . . . " Douglas then added: "Justice Holmes wrote those words before the atomic bomb and the hydrogen bomb had made war 'a Frankenstein to destroy both sides'. . . . "[6]

With due respect for Holmes and Douglas, I must confess that I am more impressed by their work as judges than by their theories about the conditions that make possible the work of judges. Both of them were continuing the debate of rationalizing theorists, while ostensibly dealing with a question that calls for empirical evidence. In particular, the theory of Holmes regarding the political consequences of relativism was insufficient evidence to settle the empirical question: What is required to establish law and order here and now, and what is required to settle disputes without mutual destruction in all other times and places?[7]

Indeed, the diverse ways of life, which inspired Holmes's relativism, would suggest that not all social orders are generated by one and the same condition. A thorough-going relativist would doubt that the preservation of order in all societies has one universal requirement. There have certainly been governments that were not supported by a moral consensus. And, even in the modern nation-states, a single sovereign power was not unchallenged for very long periods of time.

Ancient theorists had identified class divisions in the larger city-states and empires: the rich and the poor, the natives and the aliens, the freemen and the slaves. Modern theorists have had to add to the list of factions: language groups, religious sects, and occupations. But, in their eagerness to find completely general principles, theorists often turned from the variety of political predicaments to the idea of one all-important confrontation of single-minded opponents, an idea that makes plausible a simple set of alternatives. They have had difficulty remembering the work of historians, like Charles Beard, who documented the complexity and variability of "the national interest." They seemed to forget the accidents of political history that render potent and active for a time odd and normally nonpolitical passions. They seemed to ignore the many governments that were created or preserved in three- and four-cornered contests.

Hume was correct when he denied that there was any one "cause" of government. He admitted that some regimes may have originated in agreements; but there were others that were created by force or fraud. Hume's *History of England* was written with the idea that the conquerors and the tricksters did not establish dynasties of long duration. Hume seemed to think that civil war might be prevented, if no politically active party held un-challenged power for very long and if the habits and inertia of nonpolitical subjects were not disturbed. As for the relations between national governments Hume held out little hope for a durable peace. Hume's scep-ticism concerning simplistic theories of power did not provide an escape on the international scene between the horns of the traditional dilemma: either order by moral consensus or order by coercion.

It is to more recent political pluralism that we now turn, asking whether a third alternative may provide a way to tolerable order.

Political Pluralism

The theory of political pluralism in our time is, I think, most convincing when it is least systematic. If we look for a complete theory to replace the theories of Hobbes or Marx, we are not apt to be satisfied with what we find in Laski, Cole, Figgis, Bentley, Dahl, T. V. Smith, Kallen, Merriam or de Jouvenel. In such writers we find the sort of thing that we found in Madison, Montesquieu and Aristotle: hints and suggestions growing out of certain political practices as empirically described.

If we try to generalize upon these hints, we talk about a pluralistic order with some such ingredients as the following:

1. the organization of more than two (but not too many) factions capable of behaving as disciplined pressure groups;

2. the acquisition of political skills by leaders who can speak for and in-fluence those pressure groups;

3. the invention of novel procedures for opposition and negotiation (although there is much disagreement about the limits beyond which novelty breeds anarchy or destructive conflict);

4. the recognition and legitimization of differences in the preferred procedures of different groups, with the result that

5. it is possible for well-informed leaders to know whether their op-ponents are playing according to the rules of any known game.

In some such fashion in certain countries and, part of the time, in inter-national conflicts, alternative ways of ritualizing and containing conflicts are now available.

A weakness of pluralistic theories has been the theorists' tendency to believe that a pluralistic peaceful order had been achieved as soon as the representatives of more than two factions were participating in a governmental process. Professor T. V. Smith, for example, was convinced that legislators and lobbyists in the United States could settle disputes that were nonnegotiable on the basis of constituents' moral principles. Smith wrote a book entitled, *Beyond Conscience.* He used "compromise" as a term of praise. In his enthusiasm for legislative representation of factions he wrote:

> But the legislature is, for all that, the only institution developed by man through the centuries which preserves individuals against gross invasion of their private rights and guarantees some minimum benefits to all groups alike in their struggle for survival and supremacy. If the legislative way can but keep the qualities of its defects, we must continue to allow it the defects of its qualities.[8]

Unfortunately, when these words were being written, Reinhold Niebuhr had already called attention to groups in American society that could not get their grievances effectively before a legislature. Niebuhr was talking about the Negro population, for example, which at that time contained the promise of future troublemaking but without the skilled organization of an election-winning pressure group. And a few years later, in 1942, I am sure that the Japanese Americans on our West Coast found it difficult to appreciate "the qualities of the legislature's defects."

It is interesting that Smith could find no political virtue in Gandhi and regarded civil disobedience campaigns as invitations to unrestricted warfare. In reviewing Gandhi's *Autobiography* Smith wrote: "When a gandhi meets a gandhi, then the blood begins to flow." This was a particularly ungenerous pronouncement, following Smith's plea for the back-door deals and engineering monstrosities that were being created by legislative compromise. It showed an appreciation of a very limited pluralism, a pluralism consisting of those pressure groups that were willing and able to engage in election campaigns and vote trading. It was a pluralism that left out millions of "citizens."

The strikes and boycotts that were organized by Gandhi had not been invented by him, although he did introduce some new rules for his strikers. Strikes and boycotts had already been extensively employed by organizations of industrial workmen. The history of labor strikes is well documented and we can precisely date the legitimization of those weapons. Some of the early strikers had been punished as conspirators. A century of turmoil was suffered in Europe and America before the legal right to strike was established. A long struggle was involved in establishing rules limiting the tactics that could be employed by strikers and their adversaries: rules against physical violence, intimidation of various sorts, secondary boycotts; and rules making negotiation compulsory.

Another set of inventions that has been supplementing legislation consists of self-regulation and unilateral concession, followed by the adversary's silent acceptance of such moves as a settlement. These inventions, not yet possessing a convenient name, have had some successes in the relations of warring trade groups and in international relations. Although the codes of trade associations contain hypocritical gestures and dead letters, they also include self-regulating rules that are now a significant substitute for much legislation and litigation. And a realistic account of international law (both public and private) can hardly ignore the silent acceptance of innumerable concessions that could not be negotiated in a formal treaty.

Other nonviolent terminations of conflict are secured by sabotage and slowdowns, bribery, nuisance tactics, and mass migrations. It is not unusual for conflicts now to be carried from one forum to another and to be contained within one nonviolent procedure after another. The quarrels of blacks and whites, for instance, have sometimes taken the form of court battles, sometimes trading among legislators and lobbyists, sometimes strikes and boycotts, sometimes arbitration, sometimes the acceptance of unilateral concessions, sometimes other forms of civil disobedience and noncooperation. The existence of this plurality of conflict forms has not prevented all violence, but it must be credited with significant accomplishments.

In recognizing the existence of alternative rituals, games or processes, I wish to make it clear that these alternatives have not been legitimatized everywhere or for all issues.[9] But the idea of alternative modes of conflict is more widely acted upon than the received theories of government suggest. The idea is accepted wherever the effective leadership of a contesting group can let adversaries and bystanders get this message: "Choose your weapons; you make a move in accordance with some recognizable rule-governed game, and we shall make a countermove."

If pressure group theory is broadened so that it recognizes a plurality of modes of combat as well as a plurality of power-wielding groups, it may be able to guide us toward a peaceful order that is grounded neither in moral consensus nor a power monopoly. It may suggest how restraints may be put upon angry and fearful partisans who have the potential for destructive conflict, even nuclear bombs and intercontinental rockets.

Philosophers' Tardy Recognition of Novel Procedures

Philosophers have not shown great alacrity in celebrating the birth of pluralistic politics. Kant and John Stuart Mill, for example, both had some awareness of nonmilitary politics in the absence of moral agreement. Kant advocated federalism. Mill recorded his experience at India House, where policy documents passed from desk to desk until, when finally released, they were the work of no one mind. Yet, Mill tried to prevent representative government by assuring a disproportionate influence for men as "enlightened" as himself. And Kant continued the old quest for a universal political principle in his systematic work on the philosophy of law.

Maritain, to name a perceptive representative of Thomism, recorded his surprise and gratification in being able to reach agreement with Moslems and atheists in working out the Declaration of Universal Human Rights, when it was manifestly impossible for the assembled delegates to agree on reasons for the agreement. But Maritain was not ready to adjust his philosophical apparatus so that this political accord could be viewed as anything other than an accident or an irrational feature of human life.[10]

John Dewey, dedicated as he was to the invention of untraditional methods, showed reluctance to go along with much of the newer politics by which previously submerged groups became in some way participants in the political process. On the one hand, he wrote:

> Democracy is belief in the ability of human experience to generate the aims and methods by which further experience will grow in ordered richness. Every other form of moral and social faith rests upon the idea that experience must be subjected at some point or other to some form of *external* control; to some 'authority' alleged to exist outside the process of experience. Democracy is the faith that the process of experience is more important than any special result attained, so that special results achieved are of ultimate value only as they are used to enrich and order the ongoing process.[11]

On the other hand, Dewey condemned most of the techniques by which large numbers of illiterates could be mobilized as a pressure group. He growled about the dangers and wickedness of propaganda nearly every time he thought about the new techniques of mass communication.

While paying my respects to the nostalgia of philosophers I should not omit mention of the Marxists. They insist that government, religion and morality comprise a "superstructure," a changeable product of a "substructure" (the changing material mode of production). Yet, when they look at twentieth-century institutions, they see almost exactly what Marx described over a century ago. The important class struggle is between two classes, one class holding productive property and the other propertyless. How little guidance this antique picture of the world has provided is evident in the Soviet Union, where there have been four about-faces in criminal law, each new policy justified by quotations from Marx's analysis of class relations in nineteenth-century England and France. Renegade Marxists have tried to get bureaucrats, soldiers, peasants, scientists and artists into the theorists' pictures—without much luck. Marxist theory continues to view "the" state as the executive committee of "the" dominant class, intent on using their power monopoly to liquidate the enemy.

Theorists are no more leery of pluralist thinking than many men of action (officials, pressure group entrepreneurs, etc.). The latter become accustomed to one set of rules and procedures. When an opposing faction opts for another set of procedures, the response is often horror and panic. Political innovations are perceived as destroying the necessary conditions of government. An unexpected order is seen, as Bergson said, as disorder. In our time there have been many instances of real disorder, anarchy and war. But on many occasions the "necessary conditions" of government are only the psychological necessities of certain participants. Government was once unthinkable without theological tests for officeholders. Secrecy is now regarded as necessary in the conduct of "public" business. Collective bargaining by government employees is often seen as "impossible." Negotiations "cannot" proceed without agreement on an agenda. Managerial prerogatives "must" be maintained on all sorts of matters. It is not within my competence to recommend new limits for political and legal processes. All that I am sure of is that numerous "unthinkable" and "impossible" procedures have helped to keep the peace in a pluralistic world.

Concepts Useful for Pluralistic Politics

A critical study of political theory tempts one to reverse the Kantian aphorism about concepts being empty and percepts being blind. But the blindness and blinding effect of certain concepts does not imply that men who perceive political facts at first hand understand them and organize them in optimum fashion. If inherited political concepts are inappropriate, perhaps they can be remodeled. And that is what is being attempted by a good many philosophers and social scientists. In order not to fall into narrowly sectarian polemics, I shall mention several recent "tendencies" and relate them to the problem of understanding and improving pluralistic politics, hoping thereby to give encouragement to conceptual work that might otherwise seem purely whimsical.

(1) First, I should like to encourage the pluralistic idea that is most widely accepted by contemporary teachers of philosophy, viz., the conception of philosophy which they use in discussing "the history of philosophy." Confronted by endlessly varying "systems," they may abandon the idea that each philosophy stands or falls according to the "truth" of its explanations of everything that happens. The classical philosophers obviously did not see life "whole and steadily." What can be said about "the whole of life and the universe" is that no mind appreciates all aspects of it at once. "All that is valuable and important" is more than any of us value at a given moment.

Of course, there are teachers who, like Hegel, exempt their own "philosophy" from the obvious partiality of the old systems by constructing an evolutionary scheme in which the patently partial philosophies are stages in the development of a "complete consciousness." But others do not offer budding intellectuals that kind of protection from the disturbing expectation of continuing coexistence with heathen adversaries. From their presentation of ancient thought students come to appreciate both the insights and the blind spots of competing points of view. They grow accustomed to the role of philosophers, not as omniscient Olympian gods, but as men "who think otherwise," struggling out of the obsessions of their own neighborhoods. If philosophers are in the company of moralizers who neglect aesthetic and scientific interests, they may, like Nietzsche, become "immoralists." If they find themselves surrounded by scientific or political fanatics, they may react as champions of religious and moral interests, as William James did. After students have been enabled to make sense of the limited but undeniable insights of famous philosophers, they should find it easier to believe that the worth of their own philosophy and the worth of opposed philosophies do not depend upon their winning universal acceptance.

(2) Also helpful to minds trying to adjust to the pluralistic predicament are recent efforts to loosen and broaden the concept of a system. In the European tradition the leading conception of a system was derived from mathematics. A system was seen as an order in which every part had logically consistent relations to every other part, all of the elements and relations being capable of exact definition. Hegel rejected the model of mathematics as inappropriate to social systems, though, unfortunately, he messed up mathematics and logic by trying to knock abstract forms out of formal systems. In more recent times social systems have been conceived by means of constructs or analogies that were admittedly imperfect models. Institutional systems have been compared to the organic relationships within plants and animals, to natural languages and art forms, to game plans, family relationships, to simplified descriptions of historic communities (ideal types). Persons who employed these models were trained to remind themselves of "discontinuities," "the open texture of the networks," "existential absurdities," "emergent novelties," and "opaquenesses." "Process" and "dialectical" philosophies have warned system builders that orderliness in theorizing should be balanced by readiness to recognize factors in the social system that were not represented in the model. Models were viewed as always suspect, lacking, as they usually do, unpredictable features that match the more or less intelligent responses of human groups and their leaders.

It will be "systems theorists," thus chastened, who have some chance of contributing intelligently to the creation of a political order that will be adequate for all mankind. That order will not please tidy housekeepers. It will, if it is inclusive enough to be a *world* order, have standards, not of uniformity but of compatibility. Its requirements will approach the sheer possibility of coexistence.

(3) A third contribution of philosophers to the conception of a pluralistic political world is the development of concepts of a moral order that does not consist of good little boys sitting in a straight row. During the past eighty years there have been many hints to the effect that the morality of individuals, no less than the morality of communities, is not reducible to either a simple system of values or a simple system of rules. Nicolai Hartmann wrote: "There is conflict in the realm of values." And C. I. Lewis concluded that (normative) ethics could not be derived from axiology alone. The English philosophers have done the best job on the concept of "rules." They have helped us appreciate the need for rules, but at the same time they have shown how defeasible rules are, how they assume that "other things are equal." So, nowadays ethical theory is more often a discussion of criteria than of "the good," and of standards rather than imperatives and directives.

I make these comments in order to commend and encourage a tendency. Unfortunately there is still, among Western philosophers, an itch to prove instead of exploring, to answer instead of questioning, to justify instead of inquiring, to define ideal solutions instead of defining problems. Even philosophers who are committed to "Freedom" seem unable to formulate intellectual tools that leave something to other people's imagination and experience.

The devising of these three conceptual aids to life in a pluralistic world may seem to be an exercise in futility. Readers, who remember the noncognitivist and deterministic contentions of (metaethical) relativists, may ask: "What effect will a few intellectuals have on opposed moral imperatives and value judgments?"

I am not suggesting that philosophers are likely to mediate a conflict that is nothing more than a disagreement of meat eaters and vegetarians. In a conflict with a single issue the old alternatives of moral consensus or military force are probably the only solutions. There is no basis for negotiation in a battle of birth controllers and anticontraceptionists, if the controversialists are divided on no other issue than birth control. The same can be said of a contest between state socialists and private capitalists who have no concern other than the ownership and control of property. But the confrontations of opposed cultures are seldom disagreements about a single practice or a single value. A culture, a way of life, a morality does not consist of a single interest and a single moral judgment. A way of life consists of a large number of practices. In a confrontation with an alien culture, as in a confrontation with uncongenial natural conditions, the members of a community have to make choices. They can't have everything they want and approve. They can't do everything that they consider obligatory. It is the multiplicity of values, interests and duties within a culture that makes possible what we call politics. Otherwise, everything would be nonnegotiable.[12]

I have been identifying what it is that makes possible some sort of restraint in the collisions of extremely different moralities, under conditions where there is the slimmest hope of peace. Obviously, the conflicts that take place *within* societies and enterprises can be mediated by much more than the unwillingness of a partisan group to die for every object of desire. This needs to be said in the 1970s, because amateur political theorists have been dazzled by the impasses of international and interclass conflicts, reported so intensively by the mass media in recent years. There are students and professors who see themselves in a civil war because their favorite does not get a raise in pay. In their vocabulary "tolerance," "due process," and "respect for opponents as persons" are dirty words. In my opinion they are cultivating the monomanias of war, even when they throw off these restraints while professing the advocacy of peace.

I don't know whether Professor Schilpp will agree with all of these conclusions, but they seem to me to elaborate the human predicament as Schilpp has diagnosed it. The teacher of philosophy comes upon a scene of discordant desires and standards, some of them suppressed by brute force and others threatening destructive warfare. The teacher can seek a way of thinking about the discord, hoping to stimulate ideas that will facilitate creation of an order that neither he nor any other partisan fully comprehends. To the extent that a political order is established for *all* of humanity, no one in his right mind can honestly say that he likes it or that it is an entirely moral order. Yet, it is his unsatisfied, parochial moral commitment that keeps him striving for a political order.

WAYNE A. R. LEYS

SOUTHERN ILLINOIS UNIVERSITY

MARCH, 1972

NOTES

¹ See Richard Brandt, *Ethical Theory* (New York: Prentice-Hall, 1959), pp. 271-94; and "Ethical Relativism," in *The Encyclopedia of Philosophy,* ed. by Paul Edwards (New York: Macmillan Co., 1967). William Frankena, *Ethics* (New York: Prentice-Hall, 1963), pp. 92-96. Charles L. Stevenson, "Relativism and Non-Relativism in the Theory of Value," *Proceedings and Addresses of the American Philosophical Association,* **35** (October 1962), 25-44.

² A careful review of Gustav Radbruch's successive views will be found in Arnold Brecht's *Political Theory* (Princeton: Princeton University Press, 1959), pp. 337, 357-61.

³ Melvin Rader, *Ethics and the Human Community* (New York: Holt, Rinehart & Winston, 1964), p. 243.

⁴ Brand Blanshard, "Morality and Politics," in *Ethics and Society: Original Essays on Contemporary Moral Problems,* ed. by Richard T. DeGeorge (New York: Doubleday & Co., Anchor Books, 1966), pp. 5-6.

⁵ Oliver Wendell Holmes, Jr., *Justice Oliver Wendell Holmes: His Book Notices and Uncollected Letters and Papers,* ed. by Harry C. Shriver (New York: Central, 1936), pp. 181, 187. (The quotations are from letters originally written in 1926 to Dr. Wu.)

⁶ William O. Douglas, *We the Judges* (New York: Doubleday & Co., 1956), p. 15.

⁷ Even H. L. A. Hart, in his effort to get away from the gunman theory of law, falls back on the old contraries: coercion versus morality. Despite occasional references to political innovations, his *Concept of Law* (New York: Oxford University Press, 1961) never squarely faces the question whether twentieth-century politics has not produced a variety of novel foundations for legal systems.

⁸ T. V. Smith, *The Legislative Way of Life* (Chicago: University of Chicago Press, 1940), p. 91.

⁹ The so-called "bull-headed pluralists" exaggerate the prevalence of pluralism, finding effective, independent power groups in places where there is a monopoly of power and even a reign of terror. See Andrew S. McFarland, *Power and Leadership in Piuralist Systems* (Stanford: Stanford University Press, 1969).

¹⁰ Jacques Maritain, *Man and the State* (Chicago: University of Chicago Press, 1951), Chap. 4.

¹¹ John Dewey, "Creative Democracy—the Task Before Us," in *The Philosophy of the Common Man: Essays in Honor of John Dewey to Celebrate His Eightieth Birthday,* ed. by Sidney Ratner (New York: G. P. Putnam's Sons, 1940), pp. 220-28.

¹² It was Bertrand Russell's failure to remember that opponents have more than one desire that kept him from reconciling his moral relativism with his own moral commitments. (See his letters to *The Observer,* October 13 and 20, 1957.) If absolutely single-minded opponents collide, Russell would have been correct that conflict can end only in the imposition of one party's will on the other. Professor Schilpp, though an admirer of some of Russell's opinions and arguments, dealt with this same defect in somewhat different terms in his article, "Is Man Without Moorings? In Defense of a Relativistic Value-Theory," *Religious Humanism,* **1** (Summer & Autumn, 1967).

STERLING M. McMURRIN

IDEAS AND THE PROCESSES OF HISTORY

I

No issue is more relevant to the control of the future than the question of the practical power of ideas, of whether and in what ways they can affect or determine the processes of history. This matter has been treated from every perspective and has generated speculation that has sometimes transformed history into metaphysics or theology and has often distorted cultural analysis by encouraging the imposition of preconceived categories for the description and explanation of cultural and social facts. Fortunately this trend has been checked by the logical and linguistic analysis of meaning which has exhibited the futility of most of what passes as the philosophy of history, at least where that philosophy purports to establish patterns of the historical process or cultural structure by the employment of social and cultural laws which exceed the limits of confirmable bio-socio-psychological generalizations.

But this is not to say that the philosophy of history should not be pushed beyond the empirical boundaries of sociology or psychology and therefore must in the end be identical with these sciences. For it is evident that even in the physical sciences the edge of creativity may be found in cosmology or ontology that is not entirely void of speculation, and certainly the work of the most respected historians is not fully amenable to rigorous empirical testing, to say nothing of its common failure to satisfy the canons of theoretical science. Moreover, considering the basic practical issue involved, of whether human decision can determine the course of history, there may be some value in guarded speculation on the nature of history if that speculation is not incompatible with the relevant theories and data of the empirical sciences. At any rate, while speculative philosophy of history has been properly chastened, having its wings clipped by the analysis of meaning, an interest in substantive matters that are neither strictly history nor strictly science is quite legitimate. It is in part within this territory that the question of ideas and the historical process must be pursued.

The complexity of the structure of even the simplest societies, the intricate interlocking of the forces that comprise the social process, the rudimentary character of the sciences upon which a responsible philosophy of culture must rest, and the impossibility of achieving a ground of objectivity in any attempt to describe and explain the facts of social and cultural history are all caveats against the temptation that curses every attempt to interpret history, whether past or contemporary—the gross oversimplification and distortion of masses of phenomena too complex to be comprehensible. Any account or explanation of the historical movement of a society or culture, however concientiously grounded in factual data or judiciously reasoned, must be judged to be at best only a partial and very limited commentary on a picture whose full design will never be grasped.

Within the limits of these constraints and warnings, nevertheless, we are in principle entitled to raise questions of the impact of ideas upon history, where those ideas may range from carefully devised empirically based theories or speculative generalizations to the vaguely articulated moral ideals or inarticulate presumptions that appear to move the masses. The exigencies attending the decisions which on a large scale affect the course of our society make it imperative that we consider such matters. They are not questions which can be answered in full, and often they cannot be answered at all. Certainly they cannot be answered with any permanency or finality. But an attempt upon them is in some sense a measure of our humanity, or at least of our sophistication. For if there is in history a region of openness and contingency, where events are unique and novelties are genuinely real, so that it is possible to say that we and our institutions are not totally the victims of a rigid determinism and the rise and fall of our societies and cultures are not entirely matters of necessity, but rather that at some juncture of forces we have the freedom to affect the course of our future, this juncture must be the point of intersection of ideas with decision and action.

In this paper I will comment first upon the task of generalizing upon the structure and history of a culture. Thereafter, I will suggest several theses on the role of ideas in the interpretation of history and will conclude with a discussion of the centrality of the idea of the individual in the contemporary movement of culture in the United States and western Europe.

II

In its most elementary phase, a descriptive study of a culture is a summary of the content of the culture embracing a wide variety of elements which taken together constitute the accrued attainment of a people and in one way or another indicate the level and character of their cultivation. For such descriptive purposes, "culture" may be defined more or less objectively on an enumerative basis as the sum of such external factors as human behavior, historic events, material creations, and social arrangements together with their internal concomitants, the emotional, ideational, and temperamental characteristics of the people. On this basis, culture must be defined to include the primary folkways, the social, economic, and political forms and processes, industry and communication as well as the science, religion, art, philosophy, and mental traits of the people and period.

Every culture is an admixture of elements, and what predominates in one may be present to a lesser degree in another. There are no simplified lines that can be drawn definitively. For general purposes, a culture may be described and differentiated on a variety of bases: is it, for example, predominantly religious or secular; is the major orientation of its thought and ideal supernaturalistic, naturalistic, or positivistic; is its logic realistic or nominalistic, its dominant method intuitive, rational, or empirical. Is its ethic absolute or relative, its common concept of the good life sacrificial or hedonistic. Is its music heroic or lyric, its poetry comic or tragic. Is its concept of society atomistic or organismic, its political arrangements aristocratic or democratic. Do its people seek dominion or peace. Do they lay waste their world or protect and nurture it. Is their social structure predominantly urban or rural, their economy industrial or pastoral. Is there abundance or scarcity; do men find joy or starvation. Is the social order founded on competition or cooperation. Do the masses await the miracle of apocalyptic fulfillment or are their hands put to social improvement. Is the moral consciousness of the people an agonized suffering of depraved conscience or delight in human possibility. Do they commune with God or with nature.

A philosophical study of culture must go beyond elemental description and engage in a search for origins and the relating of the cultural elements causally to each other and to noncultural factors such as ethnological composition and natural environmental conditions. Such a study of cultures inevitably becomes an attempt to ascertain the nature of the cultural process. This necessitates a careful identification of those factors both within and external to a culture which most completely determine its internal development and affect the production of its outward manifestations. Where social and technical developments are rudimentary, the location of such basic factors may not be difficult as, for instance, extremes in temperature, scarcity of arable land, or the proximity of natural enemies. But as a society becomes more extensive and its institutions more complex the underlying determining forces may not be readily evident, especially since some are themselves cultural products.

As a society develops in its compositeness, its internal intricacies, and the complexity of its external relations, there is a concomitant increase in the subtlety of the forces that determine its course. To identify those factors, nevertheless, and to explain the cultural process by discerning the numerous causal relations which obtain within the total complex is primary to the task of a philosophy of history or culture.

It is at this point that success or failure in cultural or historical analysis is determined. I have already confessed that a primary offense of philosophies of history is their gross oversimplification of the historical process. Such oversimplification is perhaps inevitable in view of the utter complexity of the structure and development of advanced cultures and the necessity in a philosophical analysis to reduce the problem to intelligible proportions. But an advance confession of guilt does not remove the temptation to undue simplification. A philosophy should be immediately suspect which undertakes to describe a highly complex culture in terms of any simple formula. Certainly the cultural processes of our own society are utterly involved, and it is naive to suppose that a single factor could account for basic transmutations unless it could be shown that, in conjunction with other elements, its impact upon the total cultural complex might be of such a nature as to produce numerous deep-seated variations in our modes of thinking and living. It seems safe to assume that ordinarily a total culture is not a function of any one of its constituent elements such that a variation in that constituent only will produce a concomitant variation in the culture as a whole.

A philosophy of culture should be a normative pursuit that goes beyond both description and rudimentary explanation through the analysis of historical determinants. In order to achieve a genuinely synoptic theory, it must ascertain those elements which not only by their generality summarize the content of a culture, and through their causal interrelationships afford an adequate insight into the historical process of the culture, but which constitute as well indices that disclose the stage of maturity of the culture by indicating the nature of its internal development. Such cultural elements can function as data for cultural philosophy because in them numerous basic traits and tendencies become articulate and recognizable. They must satisfactorily represent both the dynamic and static features of a culture, both its external and internal elements, its particular achievements and the general format of its development. In brief, they must represent the culture with such adequacy that a discussion of them may in effect be a shorthand discussion of the total cultural complex.

When an inquiry is made into possible factors that may serve as key principles for the analysis of culture and history, a variety of items present themselves. Some of these express the material, others the ideal elements of the culture. Some emphasize its external, others its internal features. My point is that in the relationship of *idea* to *action* there can be found a cultural principle of unusual adequacy that can serve a variety of purposes both analytical and synthetic. The idea-action relationship is the meeting ground of both opposing and complementary factors—of theories to decisions; the ideal to the material; internal attitudes and dispositions to external action and achievement; generalities to particulars; thought and reason to conduct. Moreover, the dynamic processes of a culture may be exhibited historically in this relationship. Indeed, it is quite possible that the study of a culture in terms of this principle, determining the role which ideas play in relation to practice and practice in relation to ideas, will articulate many of the fundamental characteristics and qualities of the culture, provide a basis for careful analytical comparisons among cultures, indicate the degree to which the culture has achieved maturity in terms of its own genius, and yield a perspective for a synoptic judgment on the culture for evaluative and possibly even predictive purposes.

It is obvious that whatever occurs or has occurred must be admissible from the standpoint of each principle of explanation, e.g., economic, theological, or geographical. Assuming the analysis to be adequate, every explanatory principle must be compatible with whatever events have taken place. The temptation to select only those events which fit the explanation must be resisted. On the other hand, the probability of achieving an adequate analysis increases with the satisfactory explanation of a historical fact by more than one cause. Here lies a very special virtue of the idea-action interpretation of cultural history. Since it is not by nature antithetical to most other possible principles of explanation, and since it cuts across the lines of some of these, it may well serve as an integrating factor among them and thereby contribute to a more adequate analysis. To treat history in terms of the practical impact of ideas does not necessarily preclude the employment, for instance, of economic, biological, or physical explanations of the same events. Such factors may combine with ideas to effect the specified action or behavior.

The selection of a principle of historical interpretation is perhaps best made by the observation of current trends that suggest a basic and general tendency which will serve as the focus of the cultural process. The selection of the idea-action relation as a principle of interpretation is by no means arbitrary. This relation is an index to many of the problems of contemporary Western culture and is an access to the historical meaning of past and perhaps also future events.

III

It should be obvious that the story of Western culture cannot be told without a recognition of the large role played in its advances and retrogressions by the idea-action factor. The major philosophical tradition is an incorporation in interpretive thought of the basic elements of the culture and may be expected, therefore, to reflect this same factor as one of its dominant characteristics. It is perhaps not too incautious to assert that much of Western intellectual history can be outlined in terms of two major efforts: (1) the attempt to construct theories adequate to the requirements of practice, and (2) the more technical attempt to construct metatheories which will adequately relate theory with practice. These efforts are evident in both secular and religious philosophy.

At the risk of the simplification against which I have warned, I will propose and illustrate several "theses" on the problem of the relation of ideas to action. "Ideas" may refer to consciously constructed theory or simply to general explanatory concepts embedded in a society's morality or articulated in its philosophic, scientific, or religious thought. I will incidentally impose upon the reader a few moral lessons which can perhaps be drawn from the examples adduced in support of the theses. These theses are not proposed as in any sense historical laws, either metaphysical or scientific, or as descriptions of invariant characteristics of cultural movement. They are suggested, rather, simply as indicators of useful directions which may be taken in the analysis of history.

First Thesis:

The failure to engage creatively in the construction of theory may set limits to the advancement of a culture and contribute eventually to its decline.

Perhaps nowhere is this thesis more clearly exemplified than in the comparative indifference to theoretical science that appears to have been a major contributor to the disintegration of Roman civilization. The decline of Rome was unquestionably the result of a complex of causes both overt and subtle, but among these was Rome's dependence upon technology while it failed to support that technology with the scientific theory that might have made it more adequate to the large problems of production, distribution, communication, and military action which plagued the empire after the Antonines. With all its genius for practicality, Rome, in failing to cultivate a traffic in ideas for their theoretical or explanatory value, failed eventually in the conduct of its practical affairs. The Romans were not indifferent to science. Their error lay in the fact that they valued science primarily not for the intrinsic value of knowledge, but rather simply for its practical uses, and they therefore severely neglected basic theory. In the same way they pursued metaphysics not so much to achieve understanding as simply to provide a basis for religion and morals. In this they were different from the Greeks, who in valuing knowledge for its intrinsic worth produced much of the theory upon which their own and later technologies were founded.

And yet the Romans were quite like many segments of American and European society today, for anti-intellectualism is a pervasive quality among us. We may well believe that the future strength of our culture will depend in part upon our overcoming this anti-intellectualism which has affected and infected even our institutions of learning. We must overcome it with a new and greater respect for ideas while yet preserving the practicality which has played such an important role in the creation of our civilization. We should not forget that the Romans excelled in those very capabilities upon which we now seem willing to depend: efficiency in administration, communication, engineering, and military organization.

Second Thesis:

In humane matters, major ideas that have developed independently of the living context of a culture, its economy and political and social life, or its art, morals, and religion, will fail to produce lasting results in the practical life of the culture.

History exhibits no more obvious case of the practical failure of such barren theorizing than the abortive monotheism of Ikhnaton in fourteenth-century Egypt, a monotheism produced without cultural roots as a metaphysical and religious idea, as compared with sixth-century Hebrew monotheism, which evolved from the complex of personal, tribal, national, and international affairs. The Egyptian monotheism appears to have been the product of an elite ruling caste which had lost touch with the moods and modes of life of the masses. The lasting power of the Hebrew monotheism, on the other hand, was no doubt due in part to its relation to the living processes of individual and group life. The values that issued from those processes became articulate in the prophetic religion and achieved a firm ideational support in the resulting theology.

Or consider the failure of the advanced religious and moral thought of nineteenth- and twentieth-century Germany to impress itself importantly on the religious and moral life of that nation—a consequence apparently of the sheltered patronage of German academic life that insulated it from its natural base in the social, moral, and political experience of the people. This meant a failure of the academic liberalism to affect the religion and social morality of the masses, a failure having consequences of far-reaching importance in the impotence of established religion in stemming the tide of political totalitarianism.

There is much for us to learn from these and similar historical examples—that human culture cannot be strengthened or transformed by executive orders and administrative procedures; that the learning of a nation must not be artificially severed from its vital processes, but that its schools must be kept close to its people; and that there must be an effective articulation of the creative capacities of a people with the dissemination and communication of ideas. Irrational decision and subsequent irrational behavior can be consequences of the detachment of thought from the life of society.

Third Thesis:

The construction of social theory in close relationship to limited social conditions but without regard to political, social, and economic trends can generate acute social and cultural crisis.

The failure of the ancient Greeks, for instance, to produce a political theory and idealism relevant to the practical need for large-scale political, social, and economic organization and action, resulting in the decline and eclipse of the polis, greatly accelerated the transformation of Greek culture into hybrid Hellenistic and eventually Roman forms.

The Greek political ideal issued from the facts of local social and economic life and a simple international commerce, but when faced with the practical requirement of a radical expansion in civic loyalties and extension of political affiliation if their status were to be preserved, the Greeks found it impossible to break with their traditional city-state political theory and parochial civic ideals. Lacking in political action the guidance of an adequate ecumenical idea and ideal, their political system passed into history and their culture was preserved mainly as an ingredient of its successors. Here is a strange and rather sad spectacle of some of the world's foremost minds out of touch with the movement of history, failing in their limited perspective to see the coming of the new imperial world which their own metaphysical and moral ideas would eventually help to shape. In statesmanship there is no substitute for breadth and depth of vision when the decisions of the present are important for the future, and a full grasp of the present is a grasp of the directions in which the social order is moving or is likely to move.

Vision in this sense was never more lacking than in those American statesmen who opposed the Louisiana Purchase or the purchase of Alaska and perhaps never more present than in St. Augustine's intuition that the Church would conquer the declining empire. But to argue for the importance of understanding social trends is not to endorse the kind of historical mysticism represented in the so-called doctrine of "manifest destiny" or other claims to a determined future. It is rather to emphasize the importance of cultivating an understanding of human individual and mass behavior through a knowledge of history and a pursuit of the social and psychological sciences. And, as in the case of decisions made by an organization like the Ford Foundation, it means measuring such things as the worth of proposed programs of action against such facts as necessary budget ceilings and other fiscal restraints.

Fourth Thesis:

When basic ideas and theories issue from the cultural process and thereafter persist but fail to positively affect decision and action, the result can be cultural lag and the possibility of cultural decline and social disintegration.

The Greeks created an advanced science under the impact of such practical demands as navigation and agriculture, but in the long run they failed to develop a technology commensurate with their own science, a technology which conceivably might have produced an economic and military strength that would have made the Macedonian invasion impossible.

A different kind of case is the failure of modern Christian fundamentalism to preserve its vital historical continuity with the socially oriented prophetic religion. As a consequence, the biblical connections of fundamentalism have often been a negative rather than a positive force in moral matters. The Bible has been used to deter rather than promote social progress. The problem of the future of today's culture is especially acute because of the fundamental methodological conflicts in our thinking where, as likely as not, we attempt to resolve the moral difficulties posed by new and unique social circumstances by the simple imposition of the old moral absolutes, or contend with difficult and subtle social issues by a recital of the personal virtues that are expected to set everything right. It is true that our knowledge of ourselves and of society has not kept pace with our knowledge of the physical world. But it is also true that our practical wisdom in moral affairs has not kept pace with our meager knowledge of human behavior. Our irrationalism is in part our refusal to act on the knowledge which we have already.

Fifth Thesis:

The achievement of a close harmony between idea and practice contributes to a stabilization of the culture that may prevent both advancement and decline.

Here a lack of intellectual initiative and adventurousness combines with a degree of practical inventiveness to produce an approximate equilibrium of thought and action. Such a condition is probably approached by most primitive societies in the absence of "civilized" invasion, as may be evidenced by the North American Eskimos in their more native condition. Such cultures are marked by an impressive measure of stability but may lack the creative and experimental capacity to survive large-scale cultural, social, or environmental crises.

On a totally different and highly sophisiticated level, there has been a most remarkable degree of stabilization in the culture of the Roman Catholic Church, where practice approximates the basic ideas in Augustinian theology and Thomistic philosophy, with the result that the religious culture persists anomalously within secular contexts often basically contradictory to it. Here there is a conceptual formulation embracing the arts and sciences, morality, politics, and natural religion in a grand theory integrated by revealed religion with the life of the individual, and, in nations predominantly Catholic, with the social process. It should be a matter of great interest to those concerned with cultural history that in this century the Church is examining many of its forms and practices in the hope of insuring its own future vitality by achieving a more authentic relevance to personal and social life. An increased vitality of the Church will probably result only from major breaks in the harmony that has so recently prevailed between the ideational structure of Catholic theology and the established practices of the Church and of Catholic society.

Sixth Thesis:

The cultivation of incompatible basic theories where none of these succeeds in the elimination of the others may produce basic practical as well as theoretical conflicts between societies as well as within single cultures.

Civil war and political revolution are often instances of such conflict in political or economic theory, and taking the world as the stage, such conflicting theories can become basic to national cultures that are thereby set in opposition. The Soviet Union and the United States exhibit this opposition in action that follows from contradiction in theory, as did the Soviet Union and Nazi Germany, even though the totalitarianisms of these last two were rooted in a common philosophic ground. The conflict between the two Chinas is perhaps today's best example of the antagonisms and transformations arising from essentially ideational forces internal to a culture.

But conflicting ideas in science or philosophy or social theory can be the occasion for the advancement of thought and the general enrichment of culture, as fundamental conflict within a culture can be a constructive good as well as a destructive evil. Revolution is often good rather than evil. There is no simple ground on which to judge the ultimate consequences of ideational differences and antagonisms.

Seventh Thesis:

A confluence of cultures whose structures are underwritten by basic ideas which are incompatible may result in a cultural movement which incorporates fundamental theoretical contradictions.

An obvious instance of a major confluence of cultures is the coming together of important Hellenistic and Hebrew elements within the context of Roman civilization to produce the foundations of Christianity. At least at two important points there were fundamental contradictions that persisted in the groundwork of Christian thought and continue even today to plague the theology and metaphysics of the religion in ways that appear to have adverse practical consequences.

Perhaps there is no more dramatic instance of conflict in basic cultural ideas than that between the dominant Greek conception of eternity, with its implicate of a cyclical theory of time and history, and the Hebrew commitment to temporality which was tied to the conception of creation and the large involvement in eschatology that characterized Judaism at the beginning of the Common Era. This conflict at the philosophical roots of religious thought was never adequately reconciled in Christian theology and metaphysics, though ingenious but sometimes devious efforts at such a reconciliation have many times been made. It now haunts the theologians, who are still hard pressed, after two thousand years of Christology, to make the eternal God relevant to his temporal creation, to make human history meaningful in a world of ultimate timelessness.

The second conflict to which I refer is related to the first. It is the attempt in Christian thought to achieve a meaningful synthesis of the impersonalistic metaphysics of the Greeks, particularly of Platonism, with the personalistic theology inherited from the Hebrew scriptures. Here again the theologians have exhibited remarkable ingenuity, but Christian theology, having opted for both Greek and Hebrew ideas, for cultural causes that are entirely obvious, has been caught in the contradictory predicament of describing the personal biblical living God of history with categories designed for the description of the Greek metaphysicians' impersonalistic conception of ultimate, motionless, timeless reality. That the personal and temporal do not join comfortably with the impersonal and eternal is no fault of the theologians and philosophers. Christian thought is in this embarrassing predicament because in the confluence of cultures important ideas that have served well in the tributaries stand a good chance of surviving in the mainstream even though their survival may not serve the cause of logic.

Eighth Thesis:

When ideas which have issued from experience and proved their practical worth become incorporated in institutions which perpetuate them and extend their influence into eras in which they are essentially foreign, cultural confusion and disintegration may result.

The anomaly of a highly influential biblical fundamentalism kept alive by ecclesiastical forms and institutions in our age of scientific intelligence may be taken as a case in point, a condition responsible for much moral, mental, and spiritual conflict and confusion. Or consider the radically atomistic concept of society, so important in the rise of capitalistic individualism, that persists today with little regard for the psychological, economic, and political facts which deny its validity and call for an organic concept of the individual in relation to society which clearly recognizes the social and cultural facets of the individual person. To liberate a culture from the dead hand of the past that reaches out continually from the society's established institutions requires a never-ending battle with custom and tradition. To achieve freedom from established forms without destroying the inheritances from the past that are precious to the present and essential to the future requires a wisdom that is far too uncommon in the decision-makers of any society.

Ninth Thesis:

When practical circumstances generate theories which are in advance of practice, those theories may become positive forces which contribute to cultural advancement and fulfillment.

It seems obvious, for instance, that the development in Hellenistic philosophy of the Stoic theory of man and his relationship to the universe, together with the rather successful incorporation of this theory into the individual practice and certainly the corporate life of large segments of Mediterranean people, contributed immeasurably to the achievement of Roman imperialism and the strength of the civilization that was built upon it. It is doubtful that the remarkable achievement of the empire in uniting so many societies of diverse origin and character would have been possible without a widely dispersed and accepted philosophy grounded in the idea of the unity of mankind combined with a cosmology that gave meaning to the conception of the universe. But this philosophy itself was quite certainly in part one of the products of the extension of Macedonian rule through the Middle East.

Not less impressive was the role played by the Christian doctrine of God and man in salvaging much of the culture of antiquity when the religion was legalized in the fourth century at the very time of the disintegration of the secular empire. Later, to cite another exhibit, the Protestant theory of man set forth in intensified individualistic terms combined with such factors as nominalistic metaphysics, population increase, experimental methodology, geographic expansion, and the improvement of navigation to establish the foundation of modern capitalistic economy.

More spectacular has been the achievement of modern advanced industrial technology with its vast complex of political, economic, and spiritual consequences in large part as the result of deductively formulated scientific theory. An important point might be made here of the practical impact of mathematics where that science has been cultivated on a formal basis.

Tenth Thesis:

Ideas which set forth philosophies of history and culture may influence the processes of history in directions compatible with their own prescriptions.

The destruction of Hebrew culture appeared imminent with the sixth-century Chaldean invasion, but the creation, under the dominion of religion, of a theory of Judaic culture and contemporary history by Ezekiel and the Second Isaiah gave a new foundation to the life of the community and a new meaning to its experience sufficient to carry it through a most precarious era. Indeed, the idea that it is the historic destiny of the people of Israel to bear the sufferings of the world gave the Jewish people the incredible strength to survive unspeakable suffering.

The early Christian doctrine of man, his relationship to God, the Church, and the state, having been established as a general theory and made articulate in St. Augustine's philosophy of history and culture marked a turning point in history as for a thousand years it was a major determinant of the structure of medieval culture erected on the ruins of antiquity.

The Yang-Yin conception interpreted as a principle of harmony of opposites in the cultural process has no doubt been an important stabilizing factor in Chinese social and political development. Or consider the impact on the social process of the dialectical materialistic interpretation of history and culture advanced by Marx which moved society so far in the direction indicated by the theory itself. Clearly there is abundant evidence that the very course of history can be influenced by ideas on the nature of culture and the historical process.

Now, by presenting these theses on the possible practical effects of ideas I do not mean to propose a logico-mechanical guide to our thinking in relationship to the processes of the culture. Nothing could be more destructive of original and inventive thought. I mean rather to exhibit the impact of ideas on history under various conditions as evidence of the creative power of ideas as determinants of the course of history. If history is free and the future is open, no one can know in advance what factors may influence the movement of a culture. The resources of a people in facing the future are many and varied—economic, political, intellectual, moral, artistic, and spiritual. No society that is conscious of its place in history can neglect the cultivation of any of these.

IV

It is possible to identify ideas or clusters of ideas that define the character of a culture and are powerful forces in determining the directions in which it moves. These may appear in diverse forms ranging from deductively formulated theories or as ideals well established in the philosophical or religious literature or moral tradition of a people, to half-articulate ideas and dispositions evident in their mythology, folk tales, hymns, governmental and business decisions, or voting records. I am not arguing for a mystical "genius" of the culture, some independently real power which moves it inexorably toward its denouement, but rather for a quite matter of fact "genius" which is an ideational and ideal focus or concentration of the culture's energies, which may identify it and signify its most distinctive qualities. But the idea-ideal which is the "genius" of the culture not only describes the culture; it is a moving power within it, a moving power not because it has some mysterious reality of its own but rather because it is a factor in the minds of men which affects their attitudes, decisions, and actions.

It is possible to say, for instance, that a dominant moving force in Jewish history has been the idea of the "chosen people," that the ideal of "world unity" was a central and powerful factor in shaping the Roman Empire, or that the religious concept of "salvation" informed much of European life and literature between Augustine and the Renaissance. It is in this sense that we can say that the "genius" of the culture of modern western Europe and America is the idea of the individual person. The currents and crosscurrents that are our intellectual and institutional history have produced a world in which the individual person is the center of concern. Perhaps there is no direction in the process of history, no creative purpose and no telos or end which determines its movement, but here and there in the course of ideas and events the worth of the individual person has emerged as the foundation of value, and the well-being of the individual as the object of social purpose and action, until now the individual person, his rights, and his responsibilities, have become the ground upon which must be fought the decisive battles of moral and political philosophy and where the large decisions affecting economic, political, and social life must be forged. Indeed, it is the battleground upon which actual wars are fought, or at least on which the people who fight them are told they are fought.

There is a sense in which individual personality is the substantive ground of our culture: our metaphysics and logic tend to be nominalistic, our religion personalistic, and our theology theistic; our morality is often intensely individualistic; and our social and political ideals are nominally democratic. The person enjoys strong traditional support from our metaphysics as well as from religion and ethics and in sometimes subtle ways is more often than not the center of our art, our literature, and certainly our civic consciousness.

The concern for the individual is especially characteristic of British and American thought, a fact obvious not only in political and legal documents and constitutions, but as well in the literature of metaphysics and moral philosophy. Perhaps there is no better instance than the exhibit of Josiah Royce in his Gifford Lectures, *The World and the Individual,* struggling to preserve the ontological status of the individual against the totalitarian proclivities of the Hegelian idealism which he had espoused. For us, indeed, the individual person is the ground upon which we must construct the edifice of values, whether private or social, and the symbol by which alone we can now invest our history with meaning and purpose. Whatever, therefore, in our thought, attitude, and practice contradicts the worth of the individual person or obstructs the securing of his values—preventing the achievement of his moral autonomy and subverting the individual freedoms that are our most precious inheritance from the past—contradicts as well the creative spirit of the culture and frustrates the realization of its high possibilities. Whatever contributes to the well-being and the realization of the inherent capabilities of the individual person, however directly or indirectly, is consonant with the central meaning of the culture. The survival and flourishing of our culture is a question of the condition of the individual person.

It is quite irrelevant that our personalism and individualism are only the current summation of a long history of the evolution of these ideal concepts, that we can with some success trace that history across the centuries through the philosophic, religious, literary, and political movements of other cultures. For those other cultures, Greek, Hebrew, Roman, Arabic, Teutonic, were in

fact the ancestors of our own, and there is no more reason why we should suppose that a dominant and moving idea should not have an ancestry than that
those who hold it should have appeared from nowhere. That Jeremiah,
Ezekiel, Socrates, and Augustine are at the foundations of our individualism
should be no more surprising than that Occam, Locke, Blackstone,
Rousseau, Jefferson, and William James are also found there.

It is irrelevant also that a strong emphasis on individualism has appeared
in other cultures quite unrelated historically to our own, for there is nothing
incongruous about value parallelisms among diverse cultures.

Finally, it is also irrelevant that the full meaning of individualism has not
been realized in practice, that we continue to leave behind us a disappointing
accumulation of failures and persist to a frightening degree on a course that
invites catastrophe for the individual. The meaning of a culture is not defined
simply by the successes in its history. It is defined rather by those very criteria
which are employed in assessing success and failure.

We are not unacquainted with the fact of decline and death of cultures,
for we can move through the ruins of past civilizations whose visible remains
may inspire admiration or contempt, or nothing more than an indifferent
curiosity, but which leave us wondering where all the people have gone, that
these monuments whether of stone or words should seem to stand apart and
belong not simply to the past but to another and strange world. Perhaps we
are not concerned with world conditions or with life on this continent a half-
million years from now, or even a thousand. But if our span of concern cannot be measured by millennia, it is at least a matter of generations. And the
rate of acceleration in the processes of history has become so great that even
without the catastrophe of total war, or the total consumption of our vital
resources, within the lifetime of millions now being born the substance and
character of our culture could be so radically transformed that future
historians, surveying their past from the perspective of time, could well
remark that at the close of the twentieth century of the Common Era the
Hellenic-Judeo-Christian culture of Euro-American civilization had already
begun its decline, and that even at the middle of that century the sure signs of
the coming fall and disintegration were clearly visible.

Those signs, they might write—if indeed some civilization of the future
retains enough humanity to produce sensitive and perceptive historians
—those signs, visible but not seen, were unheeded warnings of the *collectivism* that effectively destroyed individuality and the *dehumanization*
that effectively destroyed the personal quality of life. For this, one of them
might observe, was a civilization, brief lived to be sure, that was in its substance and ideal a coming together of the best ingredients of the classic

Hellenic culture, its love of formal beauty and its profound respect for reason and knowledge, the best of the Judaic religious culture, its reverence for the mystery of being and the grounding of its life in the moral will, and the best of Roman civic culture, its conception of law and order and unity. These joined eventually in an uneasy and unstable association, for even after two thousand years they were in frequent and serious conflict. But they became the foundation, nevertheless, of a culture whose art, science, religion, and morality conspired mutually to magnify the individual person in reality and worth and importance, not only ideally but even with some success in practice. That success was always partial and often transient, but nevertheless real.

The struggle for the individual and his freedom, he might continue, was long and sometimes bitter and was fought against the most overwhelming odds—the oppressive force of social habit and custom, ignorance, irrationalism, anti-intellectualism, moral indifference, secular and ecclesiastical authoritarianism, commercial exploitation, national enmities, cruelties, hypocrisies, bigotries, and tyrannies of every kind. Yet with all its failures, this was a civilization of high intelligence, strong determination, and an abundance of good will, and by the close of the twentieth century there had been achieved in western Europe and North America a quite remarkable degree of political equality and social equity. Civil rights were generally guaranteed to everyone and with the universalizing of education and literacy, together with the vast increase in material productivity made possible by a steadily advancing technology and the progressive destruction of trade barriers, there was general prosperity and equality of economic opportunity. The effective deployment of political and military power secured a tenuous peace and there was a social stability and efficiency in human affairs that had theretofore been quite undreamed of. Much that had formerly been mostly ideal was actually accomplished.

But, our historian might well continue, in the achievement of these ends the individual was in some way lost—not obviously nor intentionally, of course, but slowly and surely through a general failure of the people to sense the full nature of the ideas and ideals of individualism and to come to grips with the multiple forces large and small that determine the character of both social and individual life. The twentieth century more and more regarded the individual as simply a political and economic animal—a voter, taxpayer, producer, and consumer—and it organized and regimented his life in the interest of governmental, industrial, and commercial efficiency. Organized it endlessly, for American and European society faced the immense social problems that were inevitable to such a highly industrialized civilization, one whose advanced science and technology conspired with nature to burden the world with an excessive population. This generated the endless vital problems associated with the crowding of great masses of humanity into gigantic cities, of increasing demands upon production, of decreasing resources, of more and more public services, more and more bureaucracy and regulation and control, and more and more destruction and desecration of the world itself.

For the most part, the individual had gained what was commonly called equality and the society had achieved a high degree of solidarity and cohesion, with a high level of law and order. But the twentieth century had failed, as all others had failed, to protect and nourish the individual in his authentic being, in his freedom and in his unique individuality. Under the stress of its overwhelming social tasks, it failed to find a way to create and maintain a secure and orderly society without sacrificing the real individual person. It failed to reconcile the authority necessary to order and stability with the freedom essential to the meaning of authentic individuality. After centuries of struggle for the liberation of the individual from the group, in the achievement of the independence of thought and expression and movement and the spontaneity, privacy, and self-determination which are the ingredients of personal freedom, and just when the economy and political order seemed to make the consummation of that liberation a real possibility, the individual was drawn back into the collective mass. His autonomy and freedom were sacrificed to the demands of organization, the mass organization that proved necessary to secure human life upon a scale so utterly complex and vast. This meant the inevitable decline of spontaneity and creativity, the destruction of uniqueness, variety, and difference, the victory of a deadening boredom and mediocrity of life.

Now, because if our culture fails another may not arise which values the individual person as we do, in looking back our historian may be far less sensitive to the loss of individuality than I have given him credit for. He would see the individual submerged in the social mechanism, because that would be visible and obvious. But he might not sense the concomitant loss of personality, the destruction of the very soul of the culture, the dehumanization of which there are already such ominous and threatening signs. Within a single generation we have seen an incredibly rapid acceleration of the technical and bureaucratic processes that convert social relationships into mechanics and human souls into things. To contend with the complexities of human relations we are developing a social technology that borrows heavily from the successes of our mechanical techniques and depends more and more on mechanics and electronics and less and less on human judgment. The concept of human engineering is becoming commonplace as we refine our skills and extend our powers for manipulating human beings. There can be little doubt that many large social problems which now seem insurmountable will be solved through social technology. But the solution of some problems inevitably produces others, and already we have learned that the creation of authentic community, the community of persons treated as persons and not as things, depends on intellectual, moral, and spiritual forces that are internal to the life of the person and cannot be generated by the processes of external social engineering.

The problem of technology and bureaucracy is not simply the external impact of machinery and organization upon men. It is even more the mechanizing of men, the dissolution of personal identity into the anonymity of function, the loss of the sense of productive vocation with nothing to replace it as a foundation of personal worth, the transformation of names into numbers, the sacrifice of the individual to efficiency, and in general the dehumanization of the quality of life in the estrangement of the individual from the ground and conditions of personal being.

That our future may be threatened with technological dehumanization does not mean that we should attempt to slow down or reverse the course of civilization and undo the great scientific and technical gains that have been made, reaching for a simpler society free from the intricate complications of modern life. This is totally impossible and clearly undesirable. The very quality of personal life that is precious to us is possible in part because of our technology. To attempt to reverse the order of technical progress or to thwart the continuing advance of science and technical achievement would be as immoral as it is impossible. We can only look ahead, not backward—but look ahead with a better knowledge and understanding of the human predicament, with a more sophisticated perspective and insight, with a more sensitive conscience and more profound wisdom, seeing more clearly that we must continue to construct and reconstruct our values within the contexts of new and greater difficulties, that the future cannot be a repetition of the past, and that it cannot be a simple extension of the present. Seeing as well that if our future is to be the consummation of the free culture of the individual person and not the culture of inhuman technology, we must cultivate an ethic which ensures that techniques as means will not dominate the moral, aesthetic, and spiritual ends and purposes which must be set by and for the autonomous person.

Notwithstanding its great failures, the culture of western Europe and America represents so much that is of supreme worth that it is difficult for us to believe it is not fated not only to survive with strength, but to move into a virtually endless future of progress and high accomplishment. We would like to believe that in some way or another there are guarantees of history on our side, that what we have done and are doing and will do conforms to nature or to the will of God or to some cosmic ground of being and righteousness. We would like to believe that our human failures are but temporary, that the dehumanization that threatens our society is but an interim passage in a vast process of growth and progress, that the alarming increase in human estrangement and alienation we see all around us is evidence of a mere surface malady that a few timely adjustments in the social order will surely cure.

But if we cannot believe these things, and must face the fact not only that our failures are great and profound, that the dehumanization is real and may increase at an accelerating rate, and that the estrangement, alienation, anxiety, meaninglessness, purposelessness, and despair are deep-rooted in the very structure of our culture, but also that we do not now know how to effectively contend with these matters, where we should turn or what we should do, we can at least believe that history and the universe are not inevitably set against us. We need not believe the myth that our civilization is fated to decline and die. We have a fighting chance to win through, to bring new strength and wisdom to our culture, to give it a new vitality and power of endurance. It is a chance that depends upon a clear vision of what constitutes the ideal greatness of our civilization and an honest recognition of the destructive character of much that we tolerate and condone. It depends upon a full marshalling of our intellectual, moral, and spiritual resources to assure that our human purposes and ends are not dominated by our technical means, that we do not permit the things that matter least to tyrannize over the things that matter most. The issue before us now is nothing less than whether humanity can set its mind and will purposefully against an indeterminate future and establish the autonomy of human freedom over an otherwise conscienceless and meaningless drift of history.

STERLING M. MCMURRIN

UNIVERSITY OF UTAH   .
JULY, 1972

ROBERT S. HARTMAN

THE VALUE STRUCTURE OF JUSTICE

"Earthly power doth then show likest God's
When mercy seasons justice."
Portia in *The Merchant of Venice,* IV, i.

1. Formal Axiology: The Synthetic A Priori of Justice

The idea of justice has been around as long as the idea of motion—and actually began its career together with it in Plato and Aristotle. But the history of the two ideas has been very different. The idea of motion has had its Galileo who converted it into geometry and hence into the basis of natural science, a synthetic a priori system which became applicable to the measurement of any kind of motion.

The idea of justice never had a Galileo. It is still defined by words rather than variables of a system, still a plaything of philosophers rather than a tool of social scientists. It is still subject to abstractions and analytic implications rather than constructions and synthetic deductions. When we think of motion today we think of systems of variables; when we think of justice we think words: "rightness," "equity," "honor," "good will"; "the lawful and the fair," to speak with Aristotle. These words can be found both in dictionaries of the English language under "justice" and in philosophical treatises of Justice—which latter are only in degree but not in kind on a higher level than everyday discourse. Each of these words is as much in need of definition as "justice" itself. A reviewer of a recent book on a theory of justice, based on a classic version of the ancient notion of fairness, wrote that "the notion of fairness, and hence Rawls's notion of justice, seems to involve attaching a sense to the notion of *deserving;* and this seems to me an utterly obscure notion."[1] In fact the more an obscure notion is "explained" the more obscure it becomes; for as Descartes observed, philosophical explanation asks for further philosophical explanation and this for further such explanation and so on ad infinitum. Philosophy, says Descartes, explicates vaguely known concepts by concepts equally vague, which in turn are explained in the same way so that eventually the original notion is explicated by a chain of concepts one link as weak as the preceding, and all on a level of abstraction infinitely removed from practical application. Words, Descartes tells us, are simply no scientific means of defining phenomena,[2] and by science he meant both natural and moral science. Justice is a fundamental phenomenon which ought to be defined by a different method than that of words.

Even the greatest jurist of our age, Hans Kelsen, writes on justice in the interrogative mood and professes at the end of his essay: "I started this essay with the question as to what is justice. Now, at its end I am quite aware that I have not answered it."[3] "My only excuse," Kelsen continues, "is that in this respect I am in the best of company."[4] For, "the many doctrines of justice that have been expounded from the oldest times of the past until today may easily be reduced to two basic types: a metaphysical-religious and a rationalistic or—more exactly formulated—a pseudorationalistic one."[5] In Kantian terms, which are still the best for those who want to make a science out of a philosophy, "justice" has been defined throughout history and until today in terms of analytic or abstracted and not in terms of synthetic or constructed concepts like those of mathematics.

It has been a prejudice—not indeed since Newton's time, for even Locke at that time believed that a science of morals was possible but a science of nature impossible "in spite of the incomparable Mr. Newton,"[6] but since the nineteenth century—that synthetic a priori construction could be applied only to natural and not to moral and social phenomena, even though this was the very essence of Kant's work. Social science continued with words and thus with explaining *ignotum per ignotius;* scientific definitions, on the other hand, as Galileo's of "motion," transformed the *ignotum,* e.g. the unknown concept of Aristotelian "movement," into sets of formulae which gave rise to systems applicable to the phenomena from which the unknown concepts were abstracted.

The present essay is an attempt at a Galilean transformation of "justice." As Galileo used *number* to transform the philosophical definition of motion—"fulfillment of the potential *qua* potential"—into a scientific, that is synthetic a priori one,—so we shall use *value* to transform the philosophical notion of justice into a scientific, that is a synthetic a priori one.

Galileo took advantage of the fact that number is structured in the a priori system of mathematics; he thus was able to express "motion" in terms of this system. We shall take advantage of the fact that value is structured in the a priori system of formal axiology,[7] and thus shall be able to express "justice" in terms of this system. The mathematical system is the application of sequential order to quantity, the axiometric system is the application of sequential order to quality. A number is a set of extensions, a value is a set of intensions. When value is thus analyzed synthetically, or rather the value system thus constructed synthetically, it will be seen that "justice" is another word for "valuation"—as philosophers have indeed held from Plato to Rawls—and that a system of valuation gives details of the value structure of justice some of which have escaped the social philosophers.

I shall, therefore, first give a very short survey of the system of axiology and then, in terms of this system, analyze the notion of justice and show its internal structure and applicability.

In an earlier essay,[8] the value system was summarized in ten points which amount to the following: Value is meaning. Meaning is richness of properties. Sets of properties are intensions. A thing has value in the degree that it fulfills the intension of its concept. The intension, as value measure, is the axiometric norm of the value. There are three kinds of concepts, which constitute three kinds of intensions: constructs or synthetic concepts, abstracts or analytic concepts, and singular concepts. Correspondingly, there are three dimensions of value—systemic value as the fulfillment of the construct, extrinsic value as the fulfillment of the abstract, intrinsic value as the fulfillment of the singular concept. Constructs are of finite, abstracts of denumerably infinite, and singular concepts of nondenumerably infinite content or cardinality. The dimensions of value form a hierarchy, with intensional cardinalities n, $\aleph_0$ and $\aleph_1$, respectively. Systemic valuation is the model of schematic thinking, extrinsic valuation that of pragmatic thinking, intrinsic valuation that of emphatic—and empathic—thinking. Systemic value (S), extrinsic value (E), and intrinsic value (I) can themselves be valued in terms of each other. Thus, intrinsic value can be valued systemically, extrinsically or intrinsically, and so can systemic value and extrinsic value. These valuations of the value dimensions in terms of each other give rise to the calculus of value. This calculus combines the three value dimensions and their respective cardinalities, n, $\aleph_0$ and $\aleph_1$. Combinations of the three value dimensions can be either compositions or transpositions. A *composition* of values is a positive valuation of one value by another, a *transposition* is a negative such valuation or a disvaluation. Each of the three values may be either valued or disvalued by the three. Hence there are $3 (3 + 3) = 18$ value combinations, half of which are compositions and half transpositions.

This is as much as we shall need for analyzing "justice" in terms of the axiological system. For greater understanding, of course, the system must be studied in detail. In particular, it must be understood that the formulae of the axiological calculus are no abbreviations of abstracted concepts such as Bentham's or Hutcheson's, but are synthetic a priori constructions. They are set-theoretical formulae, based on the axiom that *a value is a set of properties.* Thus, a value composition, say E^S, means not only that an extrinsic value (E) is valued systemically (S), but also that a denumerably transfinite set of properties ($\aleph_0$) is exponentiated a finite number of times $(^n)$, so that the formula is an authentic mathematical formula, $\aleph_0{}^n = \aleph_0$.[9]

2. The Axiological Definition of Justice

Our definitions are the following:
Distributive justice is value composition.
Injustice is value transposition.
Corrective justice is relevant disvaluation of value transposition.

We symbolize by "U," "V" any two values, intrinsic, extrinsic or systemic ("I," "E," or "S"). We represent by "U^V" a composition, and by "U^{-V}" or "U_V" a transposition of values. The formula for distributive justice then, is U^V, for injustice U_V, and for corrective justice $(U_V)_U V$. Corrective justice must be the relevant disvaluation of the injustice. This means that the justice in question must *invert the act of injustice and through this inversion disvalue the injustice.*

As is seen, the most interesting and complex cases are those of corrective justice. But all three formulae give us insight into the structure of justice. Before we examine each of the three definitions we shall mention two of their corollaries.

The first concerns the fundamental *kinds* of justice. Since "U" and "V" stand for *any* kind of value, we can substitute for these variables those of any of the value dimensions, "S", "E" or "I". Correspondingly, we have three fundamental kinds of justice, as well as of injustice and corrective justice. (By "justice" we shall in the following mean "distributive justice", as the basic kind of justice.) These fundamental or pure kinds are systemic, extrinsic, and intrinsic justice. The first is *legal* justice (S^S) (or any other kind of systemic justice), the second *social* justice (E^E), the third *moral* justice (I^I). There are, moreover, mixed forms where the act of justice consists of different value dimensions, for example I^S, which is a systemic valuation of an intrinsic value. This is an act of justice which is both legal and moral; or E_S which is a social-legal injustice. By definition, any composition of value is a justice. It is a peculiarly illogical feature of language and a sign of lacking articulation in axiological thinking, that we can speak of *an* injustice but not of *a* justice. Still, we shall use this expression for an act of justice. By definition, then, any composition of values is a justice, any transposition of values an injustice, any composition which corrects, that is disvalues, a transposition of values is a corrective justice.

The second corollary concerns the *normative* nature of justice. Any valuation is the fulfillment of a norm, any disvaluation the nonfulfillment or violation of a norm. We therefore may also define *distributive justice as the fulfillment of a norm, injustice as the violation of a norm, and corrective justice as the corrective fulfillment of a norm that had been violated, or the disvaluation of the violation of a norm by the corresponding fulfillment.* In this formulation, the definition of justice depends on the axiometric definition of "norm." There are, in formal axiology, three different kinds of norm, depending on whether the axiometric intension consists of synthetic, analytic or singular concepts. From these three kinds of norm derive the three kinds of justice, namely *legal* justice the norm of which is the synthetic concept or construct; *social* justice the norm of which is the analytic concept or abstract; and *moral* justice the norm of which is the singular concept. The first is systemic, the second extrinsic, the third intrinsic value.

3. Distributive Justice

(a) Legal Justice

In the widest sense, any kind of systemic valuation would be the fulfillment of a systemic concept, and hence an act of systemic justice. Thus, when an accountant keeps his books in terms of the system of mathematics and of numbers which correctly signify the receipts and expenditures of the business, then "he does justice" to the situation, his accounting is done correctly, justly, and will not give rise to procedures due to violations of the norm. The corresponding formula is "S^S." Similarly, when a mathematician does a calculation, then, in this widest sense, he does justice to the science of mathematics; and if he does not he is doing it injustice. In the narrow sense, of course, the systems in question must be those which apply to human affairs, and here the norms of the legal system are paramount. If these are applied correctly justice is done.

Pure cases of legal justice, that is of the formula S^S, are relatively rare for they mean that the legal rule (S) is applied to a rule (S). Thus, in cases of mortgages, checks, or promissory notes, both the legal rule and the facts of the case, its "material" reference, are defined by strict rules. The rules of mortgages *construct* the mortgage. But the vast majority of legal acts are of the mixed form S^E,[10] that is, the extrinsic valuation of systemic value: the situational interpretation of a legal rule. In the field of distributive justice, we have here cases of the law of obligations, sales contracts, any case where actions are performed which are legally regulated, also legally regulated social relations such as labor relations, even family relations such as matrimony insofar as they are subject to the law. In the law, these relations do not have their intrinsic dimension; so that Kant, for example, could define matrimony as "the mutual lease of the sex organs."

The most interesting cases of mixed formulae are those of the formula S^I [11] that is intrinsic determinations of legal rules where the essence of human life determines the legal interpretation. It is very rare for such a case to come before the courts when it is one of distributive rather than corrective justice, and no violation of intrinsic value has occurred. But there are some cases where the intrinsic value of the human being is the very core of the case without an explicit violation of such a value. An instance is Bridges vs. Wixon.[12] Harry Bridges, an alien who entered the United States in 1920 and became a labor leader, was to be deported for being an alien and affiliated with an organization advocating overthrow of the government by force. The Supreme Court held that legally serious guilt cannot be acquired by mere association; human persons are unique and individual entities each of whom may claim to be tried and judged on his own acts and pronouncements severed from those of all others. There are other cases, where intrinsic value is legally regarded, as for example the award of the Nobel Prize to a person, which presupposes total dedication to his work. These awards give the person a legal right to the prize and this may be violated, as is seen strikingly in the case of Alexander Solzhenitsyn. Here also belongs any case of reward to a person on the ground of his intrinsic value, his sincerity, honesty, authenticity, or self-sacrifice, as a reward of a lifesaver or rewards for morals, e.g. a medal, if such rewards are legally founded. In these cases legal justice is founded not on a rule (S^S) nor a situation (S^E) but on human dignity and self-respect (S^I).

(b) Social Justice

Here we have the cases of the formula E^E. They are of greater interest because they concern everyday life and have historical relevance for philosophy. The classic notions of justice are based on the correct valuation of extrinsic (or social) values. The formula E^E means that an abstracted concept is applied to its correct referent, that is, an instance of the kind from which it was abstracted. The very notion of goodness is based on this kind of valuation, in classical treatises of both the Western and the Eastern world, and so is the correspondence of goodness and justice. When a chair is judged as either good or bad the norm for the judgment is the concept "chair", and not any other concept. A chair is good if it fulfills the correspondence definition, that is, if it has all the properties a chair is supposed to have. If it lacks some it is not a good chair. The same is true of a human being. He is socially good if he fulfills his role in society or if, in Plato's words, "he does his own proper work." And this is at the same time Plato's definition of justice, "this principle of doing one's own proper work" *(to ta hautou prattein)*.[13] Plato's definition of justice was a social definition; it became moral only when applied to the parts of the soul. Justice was a universal requirement for the "founding of our city" and "what we did lay down, and often said, if you recall, was that each man must perform one social service in the state for which his nature was best adapted." Then follows the definition. "And again, that to do one's own proper work and not be a busybody *(polypragmonein)* is justice."

This doing everyone his own business is a specific case of the rule that a concept must be applied to its referent and not to something else—that names must be correctly applied. "A carpenter undertaking to do the work of a cobbler or a cobbler of a carpenter, or the interchange of one another's tools or honors or even the attempt of the same man to do both—the confounding of all other functions would not, think you, greatly injure a state, would it?"[14] The general principle that goodness is the application of the right name to the right referent, was developed by Plato in *Cratylus or On the Correctness of Names*. Just as a shuttle is an instrument for separating the web so is a name an instrument for distinguishing one thing from another according to differences in nature. "The weaver, then, will use the shuttle well—and 'well' means like a weaver, and the teacher will use the name well—and 'well' means like a teacher."[15] The right name will correctly characterize the thing named, and the thing when characterized correctly will correspond in nature to what the name says. It will then be doing "well" what the name says it is doing. This means that *the name serves as the standard of good.* Socrates uses the etymology of proper names to determine their meaning, and compares the character of the name's bearer with the "characters" of the name. He makes the name the standard of value of the thing named. This is what in Plato we may call the nominalistic solution of the problem of good: a thing is good if it is correctly named, and corresponds fully to its name. From *Cratylus* to the theory of ideas is a long way—but *Cratylus* is the origin of the theory of ideas. The ideas are standards of values; they grow out of general names, and general names, or concepts, grow out of the kind of names discussed in *Cratylus.* In *Cratylus,* the correct name is a correct description; its letters take the place taken by the attributes of the concept, and etymology takes the place taken by conceptual logic.[16]

For Plato, this solution was an experiment, no sooner made than dis carded. It became, in a different sense, the solution of Aristotle for the notion of goodness: "the good is that toward which all things strive," where what they strive toward is teleologically their essence and logically their definition But again, Aristotle did not develop this general principle; he held, rather that there is no *common* idea of goodness to all things. Good is a homonym.[1] For this reason, in the *Politics,* which is based on the same principle of goodness, he is unable to clarify what "sort of equality" justice is. "Equality or inequality of what? Here is a difficulty which calls for politica speculation."[18] Actually, it calls for *logical* speculation; for, as the subsequent "obscure" discussion intimates, *the sort of equality in question is that of the concept ruling the members of a class.*

The nominalistic definition of good, even though it reappears again and again in Western philosophy, as in Thomas of Aquinas,[19] Spinoza,[20] ever Kant,[21] was not taken seriously in Western philosophy, either as basis of valuation or of justice. But it was in Eastern philosophy, where it had a long history in the philosophy of Confucius—never, to be sure, systematically developed but instead socially effective. "Confucius, when asked what should be the first step in governing a country replied: *'Rectify names' (Jen Min)* Let the ruler be a ruler, the minister a minister, the father a father, and the son a son. For when things no longer mean what their names indicate then says Confucius, the people are confused and know not how to move hand and foot."[22] "To rectify by taking action" is the character *Jen,* "to govern" or "government" is *Min.* "The art of government simply consists in making things right, or putting things in their right places."[23] "If you lead on the people with correctness who will dare not to be correct?"[24] The Confucian notion of *Li* gives the fundamental concept of order, "the order of things."[25] A corollary of the doctrine of *Li* is the importance of terminology: everything should be called by its right name.[26] Confucius said: "A melon cup that no longer resembles a melon cup, and people still say, 'A melon cup! A melon cup!' "[27]

Our formula E^E for social justice, namely valuing a thing extrinsically as a member of its class, is precisely the formula of Confucius. Name a thing by its right name and you do it justice, whether this thing is a cup or a human being. In the strict sense, of course, it means that a human being should be treated in accordance with his own social role and not with any other role. Thus, to judge whether a person is a good bookkeeper one has to judge him by the rules for bookkeepers and not by those for bakers. And these rules are the characteristics or notes of the concept "bookkeeper." When I judge a professor of philosophy for a promotion I have to judge him by the definition of "professor of philosophy" and the content of this concept, and not by any other. In general, to do justice to a person in his social role means to apply to him the concept of this role and not any other concept.

Using the concept of the class to which a being belongs as *norm* for judging the being in his role in the class, makes *justice a function of correct judgment.* This is of incalculable importance. It makes *the activity of judging the instrument of justice.* It solves at one stroke, and as a matter of course, the problem of applying justice to individual situations and illuminates the "utterly obscure" notion of *deserving.* A person deserves reward for social behavior in the degree that he fulfills the concept of his role. The more properties of the concept "foreman" a foreman fulfills, the more deserving a foreman he is.[28] The more properties of the concept "fluteplayer" a fluteplayer fulfills, the more deserving a fluteplayer he is; "he ought to have the best flutes given to him."[29] Attributing to him the properties he fulfills in the degree of his actual fulfillment is correct judgment; and acting upon this judgment is socially just action. *We act justly in an individual situation in the degree that we judge it correctly and act upon this judgment.* It makes conceptualization itself the powerful and effective instrument of just action; and traces an injust action to an incorrect judgment.

Social justice, in a word, is a *function of judgment.*[30] Judgment is learned when we learn to apply concepts to objects. In the last instance, *we learn to be just when we learn to speak.*[31]

The mixed forms of social justice are E^S and E^I. The first means the correct systemic valuation of an extrinsic situation and is the application of a legal rule to a situation, a social-legal valuation; it is the complement to the form S^E discussed in Section 3 (*a*), the situational interpretation of a legal rule. The second form, E^I, is the instrinsic valuation of an extrinsic situation, a social-moral valuation, the complement of which is the moral-social valuation, I^E, which will be examined in the next section. The form E^I means that a social situation is seen not only in its legal (E^S) or its social (E^E) but its moral dimension, it adds *compassion* to social justice; it means *social passion.* Here belong all the efforts at social improvement, from the Factory Commissioners in Karl Marx's England to today's ecologists, pacifists, and blacks, and women's liberators. Here social justice is done out of passion and compassion.

(c) Moral Justice

Moral justice is the application of the rule I^I, that is, the intrinsic valuation of an intrinsic value, especially of a human being. Axiologically, a thing is good if it fulfills its definition. The human person is defined, in formal axiology, as that being which has its own definition of itself in itself—the being which defines itself. Self-definition is the answer to the question, "Who am I?" The answer for each person is "I am I." To fulfill this definition, a person has to *be* himself; to be authentic, genuine, true to himself, honest, sincere—all the words of personal ethics.[32] An act of justice toward a person, therefore, is based on judging the person in accordance with his intrinsic self, his autonomy, his dignity and self-respect. Any violation of these is an act of moral injustice which must awaken the sense of intrinsic injustice called *compassion.* The prototype of intrinsic corrective justice is the case of the Good Samaritan. The prototype of distributive intrinsic justice is the Saint, the person who out of the fullness of his heart, *out of love,* gives each his due. Compassion presupposes the violation of the other's person, love presupposes the other's personal nature and his claim to be given his due as the person he is. In saints such as St. Francis and Albert Schweitzer, the superabundant sympathy and empathy with all beings extends not only to humans but to animals and things. "Be careful, Friar Leo," said St. Francis when his coat caught fire and Friar Leo poured water on it, "be careful, Friar Leo with Friar Fire!" "It hurts me," said Albert Schweitzer, "to have to kill bacteria when I operate." These expressions, we may say, are the most general forms of moral distributive justice. Here every being becomes a Thou, in the sense of Martin Buber. The categorical imperative of pure moral distributive justice is Jesus' command "Love thy neighbor as thyself." In Christian ethics, love and justice have seldom been included in one another, mainly because the notion of moral or intrinsic distributive justice has not been clearly formulated. Thomas of Aquinas, although he connects love and charity with justice, does not include them in the notion of intrinsic justice. Peace, he writes is *the work of justice indirectly* insofar as justice removes the obstacles to peace; but it is the *work of charity directly,* since charity, according to its very nature, causes peace; *for love is a unitive force.* The bonds of love and friendship unite men where justice merely governs their interaction. What men do for one another out of the generosity of love far exceeds the commands of justice. That is why mercy and charity are called upon to qualify justice or even to set it aside. Justice is seen merely systemically. On the Protestant side, Henry N. Wieman makes a strict distinction between love and justice.[33] Actually, mercy and compassion are synthetic a priori, universal and necessary forms of justice when justice is defined as correct valuation and all three forms of valuation, systemic, extrinsic, and intrinsic, are applied.

In this sense, R. Carpentier defines justice as "the moral virtue which causes us to respect the person of our brother in Christ, at least in what concerns his rights";[34] and Emil Brunner points out the desiccation of the term "justice" in modern as against biblical usage, and substitutes the word "love" for much of what has been lost. In the biblical sense, says Brunner, the kindly, devout, charitable, grateful and God-fearing man was called just; today, justice has become a captive of systems.[35] Jesus himself never tried to make clear both the connection and the distinction between legal and moral, systemic and intrinsic justice. "Judge not, that ye be not judged. For with what judgment ye judge, ye shall be judged: and with what measure ye mete, it shall be measured to you again. . . . Therefore all things whatsoever ye would that men should do to you do ye even so to them."[36] Here Jesus complements the imperative of intrinsic distributive justice (I^I) by the prohibition of its systemic (I^S) and the recommendation of its extrinsic (I^E) mixed form. So does Paul;[37] while in the letter to Philemon he asks the master to receive his former slave and thief Onesimus back as a brother and the apostle's child—a pure case of intrinsic distributive and corrective justice.[38]

In formal axiology, intrinsic value is not in space and time so that the human being as intrinsic value is not separated from other human beings. Rather, as Ortega y Gasset has shown in *Man and People,* the "I" which each human person fulfills in being himself is the same "I" that everyone fulfills. It is that of the Kingdom of Ends in the Kantian sense, the Kingdom of God in the sense of Jesus, the Universal Community in the sense of Royce: intrinsically we are one with every other person. Hence an injustice done *to* us is done to all, and an injustice done to another is done to us. On this intrinsic oneness of all persons is based the nature of *compassion.* Similarly, any injustice done *by* us is done by all. Hence the nature of *conscience,* as the complement of compassion. But also, any justice or injustice done by us is done by all and any justice or injustice done to us is done to all. Moral justice includes not only compassion and conscience but also the categorical imperative.

The Kantian categorical imperatives illustrate the mixed form, I^S. These imperatives are matters, of course, of moral distributive justice, but instead of being based on moral passion for oneself and humanity within oneself (I^I) they are based on one's self-definition as an autonomous rational being (I^S)—on systemic rather than intrinsic self-valuation. "Act only according to that maxim by which you can at the same time will that it should become a universal law." In the *pure* form of moral justice, (I^I), this law is intrinsic knowledge, intuition, compassion rather than a systemic rule. The systemic nature of the Kantian imperative becomes even more clear in the second form: "Act as though the maxim of your action were by your will to become a universal law of nature." The third formulation is teleological. Here an extrinsic process is applied to the self. The formula is I^E.[39] "Act so that you treat humanity whether in your own person or in that of another always as an end and never as a means only." This is the teleological formulation of the rule of intrinsic distributive justice. It illustrates the second mixed form of this kind of justice. In Kant's *Ethics,* thus, the forms I^1, I^S, and I^E of moral justice are intermixed. The Kingdom of Ends, *das Reich der Zwecke,* is the pure form I^1, the intrinsic valuation of intrinsic value, in a noumenal realm beyond space and time. In the first two forms of the categorical imperative we have the systemic universalizing function of the rational will (I^S), and in the teleological formulation the extrinsic command which distinguishes the means and the end of an action in space and time (I^E). The formula I^S, the systemic valuation of an intrinsic value, when applied to the State, is the formula for the legal freedom of the human person, guaranteed by the State. Hence the foundation of the Kantian imperative in freedom and the corresponding legislative analogies make good axiological sense.

As we have seen, the form I^E was recommended by Jesus and the Apostles: value the eternal self (I) in such a way that its earthly way (E) will be smooth and helpful. Make love effective in human affairs. Make the material serve and not alienate the spirit. The first Christian community lived these moral-social rules, the extrinsic imperatives of intrinsic distributive justice: "The whole body of believers was united in heart and soul. Not a man of them claimed any of his possessions as his own but everything was held in common. They had never a needy person among them, because all who had property in land or houses sold it, brought the proceeds of the sale, and laid the money at the feet of the apostles; it was then distributed to any who stood in need."[40] Throughout history, Christians have in isolated communities, patterned their lives in accordance with these extrinsic rules of intrinsic, moral justice; and today many youth communes live this way, as do the Israeli kibbutzim. But the nations have not followed suit. While communist nations fail in *systemic* moral distributive justice (I^S), the recognition of fundamental *legal* human rights, that is, Liberty, the capitalist nations fail in *extrinsic* moral distributive justice (I^E), the recognition of *social* human rights, that is *Security.* The extrinsic valuation of man's intrinsic value means to guarantee a person the material benefits due to his human dignity, his right to a dignified nonalienating job and remuneration, to housing and all the other demands of social justice in the intrinsic or moral sense. Here belong all demands for social welfare; "Welfare" supplies the intrinsic dimension to social justice.

We have, in the mixed forms of moral justice, I^S and I^E, the axiological bases for welfare and human rights legislation.[41]

4. Injustice

Injustice is value transposition. Value transposition is the inversion of value composition, the latter being distributive justice. Thus, in order to understand injustice, we invert the fulfillment of the norms which we discussed in the previous section, and get nonfulfillment or violation of these norms. To the general formula for justice, U^V, then corresponds the formula for injustice, U_V, and to the three pure forms of justice S^S, E^E, and I^1, the formula for *legal* injustice, S_S; *social* injustice, E_E; and *moral* injustice, I_1, with the corresponding mixed forms in each dimension: S_E and S_1; E_S and E_1; I_S and I_E.

(a) Legal Injustice

We have legal injustice in the pure sense (S_S) if a legal rule is used to undo a legal rule. Here belong faulty legal constructions, as of mortgages. But here also belong illegal laws, as those of the Hitler state (which were pronounced illegal by the courts of the German Federal Republic).[42] More generally, and strikingly so, here belong all the bureaucratic rules and red tape that make injustices legal[43] and legalities unjust. Here belong all the cases so heartbreakingly and pitilessly described by Kafka especially in *The Trial* and *The Castle*. Kafka's world is a world of *systematic chaos,* the pure case of the formula S_S. Other chilling accounts of legal counterworlds are Rousset's and Kogon's descriptions of the Nazi system,[44] and Menotti's opera *The Consul.* In all these cases, what is legally devalued is the legal system itself; but behind it it is the human person whose freedom is guaranteed by this system. So, what the formula S_S indirectly means is the formula $(I^S)_S$, the legal devaluation ($_S$) of man's legal valuation (I^S). Only because the latter, the legal valuation of the human person, human freedom, does not appear in the theory and practice of legal illegality (S_S), does the latter appear "banal." The banality of evil is the banalization of evil by its legalization.[45] All Eichmann did was approve railroad schedules; he never killed anyone. That the trains transported people to the fire of incineration did not concern him. He was a transportation specialist. But so is a Polaris captain. At a command, his missiles will incinerate cities. But all he does is navigate a submarine. He too is a transportation specialist, not of people to the fire but of fire to the people. War, too, axiologically seen, is systematized chaos. The systematization of it makes its evil appear banal. The formula S_S hides monstrosities under the veil of legitimacy—the violations of the law *by means of the law.* The reason is the merely instrumental, amoral nature of positive law—a fact that was to haunt Kelson.

The mixed form S_E is the extrinsic disvaluation of the legal system, the disruption of the system by material things, for example a bribe to a judge or the selection of false facts in a trial. "Much depends upon choice of facts on the one hand and choice of rules on the other. Since testimony and documents are susceptible of various appreciations, the judge and jury are free within astonishingly wide limits to choose their facts."[46]

The second mixed case is a worse legal injustice, S_I, for here the rule (S) is violated by means of an intrinsic value (I), that is, a human being: a human being is used in order to violate the legal rule. The violation of the rule is the end and the human being is the means to that violation. Thus, to burn a human being in order to uphold a dogma is, in reality, the violation of the dogma by the act of burning. As Castellio said in the case of Calvin's burning of Servetus: "To burn a man alive does not defend a doctrine but slays a man."[47]

(b) Social Injustice

Here we have any case in which an abstracted concept is used incorrectly, that is, not with reference to a member of the class in question, hence as an incorrect norm (E_E). Thus, to judge our bookkeeper as a baker and act accordingly, or Plato's carpenter as a cobbler and vice versa, or our professor of philosophy as a bureaucrat and deny him promotion because he isn't at the office often enough even though he does his work conscientiously, we act extrinsically or socially unjustly. In the more general sense, we do injustice to a thing when we apply to it the wrong concept; when, to speak with Confucius, we continue saying about something that no more is a melon cup: "A melon cup! A melon cup!" In the strict sense, "doing injustice" only applies to human roles and actions, so that social injustice is applying the incorrect concept, in judgment and action, to such a role or action. Thus, when Vice President Agnew said that the North Vietnamese invasion of South Vietnam in Spring 1972 was the first real invasion of a country since Hitler's invasion of Poland, he forgot to subsume under the concept "invasion" those of Russia into Hungary and Czechoslovakia, of North Korea into South Korea, of China into Tibet and India, of the United States into Guatemala and the Dominican Republic. He committed an act of social injustice E_E (which was accompanied by waves of B-52's over Vietnam, acts of moral-social injustice, E_I). These and other kinds of social and moral injustices are the realizations of the thought pattern of *systematic chaos,* S_S, which leads to, and is, war.

All the kinds of injustice can be done not only to others but to ourselves as well. Thus, we do social injustice to ourselves if we do not find ourselves worthy of rewards others hold us worthy of. We do a systemic injustice to ourselves when we are confused about our self-concept (cases treated especially by Karen Horney)[48] and we do moral injustice to ourselves when we hate ourselves (a frequent reason for suicide). In short, all the confusions which are at the basis of injustice can be turned by ourselves against ourselves.

The cases of social injustice, in particular, are all the fundamental confusions which for Plato and Confucius were the bases of injustice in general.

The mixed formula E_S, the legal disvaluation of a role, or social-legal injustice, would exist in the case of laws which forbid a person to perform his role, as did the Nuremberg laws in Germany; or as a righteous prostitute may find the laws against prostitution if she regarded her profession not only as the oldest but also the most honorable. Here belongs the attitude of Alfredo in *La Traviata* (or Armand in Dumas's *Camille*), against that of his father.

The mixed form E_1 again is a more serious injustice, when namely a status situation or condition is disvalued by means of a human being. Thus, if people keep themselves alive by eating a companion, as in the case of Queen vs. Dudley, 14 Q. B. D. 273 (1884) where Dudley and Stephens drifted on the ocean for twenty days and in their final desperation stuck a knife into the throat of a helpless companion and fed on the body, the companion is used to uphold the situation, but actually his murder was an intrinsic devaluation of the situation. Here also belong cases of sadism and indignities against slaves or workers insofar as these are regarded as extrinsic values. Moreover, here belong actions against "targets" which do irreparable human harm, as the bombing of cities such as Warsaw or Haiphong.

(c) Moral Injustice

Here we have the intrinsic disvaluation of intrinsic value, I_1. The most hideous crime on record, the Nazi Irma Greese's, who tied women's legs in labour and used life to kill life belongs here, but also any murder such as Raskolnikov's, indeed any indignity to a person. For Jesus, the intrinsic disvaluation of an intrinsic value and thus moral injustice was already done when the mere thought of an indignity to another crossed the mind,[49] and for St. Paul it was murdering Jesus when the holy communion was taken in a spirit of eating.[50]

Subsidiary forms of moral injustice are the mixed formulae I_S and I_E. The former is the systemic disvaluation of a human being; which is being felt by soldiers in the military, prisoners in jails, the sick in asylums, workers on the production line, in short, by persons in all situations where a system devalues their intrinsic value. This system may even be the world system itself, as in some of the French existentialists.[51] Aristotle's theory of natural slavery belongs here, seen from today's viewpoint. From Aristotle's viewpoint, the slave was no intrinsic but an extrinsic value, not a person but a thing. We have here a particularly good example of the incorrect use of names and the corresponding injustice of disvaluing a human being (I_S). Aristotle's theory was based on a supposition of natural inequality which was thought to justify the enslavement of some men and the freedom of others. This particular injustice came to a historical high point in the encounter between Bartolomé de las Casas and Juan Ginés de Sepúlveda before Charles V on the question whether Indians were humans. Las Casas held that "all the peoples of the world are men," while Sepúlveda kept to the Aristotelian notion that the Indians were natural slaves. "People so uncivilized, so barbaric, so contaminated with so many sins and obscenities . . . justly conquered by such an excellent, pious and most just King as was Ferdinand the Catholic and is now Emperor Charles, and by such a human nation which is excellent in every kind of virtue." The Indians are as different from Spaniards as cruel people are from mild people. They are "homunculi in whom you will scarcely find even vestiges of humanity."[52] Sepúlveda, says Las Casas, seems to value the State more highly than the divine right, and the service to his earthly lord higher than his service to God's cause.[53] Here also belong every kind of systemic disvaluation of the human person, whether legal or not, such as unjust rules of work, unjust limitations of human autonomy by any kind of rules. When these rules are of the State they are "legal," such as the Nuremberg laws in Germany. The State is a systemic value; but very often in human history it has been regarded as an instrinsic value. Axiologically, this is a confusion which results in fetishism. Due to it, systemic limitations of human personality by the State have been regarded as privileges rather than deprivations; and mothers have been proud over the death of their sons in battle. Against such perversions of values, the German President Gustav Heinemann coined the now famous rejoinder: "I don't love the State, I love my wife."[54]

The second mixed form of moral injustice is the formula "I_E", the extrinsic disvaluation of intrinsic value. Here persons are regarded as functions, the self is being alienated by its own role in society (Marx), a spiritual value is seen as a material thing, an idol, and spiritual values are degraded by material actions, from the orgies of Christmas shopping to the worldly roles of spiritual rulers. Here also belong acts of killing when the emphasis is on the instrument rather than the murderous will, as in penal procedure or a detective novel.

A very deep and not yet clarified problem is the fact that any kind of injustice brings about Violence, that is, physical force. The only explanation seems to be that while rationality, i.e. justice, is antientropic, in the sense of Schroedinger, irrationality, i.e. injustice, is entropic which means that it is necessarily accompanied by force.

5. Corrective Justice

Corrective justice is relevant disvaluation of value transposition, or relevant disvaluation of disvaluation. It shows up the injustice of injustice, correcting it by justice.

The formula here is $(U_V)_U V$, the correction of an injustice by the corresponding justice, or the correction of the violation of a norm by the corresponding observance of the norm. Actually, the formula admits of two different corrections, by U^V and V^U. Hence, beside the formula $(U_V)_U V$ there is the formula $(U_V)_V U$.

By "correction" of the injustice here is meant its disvaluation by justice. The justice must be relevant, it must correspond to the injustice; it must be the valuation corresponding to the disvaluation, or the composition corresponding to the transposition. The transposition being U_V, the corresponding composition is U^V, and may also be V^U.

These general formulae give us three pure formulations each, depending on whether both U and V are substituted by either I, E or S. The results are the pure forms of extrinsic, systemic, and intrinsic, or *legal, social,* and *moral* injustice. Each of these has four mixed forms, as will be seen. There are, then, in total, five different kinds of injustice in each of the three value dimensions, or fifteen kinds in all. With the nine kinds of distributive justice and the nine kinds of injustice explained, there are in all thirty-three fundamental kinds of justice (see table 1).

The three pure forms of corrective justice are $(S_S)_S S$, $(E_E)_E E$, $(I_I)_I I$. The mixed forms are those where the values V and U are not of the same but of different dimensions, e.g. $(I_S)_I S$. These forms have each an alternative where the compositional subscript is inverted. Thus, the alternative form to $(I_S)_I S$ is $(I_S)_S I$. Let us take this latter form as an example. Here we have, within the parenthesis, the systemic devaluation of an intrinsic value (I_S), the inhuman use of a system. This disvaluation is inverted by the intrinsic valuation of the system (S^I), the human use of the system; and this inversion *disvalues* the original disvaluation, or shows up and corrects the injustice of the original injustice. In other words, the inhuman use of a system is corrected by the human use of the system. A large example of this kind would be an equivalent to war which would use the vast war machine for a peaceful purpose, not only beating swords into plowshares (Isa. 2:4) but, say, convert the whole Pentagon into NASA—change the conquest of earth into that of space. A small example is the following, an actual case. A German tourist in the United States on a visit to Niagara Falls went out on the International Bridge to admire the Falls. On returning, the U.S. Immigration officer does not let him pass because he forgot his passport in the hotel. The tourist goes to the Canadian side, but they don't let him in either for the same reason. He is caught between the two systems. Should he pass the rest of his life on the bridge? In this dilemma, the Immigration officers used the system to undo the system. The Canadians allowed him to put one foot into Canada so that they could expedite an expulsion order. This satisfied the requirements of the U.S. Immigration officer and the tourist could leave the bridge. The human use of a systemic rule (S^1) annulled the inhuman use of another rule of the system (I_S). During World War II, unfortunately, no such human use was made of systems, legal injustices remained uncorrected, refugees were caught on international bridges to die, and ghost ships plied the oceans from port to port only finally to deliver their human cargo to the hells of Auschwitz and Treblinka.[55]

Each of the theoretically possible rules of the structure $(U_V)_U V$ and $(U_V)_V U$ has an infinity of applications. *Justice is a pattern of infinite variety under strict form.* It is a formal pattern, in the sense of logic, not merely of jurisprudence. Let us remember, in particular, that the formulae are not just abbreviations and hence plays with concepts which could just as well be put into words, but that all their variables have a mathematical value representing numbers of properties, so that each formula has itself a specific mathematical value.

Moreover, the formulae of formal axiology far transcend their use in the pattern of Justice. There is, for example, a striking and profoundly significant parallelism to the formulae of corrective justice in certain psychotherapeutic techniques where the transposition of values which is the syndrome of the patient, is being corrected by exactly the valuation of what the patient devalues. Thus, in Viktor Frankl's logotherapeutic techniques, there is the instrument of "paradoxical intention." This means that the patient is encouraged to do or wish to happen the very things he fears. The pathogenic fear is replaced by a paradoxical wish. As a result, the patient may be suffering from anxiety only, but not from anxiety over anxiety. In many phobias, the fear of the fear situation is worse than the feared situation itself; and it is this fear of fear that is being counteracted. Thus, a person who stutters is asked to stutter, that is, instead of devaluing his stuttering is asked to value it; and he will soon not be able to stutter any more. He cannot do consciously what he was impelled to do unconsciously. What is affected here are the patient's standards and ideals, his thought pattern or, axiologically speaking, his value pattern. This treatment has proved successful. In replacing the pathogenic fear by a paradoxical wish the wind is taken out of the sails of anticipatory anxiety. Axiologically, the technique of paradoxical intention is the same as that of corrective justice, that of overcoming evil by the corresponding good, of disvaluing a disvalue situation by the values of the situation. Thus, if in a phobia, a self is intrinsically devalued by an obsessive idea, e.g. that of being unable to cross an open space, then this intrinsic *devaluation* is in turn intrinsically *devalued* by the intrinsic *valuation* of that idea, namely the idea that one with all one's might wishes to do what before one feared—by inverted intention.[56] Not only is the logotherapeutic cure an overcoming of evil by good as in corrective justice, *the evil itself is the same as that of injustice*—faulty judgment. The unjust person, as Plato already held, is sick; and the mentally sick cannot possibly be just. Justice and sanity are two sides of the same coin, and so are injustice and insanity.

(a) Legal Corrective Justice

The value formula of legal corrective justice is $(S_S)_S S$: a legal rule is legally violated, and this legal violation of the legal rule is disvalued by the legal valuation of the legal rule violated. Thus, if through a bureaucratic delay a legal rule was violated (S_S) then the correction lies in the invalidation of this violation by the legal valuation (S^S) of the rule violated. If, for example, in Kafka's *Castle,* a person would suddenly have appeared which would have put into force the rules that K. was trying to apply and would thus have undone the anonymous delays and brought the procedure to a good end; or if, in *The Trial,* a person would have appeared as a legally effective advocate for K. who would have forced the accusers to show their faces and formulate their accusations, then corrective justice would have been done in the case of K. Here we have the pure kind of legal, or in general, systemic corrective justice.

The legal-social mixed kind is the one where the devaluing value is E rather than S, namely $(S_E)_S E$ or $(S_E)_E S$. The subversion of the legal system by material goods, e.g. the bribed judge (S_E), which was discussed on p. 142 above, is here being disvalued by either the correct material valuation of the legal system (S^E) or the legal valuation of material goods (E^S). In other words the injustice will be shown up by the material well-being of the judge (S^E) or the systemic value of money in the legal system (E^S), its correct use in the system, for paying fees but not for bribing judges. The judge is seen here not in his intrinsic value as a human person but strictly in his systemic position, as an element of the legal system. In his intrinsic value, as a person, he would be put into prison. In this case he would be seen as a human being who devalues himself by money and values his own devaluation by taking the money $(I_E)^I$. This situation is devalued by the systemic disvaluation of the intrinsic value (I_S), that is the imprisonment of the judge as a person; so that the total formula is $((I_E)^I)_I)_S$—a very much more complicated case of corrective justice than the fundamental cases here discussed. Actually, to imprison the bribed judge is not a case of corrective justice in our sense, because imprisonment does not invert the original disvalue, the bribe. The corrective formula would rather belong into moral corrective justice and be $(I_E)_1E$. This would mean that the judge as a human being who corrupts his character by money, the bribe, is doing a moral injustice to himself (I_E), which would be corrected by his correct self-valuation in terms of money (I^E) or the repayment of the bribe. This punishment would fit the crime. Imprisonment, as the formula shows, does not fit in naturally with the fundamental cases of corrective injustice which correct themselves by their own means rather than by intervention of the State, imprisonment and the like. The actual condition of the penal system in all countries demonstrates that it has no natural axiological base.[57]

The third kind of corrective systemic or legal justice is the legal-moral mixed kind, $(S_I)_SI$ or $(S_I)_1S$. Returning to the case of the heretic being condemned to burn to uphold the system (above p. 142), this judgment (S_I) would in corrective justice have been annulled by the correct systemic valuation of the heretic as a human being rather than a heretic (S^I), so that the total formula $(S_I)_SI$ would mean the correction of the injustice by the intrinsic valuation of the system, seeing it in spiritual rather than worldly terms. This reminds me of the statement of Bartolomé de Albornoz concerning the discussion between Las Casas and Sepúlveda: "I do not find in the law of Jesus Christ that the liberty of the soul must be paid for with slavery of the body."[58]

(b) Social Corrective Justice

The fundamental formula here is $(E_E)_EE$. This means that an incorrect use of a concept is to be repaired by the correct use. Thus, the wrong valuation of our bookkeeper or philosopher is corrected by their correct valuation, E_E is corrected by E^E. In general, any incorrect valuation or injustice, as the mix-up of Plato's cobbler and carpenter, is corrected by the corresponding form of distributive justice. When a melon cup is not a melon cup anymore it should not be called anymore: "A melon cup! A melon cup!"

The first mixed form, $(E_S)_ES$, is the disvaluation of an extrinsic value by a systemic one and its correction, i.e. the disvaluation of a role or a life situation by a system and the corresponding correction. Here belong all the perversions of language and action we find in Orwell's *1984* or Thomas Merton's "War and the Crisis of Language,"[59] and the gobbledygook of officialese, from Washington to K.'s Prague, with its accompanying monstrosities. The corrections would be to replace the systemic corruption of situations (E_S) by the corresponding systemic purifications (E^S), and name things by their correct names. This would help to bring about correct action. Thus, the Department of Defense is actually the Department of Nuclear War, and this war would bring about the end of the world. If it were called "Department of the End of the World" people would be less inclined to ask for the use of nuclear weapons to "defend" real estate. In the strict sense, we have here the social-legal injustices or disvaluations discussed in Section *4 (b)* above, corrected by the corresponding social-legal justices or valuations, that is, the correct legal valuations of the transposed situations in question. The Nuremberg laws were declared illegal in Germany after the war. On the other hand, prostitution which had been declared illegal in some countries, was declared legal, and shares in brothels were traded in the stock exchange.

The second mixed form $(E_S)_S E$ is, as the first, a social-legal form of corrective justice. *In general,* the formula means that a disvaluation of a situation in terms of the wrong word is to be corrected by the situational understanding of the word (rather than the systemic understanding of the situation, as in the first case). Here would fit in a science of situational semantics, of how words are to be situationally used. The emphasis of the Oxford School on the use of words is of importance here. These misuses of words are systemic injustices in the field of social relations. If the injustices are committed by laws rather than by everyday words we have the legal-social injustices in the strict sense mentioned above. The corrections are the corresponding ones, the offending laws (E_S) are invalidated and replaced by laws that fit the situation (S^E).

The second group of mixed forms are those where the social injustice is moral or intrinsic rather than legal or systemic, $(E_I)_I E$. These are the forms of social-moral injustice or disvaluation examined in Section *4(b)*, corrected by the corresponding justices or revaluations. Thus, the bombing of cities in war (E_I) is corrected after the war by the rebuilding of the cities with infinite care (E^I), as in the rebuilding of Warsaw, or by material compensation to the victims (I^E).

In general, these forms mean that the intrinsic disvaluation of an extrinsic value is corrected by either the intrinsic valuation of the extrinsic value or the extrinsic valuation of the intrinsic value. Thus, if I hate the philosopher mentioned before because I do not agree with his handling his job, then this hate (E_I) is overcome by loving him in his role (E^I) or by extrinsically, namely as the philosopher he is, valuing his human dignity (I^E).

As all the formulae of corrective justice, these formulae demonstrate how evil can be overcome by good. The evil is the injustice or disvaluation in question, and the good which depreciates the evil is the corresponding justice or valuation.

(c) Moral Corrective Justice

Here we have the fundamental formulae $(I_I)_I I$, which means that hate (I_I) must be overcome by love (I^I), death by life, the intrinsic disvaluation of a human being by his intrinsic valuation. Here we see how intrinsic justice is compassion, both in the distributive as in the corrective sense. The prototype of moral corrective justice, as was mentioned before, is the parable of the Good Samaritan, which in turn is the model for the whole doctrine of Jesus: "A certain man went down from Jerusalem to Jericho, and fell among thieves, which stripped him of his raiment, and wounded him, and departed, leaving him half dead. And by chance there came down a certain priest that way: and when he saw him, he passed by on the other side. And likewise a Levite, when he was at the place, came and looked on him and passed by on the other side. But a certain Samaritan, as he journeyed, came where he was: and when he saw him, he had compassion on him, and went to him, and bound up his wounds, pouring in oil and wine, and sat him on his own beast, and brought him to an inn, and took care of him" (Luke 10:30-34). Here an intrinsic evil done to a man was repaired by compassion, the corresponding corrective justice.

A second classic case is Paul's letter to Philemon. Philemon's slave Onesimus, had escaped with loot, and became a convert to Paul. Paul wrote to his former owner this moving letter: "I beseech thee for my brother Onesimus . . . whom I have sent again: thou therefore receive him, that is, mine own bowels: whom I would have retained . . . but without thy mind would I do nothing; that thy benefit should not be as it were of necessity, but willingly. For perhaps he therefore departed for a season, that thou shouldest receive him for ever; not now as a servant but above a servant, a brother beloved, specially to me, but how much more unto thee . . . ? If thou count me therefore a partner, receive him as myself. If he hath wronged thee ought, put that on mine account." The indignity Onesimus did to his master (I_1) is redeemed by the salvation of his own soul and that of the master! (I^1) through the apostle.

The mixed cases of moral corrective justice are those where the devaluing value is systemic and where it is extrinsic, the moral-legal and the moral-social cases. In the former, we have the formulae $(I_S)_I S$ and $(I_S)_S I$, damage done to the human being by legal (or other systemic) devaluation and the correction of this damage by the corresponding legal valuation. Here again belong the Nuremberg laws with their indignities against the Jews, which were corrected by the German Federal Republic, by laws that confirmed human dignity (I^S) and were themselves highly regarded by the new Germany (S^1). In the Spanish case of the American Indians, the correction was not so complete. The so-called New Laws adopted after the discussion between Las Casas and Sepúlveda (1542) confirmed the human nature of the Indians (I^S) but the laws were not highly regarded, indeed, were disregarded and fought

(S_I rather than S^1) and their humanitarian purpose was frustrated. In general, the human disvaluation by a system must in corrective moral-legal justice be made up by the corresponding human valuation by the system. This will be the case when, in the fields mentioned in Section *4 (c)* above, the soldier will be valued in his human dignity by the military state, the insane by the mental institution, the prisoner by the jailor, the worker by the employer—and the French existentialist, lost in the world, by his own conscience.

In some cases the legal system will open itself up to intrinsic valuation in the form of Mercy. In these cases, the legal rules (S) are made subject to the facultative exercise of pure moral judgment (I): it is legally permitted to value them from the intrinsic or moral point of view (S^1); and implicitly the affected person in the same manner (I^1). In these cases the legal administrator may act not only as legal authority but as fellow human—and this latter attitude is infinitely more valuable than the former. In this specific sense, the formula $(I_S)_S I$, which may be said to be the formula for Mercy in its legal aspects, changes into $(I_1)_1 I$, the formula for pure moral corrective justice: a person has been done a moral injustice—not just a legal one—and this is rectified by moral justice.[60]

The second group of kinds of mixed moral corrective justice are the cases of moral-social corrective justice, $(I_E)_1 E$ and $(I_E)_E I$. Here we have the damage done to the individual by society in the alienation of work, the material disvaluation of spiritual values in idols, the worldly roles of spiritual rulers, all corrected by the corresponding valuations. Thus, workers alienated by their work (I_E) will become proud of it and of themselves as their work will value (I^E) rather than disvalue (I_E) them; when for example, they share the profits or become coowners or owners of the factory (but not when the State does); and in these cases the work itself will be prized (E^1). Or, when in the Golden Calf the spiritual values are degraded by being idolized (I_E) the thunder of Moses makes the people understand that the spiritual is honored by everyday living in the fear of God (I^E), but not by making images. Here, again, the correction was not complete because of the absolute prohibition to make molten or graven images of God (E_1); complete correction would include the adoration of God by beauty (E^1), as was done later in the Renaissance. In Constantinople, the two forms, E_1 and E^1, fought for centuries, the former as iconoclasts, the latter as icon makers, creators of divine forms of beauty. And, the last example, spiritual rulers in their worldly roles (I_E) are illustrated by those Popes who commit injustices in the name of God, as Pius X in the play of Hochhut and Paul VI in the eyes of a majority of the faithful, as against those who fuse their role with their spiritual being

(I^E) and spiritualize their role (E^I), as John XXIII did in the eyes of every human.

Finally, we may mention here the cases in which "E" does not mean society but an instrument. These are the cases where damage is done to a human being by means of a material thing (I_E), say, the violation of a man by a hatchet. This is corrected by the correct extrinsic valuation of the person in his role in the material world (I^E) or, a peculiar but significant case, the intrinsic valuation of the instrument (E^I). This latter case is exemplified by the relics of the saints, the Cross of the Crucifixion, and, in the museums of all nations, the grisly-holy mementoes of national awe and pride. Thus, the London Tower and the Musée Carnavalet in Paris, we can see the hatchets that took the lives of Anne Boleyn and Marie Antoinette, and the blocks upon which fell their heads, together with the locks from these heads. Here justice is done by history and, intrinsically, the veneration of the faithful.

6. Formal Axiology as Natural Law

The cases discussed are the fundamental kinds of justice. There are more complex forms, as we have seen (Sec. 5[a]), but they all yield to the axiological calculus.

The axiological pattern here developed may take the place natural law was supposed to take in legal history. It never was efficiently used, though, because it was not articulated. Formal axiology, as can be seen, is extremely articulate, to a point that one who is not used to its terminology and symbolism, might even consider its articulateness exaggeratedly complex. Yet, considering the infinite variety of possible cases, the symbolism is economic indeed. Every law which contains one of the value transpositions, that is, of the injustices mentioned, is an invalid law, a nonlaw. It is legally, socially, or morally unjust, and hence it is not law. Natural law is law insofar as its violation by a positive law negates the legal character of this law. This rule can, and could, not be enforced because of the vagueness of natural law. It could never be stated with precision either in which way it was natural or in which way it was law. Formal axiology may take its place, and the principle just stated may be reformulated as follows: *The value pattern of justice is law insofar as its violation by a positive law negates the legal character of this law.*

An instructive case for the vagueness yet inherent power of natural law is the Remer case, decided by the German court of Braunschweig.[61] Remer, a member of a neo-Nazi party, had in a political speech called the plotters against Hitler, of July 20, 1944, "traitors." The sons and relatives of some of the conspirators sued Remer for slander. The court had to decide whether the conspirators had been traitors or patriots. After voluminous opinions by legal, philosophical, religious and other experts, the court decided that "a state whose government not only tolerates injustice but consciously executes or permits its realization in order to fulfill its own political objectives without consideration of the inconditional human rights, cannot pretend to be a legal state. . . . The national-socialist state must be considered, therefore, in this sense an *Unrechtsstaat,* an unlawful state, a state of injustice."[62] Its citizens, the court held, not only have the right but the duty to destroy the unjust leaders.[63] The conspirators were patriots not traitors; and Remer was condemned to three months in prison for defamation.

Once formal axiology is recognized as the articulation of natural law its detailed account of justice and injustice will make natural law truly deserving of its name.

In philosophy in general, and legal and social philosophy in particular, the value pattern here developed can be used to bring order into the treatises on justice and, indeed, to write commentaries on them that may give exact meaning to their often rhapsodic and essentially obscure statements.

Finally, as we have seen, the value formulae which define justice connect justice with other fields of value and thus make the phenomena of justice an exactly defined part of the total world of valuation.

The following table summarizes the thirty-three forms of the value pattern of justice we have presented.

TABLE 1

Name	General Formula	Pure Form			Mixed Form		
		Legal	Social	Moral	Legal	Social	Moral
Distributive Justice	U^V	S^S	E^E	I^I	S^E,S^I	E^S,E^I	I^S,I^E
Injustice	U_V	S_S	E_E	I_I	S_E,S_I	E_S,E_I	I_S,I_E
Corrective Justice	$(U_V)_UV$	$(S_S)_SS$	$(E_E)_EE$	$(I_I)_II$	$(S_E)_SE$ $(S_I)_SI$	$(E_S)_ES$ $(E_I)_EI$	$(I_S)_IS$ $(I_E)_IE$
	$(U_V)_VU$				$(S_E)_ES$ $(S_I)_IS$	$(E_S)_SE$ $(E_I)_IE$	$(I_S)_SI$ $(I_E)_EI$

Robert S. Hartman

Cuernavaca, Mexico
April, 1972

NOTES

[1] Stuart Hampshire, "A New Philosophy of the Just Society," *The New York Review,* February 24, 1972, p. 6.

[2] Descartes, *Principia Philosophiae,* I, LXXIV; *Regulae,* XII, XIII.

[3] Hans Kelsen, *What Is Justice?* (Berkeley: University of California Press, 1957), p. 24.

[4] Ibid.

[5] Ibid., p. 11. While Rawls bases justice on the rationality of egoists, Kelsen bases it on rationality itself, as do we; but he confuses the rational order, which is that of logic, with positive law. He thus commits what we call the fallacy of method. (Robert S. Hartman, *The Structure of Value: Foundations of Scientific Axiology* [Carbondale, Ill.: Southern Illinois University Press, 1967, 1969], pp. 126-31.)

[6] Locke, *Letter on Education,* 1695.

[7] *Structure of Value,* passim.

[8] Robert S. Hartman, "Formal Axiology and the Measurement of Values," *The Journal of Value Inquiry,* **1,** No. 1 (1967), 38-46.

[9] Hartman, *Structure of Value,* pp. 357 f., n. 32. It is due to the inherent mathematical pattern that the calculus of value works strikingly in practice, in an axiological test. There the testee orders items representing the 18 binary value compositions according to his own preference. Actual sequences correlate with the theoretical sequence 89 to 99 percent. For details see "Formal Axiology and the Measurement of Value"; *The Structure of Value,* pp. 265-93; *The Hartman Value Profile: Manual of Interpretation* (Alcoa, Tenn.: Axiometric Testing Service, 1972).

[10] Hartman, *Structure of Value,* p. 272, No. 7.

[11] Ibid., p. 272, No. 3.

[12] Bridges vs. Wixon, 326 U.S. 135 (1945).

[13] Plato, *Republic,* IV, 433. Today's definition of a person's goodness, as doing his own thing, is not an extrinsic but an intrinsic definition, meaning he ought to do what makes him intimately the human being he is, honest, genuine, authentic and true to himself, as we shall see when discussing moral justice, the formula "I^1."

[14] *Republic,* IV, 434.

[15] Plato, *Cratylus,* 388 C.

[16] The investigations of Ernst Cassirer on the development of concepts from onomatopoetic forms and proper names, and the "overcoming of the Heraclitian flux of change: by language, treat the same problem as that of the *Cratylus.* Ernst Cassirer, *The Philosophy of Symbolic Forms,* Vol. I, Chaps. II and IV, Secs. I and II, English ed. (New Haven: Yale University Press, 1953), pp. 190 ff., 280ff., 295 ff. On *Cratylus* as introductory to the logical theories of the *Phaedo* and presupposing the conclusion of ethical inquiries summed up in *Gorgias,* see W. Lutoslawski, *The Origin and Growth of Plato's Logic* (New York: Longmans Green and Co., 1897), p. 231. Also cf. Morris Henry Partee, "Plato's Theory of Language," *Foundations of Language,* **8,** No. 1 (January 1972), 113-32.

[17] Aristotle, *Nicomachean Ethics,* Book I, Chap. 6.

[18] Aristotle, *Politics,* 1282 b, 23.

[19] Thomas Aquinas, *Summa Theologica,* Q. 5, Art. 5.

[20] Spinoza, *Ethics,* Part IV, Preface, Defs. I, II.

[21] Kant, *Critique of Judgment,* Par. 4; Sieben kleine Aufsätze, Werke, ed. by Ernst Cassirer (Berlin, 1913), Vol. IV, pp. 527 f.

[22] Confucius, *Analects,* Book XIII. Cf. Rose Quong, *Chinese Written Characters, Their Wit and Wisdom,* rev. ed. (New York: Cobble Hill Press, 1968); originally titled *Chinese Wit, Wisdom, and Written Characters* (1944).

[23] Lin Yutang, *The Wisdom of Confucius* (New York: Modern Library, 1938), p. 218.

[24] Alfred Doeblin, *The Living Thoughts of Confucius* (Philadelphia: David McKay Co., 1940), p. 108.

[25] *Liki,* XXVIII.

[26] Lin Yutang, *Wisdom of Confucius,*p. 17.

[27] Confucius, "The Aphorisms of Confucius," in *The Wisdom of China and India,* ed. by Lin Yutang (New York: Random House, 1942), p. 826.

[28] See Hartman, *Structure of Value,* p. 216.

[29] Aristotle, *Politics,* 1283 a, 1.

[30] Here may lie a deep reason why we cannot say "a justice" but only *"an injustice", so that this asymmetry may have a good axiological reason. "If justice has been done in a particular act, that act is determined by universal law, an ennoblement that finds recognition even in the linguistic form by not placing it on the same level as the dead particularly of 'an' unjust act" (Dr. Wolfgang Schwarz in a letter to me of July 1, 1972).*

[31] Jean Piaget, *The Moral Judgment of the Child* (Glencoe, Ill.: The Free Press, 1932), pp. 197 ff.; F. R. Bienenfeld, *Rediscovery of Justice* (London, 1947), pp. 19-27; Edgar Bodenheimer, *Jurisprudence: The Philosophy and Method of the Law* (Cambridge: Harvard University Press, 1962), p. 196.

[32] Here belong, beside the ethics of Kant, works of Ortega y Gasset, Berdyaev, and of the existential psychologists, Viktor Frankl, Abraham Maslow, Rollo May and others. See Hartman, *Structure of Value,* pp. 114 f., 293, 306, 308, 311.

[33] Henry N. Wieman, *The Source of Human Good* (Chicago: University of Chicago Press, 1946), pp. 258 ff.

[34] Gérard Gilleman, S. J., *The Primacy of Charity in Moral Theology* (Westminster, Md.: Newman Press, 1959), p. 341. Cf. Gerhard Uhlhorn, *Die christliche Liebestaetigkeit* (Neukirchen: Kreis Moers, Neukirchener Verlag, 1959).

[35] Emil Brunner, *Justice and The Social Order* (New York: Harper & Brothers, 1945), pp. 110 ff.; Paul Ramsey, *Basic Christian Ethics* (New York: Charles Scribner's Sons, 1950), pp. 2 f.

[36] Matt. 7:1, 2, 12.

[37] Rom. 13:7; 2 Cor. 8:21; Col. 4:1.

[38] See my Sec. 5(c).

[39] For details see Robert S. Hartman, "Die Wissenschaft vom Entscheiden," *Wissenschaft und Weltbild,* Vienna (June, 1966), 81-99.

[40] Acts 4:32-35.

[41] See Alfred Moser, *Die Rechtskraft der natürlichen Lebenswerte* (Heidelberg: Kerle, 1962).

[42] See below, n. 56.

[43] Hartman, *Structure of Value,* p. 273, No. 10.

[44] Eugen Kogon, *Der SS-Staat* (Stockholm: Bermann-Fischer Verlag, 1947); *The Theory and Practice of Hell* (New York: Farrar, Strauss, 1950); David Rousset, *The Other Kingdom* (New York: Reynal, 1947).

[45] Hannah Arendt, *Eichmann in Jerusalem: A Report on the Banality of Evil* (New York: Viking Press, 1963); Günther Anders, *Wir Eichmannsöhne* (Munich: C. H. Beck, M., 1964).

[46] Edmond N. Cahn, *The Sense of Injustice* (New York: New York University Press, 1949), p. 34.

[47] Stefan Zweig, *The Right to Heresy: Castellio Against Calvin* (Boston: Beacon Press, 1951), p. 182.

[48] Karen Horney, *Our Inner Conflicts: A Constructive Theory of Neurosis* (New York: W. W. Norton & Co., 1945), pp. 96-114; *Neurosis and Human Growth* (New York: W. W. Norton & Co., 1950), pp. 155-75.

[49] Matt. 15:19.

[50] 1 Cor. 11:27; Hartman, *Structure of Value,* pp. 279, 359, 273, Nos. 10-18.

[51] Here belongs the literature on systemic disvaluation of the human person, by the legal (the "Chicago Seven"), the military (Heller, Hasek, Kirst), the penal ("Papillon," Leon-Sánchez), the industrial (Whyte, Argyris), even the world system (Camus, Sartre).

[52] Lewis Hanke, *Aristotle and the American Indians* (Chicago: Henry Regnery Co., 1959), p. 47. Reinhold Schneider, *Las Casas vor Karl V.* (Leipzig: Insel-Verlag, 1955).

[53] Schneider, *Las Casas vor Karl V.,* p. 66.

[54] On the perversion of human values by the State, see Jacques Maritain, *Man and the State* (Chicago: University of Chicago Press, 1951).

[55] Arthur D. Morse, *While Six Million Died: A Chronicle of American Apathy* (New York: Random House, 1968).

[56] Viktor E. Frankl, *The Will to Meaning* (New York: World Publishing Co., 1969).

[57] The formula for imprisonment $(I_E)^1)_1)_S$ has mathematically *intrinsic disvalue* $(\aleph_2^{-1})$ whereas the formula for intrinsic corrective justice $(I_E)_1 E$ has intrinsic value $(\aleph_2)$. Hirst-Perkins "Axiological Tables" (unpublished MS), pp. 53, 54. (See Hartman, *Structure of Value* [1969], p. xix.)

[58] Hanke, *Aristotle and the American Indians,* p. 80.

[59] Thomas Merton, "War and the Crisis of Language," in *The Critique of War,* ed. by Robert Ginsberg (Chicago: Henry Regnery Co., 1969), pp. 99-119.

[60] For a general discussion, see Claudia Card, "On Mercy," *The Philosophical Review,* **81,** No. 2 (April 1972), 182-207.

[61] *Die im Braunschweiger Remer Prozess erstatteten moral-theologischen und historischen Gutachten nebst Urteil,* herausgegeben von Dr. jur. Herbert Kraus (Hamburg, 1953).

[62] Ibid., pp. 123 f.

[63] See Bodenheimer, *Jurisprudence: The Philosophy and Method of the Law,* p. 226; Otto Kirchheimer, *Political Justice: The Use of Legal Procedure for Political Ends* (Princeton: Princeton University Press, 1961), pp. 319-23.

RICHARD WASSERSTROM

THE LAWS OF WAR*

Many persons who consider the variety of moral and legal problems that arise in respect to war come away convinced that the firmest area for judgment is that of how persons ought to behave in time of war. Such persons feel a confidence about dealing with questions of how war ought to be conducted that is absent when other issues about war are raised. They are, for example, more comfortable with the rules relating to how soldiers ought to behave vis-à-vis enemy soldiers and enemy civilians—the laws of war—then they are with the principles relating to when war is permissible and when it is not. Thus, most commentators and critics are uneasy about the applicability to the American scene of that part of Nuremberg that deals with crimes against peace and crimes against humanity. But they have no comparable uneasiness about insisting that persons who commit war crimes, violations of the laws of war, be held responsible for their actions.

I propose to consider several features of this view—and I do think it a widely held one—which accepts the moral significance and urges the primacy of the laws of war. I am not interested in providing a genetic account of why this view gets held. I am, rather, concerned to explicate at least one version of this view and to explore the grounds upon which such a view might rest. And I want also to show why such a position is a mistaken one: mistaken in the sense that this conception of the laws of war is a morally unattractive one and one which has no special claim upon our attention or our energies.

* From the "Philosophy and Public Policy" issue of *The Monist*, **56**, No. 1 (January, 1972), published by the Open Court Publishing Company.

There are two general, quite distinct arguments for this notion of the primacy of the laws of war. One is that the laws of war are important and deserving of genuine respect and rigorous enforcement because they reflect, embody and give effect to fundamental moral distinctions and considerations. The other is that, considered simply as laws and conventions, they merit this dominant role because general adherence to them has important, desirable effects. The former of these arguments emphasizes the contents of the laws of war and the connection they have with more basic moral ideals. The latter argument emphasizes the beneficial consequences that flow from their presence and acceptance.

The arguments are clearly not mutually exclusive; indeed, they are related to each other in several important respects. Nonetheless, it is useful to distinguish sharply between them for purposes of analysis and to examine the strengths and weaknesses of each in turn. Before I do so, however, it is necessary to explicate more fully the nature of the laws of war with which I shall be concerned. This is so because it is important to see that I am concerned with a particular view of the character of the laws of war and the related notion of a war crime.[1] I believe it to be the case that this account constitutes an accurate description of the existing laws of war and the dominant conception of a war crime. That is to say, I think it is what many if not most lawyers, commentators, military tribunals, and courts have in mind when they talk about the laws of war and the responsibility of individuals for the commission of war crimes. In this sense at least, the sketch I am about to give constitutes an actual, and not merely a possible, conception of the laws of war. If I am right, the criticisms that I make have substantial practical importance. But I may of course be wrong; I may have misstated the actual laws of war and the rules for their applicability. To the degree that I have done so, my criticism will, perhaps, less forcefully apply to the real world, but not thereby to the conception of the laws of war I delineate below.

I

The system I am concerned to describe and discuss has the following features. There are, to begin with, a number of formal agreements, conventions, and treaties among countries that prescribe how countries (chiefly through their armies) are to behave in time of war. And there are, as well, generally accepted, "common law" rules and practices which also regulate behavior in warfare. Together they comprise the substantive laws of war. For the most part, the laws of war deal with two sorts of things: how classes of persons are to be treated in war, e.g. prisoners of war, and what sorts of weapons and methods of attack are impermissible, e.g. the use of poison gas. Some of the laws of war—particularly those embodied in formal documents—are narrow in scope and specific in formulation. Thus, Article 4 of the Annex to the Hague Convention on Land Warfare, 1907, provided in part that all the personal belongings of prisoners of war, "except arms, horses, and military papers," remain their property. Others are a good deal more general and vague. For example, Article 23(e) of the same Annex to Hague Convention prohibits resort to " . . . arms, projectiles, or material calculated to cause unnecessary suffering." Similarly, Article 3 of the Geneva Conventions on the Laws of War, 1949, provides in part that "Persons taking no active part in the hostilities . . . shall in all circumstances be treated humanely. . . . " And at Nuremberg, war crimes were defined as follows:

> . . . violations of the laws or customs of war. Such violations shall include but not be limited to, murder, ill-treatment or deportation to slave-labour or for any other purpose of civilian population of or in occupied territory, murder or ill-treatment of prisoners of war or persons on the seas, killing of hostages, plunder of public property, wanton destruction of cities, towns or villages, or devastation not justified by military necessity.[2]

The most important feature of this conception of the laws of war is that the laws of war are to be understood as in fact prohibiting only violence and suffering that are not connected in any direct or important way with the waging of war. As one commentator has put it, the laws of war have as their objective that " . . . the ravages of war should be mitigated as far as possible by prohibiting needless cruelties, and other acts that spread death and destruction and are not reasonably related to the conduct of hostilities."[3]

This is reflected by the language of many of the laws themselves. But it is demonstrated far more forcefully by the way, even relatively unambiguous and absolute prohibitions, are to be interpreted. The former characteristic is illustrated by that part of the Nuremberg definition of war crimes which prohibits the " . . . *wanton* destruction of cities, towns or villages." The latter characteristic is illustrated by the following commentary upon Article 23(c) of the Hague Convention quoted above. That article, it will be recalled, prohibits the resort to arms calculated to cause unnecessary suffering. But "unnecessary suffering" means suffering that is not reasonably related to any military advantage to be derived from its infliction. "The legality of hand grenades, flame-throwers, napalm, and incendiary bombs in contemporary warfare is a vivid reminder that suffering caused by weapons with sufficiently large destructive potentialities is not 'unnecessary' in the meaning of this rule."[4]

Another way to make the same point is to indicate the way in which the doctrine of "military necessity" places a central role in this conception of the laws of war. It, too, is explicitly written into a number of the laws of war as providing a specific exception. Thus, to quote a portion of the Nuremberg definition once again, what is prohibited is " . . . devastation not justified by military necessity."

The doctrine of military necessity is, moreover, more firmly and centrally embedded in this conception of the laws of war than illustrations of the preceding type would suggest. The doctrine does not merely create an explicit exception, i.e. as in "devastation not justified by military necessity." Instead, it functions as a general justification for the violation of most, if not all, of even the specific prohibitions which constitute a portion of the laws of war. Thus, according to one exposition of the laws of war, the flat prohibition against the killing of enemy combatants who have surrendered is to be understood to permit the killing of such persons where that is required by "military necessity." There may well be times in any war when it is permissible to kill combatants who have laid down their arms and tried to surrender.

> Small detachments on special missions, or accidentally cut off from their main force, may take prisoners under such circumstances that men cannot be spared to guard them or take them to the rear, and that to take them along would greatly endanger the success of the mission or the safety of the unit. The prisoners will be killed by operation of the principle of military necessity, and no military or other court has been called upon, so far as I am aware, to declare such killings a war crime.[5]

Or, consider another case where, according to Taylor, the doctrine of military necessity makes ostensibly impermissible conduct permissible. In 1930, a number of nations signed the London Naval Treaty. That treaty required that no ship sink a merchant vessel "without having first placed passengers, crew and ship's papers in a place of safety." The provisions of this treaty were regularly violated in the Second World War. Nonetheless these violations were not war crimes punished at Nuremberg. This is so, says Taylor, for two reasons. First, the doctrine of military necessity makes the treaty unworkable. If submarines are to be effective instrumentations of war, they cannot surface before they attack merchant ships, nor can they stand around waiting to pick up survivors. The answer is not that it is wrong to use submarines. Rather it is that in the interest of military necessity the prohibitions of the treaty cease to be prohibitions. And second, even if considerations of military necessity were not decisive here, violations of the London treaty would still not have been war crimes because the treaty was violated by both sides during the Second World War. And nothing is properly a war crime, says Taylor (at least in the absence of a genuine international tribunal) if both sides engage in the conduct in question.

> As long as enforcement of the laws of war is left to the belligerents themselves, whether during the course of hostilities or by the victors at the conclusion, the scope of their application must be limited by the extent to which they have been observed by the enforcing party. To punish the foe—especially the vanquished foe—for conduct in which the enforcing nation has engaged, would be so grossly inequitable as to discredit the laws themselves.[6]

Finally, the question of the legality of aerial warfare is especially instructive and important. Once more I take Telford Taylor's analysis to be illustrative of the conception I have been trying to delineate. The bombing of cities was, he observes, not punished at Nuremberg and is not a war crime. Why not? For the two reasons he has already given. Since it was engaged in by the Allies—and on a much more intensive level than by the Germans or the Japanese—it would have been improper to punish the Germans and the Japanese for what we also did. But more importantly the bombing of cities with almost any kind of bomb imaginable is perfectly proper because bombing is an important instrument of the war.

There is nothing illegal about bombing population centers; there is nothing impermissible about using antipersonnel bombs. To begin with, it is not a war crime because aerial bombardments were not punished at Nuremberg. Nor, more importantly, should they be proscribed. For bombs are important weapons of war. But what about the fact that they appear to violate the general prohibition against the killing of noncombatants? They certainly do end up killing lots of civilians, Taylor concedes. But that just cannot be helped because a bomb is, unfortunately, the kind of weapon that cannot discriminate between combatants and noncombatants. What is more, bombing is an inherently inaccurate undertaking. The pilots of fast-moving planes—no matter how carefully they try to annihilate only enemy soldiers—will invariably miss lots of times. And if there are civilians nearby, they will, regrettably, be wiped out instead.

The general test for the impermissibility of bombing is, says Taylor, clear enough. Bombing is a war crime if and only if there is no proportioned relationship between the military objective sought to be achieved by the bombing and the degree of destruction caused by it.

This collection of specific prohibitions, accepted conventions, and general excusing and justifying conditions is the conception of the laws of war with which I am concerned. I want now to examine the deficiencies of such a view and to indicate the respects in which I find unconvincing the two general arguments mentioned at the beginning of the paper.

II

I indicated at the outset that one argument for the importance and value of the laws of war is that they in some sense reflect, embody or give effect to fundamental moral distinctions and considerations. I can help to make clear the character of my criticism of this argument in the following fashion. There are at least three grounds upon which we might criticize any particular criminal code. We might criticize it on the ground that it contained a particular criminal law that ought not to be there because the behavior it proscribed was behavior that it was not morally wrong for people to engage in.[7]

So, we might criticize our criminal code because it punishes the use of marijuana even though there is nothing wrong with using marijuana. Or, we might criticize a criminal code because it is *incomplete.* It proscribes a number of things that ought to be proscribed and regards them with the appropriate degree of seriousness, but it omits to punish something that ought, *ceteris paribus,* to be included in the criminal law. So, we might criticize our criminal code because it fails to make criminal the commission of acts of deliberate racial discrimination.

Compare both of these cases with a criminal code that made criminal only various thefts. Such a code would be incomplete in a different way from the code that just omitted to prohibit racial discrimination. It would be systematically incomplete in the sense that it omitted to forbid many types of behavior that any decent criminal code ought to prohibit. It would, I think, be appropriate to describe such a code as a morally incoherent one and to regard this incoherence, by itself, as a very serious defect. The code would be incoherent in that it could not be rendered intelligible either in terms of the moral principles that ought to underlie any criminal code or even in terms of the moral principles that justified making theft illegal.[8] One could not, we might say, make moral sense out of a scheme that regarded as most seriously wrong (and hence a fit subject for the criminal law) a variety of harmful acts against property, but which permitted, and treated as in this sense legitimate, all acts of violence against persons. It would be proper to regard such a code as odious, it should be noted, even though one thought that thefts were, on the whole, among the sorts of things that should be prohibited by the criminal law.

As I hope the following discussion makes clear, it is this last kind of criticism that I am making of the conception of the laws of war set out above. So conceived, the laws of war possess the kind of incompleteness and incoherence that would be present in a criminal code that punished only theft.

The chief defense to the accusation that the laws of war are in this sense incomplete and incoherent would, I think, rest on the claim that the laws of war are complete and coherent—the difference is that they set a lower standard for behavior than that set by the typical criminal code. Even in war, so the argument would go, morality has some place; there are some things that on moral grounds ought not be permitted even in time of war. Admittedly, the argument might continue, the place to draw the line between what is permissible and impermissible is different, is "lower," in time of war than in time of peace, but the guiding moral principles and criteria remain the same. The laws of war can quite plausibly be seen as coherently reflecting, even if imperfectly, this lower but still intelligible morality of war. Thus, the argument might conclude the laws of war are not like a criminal code that only punishes theft. Rather, they are like a criminal code that only punishes intentional homicides, rapes, and serious assaults and thefts.

Although I do not argue the point at length in this paper, I accept the idea that even in war morality has some place. What I do challenge, therefore, is the claim that the laws of war as I have sketched them can be plausibly understood as reflecting or embodying in any coherent fashion this lower, but still intelligible morality of war.

Consider first the less permissive (and hence morally more attractive) conception of the laws of war, the conception that does not always permit military necessity to be an exception or an excuse. It cannot be plausibly claimed, I submit, that this scheme of what in war is permissible and impermissible reflects simply a lowering of our basic moral expectations or standards. The most serious problem, I think, is that the distinction between combatants and noncombatants is not respected by the laws of war—particularly as they relate to aerial warfare and the use of weapons of mass destruction. This constitutes a deviation in kind and not merely a diminution of standards in respect to our fundamental moral notions. This is so because the failure meaningfully to distinguish between combatants and noncombatants obliterates all concern for two basic considerations: the degree of choice that persons had in getting into the position in which they now find themselves, and the likelihood that they are or are about to be in a position to inflict harm on anyone else. The distinction between combatants and noncombatants is admittedly a crude one. Some noncombatants are able in reasonably direct ways to inflict harm on others, e.g. workers in a munitions factory. And some noncombatants may very well have knowingly and freely put themselves in such a position. Concomitantly, many combatants may have been able to exercise very little choice in respect to the assumption of the role of a combatant, e.g. soldiers who are drafted into an army under circumstances where the penalties for refusing to accept induction are very severe. Difficulties such as these might make it plausible to argue that the laws of war cannot reasonably be expected to capture perfectly these distinctions. That is to say, it would, I think, be intelligible to argue that it is unreasonable to expect anyone to be able to distinguish the conscripts from the volunteers in the opponent's army. It would, perhaps, even be plausible to argue (although less convincingly, I think) that civilians who are engaged in activities that are directly connected with the prosecution of the war can reasonably be expected to understand that they will be subject to attack. If the laws of war even preserved a distinction between soldiers, munitions workers, and the like on the one hand and children, the aged, and the infirm on the other, one might maintain that the laws of war did succeed in retaining—at a low level and in an imprecise way—a distinction of fundamental moral importance. But, as we have seen, the laws of war that relate to aerial warfare and the use of weapons of mass destruction do not endeavor to preserve a distinction of even this crudity.

A similar point can be made about those laws of war that deal primarily with combatants. Here, though, there is a bit more that can be said on behalf of the rationality of some of the relevant laws of war. The strongest case is that for the special, relatively unequivocal prohibitions against the mistreatment of prisoners of war and the infliction of damage upon hospitals and medical personnel. Someone might object that these make no sense, that there is no difference between attacking a wounded soldier in a hospital and attacking an unwounded soldier with a weapon against which he is defenseless, e.g. strafing or bombing infantrymen armed with rifles. Similarly, it might be objected that there is no coherent principle that distinguishes the wrongness of killing (generally) prisoners of war and the permissibility of killing enemy soldiers who are asleep.

Such an objection would be too strong, for there does seem to be a morally relevant distinction between these two kinds of cases. It is the distinction between those who have obviously been rendered incapable of fighting back (the wounded and the prisoners of war) and those who only may be incapable of fighting back.

It would be wrong, however, to make too much of this point. In the first place, for the reasons suggested earlier, distinctions among combatants are morally less significant than the distinction between combatants and noncombatants. And in the second place, the principle justifying this distinction among combatants is a pretty crude and not wholly attractive one. In particular, it does not very convincingly, I think, establish the obvious appropriateness of using deadly force against combatants who pose no direct threat and who are defenseless against the force used.[9]

Be that as it may, this is the strongest case for these particular laws of war. There are others for which no comparable rationale can be urged. Thus, it cannot be argued successfully that the laws of war concerning combatants can be generally understood to be a reflection or embodiment of a lower, but coherent set of standards relating to how combatants ought to behave toward one another. More specifically, it cannot be maintained, as persons sometimes seek to maintain, that the laws of war relating to which weapons are permissible and which are impermissible possess a similar coherence. Someone might argue, for example, that there are some ways of killing a person that are worse, more inhumane and savage than other ways. War both permits and requires that combatants kill one another in a variety of circumstances in which, in any other context, it would be impermissible to do so. Nonetheless, so the argument might continue, the laws of war do record and give effect to this perception that some techniques of killing are so abhorrent that they ought not be employed even in war.

Once again, my response is not a direct challenge to the claim that it may be possible to distinguish on some such ground among methods of killing. Indeed, were such a distinction to be preserved by the laws of war, important and desirable alterations in the nature of war would almost surely have to take place. What I am concerned to deny is that the laws of war that deal with weapons can be plausibly viewed as reflecting distinctions of genuine moral significance. Since it is permissible to kill an enemy combatant with an antipersonnel bomb, a nuclear weapon, or even a flamethrower, it just cannot be plausibly maintained that it is a war crime to kill a combatant with poison gas because it is morally worse to use poison gas than to invoke the former methods of human destruction.

It must be observed that so far I have been concerned with that morally more attractive view of the laws of war which does not permit a general exception to all of the laws on grounds of military necessity. Once such a general exception is permitted, whatever plausibility and coherence there is to this conception of the laws of war is diminished virtually to the vanishing point. That this is so can be shown in the following fashion.

To begin with, it is important to notice that the doctrine of "military necessity" is employed in an ambiguous and misleading fashion. "Necessity" leads us naturally to think of various sorts of extreme circumstances which excuse, if they do not justify, otherwise impermissible behavior. Thus, the exception to the rule about taking prisoners is, perhaps, a case where necessitarian language does fit: if the prisoners are taken by the patrol deep in enemy territory the captors will themselves almost surely be captured or killed. They cannot, in such circumstances, be held to the rule against killing prisoners because it is "necessary" that the prisoners be killed.

Now, one may not be convinced that necessitarian language is appropriately invoked even in this case. But what should nonetheless be apparent is the inappropriateness of describing the doctrine that justifies aerial warfare, submarine warfare, or the use of flamethrowers as one of military *necessity*. Necessity has nothing whatsoever to do with the legitimacy of the aerial bombardment of cities or the use of other weapons of mass destruction. To talk of military necessity in respect to such practices is to surround the practice with an aura of justification that is in no way deserved. The appeal to the doctrine of military necessity is in fact an appeal to a doctrine of military utility. The laws of war really prohibit (with only a few minor exceptions) some wrongful practices that also lack significant military value. The laws of war permit and treat as legitimate almost any practice, provided only that there is an important military advantage to be secured.

The more that *this* doctrine of military necessity permeates the conception of the laws of war, the less intelligible and attractive is the claim that the laws of war are a coherent, complete, or admirable code of behavior—even for the jungle of warfare. Given the pervasiveness of this doctrine of military utility, the laws of war are reducible in large measure to the principle that in war it is still wrong to kill (or maim or torture) another person for no reason at all, or for reasons wholly unrelated to the outcome of the war. But the laws of war also tell us what it is permissible and legitimate to do in time of war. Here the governing principle is that it is legitimate, appropriate (and sometimes obligatory) to do almost anything to anybody, provided only that what is done is reasonably related to an important military objective. It is, in short, to permit almost all possible moral claims to be overridden by considerations of military utility. Whatever else one may wish to claim for the preservation of such a system of the laws of war, one cannot, therefore, claim that they deserve either preservation or respect because of the connection these laws maintain with the idea of morality.

Finally, it should be noted, too, that the case is hardly improved by the condition that a practice which is otherwise prohibited ceases to be so, if the practice was engaged in by both sides. As I indicated earlier, this may not be the way to interpret the argument for not punishing the Germans for, say, engaging in unrestricted submarine warfare. But if part of the idea of a war crime is, as some of the literature surely suggests it is, that an offense ceases to be an offense once the practice becomes uniform, then this, too, must count against the possibility of making the case for this conception of the laws of war rest on moral grounds.

III

As I indicated at the outset, there is another way to approach the laws of war and to argue for their worth and significance. This route emphasizes the beneficial consequences of having and enforcing the laws of war, and is relatively unconcerned with the "intrinsic" morality of the rules. The arguments in support of such a view go something like this.

Despite some real fuzziness about the edges (or even closer to the center) many of the laws of war are reasonably precise. A number of the laws of war are written down and embodied in rather specific conventions and agreements. It is relatively easy, therefore, to tell, at least in a good many cases, what is a war crime and what is not. It is certainly simpler to decide, for example, what constitutes a war crime than it is to determine whether a crime against peace or humanity has been committed. And the fact that the laws of war are more readily ascertainable has certain important consequences of its own.

To begin with, there is first the intellectual confidence that comes from dealing with rules that are written down and that are reasonably specific and precise. More to the point, it is this feature which makes it quite fair to hold persons responsible for violations of the laws of war. The laws of war can be ascertained in advance by the individuals concerned, they can be applied impartially by an appropriate tribunal, and they can be independently "verified" by disinterested observers. They are, in sum, more like typical criminal laws than any of the other rules or principles that relate to war.

A second argument for the primacy of the laws of war also concerns their enforcibility.

It goes like this. It is certainly not wholly unrealistic to imagine the laws of war being enforced, even while a war is going on. More importantly it is not wholly unrealistic to imagine the laws of war being enforced by a country against members of its own armed forces, as well as against members of the opposing army. Such has indeed been the case in the United States as well as in other countries. Once again, the contrast with crimes against peace is striking. It is quite unlikely that the perpetrators of crime against peace, who will be the leaders of the enemy, will ever be caught until the war is over. It is surely unlikely, therefore, that the existence of rules making the waging of aggressive war a crime will ever deter leaders from embarking on aggressive war. If they win, they have nothing to fear. If they lose, they expect to die whether they are guilty or not.

The case is more bleak still where the perpetrators of crimes against peace are the leaders of one's own country. While one can in theory imagine the courts of a country holding the leaders of the country liable for waging aggressive war, this is a theoretical but not a practical possibility. While a war is going on the one thing that national institutions are most unlikely to do is to subject the conduct of the leaders of the nation to cool, critical scrutiny. The leaders of a country are hardly likely to be deterred by the prospect that the courts of their own country will convict them of having committed crimes against peace.

The situation in respect to crimes against war is markedly different in both cases. Soldiers fighting on the opposing side do run a real risk of being caught while the war is on. If they know that they may be captured, and if they also know that they may be punished for any war crimes they have committed, this can have a significant effect on the way they behave toward their opponents. Similarly, the knowledge that they may be punished by their own side for misbehavior toward the enemy can influence the way soldiers in the army go about fighting the war. Hence there is a genuine prospect that the members of both armies will behave differently just because there are laws of war than they would have were there no such laws.

What all of this shows is that the laws of war will influence the behavior of persons in time of war. There are additional arguments, connected with those that have just been presented, to show that the behavior will be affected in ways that are both desirable and important.

The first such argument is that, despite all of their imperfections, the laws of war do represent the consensus that does at present exist about how persons ought to behave in time of war. The fact that the laws of war are embodied in conventions and treaties, most of which have been explicitly ratified by almost all the countries of the world, means that we are dealing with conduct about whose character there can be relatively little genuine disagreement. To be sure, the conventions may not go as far or be as precise as we might like. The laws of war may be unambitious in scope and even incoherent in the sense described earlier. Nonetheless, they do constitute those rules and standards about which there is universal agreement concerning what may not be done, even in time of war. And the fact that all nations have consented to these laws and agreed upon them gives them an authority that is almost wholly lacking anywhere else in the area of morality and war.

Closely related to, but distinguished from, the above is the claim that past experience provides independent evidence of the importance and efficacy of having laws of war. They have worked to save human life. If we look at wars that have been fought, we see that the laws of war have had this effect. Perhaps this was because the participants were deterred by the threat of punishment. Perhaps this was because the laws of war embody standards of behavior that men, even in time of war, thought it worth respecting. Perhaps this was because countries recognized a crude kind of self-interest in adhering to the conventions as a means of securing adherence by the other side. It does not matter very much why the laws of war were respected to the degree that they were—and they were respected to some extent in the total wars of the Twentieth Century. What matters is that they were respected. Telford Taylor has put the matter this way:

> Violated or ignored as they often are, enough of the rules are observed enough of the time so that mankind is very much better off with them than without them. The rules for the treatment of civilian populations in occupied countries are not as susceptible to technological change as rules regarding the use of weapons in combat. If it were not regarded as wrong to bomb military hospitals, they would be bombed all of the time instead of some of the time.
>
> It is only necessary to consider the rules on taking prisoners in the setting of the Second World War to realize the enormous saving of life for which they have been responsible. Millions of French, British, German and Italian soldiers captured in Western Europe and Africa were treated in general compliance with the Hague and Geneva requirements, and returned home at the end of the war. German and Russian prisoners taken in the eastern front did not fare nearly so well and died in captivity by the millions, but many survived. Today there is surely much to criticize about the handling of prisoners on both sides of the Vietnam war, but at least many of them are alive, and that is because the belligerents are reluctant to flout the laws of war too openly.[10]

The final argument for the preservation of the laws of war concerns the effect of the laws—or their absence—upon the moral sensibilities of individuals. Were we to do away with the laws of war, were we to concede that in time of war anything and everything is permissible, the effect upon the capacity of persons generally to respond in accordance with the dictates of morality would be diminished rather than enhanced. This, too, is one of Telford Taylor's main theses. "All in all," he argues, "this has been a pretty bloody century and people do not seem to shock very easily, as much of the popular reaction to the report of Son My made depressingly plain. The kind of world in which all efforts to mitigate the horrors of war are abandoned would hardly be a world sensitive to the consequences [of total war]."[11]

The consequences for military sensibilities are at least as important, Taylor continues, as are the consequences for civilian sensibilities. The existence of the laws of war and the insistence upon their importance prevent combatants from becoming completely dehumanized and wholly vicious by their participation in war. The laws of war, Taylor asserts, are

> . . . necessary to diminish the corrosive effect of mortal combat on the participants. War does not confer a license to kill for personal reasons—to gratify

perverse impulses, or to put out of the way anyone who appears obnoxious, or to whose welfare the soldier is indifferent. War is not a license at all, but an obligation to kill for reasons of state; it does not countenance the infliction of suffering for its own sake or for revenge.

Unless troops are trained and required to draw the distinction between military and nonmilitary killings, and to retain such respect for the value of life that unnecessary death and destruction will continue to repel them, they may lose the sense for that distinction for the rest of their lives. The consequence would be that many returning soldiers would be potential murderers.[12]

It should not be difficult to foresee the sorts of objections that I believe can most tellingly be raised against these arguments. I will state them very briefly.

It is, to begin with, far less obvious than the argument would have it that the laws of war possess the kind of specificity we typically require of an ordinary criminal law. In particular, the pervasive character of the doctrine of military "necessity" comes close to leaving as unambiguously criminal only senseless or gratuitous acts of violence against the enemy.

Similarly, the fact that countries have been able to agree upon certain conventions does not seem to me to be a matter of particular significance. At the very least, it is certainly a mistake to infer from this fact of agreement that we have somehow succeeded in identifying those types of behavior that really matter the most. Indeed, it is at least as likely as not, that agreement was forthcoming just because the issues thereby regulated were not of great moment. And it is surely far more likely than not that agreement was forthcoming just because it was perceived that adherence to these laws would not affect very much the way wars got fought.

This leads me to what seem to me to be the two most significant criticisms that can be made against the assertion that beneficial consequences of various sorts flow from respecting and enforcing the laws of war. There is first the claim that adherence to the laws of war teaches important moral lessons (or prevents soldiers from becoming totally corrupt). Just what sort of things about killing do the laws of war (in theory, let alone in practice) teach soldiers; will someone who has mastered the distinctions established by the laws of war thereby be less a potential murderer? It is difficult to see that getting straight about the laws of war will permit someone to learn important moral lessons and to maintain a decent respect for the value of human life. It is difficult to be at all confident that soldiers who have mastered the distinctions established by the laws of war will be for that reason turned away from the path of murder. This is so just because the laws of war possess the kind of incompleteness and incoherence I described earlier. We can, of course, teach soldiers to obey the laws of war, whatever their content may happen to be.

But we must not confuse that truth with the question of whether we will have, through that exercise, taught them to behave in morally responsible ways.[13]

The issue is made more doubtful, still, because the laws of war inescapably permit as well as prohibit; they make some conduct criminal and other conduct legitimate. The evidence is hardly all in, either from the Twentieth Century in general or Vietnam in particular. It will probably never be in. But it surely appears to be at least as likely as not that the laws of war—if they have taught anything at all—have taught soldiers and civilians alike that it is permissible and lawful to kill and maim and destroy, provided only that it will help to win the war. And I do think this constitutes morally retrograde movement.

But this still leaves unanswered what may appear to be the most important argument of all, the argument put forward by Telford Taylor and others that the laws of war are important and deserving of respect because they work. Isn't it sufficient that even somewhat irrational, incoherent and incomplete rules have the consequences of saving lives? Even if it is permissible to kill women and children whenever military necessity requires it, isn't it important to save the lives of those women and children whose deaths are not necessitated by military considerations?

The argument is both sound and deceptive. Of course it is better to save some lives rather than none at all. If adhering to the laws of war as we now have them will save the lives of persons (and especially "innocent" persons) in time of war, that is a good reason (but not a decisive one) for maintaining these laws of war. If punishing soldiers (like Lieutenant Calley) for war crimes will keep other soldiers from gratuitously killing women and children, among others, in Vietnam, that is a good reason for punishing persons for the commission of these war crimes.

But to concede this is not to put an end to the matter at hand. For reasons I have tried to make plain there are costs as well as gains from concentrating our attention upon the laws of war and their enforcement. There is to put it simply a risk to human life that is quite substantial. The risk is that we inevitably and necessarily legitimate behavior that is morally indefensible, that is, truly criminal. The cost—and it is a cost in human life—is, for example, that the sanitized war in Vietnam that would result from a scrupulous adherence to the laws of war will increase still further our tolerance for and acceptance of the horror, the slaughter, and the brutality that is the essence of Twentieth Century war. There is something genuinely odious about a code of behavior that says: if there is a conflict between the attainment of an important military objective and one or more of the prohibitions of the laws of war, it is the prohibitions that quite properly are to give way. And there is something dangerous about a point of view that accepts such a system and directs us to concentrate our energies and our respect upon its enforcement. The corrosive effect of living in a world in which we embrace such a code and insist upon its value seems to me appreciably more dangerous than the effect of a refusal to accord a position of primacy to the sometimes bizarre, often morally incoherent laws of war.

The answer is not, of course, to throw out the laws of war with a view toward inculcating in us all the belief that in war anything goes. But neither is it an acceptable answer to take as given the nature of modern war and modern weapons and to conform, as best one can, the laws of war to their requirements. This, it seems to me, is the fatal flaw in the conception of the laws of war with which I have been concerned. The beginning of a morally defensible position is surely to be found in a different conception of the laws of war. A conception sufficiently ambitious that it refuses to regard as immutable the character of contemporary warfare and weaponry, and that requires instead, that war itself change so as to conform to the demands of morality.

RICHARD WASSERSTROM

UNIVERSITY OF CALIFORNIA
AT LOS ANGELES
MAY, 1971

NOTES

[1] For my purpose I treat the laws of war and war crimes as identical phenomena. I recognize that for other purposes and in other contexts this would be a mistake. See, e.g., Richard Falk, Gabriel Kolko, and Robert Lifton, eds., *Crimes of War* (New York: Random House, 1971), p. 33.

[2] *The Charter of the International Military Tribunal*, Article Six (b).

[3] Telford Taylor, *Nuremberg and Vietnam: An American Tragedy* (New York: Quadrangle Books, 1970), p. 20.

[4] Georg Schwarzenberger, *The Legality of Nuclear Weapons* (London: Stevens, 1958), p. 44.

[5] *Nuremberg and Vietnam*, p. 36. There is an ambiguity in this quotation that should be noted. Taylor may not mean that the laws of war permit an exception in this kind of case. He may mean only that the law is uncertain, that he knows of no court decision which authoritatively declares this to be either a war crime or a permitted exception. It is sufficient for my purposes if he means the weaker claim, that it is an open question.

A more serious objection to my assertion that I am accurately characterizing the existing laws of war would call attention to the following quotation from the *U.S. Army Field Manual, The Law of Land Warfare*, Chap. I, Sec. I.3:

"The law of war places limits on the exercise of a belligerent's power in the interests mentioned in paragraph 2 and requires that belligerents refrain from employing any kind or degree of violence which is not actually necessary for military purposes and that they conduct hostilities with regard for the principles of humanity and chivalry.

"The prohibitory effect of the law of war is not minimized by 'military necessity' which has been defined as that principle which justifies those measures not forbidden by international law which are indispensable for securing the complete submission of the enemy as soon as possible. Military necessity has generally been rejected as a defence for acts forbidden by the customary and conventional laws of war inasmuch as the latter have been developed and framed with consideration for the concept of military necessity."

I leave it to the reader to decide exactly what this means. It seems to anticipate, on the one hand, that the laws of war and the doctrine of military necessity can conflict. It seems to suppose, on the other hand, that substantial conflicts will not arise either because the laws of war prohibit militarily unnecessary violence or because they were formulated with considerations of military necessity in mind. In substance, the view expressed in the quotation is not inconsistent with the conception I am delineating.

⁶ *Nuremberg and Vietnam,* p. 39. Once again, there is an ambiguity here. Taylor may mean that it is procedurally unfair to punish the loser but not the victor for the same act. He may also mean, though, that there is a principle at work which legitimizes a practice which was previously proscribed on the ground that the practice has now become widespread. He does not distinguish these two positions in his book and he seems to me to hold both.

⁷ I recognize that this is vague. For my purposes it does not matter. It does not matter, that is, whether the law is criticized because the behavior is not immoral, or because the behavior is immoral but not harmful, or because the behavior is harmful but not sufficiently so to justify the use of the criminal law, etc.

⁸ Of course, there is still a fourth possible code. It would make illegal only those things that it is morally right and permissible to do, or that ought, on other grounds, never be made illegal. Such a code would certainly be the very worst of all. I am not claiming, it should be emphasized, that the laws of war are like this fourth possible case.

⁹ It is, for example, legitimate to bomb the barracks of soldiers who are not at the front lines, to ambush unsuspecting (and possibly even unarmed) enemy soldiers, and to use all sorts of weapons against which the particular combatants may be completely defenseless. At some stage it just ceases to be very satisfactory to insist that this is unobjectionable because the combatants could defend themselves if they chose and because they chose to be combatants in the first place. For both claims about the combatants may in fact be false and known to be such.

¹⁰ *Nuremberg and Vietnam,* p. 40.

¹¹ Ibid., p. 39.

¹² Ibid., pp. 40-41.

¹³ Unless, of course, one holds the view that teaching persons to obey orders, or even laws, whatever they may happen to be is an important constituent of the curriculum of moral education. It is not a view I hold.

HUGO ADAM BEDAU

COMPENSATORY JUSTICE AND THE BLACK MANIFESTO*

In May, 1969, James Foreman interrupted a religious service at River-side Church in New York to deliver "The Black Manifesto," which included a stunning "demand" of $500 million in "reparations" for black Americans from the white religious establishment. In the period since that date, The Manifesto has aroused rather less serious discussion than one might have thought it would.[1] No doubt, the burden of The Manifesto has struck many whites and some blacks as so outrageous in its morality, so unrealistic in its politics, so unfeasible in its economics, that intellectuals may have done a public service by consigning The Manifesto to relative neglect.[2] Not that The Manifesto has had only unfavorable publicity, nor that the churches have ignored it; quite the contrary. What remains true, however, is that the crucial burden of The Manifesto, indeed, the precise *argument* it advances for reparations and compensatory justice, has not so far as I can tell received the thoughtful attention it deserves. Until it does, and is appraised with care and fairness, it is impossible either to support or to reject The Manifesto's "demands." Let us try, then, however belatedly, to state and assess the argument of The Black Manifesto.

The full text of The Manifesto runs to less than three thousand words; its "Introduction" adds another two thousand words. What is needed, however, is neither quotation, excerpt, or summary of these texts but a reconstruction

* From the "Philosophy and Public Policy" issue of *The Monist,* **56,** No. 1 (January, 1972), published by the Open Court Publishing Company.

of the argument they contain, since it is the merits of that argument which demand scrutiny and appraisal. The problem immediately evident to any reader of The Manifesto is that its argument is elliptical and obscure. The rhetoric of revolution, plain indignation, threats, predictions, and the sketch of how the reparations are to be used once they are in hand—all these confuse and fail to advance the argument implicit in The Manifesto and upon which whatever merit it has rests. My first task, therefore, is to take it as it is written and to reconstruct the argument it must contain if its central explicit and manifest assertions and accusations are meant seriously. As a first approximation to a complete reconstruction I offer the following sixteen premise version. Premises not tagged with a page citation (only a minority are not so tagged) are my interpolations of what I take to be among the tacit assumptions relied upon by the explicit assertions to be gleaned from the published text of The Manifesto. Expanded though the argument in my reconstructed version is, I have not tried to make it formally valid; no doubt that could be done, but it is not essential to my purposes here to try to do so. All the really interesting tacit premisses I have tried to state.

The Argument of the Black Manifesto[3]

(1) Blacks in U.S.A. since 1619 have been "exploited and degraded, brutalized, killed and persecuted" by whites (p. 120).

(2) This has been the objective effect of the commitment to "racism, capitalism and imperialism" practiced by the white power structure (pp. 116-17, 118, 124).

(3) The historic white Christian and Jewish religious establishment is "part and parcel" of the white power structure, "another form of government in this country" (p. 125); it has actively supported and continues to support this systematic objective exploitation of blacks (pp. 119, 126).

(4) Corporate black America is the heir of the historic victims—and includes in its heritage the harm and injury suffered by the parents, grandparents, etc., of living blacks.

(5) The existing white religious establishment is liable to living blacks for whatever harm has been inflicted by its historic organizational forebears upon blacks.

(6) The chief purpose of slavery and its racist aftermath was to develop "the industrial base" of America (pp. 119, 123).

(7) The wealth exacted by this exploitation has been astronomical—in the thousands of billions.

(8) Much of this profit is owned or controlled or has otherwise been diverted to the benefit of the white religious establishment—"the white Christian churches and synagogues" (p. 120).

(9) Little if any of that profit has been returned over the centuries for the benefit of those who were exploited to earn it.

(10) This profit constitutes an unjust enrichment in the hands of white America, including the white religious establishment.

(11) Such unjust enrichment constitutes a basis for justifiable compensation (restitution being impossible in the nature of the case), or "reparations" (pp. 119, 120, 122, 123, 126).

(12) The compensation owed should be paid to and on behalf of "all black people," by the white religious establishment (p. 126).

(13) Just reparations are a sum which will fund the development of those institutions, skills, and services for living blacks and their heirs of which their heritage has deprived them and in virtue of which they can not compete today as the socioeconomic equals of whites (pp. 120-22).

(14) $500,000,000 (or "$15 per nigger") is part of such a sum (pp. 119, 120, 122); but "it is only a beginning of the reparations due" (pp. 120, 126).

(15) The white religious establishment can afford to pay such a sum; it has "tremendous wealth" (p. 120).

(16) The white religious establishment in U.S.A. must pay $500,000,000 indemnity to corporate black America.

There are, at the onset, three kinds of objections to the argument of The Manifesto which I wish to state here so as to be relieved of any need to discuss them later. Some will object, first, that The Manifesto advances a claim ostensibly for reparations based on past wrongs, when in fact this only disguises the real argument for *redistribution* of currently available social resources given the present unfair disadvantages of blacks. In other words, some will say that the argument for compensatory justice in The Manifesto is really a disguised argument for distributive justice.[4] Others will object, second, that the real argument is not one for reparations nor is it a disguised argument for distributive justice. They will argue that it is really a disguised argument of an entirely different sort, namely, for special benefits to blacks given their special needs, on the ground that the *net social welfare* is maximized by this treatment. These critics of The Manifesto think that the entire appeal to justice (compensatory or distributive) is a deception, because the point to be made really relies upon the utility of redistributed wealth. Still others will object, third, that the argument of The Manifesto is disguised *extortion,* a veiled threat of violence unless half a billion dollars is transferred from white control to black. Those who view the argument in this third way see nothing moral in it at all.

All of these objections, one must concede, have some force. No doubt the third has the least plausibility, certainly in retrospect. Yet even this notion is not wholly absurd; after all, people do sometimes threaten to harm those whom they believe owe them compensation, especially if the plea for compensation falls on deaf ears. Nevertheless, I urge that we put aside this third possibility, and also the first two as well, because in a certain sense they are neither controversial nor interesting (except among politicians, perhaps, and racists). Hardly anyone (else) denies or contests the claim on behalf of living black Americans to a larger share of the total wealth and power in the nation. Hardly anyone (else) denies it would do them good to have a larger share in the nation's affluence and in its control, quite apart from the debatable question of the advisability of accomplishing these results by granting the demands contained in The Manifesto. Nor is it doubtful that present injustices in the distribution of social wealth provide a sufficient justification for transfer of wealth from white hands to black on a scale even greater than that contemplated by The Manifesto. Indeed, it may even be that the redistributive or the utilitarian version of the argument of The Black Manifesto is really the best way to construe it, given the political and economic realities of the 1970s.[5] After all, one need not shut his eyes to the possibility that the point of a manifest argument for reparations is in fact contained in a coordinated but concealed argument for distributive justice or social welfare.

Nevertheless, all these possibilities should be put clearly off to one side, because they are all alike in being *reinterpretations* of the argument evidently being advanced, and to that extent at least, they are evasions or repudiations of The Manifesto. It is as an argument for reparations, for compensatory justice, that The Manifesto makes its plain claim upon our understanding, and it simply cannot be taken seriously unless its force (and limitations) as *this sort* of argument are granted at the onset and without reservation.

Let us turn, then, to those objections which take the argument of The Manifesto at face value. Fundamentally, of course, any such counterargument is going to proceed by alleging either that the argument-form itself is invalid, or that some explicit or implicit factual or moral premise is false. We know in advance, thanks to elementary logic, that only if at least one of these faults obtains can the argument be rejected. At the risk of being excessively contentious I propose to canvass possible objections and then rebut them as well as I can, and I shall begin with the least plausible objections and move to the more perplexing and complex ones. My survey will not be thorough, for I shall not try to dissect the reconstructed argument premise by premise, but I think the full range of possible obstacles to accepting the argument will at least be sketched and, I hope, the gravest objections directly stated and answered.

Objection (1). The figure of "$15 per nigger," mentioned in premise (14), is an arbitrary and really senseless sum because it bears no relation to any assessment of the injury suffered or the benefits exploited by whites from blacks.

This objection is partly wrongheaded. It regards the figure of $15 as a charge per head, whereas that figure is merely an arithmetic artifact produced by dividing $500 million by the number, roughly, of living black Americans. Besides, The Manifesto does not attempt to show that $15 per head is the upper limit, or anywhere near it, of the liability owed. It claims only that the lower limit of the liability is not below this sum. Whether that is so depends on certain calculations, and I return to this topic below in connection with Objection (10).

Objection (2). The Manifesto ignores the fact that the white religious establishment, mentioned in premises (5) and (8), of which white churches are alleged to be a part, is not "lily white" at all. For some decades, black Americans have been part of the congregations and, increasingly, of the clergy in all major national Protestant denominations and in the Catholic church, too. If so, then part of the current wealth and power of these churches has been contributed to them by some of the very group on whose behalf the claim of exploitation is made. This is doubly paradoxical: First, because from this fact of black membership in allegedly white churches, the victim turns out to be at one, as a member in a common institution, with his oppressor; and second, because the wealth of the oppressor has been given to him and not extorted or exploited by him from his victims.

The way to dissolve these paradoxes is by insisting that in fact the numbers of black persons in white churches is insignificant (perhaps one in a hundred, or in a thousand); and consequently, that the portion of white church wealth today which has been obtained from the voluntary contributions of black church members and clergy is equally negligible. The objection, then, is sound in implicitly raising the point (*pace* Hobbes) that a person or a class cannot "injure" himself, and a fortiori cannot hope to obtain redress for that injury from himself. It is wrong, however, in that the facts in this case do not permit application of this point.

It may also be part of this objection that it is inconceivable that the churches, as institutions, should owe reparations to blacks. This is a complex question, and I shall deal with part of it in my reply to Objection (4) and with more of it in my reply to Objection (10). Here, I would point out that The Manifesto asserts racist bias in the historic white churches of America, it implies racist exploitation among the lay and clerical members of white churches, and I think it also assumes corporate continuity of today's predominantly white churches with the historic "lily white" churches. If so, the antiracism of the contemporary white church will fail to be a barrier against the demand for reparations to the extent that today's churches cannot legitimately deny continuity with their racist predecessors nor point to prior acts of reparation of their own or of their predecessors.

Objection (3). The idea (introduced in premise (4)) of corporate black America being indemnified is absurd and unworkable. Blacks are no more a corporate body in America than are W.A.S.P.'s. And the Black Economic Development Conference, which first formulated and publicised The Manifesto, cannot claim to speak for blacks; it has no authority to act as their representative or trustee. So, even if the argument were sound, there would be no legitimate body to receive and disburse the indemnification. (One might argue the other way, and claim that insofar as blacks can be thought of corporately or as a class, they can be so only as Jews or W.A.S.P.'s are, viz., as a consequence of self-identification and group acceptance. But these two conditions are too imprecise and unpredictable in their actual operation to be sufficient for the purpose of granting the assumption of The Manifesto.)

The reply, I believe, is that it is not impossibly difficult to think of ways in which all and only living black Americans might be convened so as to create a truly representative body, or anyway a body with genuine ethnic legitimacy and authority, to receive and administer these reparations. It is not necessary that blacks undertake to effect physical, economic, or legal separation from their white fellow citizens in America in order to be, for the purposes of these reparations, identifiable as a nation within a nation. Likewise, B.E.D.C. or its successor could be established as a trustee, holding the monies received in indemnity until such a legitimate representative of corporate black America emerged. As for criteria of membership in black America, a suitable "grandfather clause" in disjunction with a nativity clause could be used to supplement self-identification and group acceptance, so as to exclude non-American blacks, e.g., Jamaican Negroes, and new black Americans, e.g., Ghanian immigrants—provided it was in fact thought necessary or desirable to limit eligibility in corporate black America in such ways.

Objection (4). The argument of The Manifesto, in being addressed to the churches, is arbitrary and unfair. The churches as corporate bodies are, if anything, less guilty of racist exploitation than other white institutions.

We may concede that The Manifesto does not make clear whether the churches are the only or simply the first white institution to be subjected to demands for reparations. In theory, The Manifesto might well be reformulated and addressed to tax-exempt foundations (typically created by the surplus profits of American commercial and industrial enterprise), institutions of higher learning (endowed from the same sources), and other non-profit organizations (such as hospitals, theatres, galleries, museums, libraries). The Manifesto explicitly does allude to demands for reparations from "private business and the United States government."[6] However, most of these other white institutions have already been asked to make quasi-restitutionary compensation, rather than monetary reparation. They have been asked to extend their services and open their jobs to blacks. It is an ironic commentary on the state of religious life in America that the chief contribution by way of compensation it is thought white churches can make to black Americans is—merely money. Whether other institutions which have more to offer could wholly discharge their debt to black America through compensatory jobs and services, however, is very doubtful, if the argument of The Manifesto is sound.

As for the complaint that among white institutions the churches are not the most guilty of racist practices, this is irrelevant in two respects. First, it remains true that the guilt of the churches would not vanish before the fact that other white institutions share or even exceed that guilt. But the truth is, the question of *guilt* is not properly at issue. Guilt carries with it the atmosphere of punitive sanctions, whereas reparations is not a punitive remedy at all. Instead, what is at issue here is corporate *liability;*[7] like guilt, liability admits of degrees and is such that the greater liability does not efface the lesser.

Second, the objection overlooks an important consideration. Churches, more than any other white institution, are specially vulnerable to a demand for reparations because such a demand can be understood perhaps best within the ancient pattern of sinfulness, contrition and penance which is inseparable from the entire historical theology of the Judeo-Christian religion. This religion, in every version and throughout history, teaches that it costs a sinner something to put himself into a right relationship with his God and his fellow-man. Surely, it is this consideration which makes the professedly religious bodies of America the very best place to begin a campaign for reparations.[8] For what other institution is equally susceptible to the demand to confess and make amends? If anything, the difficulty raised by Objection (4) lies in quite the reverse direction. If the importance of the pattern of sinfulness, confession and penance—true repentance—is stressed as central to the setting in which this demand for reparations is made, then it will entail that the argument of The Manifesto has little or no application to any other white institution! Certainly, no secular corporation, whether it makes a profit or not, will be or will think of itself as susceptible to a demand for reparations cast in this form. Nor is this an idle and inconsequential consideration. If white America owes reparations to black America, then the vast non-church-going bulk of the white population today in this country will evade paying its share of the corporate indemnity, simply by virtue of confining the argument of The Black Manifesto exclusively to white churches. Obviously, this was not the intent of The Manifesto's authors and supporters.

There remains, then, a certain tension in the fact that it is the churches to whom The Manifesto is officially and initially addressed. If the aptness of addressing the churches is stressed, then no other institutions will be subject to reparations, at least, by the terms of this argument. This is a considerable price to have to pay in order to avoid the charge of unfair and arbitrary selection of the churches as the sole target of The Manifesto, when one considers the relatively small percentage of the nation's total wealth in church control.

Since, however, the argument of The Manifesto relies upon the idea of corporate black America, and since according to the argument every white American is in some way and to some degree accountable for historic harms visited upon blacks, why doesn't The Manifesto ignore all white institutions, such as the churches, and address itself directly to corporate white America? If corporate black America can be viewed as the injured party and the party deserving reparations, why not serve the demand for reparations against corporate white America?

The answer, I think, is twofold. Corporate white America is too unrepresented, too disorganized, too diffuse to be effectively approached by anybody for anything, much less by black spokesmen for something as disturbing as reparations. The churches, by contrast, are well organized and like other voluntary organizations are accessible to black leaders; they meet weekly to transact their spiritual business behind open doors. The Black Manifesto is obviously already symbolic enough without being reduced to pure gesture, as it would be if it were addressed to corporate white America as such. Thus, while from a logical point of view, the ideas of corporate black and corporate white America are on precisely equal footing, from a practical point of view as regards the motive for organizing under such a rubric, they could not be farther apart. Moreover, since the churches might be said to be the functional conscience of the nation, addressing The Manifesto to them might be viewed legalistically as placing the churches in subrogation for corporate white America: the white churches are made to answer for the liability of all white Americans. (Once again, however, if we accept this latter interpretation, only the churches can ever be made liable for reparations.)

Objection (5). The argument, if not strictly inconsistent, at least poses a dilemma for its advocates. It begins with a radical Marxist critique in its complaint of "exploitation," in premises (1), (3), and (6)-(7). But before it ends, in premises (10)-(12), it shifts into a conventional Liberal demand for "justifiable compensation." Now, the argument cannot be both Marxist and Liberal. If it is the former then it should demand expropriation of the exploiters, a revolutionary redistribution of the product of the workers' labor to all the people, public ownership of the means of production and distribution, etc.[9] For this version of the argument to be sound, it is essential to establish that current wealth in white institutions is the causal product of historic capitalist exploitation. But if the argument is merely Liberal and reformist, as it seems in the end to be, then the initial complaint of exploitation (like the alleged surplus profits) is irrelevant. It is sufficient on this version of the argument to establish only that blacks still suffer from uncompensated wrongs while others (whites) still enjoy the undeserved benefits of those historic wrongs.

The reply to this alleged dilemma is twofold. There is nothing wrong, in Marxist theory, with arguing for half a loaf rather than all. In a pre- or non-revolutionary situation, there is no reason why a sincere and consistent Marxist should not appeal to reparations, redistribution, or to any other familiar Liberal principle of social justice provided it will succeed in persuading a nominally Liberal (and unquestionably anti-Marxist) society to shift the current allocation of its resources away from protecting the propertied class to assisting the workers. In any case, Liberals have ample reason to press the purely Liberal version of the argument to its conclusion, quite apart from the evident Marxist overtones in the argument as it stands. For others, who are sympathetic to if not imbued with Marxist theory, one might insist that the notion of exploitation used in The Manifesto's argument is truly equivocal. The labor of generations of blacks has created surplus profits of slight or no benefit to them, and this labor was originally stolen and thenceforth made captive under conditions of structured injustice which a Hume, a Mill, or a Rawls would be able to recognize as such. The slave and Jim Crow heritage, therefore, constitutes both a moral and an economic exploitation. Blacks in America have been doubly exploited, so their argument for compensation is entitled to take this into account and it does. To put it another way, we might view The Black Manifesto as attempting to invoke not merely one or another version of conventional Liberal principles of justice, nor of Marxist justice—if there is such a thing[10]—but what might be called *socialist justice* (the full outline of which, I would concede, is nowhere as yet stated).

Objection (6). The Manifesto's argument rests on racist (i.e., immoral racial) assumptions. It concedes that the claimant is not the party directly injured, and that the party liable to pay up is not the party who directly inflicted the injury. Yet it argues that it is just to make the heirs of the former pay the heirs of the latter because the one continues to profit from the injury as the latter continues to suffer from it. But to do this the argument must imply that blacks as a class or a race have been injured; how can this be true unless every black has been injured? Likewise, if whites as a class have inflicted the injury, is not every white responsible? But these implications are very probably false and certainly not proved. True, The Manifesto's argument does not impute fault to every white distributively, any more than it imputes benefits to every white distributively from the slavery of blacks and its aftermath. But it does allege that whites as such have benefited and blacks as such have suffered at white hands. This pattern of reasoning does, therefore, rely upon the idea of liability or responsibility (if not guilt) by mere racial association, as well as the suffering of injury by mere racial association. Any argument relying upon such concepts is morally unsound. Moreover, the nature of the argument is such that no evidence of good faith, either individually or collectively, by whites or white institutions towards blacks prior to the levy of the demand for reparations in The Manifesto would seem to exempt such whites from its thrust.

The basis of the rebuttal must lie in the incontestable fact that blacks in America have been regarded as a class historically by slave and postslavery segregation legislation and coordinate social practices. However difficult it may be, according to anthropologists, to develop an adequate empirical basis for a sound theory of races, this difficulty has not stood in the way of a practical development of the concept of a *black* as distinct from a *white* race in this country. Consequently, it is possible that various other practical relations, including injury, liability, benefit, and redress should obtain between the parties so defined, despite spatial, temporal, and hereditary dispersals among the members of the two classes (races). There is, in short, no purely logical or conceptual reason why there should not be liability and the rest by virtue of merely racial association or membership in a racially defined class. Whether there is any factual basis for such a doctrine is a separate question.

As for guilt by association, where criminal guilt before a court of law is the question, it is perfectly fitting that such guilt should be attacked and repudiated. Criminal guilt and individual fault, however, are not in question here. Therefore, any criticism of The Manifesto based on complaint against the immorality of guilt by association is simply beside the point. The appeal to corporate or institutional liability is legitimate just in case the facts show participation in and profit from racial slavery and segregation by the institution in question. The record is far from complete, but in so far as the liability of the white churches of America is in question, it would appear—even without the exhaustive researches scholars have yet to provide—that it ill-behooves contemporary defenders of the major American religious denominations to repudiate the moral legitimacy of the notion that their churches as institutions are liable for claims of reparations based on the fact that they are beneficiaries and preservers of racist practices against blacks.[11]

Objection (7). The argument of The Manifesto relies upon tacit analogy either with reparations exchanged between sovereign nations (as in German war reparations, under the Versailles Treaty) or with indemnities granted by a sovereign nation to one of its dependent or custodial peoples (as in our government's indemnities to certain American Indian tribes). Neither analogy is plausible. In the latter class of cases, there is always some specific treaty violation which serves as the basis of the claim for reparations; but no such treaty exists between black and white America. In the former class of cases, we have a very dangerous analogy because only the defeated ever pay war reparations and they look upon them not as just compensation owed to the victims of their unjust aggressive war, but rather as the tribute exacted from the loser under the time-honored doctrine that to the victor belongs the spoils.

First, while it is of course true that no legal treaty binds black and white Americans together, the federal Constitution and the host of federal "Civil Rights" legislation and decisional law do testify to a kind of implicit social contract among racial equals. Black Americans are entitled to argue that individually they are parties to this implicit contract but that as a class they have yet to receive their full and fair share under its terms. Second, the parallel with war reparations only points to the truth that it is unreasonable to demand reparations from a party who has made no concession of liability, and today it is doubtful whether white America has conceded its liability for wrongs visited upon black America. Yet one can make too much of this. It is true that it is unreasonable, in the face of white intransigence and the absence of overwhelming black power, to *demand* reparations, just as it is futile to threaten to *take* property or services valued in the amount of the reparations demanded unless they are paid promptly and in full. Some may have found such intentions in The Manifesto, because near its end we read: " . . . we are not opposed to force and we are not opposed to violence."[12] However, it is not necessary to construe this remark as a genuine threat. For those without any access to an appropriate court room, part of an effective strategy to get someone who is liable for reparations to accept that liability is to press upon him a well-reasoned argument imputing liability and demanding compensation. This is what (with perhaps less than perfect success) The Black Manifesto attempts to do.[13]

A better rebuttal to the complaint based on the weakness of the analogy proceeds by denying that the argument relies on any such analogy at all. The argument of The Manifesto, as I have reconstructed it, relies not on analogy with treaty violations or war reparations, but upon the common legal notion of *unjust enrichment* (see premises (6)-(12)). Arnold Kaufman has correctly emphasized this idea, though without using the term, when he asserted:

> The sons of privilege are being asked to compensate the sons of slaves whether or not the former are responsible for the disabilities of the latter. . . . The sons of slave masters continue to profit, the sons of slaves to suffer the disabilities of the original iniquity. Under these conditions the sons of slaves have rights of compensation against the sons of slave masters.[14]

In this, there is no argument by analogy at all. Instead, there is a straight-forward appeal to the fundamental principles of compensatory justice on the assumption that the facts of the situation of black Americans today vis-à-vis white Americans (or, at least, the white churches of America) satisfy those principles.[15] Moreover, there is reason to see some disanalogy between compensation for black Americans and the German war reparations, because the latter case does not rely upon the notion of unjust enrichment. It relies upon the idea of criminal harm, or at least tortious injury: the deliberate waging of aggressive and unprovoked warfare with peaceful neighbors. But an analogous complaint against the churches is at most obliquely asserted in The Manifesto.

Objection (8). The argument of The Manifesto is sufficiently legalistic that it invites criticism on at least two legalistic grounds: *(a)* the defense of belatedness of claim, and *(b)* the defense of unsought benefits. *(a)* Claims of compensatory desert based on harms that occurred decades, generations, even centuries ago are not payable because civilized society cannot be expected to entertain such claims on grounds of justice over an indefinitely long period. The parties who were originally liable are not now around to pay up, and it is unfair to expect their unknowing and innocent heirs to pay in their stead. Blacks as a class have no right today to ask the white churches or any other white institutions for reparations for ancient wrongs. *(b)* "A person is not ordinarily required to pay for benefits which were thrust upon him with no opportunity to refuse them. The fact that he is enriched is not enough, if he cannot avoid the enrichment."[16] But if The Manifesto's assumptions about racism in America are correct, this is precisely the predicament of most whites, including white institutions, in this society. The wealth which the churches have is obtained entirely through their member's voluntary contributions and the subsequent profitable investment of the unspent portions. This wealth derives from persons all of whom possess the unsought advantages of color and race, advantages of which they cannot divest themselves. There is a certain tragedy and pathos in this for blacks, but no occasion for reparations from whites.

The objection in *(b)* is easily met. The defense of unsought benefits in law is clearly designed to protect the recipient of a gift forced upon him from having to make restitution to the donor upon demand at a later date. The donor is entitled to restitution only when he affords the donee an opportunity to decline the benefit or else has a reasonable excuse for failure to do so.[17] But the special advantages accruing to whites in virtue of their race and color are not benefits given to or conferred upon whites by blacks. Historically, they have been exacted from blacks by whites only by the utmost use of terror and violence. So, while it may be true that many whites have enjoyed unsought advantages deriving from their race and color, it is false that these advantages were somehow inherent in race and color themselves, just as it is false that these advantages were thrust upon whites by blacks choosing to disadvantage themselves.

The objection in *(a)* is based on what might be called a moral statute of limitation, or a moral analogy to the legal bar of laches. Equity, we are told in an old maxim, aids only the vigilant; and a victim of another's injustice who is negligent in the assertion of his right to compensation may discover that his negligence bars him from remedy. The passage of time may result in unfair hardship for the defendant, or for third parties, or increase the likelihood of substantial change or error regarding the relevant facts.[18] It is for these reasons that statutes of limitation and the equitable defense of laches are available to protect defendants. No doubt they have comparable force in the forum of conscience as well. Whether they should work to defeat the claim for reparations advanced in The Black Manifesto is doubtful. One might argue persuasively that it is only in recent years that black spokesmen have been in a position to advance and press a claim for reparations, and thus that their failure to do so in earlier decades is not evidence of black negligence so much as it is a measure of the severity of black disabilities. In addition, the churches cannot plead that they are unable to pay the compensation demanded or that it would bankrupt them to do so. But only this kind of severe hardship enables a defendant to successfully invoke laches. Whether, however, the enormous passage of time—more than three centuries, over which the injury to blacks was inflicted and the unjust enrichment by whites was reaped—is so great as to make incalculable the injury and the benefit, and for this reason something like laches should enter, this is a difficulty to which I will turn in Objection (10).

Objection (9). Although The Manifesto claims that "black people are the most oppressed group of people inside the United States,"[19] its authors do not and could not claim that blacks alone have been exploited by others to create profits in which they have not shared, because the same is true of most white and other nonwhite immigrants throughout the history of the nation. This creates the possibility of destroying the argument of The Manifesto by reducing it to absurdity through constructing parallel arguments for compensatory reparations on behalf of other exploited and disadvantaged groups. The aboriginal American Indians are survived by tribes whose title to such reparations is every bit as good of that of erstwhile African blacks; the same is true of Mexican Americans in the Southwest and of Puerto Ricans on the Eastern seaboard. But then the same is also true of the East Boston Irish, the North End Italians, the West End Jews, etc., etc. Every minority has been exploited by the established society of its day, so the heirs of every exploited minority have a right to file a claim comparable to that levied in The Manifesto. Now, since each such argument is valid only if all are valid, none is valid—because it is absurd for all to be valid. It is simply preposterous to imagine seriously working out the details of the cross-claims for class-indemnities which would be established by this multitude of valid claims for reparations.

Again, there are two replies to this objection, one of which concedes the assumption in question and the other of which denies it. It is true that the spectacle of a whole series of claims and cross-claims for compensation by each American ethnic group against all others boggles the mind. But this is not a theoretical objection to entertaining such a complex set of intertwined claims. Lawyers are paid every day to work on cases nearly as complex. Practically, of course, it would be extremely difficult to work out a suitable scale of historic injury and to parcel out the relative degrees of liability among the various groups in question. One might hypothesize, on behalf of The Manifesto's authors, that if such cross-claims in indemnity were worked out, we would discover that they would cancel out so far as all the claims among white ethnic groups are concerned, leaving only the massive claim of blacks against whites, one portion of which is the explicit preoccupation of The Manifesto.

However, I think it is more likely to suppose that the authors of The Manifesto did not anticipate this kind of objection, because it seems in fact to be frivolous. It may be that The Manifesto's claim of compensation rests upon the assumption that blacks are historically only the nation's most exploited and least rewarded ethnic group, and that for this reason only their claim for compensation goes to the the head of the list. Certainly, nothing in The Manifesto as such implies that no other ethnic group in America also deserves reparations from whites. But the economic, psychological, and other societal facts have convinced most observers that the unique history of forced immigration (in contrast to free immigration) and chattel slavery (in contrast to indentured servitude and "wage slavery") has left a heritage of defeat among blacks incomparably more devastating than that suffered by any other initially disadvantaged immigrant minority group. Likewise, the evidence that blacks as a class, like Irish, Italian, Jewish, and other non-W.A.S.P. immigrants, can take the upwardly mobile route to their own economic prosperity and social diffusion throughout society at all levels without special compensatory efforts is doubtful at best.

There is, nevertheless, one other rival claimant to the unique status advanced by The Manifesto on behalf of blacks: the Indians. Only the American Indian as an ethnic minority has suffered what might be called (after British criminal law) 'constructive genocide', a fate even more brutal in its effects than forced immigration and chattel slavery. The legitimacy of the Indians' claim, on Liberal if not on Marxist assumptions, is if anything more valid and incontestable than the claim of blacks.[20] Without the mineral resources and real estate bargained, wrested and stolen from the Indians, white culture in this nation would lack the material base for the past century's agricultural and industrial growth and the ensuing wealth in its possession. One reply to this objection, therefore, is that the Indians are entitled to make a claim against whites in terms no less stark than those used in The Manifesto. What we need alongside The Black Manifesto is a Red Manifesto; but this concession is not sufficient to establish a *reductio ad absurdum* at all.

Finally, we should not overlook a purely logical point. The argument of The Manifesto cannot be shown to be unsound merely by the possibility that if the form of argument it employs were valid, then infinitely many other versions of the same argument would also be valid. For this is uninteresting unless it is likely that because The Manifesto's argument is sound, so are all or many of these other compensatory arguments. However, that cannot happen so long as at least one premise is false in every other version of the argument. In my criticism above, I have relied on precisely this outcome, with the one notable exception already discussed.

Objection (10). In order to make out a claim for compensatory justice, one needs to know the value of the loss suffered, the benefit derived therefrom by another, the causal connection between the injured and injuring parties, and the acts committed by the latter upon the former for which reparations are sought. But in this case, we cannot (and The Manifesto does not) identify with sufficient precision the specific harm suffered by blacks as a class nor the specific benefits secured by and on behalf of the white churches, nor the causal relation between the two. The argument for recompense depends on some assessment of how blacks would be today as a class if they had not been exploited historically. Otherwise, their loss cannot be calculated; but there is no way to establish the value of this loss, nor the wealth unjustly in white hands. The result is that the demand of any given amount in reparations is hopelessly unmoored from the necessary factual base. It is hardly surprising that the militant authors of The Manifesto themselves are unable to settle upon a proper sum for reparations. Although they initially announced the sum as $500 million, within two months they had raised it by a factor of six.[21]

Many will think this is the most fundamental and unanswerable objection of them all, so it deserves careful consideration. To take the last point first, the fact that the authors of The Manifesto upped their claimed indemnity is perhaps owing as much to the rapid change in their knowledge of the assets controlled by white churches as it is either to greed or to the sobering costs of the programs to be financed with the reparation money. Quite apart from any other considerations, if reparations are owed blacks as a class by the white churches, it does not seem unreasonable that they should amount to a sum equivalent to (what has been reasonably estimated as) 3 percent of the total real estate holdings of the churches,[22] or perhaps one year's worth of Sunday morning church offerings.

The Manifesto is not clear as to the precise mechanisms of white enrichment at the expense of black slavery and discrimination, and a certain sympathetic inventiveness of behalf of the authors of The Manifesto is required if we hope to do justice to their argument. I suggest that we view the wealth of the churches as created by white membership and administered by white clergy on behalf of implicitly racist (or with indifference to antiracist) policies, in which the actual creation and perpetuation of slavery itself played an important but not decisive part. Thus, whether black chattel slavery was or was not itself a profitable institution on these shores (a matter much debated by historians)[23] is not crucial to The Manifesto's complaint at all. We are to think of the wealth in the churches today as created bit by bit over the generations, and as representing in part the surplus profits available only to whites because of the racist character of the larger society. Presumably, if blacks had been paid their fair share (i.e., at the same rates as whites doing equivalent jobs) during these centuries for the services they rendered to white employers, there would have been proportionately less wealth now in the control of the white churches, and the position of blacks today would be more nearly that of whites as well.

Blacks, we know, arrived on these shores virtually penniless and with few exceptions remained that way generation after generation, thanks to the repressive forces harnessed in slavery. Economic research, theoretically at least, should be able to give us estimates at, say, fifty-year intervals throughout our entire history and at decennial intervals during the past century of the total wealth in the control of corporate black America and corporate white America, respectively. If we were to plot these data on a graph, so as to get a representation of the economic growth rate of blacks versus whites in America since the earliest days, we know without any question both that *(a)* the rate of slope for black growth would be much shallower than for whites, and that *(b)* the growth curve for blacks would start at the point of origin on the graph and remain nearly there for decades, whereas the comparable curve for whites would begin above zero and without faltering would continue to rise. What we don't know and could not calculate is the shape the curve for blacks would have taken had they been free men from the start and had they suffered discriminations in degree and in kind no worse than the average of those discriminations imposed by the dominant white groups upon the immigrant white groups. We might get some idea of what that curve would look like by plotting, if we could, on our graph the economic growth rate for every other identifiable ethnic group which has landed on these shores. One can assert with fair confidence that *(a)* and *(b)* above will be true no matter what white ethnic group's growth rate curve is compared with the blacks!

Given, then, that The Manifesto's argument is entitled to rely upon proof of continuous severe racial discrimination by whites against blacks in this country, proof of continuous severe economic disadvantages for blacks as against whites, proof that the latter is in considerable part explained by the former, the only fundamental question which remains is whether $500 million (or $3 billion, or any given amount) can be said to be an adequate measure of the reparations owed, given the cost to blacks of their losses and the unjust wealth accrued by whites and transferred to their churches? The only honest thing one can say is that we do not know whether it is or whether it isn't.[24] Between ludicrous extremes (such as asking for $10,000 in reparation, or asking for black control of the total wealth and income of all the churches) there are many equally plausible sums to fix upon, because our economic knowledge about the matters discussed in this and the preceding paragraph is too vague for more precision. Both $500 million and $3 billion seem to me to be within that plausible range and not at all ludicrous. Beyond that I cannot venture. One sympathizes with the predicament of white church leaders and the black authors of The Manifesto, for none of them has knowledge on these economic questions adequate to being more confident and more precise than I have been.

Yet further difficulties beyond the ten objections I have discussed can be imagined. It might be argued that if whites as a class are liable to blacks as a class for reparations, then not even if all voluntary nongovernmental white institutions make reparations will all whites have paid their fair share; only the government, through the use of its tax monies, can truly compensate blacks for centuries of slavery, injury, and degradation. Or, as another objection, one might urge that the entire argument of The Manifesto, resting as it does, upon the concept of desert, is anachronistic, because desert is a concept of declining relevance in the adjustment of social relations where inequalities suffered on the scale of those which burden American blacks are concerned.[25] Or one could argue that The Manifesto constitutes an example of what has elsewhere been called "inflated desert" claims; that is, The Manifesto commits the fallacy of inferring from the true conclusion that blacks as a class *deserve* reparations to the unproved further conclusion that blacks as a class *ought* to be paid $3 billion in reparations.[26] Or, to mention a fourth possibility, one might object that

> . . . the Negro's past suffering seems beyond the remedy of society to redeem. There is no payment that can supply its balance. It would be a sign of contempt for the Negro should the white community offer to compensate this debt, for there are trials of the spirit too large and awesome to stand comparison with any good that might be proposed as their measure. . . . The strictly compensatory act of payment for *past* suffering is impossible. . . . [27]

There is no end to the objections that might be raised.

Perhaps, however, it is enough to have come as far as we have. I hope I have shown what the basic structure of the argument of The Black Manifesto is, and that although it can be subjected to various criticisms, these in turn, with varying degrees of finality, can be rebutted. Little I could add now would make the argument significantly more persuasive for those to whom it is addressed. Nor do I wish to stand in impartial judgment on the demands of The Manifesto and deliver any final verdict. Once in a while, at least, it ought to be enough for philosophers to try to understand and not at the same time to judge, much less change, the world.[28]

HUGO ADAM BEDAU

TUFTS UNIVERSITY
JUNE, 1971

NOTES

[1] See, however, Murray Kempton, "The Black Manifesto," *New York Review of Books,* July 10, 1969, pp. 31-33; Michael Harrington and Arnold S. Kaufman, "Black Reparations—Two Views," *Dissent* (1969), pp. 317-20; Robert S. Lecky and H. Elliot Wright, eds., *Black Manifesto: Religion, Racism, and Reparations* (New York: Sheed and Ward, 1969); Arnold Schuchter, *Reparations* (Philadelphia: Lippincott, 1970).

[2] The Manifesto, said Murray Kempton (p. 31), is "not so much argument as incantation"; according to Michael Harrington, it is an "outlandish scheme" (p. 317), and an "impossible vision" (p. 318).

[3] All page references are to the version published by Lecky and Wright, *Black Manifesto,* pp. 114-26. The full text is also available in Kempton, and in Schuchter.

[4] The chief difference between compensatory and distributive justice lies in whether the recipient deserves a benefit on account of, respectively, some injury he has suffered or on some other ground, e.g., his right to a fair share. Recent discussions of justice by Rawls, Rescher, Runciman and others have not adequately developed the relation between compensation and distribution. Indeed, thanks to the notion of redistributive justice, the contrast between the two may even seem to break down. See Bertrand de Jouvenal, *The Ethics of Redistribution* (Cambridge: Cambridge University Press, 1951).

[5] Thus, Michael Harrington objected to The Black Manifesto mainly on the ground that taking it seriously would "divert precious political energies from the actual struggle" to remedy "unequal income distribution in America" (p. 318). Murray Kempton went even farther in the direction of repudiating the apparent burden of The Manifesto, for he insisted that its "indictment" was "not of a genuine deprivation but of a totally fancied reward" (p. 31). Arnold Kaufman, while emphasizing the legitimacy of its literal compensatory nature, endorsed the argument because he thought it would "strengthen . . . the political will to support vast enlargement of compensatory *governmental* programs" (p. 319; italics in original). Similarly, Calvin B. Marshall, chairman of the Black Economic Development Conference, has criticized the failure of the churches to respond to The Manifesto's appeal as evidence of their "refusing to consider human need . . ." (*New York Times,* June 10, 1970, p. 53). But "human need," like "unequal income distribution," and the rest, are not concepts central to an argument for *reparations* and *compensatory* justice.

[6] Lecky and Wright, *Black Manifesto,* p. 126.

[7] For a discussion of the difference between the idea of (criminal) guilt and the idea of (civil) liability, and of the need to confine corporate responsibility to the latter, see Joel Feinberg, "Collective Responsibility," in his *Doing and Deserving* (Princeton: Princeton University Press, 1970), pp. 231-33.

[8] This point is persuasively argued by William Stringfellow, "Reparations: Repentance As a Necessity to Reconciliation," in Lecky and Wright, *Black Manifesto,* pp. 52-64.

[9] The "Introduction" to The Manifesto does speak of "taking the wealth away from the rich people such as General Motors, Ford, Chrysler, the DuPonts, the Rockefellers, the Mellons . . ." (p. 117). The Manifesto continues, ". . . we are dedicated to building a socialist society inside the United States where the total means of production and distribution are in the hands of the State . . ." (p. 118).

[10] ". . . The common image of Marx as a prophet of social justice is a false one. . . . To Marx's mind . . . socialists like Proudhon who preached social justice . . . were misguided because they failed to see the irrelevance of the idea of justice to the social problem." Robert Tucker, "Marx and Distributive Justice," in *Nomos VI: Justice,* ed. by Carl J. Friedrich and John M. Chapman (New York: Atherton Press, 1963), pp. 309, 323.

[11] See Schuchter, *Reparations, passim,* and esp. Appendix B, "Slavery and the Churches."

[12] Lecky and Wright, *Black Manifesto,* p. 126.

[13] In the first year after it released The Manifesto, B. E. D. C. admitted it had raised only 1/170 of the $500 million originally sought from the churches. It was also reported, however, that as much as one-third of the total had been pledged. *New York Times* (see n. 5 above).

[14] Kaufman, "Black Reparations—Two Views," p. 319.

[15] I have tried to set out those principles in a general analysis of compensatory justice in another paper (unpublished), versions of which were presented to several audiences in conjunction with earlier versions of this paper.

[16] John W. Wade, *Cases and Materials on Restitution,* 2d ed. (Brooklyn, New York: Foundation Press, 1966), p. 1198.

[17] Ibid., p. 1212.

[18] Ibid., pp. 455-56.

[19] Lecky and Wright, *Black Manifesto,* p. 116; cf. p. 117.

[20] See, e.g., Dee Brown, *Bury My Heart at Wounded Knee* (New York: Harper, Row and Winston, 1971) and Vin de Loria, ed., *Of Utmost Good Faith* (San Francisco: World Publishing Co., 1971). Much the same point has been made, along with other valuable suggestions, in Graham Hughes, "Reparations for Blacks?" *New York University Law Review,* **43** (1968), pp. 1063-74.

[21] See Lecky and Wright, *Black Manifesto,* p. 50, and *New York Times* (see n. 5 above).

[22] For evidence as to the wealth of the churches in the United States, see Lecky and Wright, *Black Manifesto,* p. 176, and Schuchter, *Reparations,* pp. 175-78.

[23] See, e.g., Eric Williams, *Capitalism and Slavery* (New York: Capricorn Books, 1966) and Robert S. Starobin, *Industrial Slavery in the Old South* (New York: Oxford University Press, 1971).

[24] If we were not required to use the model of unjust enrichment, we could take a very different approach to this question. It is clear from actual cases at law where compensation is successfully sought for incommensurables (e.g., an eye blinded in industrial accident, a reputation damaged by libel or slander), the injured party can accept a certain sum as his indemnity and it will be adequate to compensate him for his loss if he decides that it is. It does not follow from this that an eye is "worth" $10,000, or an unsullied reputation "worth" $50,000, because these sums are not to be construed as measures of the value of the thing, but only as compensation for injury to them, and an imperfect remedy at best.

[25] Cf. Brian Barry, *Political Argument* (New York: Humanities Press, 1965), p. 113.

[26] Cf. Joel Feinberg, "Justice and Personal Desert," in Friedrich and Chapman, eds., *Nomos VI,* p. 94.

[27] Richard Lichtman, "The Ethics of Compensatory Justice," *Law in Transition Quarterly,* **1** (1964), 87; italics in original. Professor Lichtman has informed me that his current views on these issues are very different from what they were when he wrote this essay.

[28] Earlier versions of this paper were read before a number of audiences during 1970 and 1971. I am especially grateful for stimulus and criticism to many colleagues who discussed it with me at colloquia arranged by the Departments of Philosophy at the University of Waterloo and at the University of Michigan, by faculty at Boston College Law School, and at the Boston Area Political Theory Conference.

M. P. GOLDING

OBLIGATIONS
TO FUTURE GENERATIONS *

The purpose of this note[1] is to examine the notion of obligations to future generations, a notion that finds increasing use in discussions of social policies and programs, particularly as concerns population distribution and control and environment control. Thus, it may be claimed, the solution of problems in these areas is not merely a matter of enhancing our own good, improving our own conditions of life, but is also a matter of discharging an obligation to future generations.

Before I turn to the question of the basis of such obligations—the necessity of the plural is actually doubtful—there are three general points to be considered: (1) Who are the individuals in whose regard it is maintained that we have such obligations, to whom do we owe such obligations? (2) What, essentially, do obligations to future generations oblige us to do, what are they aimed at? and (3), To what class of obligation do such obligations belong, what kind of obligation are they? Needless to say, in examining a notion of this sort, which is used in everyday discussion and polemic, one must be mindful of the danger of taking it—or making it out to be more precise than it is in reality.

This cautionary remark seems especially appropriate in connection with the first of the above points. But the determination of the purview of obligations to future generations is both ethically and practically significant.

* From the "Philosophy and Public Policy" issue of *The Monist*, **56**, No. 1 (January, 1972), published by the Open Court Publishing Company.

It seems clear, at least, who does not come within their purview. Obligations to future generations are distinct from the obligations we have to our presently living fellows, who are therefore excluded from the purview of the former, although it might well be the case that *what* we owe to future generations is identical with (or overlaps) what we owe to the present generation. However, I think we may go further than this and also exclude our most immediate descendants, our children, grandchildren and greatgrandchildren, perhaps. What is distinctive about the notion of obligations to future generations is, I think, that it refers to generations with which the possessors of the obligations cannot expect in a literal sense to share a common life. (Of course, if we have obligations to future generations, understood in this way, we a fortiori have obligations to immediate posterity.) This, at any rate, is how I shall construe the reference of such obligations; neither our present fellows nor our immediate posterity come within their purview. What can be the basis of our obligations toward individuals with whom we cannot expect to share a common life is a question I shall consider shortly.

But if their inner boundary be drawn in this way, what can we say about their outer limits? Is there a cutoff point for the individuals in whose regard we have such obligations? Here, it seems, there are two alternatives. First, we can flatly say that there are no outer limits to their purview: all future generations come within their province. A second and more modest answer would be that we do not have such obligations towards any assignable future generation. In either case the referent is a broad and unspecified community of the future, and I think it can be shown that we run into difficulties unless certain qualifications are taken into account.

Our second point concerns the question of what it is that obligations to future generations oblige us to do. The short answer is that they oblige us to do many things. But an intervening step is required here, for obligations to future generations are distinct from general duties to perform acts which are in themselves intrinsically right, although such obligations give rise to duties to perform specific acts. Obligations to future generations are essentially an obligation to produce—or to attempt to produce—a desirable state of affairs *for* the community of the future, to promote conditions of good living for future generations. The many things that we are obliged to do are founded upon this obligation (which is why I earlier questioned the necessity of the plural). If we think we have an obligation to transmit our cultural heritage to future generations it is because we think that our cultural heritage promotes, or perhaps even embodies, good living. In so doing we would hardly wish to falsify the records of our civilization, for future generations must also have, as a condition of good living, the opportunity to learn from the mistakes of the past. If, in addition, we believe lying to be intrinsically wrong we would also refrain from falsifying the records; but this would not be because we think we have any special duty to tell the truth to future generations.

To come closer to contemporary discussion, consider, for example, population control, which is often grounded upon an obligation to future generations. It is not maintained that population control is intrinsically right—although the rhetoric frequently seems to approach such a claim—but rather that it will contribute towards a better life for future generations, and perhaps immediate posterity as well. (If population control were intrinsically anything, I would incline to thinking it intrinsically wrong.) On the other hand, consider the elimination of water and air pollution. Here it might be maintained that we have a definite duty to cease polluting the environment on the grounds that such pollution is intrinsically bad[2] or that it violates a Divine command. Given the current mood of neopaganism, even secularists speak of the despoilment of the environment as a sacrilege of sorts. When the building of a new dam upsets the ecological balance and puts the wildlife under a threat, we react negatively and feel that something bad has resulted. And this is not because we necessarily believe that our own interests or those of future generations have been undermined. Both views, but especially the latter (Divine command), represent men as holding sovereignty over nature only as trustees to whom not everything is permitted. Nevertheless, these ways of grounding the duty to care for the environment are distinguishable from a grounding of the duty upon an obligation to future generations, although one who acknowledges such an obligation will also properly regard himself as a trustee to whom not everything is permitted. Caring for the environment is presumably among the many things that the obligation to future generations obliges us to do because we thereby presumably promote conditions of good living for the community of the future.

The obligation—dropping the plural again for a moment—to future generations, then, is not an immediate catalogue of specific duties. It is in this respect rather like the responsibility that a parent has to see to the welfare of his child. Discharging one's parental responsibility requires concern, seeking, and active effort to promote the good *of* the child, which is the central obligation of the parent and out of which grow the specific parental obligations and duties. The use of the term "responsibility" to characterize the parent's obligation connotes, in part, the element of discretion and flexibility which is requisite to the discharging of the obligation in a variety of antecedently unforseeable situations. Determination of the specific duty is often quite problematic even—and sometimes especially—for the conscientious parent who is anxious to do what is good for his child. And, anticipating my later discussion, this also holds for obligations to future generations. There are, of course, differences, too. Parental responsibility is enriched and reinforced by love, which can hardly obtain between us and future generations.[3] (Still, the very fact that the responsibility to promote the child's good is an obligation means that it is expected to operate even in the absence of love.) Secondly, the parental obligation is always towards assignable individuals, which is not the case with obligations to future generations. There is, however, an additional feature of likeness between the two obligations which I shall mention shortly.

The third point about obligations to future generations—to what class of obligation do they belong?—is that they are *owed*, albeit owed to an unspecified, and perhaps unspecifiable, community of the future. Obligations to future generations, therefore, are distinct from a general duty, when presented with alternatives for action, to choose the act which produces the greatest good. Such a duty is not owed to anyone, and the beneficiaries of my fulfilling a duty to promote the greatest good are not necessarily individuals to whom I stand in the moral relation of having an obligation that is owed. But when I owe it to someone to promote his good, he is never, to this extent, merely an incidental beneficiary of my effort to fulfill the obligation. He has a presumptive *right* to it and can assert a claim against me for it. Obligations to future generations are of this kind. There is something which is due to the community of the future from us. The moral relation between us and future generations is one in which they have a claim against us to promote their good. Future generations are, thus, possessors of presumptive rights.

This conclusion is surely odd. How can future generations—the not-yet-born—*now* have claims against us? This question serves to turn us finally to consider the basis of our obligations to future generations. I think it useful to begin by discussing and removing one source of the oddity.

It should first be noticed that there is no oddity in investing present effort in order to promote a future state of affairs or in having an owed obligation to do so. The oddity arises only on a theory of obligations and claims (and, hence, of rights) that virtually identifies them with acts of willing, with the exercise of sovereignty of one over another, with the pressing of demands—in a word, with *making* claims. But, clearly future generations are not now engaged in acts of willing, are not now exercising sovereignty over us, and are not now pressing their demands. Future generations are not now making claims against us, nor will it be *possible* for them to do so. (Our immediate posterity is in this last respect in a different case.) However, the identification of claims with making claims, demanding, is plausible within the field of rights and obligations because the content of a system of rights is historically conditioned by the making of claims. Individuals and groups put forward their claims to the goods of life, demand them as their right; and in this way the content is increasingly expanded towards the inclusion of more of these goods.

Nevertheless, as suggestive a clue as this fact is for the development of a theory of rights, there is a distinction to be drawn between *having* claims and *making* claims. The mere fact that someone claims something from me is not sufficient to establish it as his right, or that he has a claim relative to me. On the other hand, someone may have a claim relative to me whether or not he makes the claim, demands, or is even able to make a claim. (This is not to deny that claiming plays a role in the theory of rights.) Two points require attention here. First, some claims are frivolous. What is demanded cannot really be claimed as a matter of right. The crucial factor in determining this is the *social ideal*, which we may provisionally define as a conception of the good life for man. It serves as the yardstick by which demands, current and potential, are measured.[4] Secondly, whether someone's claim confers an entitlement upon him to receive what is claimed *from me* depends upon my moral relation to him, on whether he is a member of my *moral community*. It is these factors, rather than any actual demanding, which establish whether someone has a claim relative to me. (I should like to emphasize that I am not necessarily maintaining that the concepts of a social ideal and a moral community are involved in a theory of every kind of obligation, but, rather, that they are required by the kind of obligation being considered here.)

The concepts of a social ideal and a moral community are clearly in need of further explanation, yet as they stand the above considerations should serve to relieve a good deal of the oddity that is felt in the assertion that future generations now have claims against us and that they are possessors of presumptive rights. There is, however, a residual sense of peculiarity in the assertion because it still remains to be shown whether future generations are members of our moral community. A discussion of the question of membership in a moral community will, I think, shed light on these subjects.

Who are the members of my moral community? (Who is my neighbor?) The fact is that I am a member of more than one moral community, for I belong to a variety of groups whose members owe obligations to one another. And many of the particular obligations that are owed vary from group to group. As a result my obligations are often in conflict and I experience a fragmentation of energy and responsibility in attempting to meet my obligations. What I ought to desire for the members of one of these groups is frequently in opposition to what I ought to desire for the members of another of these groups. Moral communities are constituted, or generated, in a number of ways, one of which is especially relevant to our problem. Yet these ways are not mutually exclusive, and they can be mutually reenforcing. This is a large topic and I cannot go into its details here. It is sufficient for our purpose to take brief notice of two possible ways of generating a moral community so as to set in relief the particular kind of moral community that is requisite for obligations to future generations.

A moral community may be constituted by an explicit contract between its members. In this case the particular obligations which the members have towards each other are fixed by the terms of their bargain. Secondly, a moral community may be generated out of a social arrangement in which each member derives benefits from the efforts of other members. As a result a member acquires an obligation to share the burden of sustaining the social arrangement. Both of these are communities in which entrance and participation are fundamentally a matter of self-interest, and only rarely will there be an obligation of the sort that was discussed earlier, that is, a responsibility to secure the good of the members. In general the obligations will be of more specialized kinds. It is also apparent that obligations acquired in these ways can easily come into conflict with other obligations that one may have. Clearly, a moral community comprised of present and future generations cannot arise from either of these sources. We cannot enter into an explicit contract with the community of the future. And although future generations might derive benefits from us, these benefits cannot be reciprocated. (It is possible that the [biologically] dead do derive *some* benefits from the living, but I do not think that this possibility is crucial. Incidentally, just as the living could have obligations to the distant unborn, the living also have obligations to the dead. If obligation to the past is a superstition, then so is obligation to the future.)[5] Our immediate posterity, who will share a common life with us, are in a better position in this respect; so that obligations towards our children, born and unborn, conceivably *could* be generated from participation in a mutually beneficial social arrangement. This, however, would be misleading.

It seems, then, that communities in which entrance and participation are fundamentally matters of self-interest, do not fit our specifications. As an alternative let us consider communities based upon altruistic impulses and fellow-feeling. This, too, is in itself a large topic, and I refer to it only in order to develop a single point.

The question I began with was: Who are the members of my moral community? Now it is true that there are at least a few people towards whom I have the sentiments that are identified with altruism and sympathetic concern. But are these sentiments enough to establish for me the moral relationship of owing them an obligation? Are these enough to generate a moral community? The answer, I think, must be in the negative so long as these affections towards others remain at the level of animal feeling. The ancient distinction between mere affection, mere liking, and conscious desire is fundamental here. Genuine concern and interest in the well-being of another must be conscious concern. My desire for another's good must in this event be more than impulsive, and presupposes, rather, that I have a *conception* of his good. This conception, which cannot be a bare concept of what is incidentally a good but which is rather a conception of the good *for* him, further involves that he not be a mere blank to me but that he is characterized or described in some way in my consciousness. It is perhaps unnecessary to add that there is never any absolute guarantee that such a conceived good is not, in some sense, false or fragmentary. Nevertheless, an altruism that is literally mindless—if it can be called "altruism" at all—cannot be the basis of moral community.

But even if it be granted that I have a conception of another's good, I have not yet reached the stage of obligation towards him. We are all familiar with the kind of "taking an interest in the welfare of another" that is gracious and giftlike, a matter of *noblesse oblige*. It is not so much that this type of interest-taking tends to be casual, fleeting and fragmentary—*"cette charité froide qui on nomme altruisme"*—and stands in contrast to interest-taking that is constant, penetrating and concerned with the other's total good. It is, rather, a form of interest-taking, however "conceptual," that is a manifestation of an unreadiness or even an unwillingness to recognize the other's claim (as distinct, of course, from his claiming), the other's entitlement, to receive his good from me. An additional step is, therefore, required, and I think it consists in this: that I acknowledge this good as a good, that his good is good-to-me. Once I have made this step, I cannot in conscience deny the pertinence of his demand, if he makes one, although whether I should now act so as to promote his good is of course dependent on a host of factors. (Among these factors are moral considerations that determine the permissibility of various courses of action and priorities of duty.) The basis of the obligation is nevertheless secured.

This conclusion, it should be clear, does not entail that I am required to concede the status of an entitlement to every demand that is made by someone in whose well-being I have an interest. Some claims (claimings), as remarked above, are frivolous. The test of this, in the case we have been considering, is my conception of the other's good. This conception is a model in miniature of what I earlier called a *social ideal*. However, the provisional definition of it—a conception of the good life for man—was unnecessarily broad. In using this term, I mean, first of all, to contrast the ideal with a personal ideal of the good life. A personal ideal of the good life is an ideal that is not necessarily maintained as desirable for others to seek to achieve. It is what an individual, given his unique interests and idiosyncrasies, sees as the private end of his striving; while it does not necessarily exclude elements of sociality, it is not social in its purview. By the term "social ideal," however, I mean primarily a conception of the good life for individuals under some general characterization and which can be maintained by them as good for them in virtue of this characterization. The term covers the possibility of a social ideal that is a conception of the good life for individuals characterized in the broadest terms, namely, as human. But a social ideal may be narrower in its scope. For example, one may have a conception of the good life for the city dweller or for the outdoors type. Since it is possible for me to maintain as good-to-me a variety of ideals bearing upon groups of individuals characterized in different ways, it is possible for me to be a member of more than one moral community. It is in such circumstances, as mentioned earlier, that I will experience the conflicting pulls of obligation and competing claims upon my energy and effort.

(There is admittedly much more to be said in explanation of the nature of social ideals, for they need not be static. The implications of our ideals are not always immediately available, and they are enriched and clarified through experience. They are adaptable to new life-circumstances. And they can also become impoverished. Just as ideals are not static, neither are the characterizations of the individuals to whom the ideals are meant to apply. Another topic that requires further study is the "logic" of the ideal-claim relationship, a study of the ways in which ideals confer entitlements upon claims. Questions also arise concerning justice and reciprocity. This list could be extended; it is only meant to be suggestive. I make no pretence that I am able to solve these problems at this time.)

So far, in the above account of the generation of my moral community, the question of membership has been discussed solely in reference to those towards whom I initially have the sentiments that are identified with fellow-feeling. But we can go beyond this. Again we take our clue from the history of the development of rights. For just as the content of a system of rights that are possessed by the members of a moral community is enlarged over time by the pressing of claims, demanding, so also is the moral community enlarged by the pressing of claims by individuals who have been hitherto excluded. The claiming is not only a claim for something, but may also be an assertion: "Here I am, I count too." The struggle for rights has also been a counterstruggle. The widening of moral communities has been accompanied by attempts at exclusion. It is important for us to take note of one feature of this situation.

The structure of the situation is highlighted when a stranger puts forward his demand. The question immediately arises, shall his claim be recognized as a matter of right?[6] Initially I have no affection for him. But is this crucial in determining whether he ought to count as a member of my moral community? The determination depends, rather, on what he is like and what are the conditions of his life. One's obligations to a stranger are never immediately clear. If a visitor from Mars or Venus were to appear, I would not know what to desire for him. I would not know whether my conception of the good life is relevant to him and to his conditions of life. The good that I acknowledge might not be good for him. Humans, of course, are in a better case than Martians or Venusians. Still, since the stranger appears as strange, different, what I maintain in my attempt to exclude him is that my conception of the good is not relevant to him, that "his kind" do not count. He, on the other hand, is in effect saying to me: Given your social ideal, you must acknowledge my claim, for it *is* relevant to me given what I am; your good is my good, also.[7] If I should finally come to concede this, the full force of my obligation to him will be manifest to me quite independently of any fellow-feeling that might or might not be aroused. The *involuntary* character of the obligation will be clear to me, as it probably never is in the case of individuals who command one's sympathy. And once I admit him as a member of my moral community, I will also acknowledge my responsibility to secure this good for him even in the absence of any future claiming on his part.

With this we have completed the account of the constitution of the type of moral community that is required for obligations to future generations. I shall not recapitulate its elements. The step that incorporates future generations into our moral community is small and obvious. Future generations are members of our moral community because, and insofar as, our social ideal is relevant to them, given what they are and their conditions of life. I believe that this account applies also to obligations towards our immediate posterity. However, the responsibility that one has to see to the welfare of his children is in addition buttressed and qualified by social understandings concerning the division of moral labor and by natural affection. The basis of the obligations is nevertheless the same in both instances.[8] Underlying this account is the important fact that such obligations fall into the area of the moral life which is independent of considerations of explicit contract and personal advantage. Moral duty and virtue also fall into this area. But I should like to emphasize again that I do not wish to be understood as putting this account forward as an analysis of moral virtue and duty in general.

As we turn at long last specifically to our obligations to future generations, it is worth noticing that the term "contract" has been used to cover the kind of moral community that I have been discussing. It occurs in a famous passage in Burke's *Reflections on the Revolution in France:*

> Society is indeed a contract. Subordinate contracts for objects of mere occasional interest may be dissolved at pleasure—but the state ought not to be considered as nothing better than a partnership agreement in a trade of pepper and coffee, calico or tobacco, or some other such low concern, to be taken up for a little temporary interest, and to be dissolved by the fancy of the parties. It is to be looked upon with other reverence; because it is not a partnership in things subservient only to the gross animal existence of a temporary and perishable nature.
>
> It is a partnership in all science; a partnership in all art; a partnership in every virtue, and in all perfection. As the ends of such a partnership cannot be obtained in many generations, it becomes a partnership not only between those who are living, but between those who are living, those who are dead and those who are to be born.
>
> Each contract of each particular state is but a clause in the great primaeval contract of eternal society, linking the lower with the higher natures, connecting the visible and invisible world, according to a fixed compact sanctioned by the inviolable oath which holds all physical and all moral natures, each in their appointed place.[9]

The contract Burke has in mind is hardly an explicit contract, for it is "between those who are living, those who are dead and those who are to be born." He implicitly affirms, I think, obligations to future generations. In speaking of the "ends of such a partnership," Burke intends a conception of the good life for man—a social ideal. And, if I do not misinterpret him, I think it also plain that Burke assumes that it is relatively the same conception of the good life whose realization is the object of the efforts of the living, the dead, and the unborn. They all revere the same social ideal. Moreover, he seems to assume that the conditions of life of the three groups are more or less the same. And, finally, he seems to assume that the same general characterization is true of these groups ("all physical and moral natures, each in their appointed place").

Now I think that Burke is correct in making assumptions of these sorts if we are to have obligations to future generations. However, it is precisely with such assumptions that the notion of obligation to future generations begins to run into difficulties. My discussion, until this point, has proceeded on the view that we *have* obligations to future generations. But do we? I am not sure that the question can be answered in the affirmative with any certainty. I shall conclude this note with a very brief discussion of some of the difficulties. They may be summed up in the question: Is our conception—"conceptions" might be a more accurate word—of the good life for man relevant[10] to future generations?

It will be recalled that I began by stressing the importance of fixing the purview of obligations to future generations. They comprise the community of the future, a community with which we cannot expect to share a common life. It appears to me that the more *remote* the members of this community are, the more problematic our obligations to them become. That they are members of our moral community is highly doubtful, for we probably do not know what to desire for them.

Let us consider a concrete example, namely, that of the maintenance of genetic quality. Sir Julian Huxley has stated:

> [I]f we don't do something about controlling our genetic inheritance, we are going to degenerate. Without selection, bad mutations inevitably tend to accumulate; *in the long run, perhaps 5,000 to 10,000 years from now,* we [sic] shall certainly have to do something about it. . . . Most mutations are deleterious, but we now keep many of them going that would otherwise have died out. If this continues indefinitely . . . then the whole genetic capacity of man will be much weakened.[11]

This statement, and others like it, raise many issues. As I have elsewhere (see footnote 1) discussed the problems connected with eugenic programs, positive and negative, I shall not go into details here. The point I would make is this: given that we do not know the conditions of life of the very distant future generations, we do not know what we ought to desire for them even on such matters as genic constitution. The chromosome is "deleterious" or "advantageous" only relative to given circumstances. And the same argument applies against those who would promote certain social traits by means of genetic engineering (assuming that social traits are heritable). Even such a trait as Intelligence does not escape immune. (There are also problems in eugenic programs having nothing to do with remoteness.) One might go so far as to say that if we have an obligation to distant future generations it is an obligation not to plan for them. Not only do we not know their conditions of life, we also do not know whether they will maintain the same (or a similar) conception of the good life for man as we do. Can we even be fairly sure that the same general characterization is true both of them and us?

The moral to be drawn from this rather extreme example is that the more distant the generation we focus upon, the less likely it is that we have an obligation to promote its good. We would be both ethically and practically well advised to set our sights on more immediate generations and, perhaps, solely upon our immediate posterity. After all, even if we do have obligations to future generations, our obligations to immediate posterity are undoubtedly much clearer. The nearer the generations are to us, the more likely it is that our conception of the good life is relevant to them. There is certainly enough work for us to do in discharging our responsibility to promote a good life for them. But it would be unwise, both from an ethical and a practical perspective, to seek to promote the good of the very distant.

And it could also be *wrong* if it be granted—as I think it must—that our obligations towards (and hence the rights relative to us of) near future generations and especially our immediate posterity are clearer than those of more distant generations. By "more distant" I do not necessarily mean "very distant." We shall have to be highly scrupulous in regard to anything we do for any future generation that also could adversely affect the rights of an intervening generation. Anything else would be "gambling in futures." We should, therefore, be hesitant to act on the dire predictions of certain extreme "crisis ecologists" and on the proposals of those who would have us plan for mere survival. In the main, we would be ethically well advised to confine ourselves to removing the obstacles that stand in the way of immediate posterity's realizing the social ideal. This involves not only the active task of cleaning up the environment and making our cities more habitable, but also implies restraints upon us. Obviously, the specific obligations that we have cannot be determined in the abstract. This article is not the place for an evaluation of concrete proposals that have been made. I would only add that population limitation schemes seem rather dubious to me. I find it inherently paradoxical that we should have an obligation to future generations (near and distant) to determine in effect the very membership of those generations.[12]

A final point. If certain trends now apparent in our biological technology continue, it is doubtful that we should regard ourselves as being under an obligation to future generations. It seems likely that the man—humanoid (?)—of the future will be Programmed Man, fabricated to order, with his finger constantly on the Delgado button that stimulates the pleasure centers of the brain. I, for one, cannot see myself as regarding the good for Programmed Man as a good-to-me. That we should do so, however, is a necessary condition of his membership in our moral community, as I have argued above. The course of these trends may very well be determined by whether we believe that we are, in the words of Burke, "but a clause in the great primaeval contract of eternal society, linking the lower with the higher natures, connecting the visible and invisible world, according to a fixed compact sanctioned by the inviolable oath which holds all physical and all moral natures, each in their appointed place." We cannot yet pretend to know the outcome of these trends. It appears that whether we have obligations to future generations in part depends on what we do for the present.

M. P. GOLDING

CITY UNIVERSITY OF NEW YORK
JOHN JAY COLLEGE OF CRIMINAL JUSTICE
JANUARY, 1971

NOTES

[1] This paper is highly speculative, and it is put forward with hesitation. It is an attempt to extend a position developed in my article "Towards a Theory of Human Rights," *The Monist,* **52,** No. 4 (1968), 521-49, wherein I also discuss some of the classical and contemporary literature on Rights. See also my paper, "Ethical Issues in Biological Engineering," *U.C.L.A. Law Review,* **15** (1968), 443-79, esp. 451-63, wherein I discuss obligations to future generations and some of the problems they provoke. I know of no other explicit discussion of the topic. The author wishes to thank the Institute of Society, Ethics, and the Life Sciences (Hastings-on-Hudson, New York) for its support.

[2] See the remarks of Russell E. Train (Chairman of the Council on Environmental Quality), quoted in *National Geographic,* **138** (1970), 780: "If we're to be responsible we must accept the fact that we owe a massive debt to our environment. It won't be settled in a matter of months, and it won't be forgiven us."

[3] Cf. the discussion of *Fernstenliebe* (Love of the Remotest) in Nicolai Hartmann, *Ethics,* trans. by Coit (New York: The Macmillan Co., 1932), Vol. II, pp. 317 ff.

[4] There is also another factor relevant to determining whether what is demanded can be claimed as a matter of right, namely, the availability of resources of goods. But I am suppressing this for purposes of this discussion.

[5] Paraphrasing C. S. Lewis, *The Abolition of Man* (New York: The Macmillan Co., paperback ed. 1969), p. 56: "If my duty to my parents is a superstition, then so is my duty to posterity."

[6] When Sarah died, Abraham "approached the children of Heth, saying: I am a stranger and a sojourner with you; give me a possession of a burying-place with you, that I may bury my dead out of my sight" (Gen. 23:3, 4). A classical commentary remarks that Abraham is saying: If I am a stranger, I will purchase it, but if I am a sojourner it is mine as a matter of right.

[7] Cf. T. H. Green, *Lectures on the Principles of Political Obligation* (New York and London: Longman's, 1959; Ann Arbor: University of Michigan Press, 1967), Sec. 140. I here acknowledge my debt to Green, in which acknowledgment I was remiss in my article on Human Rights.

[8] I think it an interesting commentary on our times that the rhetoric of obligation to future generations is so much used just when the family bond has become progressively tenuous.

[9] Edmund Burke, *Reflections on the Revolution in France* (London: Dent, 1910), pp. 93-94.

[10] The author at last begs pardon for having to use such an abused word.

[11] In *Evolution after Darwin,* ed. by S. Tax (Chicago: University of Chicago Press, 1960), Vol. III, p. 61. Emphasis added.

[12] On this and other arguments relating to the problem, see Martin P. Golding and Naomi H. Golding, "Ethical and Value Issues in Population Limitation and Distribution in The United States," *Vanderbilt Law Review,* **24** (1971), 495-523.

.

GERALD DWORKIN

PATERNALISM*

"Neither one person, nor any number of
persons, is warranted in saying to another
human creature of ripe years, that he shall
not do with his life for his own benefit what
he chooses to do with it."

MILL

"I do not want to go along with a volunteer
basis. I think a fellow should be compelled
to become better and not let him use his
discretion whether he wants to get smarter,
more healthy or more honest."

GENERAL HERSHEY

I take as my starting point the "one very simple principle" proclaimed
by Mill in *On Liberty* . . . "That principle is, that the sole end for which
mankind are warranted, individually or collectively, in interfering with the
liberty of action of any of their number, is self-protection. That the only purpose for which power can be rightfully exercised over any member of a civilized community, against his will, is to prevent harm to others. He cannot
rightfully be compelled to do or forbear because it will be better for him to do
so, because it will make him happier, because, in the opinion of others, to do
so would be wise, or even right."[1]

* From the "Philosophy and Public Policy" issue of *The Monist,* **56,** No. 1 (January, 1972),
published by the Open Court Publishing Company.

This principle is neither "one" nor "very simple." It is at least two principles; one asserting that self-protection or the prevention of harm to others is sometimes a sufficient warrant and the other claiming that the individual's own good is *never* a sufficient warrant for the exercise of compulsion either by the society as a whole or by its individual members. I assume that no one with the possible exception of extreme pacifists or anarchists questions the correctness of the first half of the principle. This essay is an examination of the negative claim embodied in Mill's principle—the objection to paternalistic interferences with a man's liberty.

I

By paternalism I shall understand roughly the interference with a person's liberty of action justified by reasons referring exclusively to the welfare, good, happiness, needs, interests or values of the person being coerced. One is always well advised to illustrate one's definitions by examples but it is not easy to find "pure" examples of paternalistic interferences. For almost any piece of legislation is justified by several different kinds of reasons and even if historically a piece of legislation can be shown to have been introduced for purely paternalistic motives, it may be that advocates of the legislation with an antipaternalistic outlook can find sufficient reasons justifying the legislation without appealing to the reasons which were originally adduced to support it. Thus, for example, it may be that the original legislation requiring motorcyclists to wear safety helmets was introduced for purely paternalistic reasons. But the Rhode Island Supreme Court recently upheld such legislation on the grounds that it was "not persuaded that the legislature is powerless to prohibit individuals from pursuing a course of conduct which could conceivably result in their becoming public charges," thus clearly introducing reasons of a quite different kind. Now I regard this decision as being based on reasoning of a very dubious nature but it illustrates the kind of problem one has in finding examples. The following is a list of the kinds of interferences I have in mind as being paternalistic.

II

1. Laws requiring motorcyclists to wear safety helmets when operating their machines.
2. Laws forbidding persons from swimming at a public beach when lifeguards are not on duty.
3. Laws making suicide a criminal offense.

4. Laws making it illegal for women and children to work at certain types of jobs.
5. Laws regulating certain kinds of sexual conduct, e.g. homosexuality among consenting adults in private.
6. Laws regulating the use of certain drugs which may have harmful consequences to the user but do not lead to antisocial conduct.
7. Laws requiring a license to engage in certain professions with those not receiving a license subject to fine or jail sentence if they do engage in the practice.
8. Laws compelling people to spend a specified fraction of their income on the purchase of retirement annuities (Social Security).
9. Laws forbidding various forms of gambling (often justified on the grounds that the poor are more likely to throw away their money on such activities than the rich who can afford to).
10. Laws regulating the maximum rates of interest for loans.
11. Laws against duelling.

In addition to laws which attach criminal or civil penalties to certain kinds of action there are laws, rules, regulations, decrees, which make it either difficult or impossible for people to carry out their plans and which are also justified on paternalistic grounds. Examples of this are:

1. Laws regulating the types of contracts which will be upheld as valid by the courts, e.g. (an example of Mill's to which I shall return) no man may make a valid contract for perpetual involuntary servitude.
2. Not allowing as a defense to a charge of murder or assault the consent of the victim.
3. Requiring members of certain religious sects to have compulsory blood transfusions. This is made possible by not allowing the patient to have recourse to civil suits for assault and battery and by means of injunctions.
4. Civil commitment procedures when these are specifically justified on the basis of preventing the person being committed from harming himself. (The D.C. Hospitalization of the Mentally Ill Act provides for involuntary hospitalization of a person who "is mentally ill, and because of that illness, is likely to injure *himself* or others if allowed to remain at liberty." The term injure in this context applies to unintentional as well as intentional injuries.)
5. Putting fluorides in the community water supply.

All of my examples are of existing restrictions on the liberty of individuals. Obviously one can think of interferences which have not yet been imposed. Thus one might ban the sale of cigarettes, or require that people wear safety belts in automobiles (as opposed to merely having them installed) enforcing this by not allowing motorists to sue for injuries even when caused by other drivers if the motorist was not wearing a seat belt at the time of the accident.

I shall not be concerned with activities which though defended on paternalistic grounds are not interferences with the liberty of persons, e.g. the giving of subsidies in kind rather than in cash on the grounds that the recipients would not spend the money on the goods which they really need, or not including a $1000 deductible provision in a basic protection automobile insurance plan on the ground that the people who would elect it could least afford it. Nor shall I be concerned with measures such as "truth-in-advertising" acts and the Pure Food and Drug legislation which are often attacked as paternalistic but which should not be considered so. In these cases all that is provided—it is true by the use of compulsion—is information which it is presumed that rational persons are interested in having in order to make wise decisions. There is no interference with the liberty of the consumer unless one wants to stretch a point beyond good sense and say that his liberty to apply for a loan without knowing the true rate of interest is diminished. It is true that sometimes there is sentiment for going further than providing information, for example when laws against usurious interest are passed preventing those who might wish to contract loans at high rates of interest from doing so, and these measures may correctly be considered paternalistic.

III

Bearing these examples in mind let me return to a characterization of paternalism. I said earlier that I meant by the term, roughly, interference with a person's liberty for his own good. But as some of the examples show the class of persons whose good is involved is not always identical with the class of persons whose freedom is restricted. Thus in the case of professional licensing it is the practitioner who is directly interfered with and it is the would-be patient whose interests are presumably being served. Not allowing the consent of the victim to be a defense to certain types of crime primarily affects the would-be aggressor but it is the interests of the willing victim that we are trying to protect. Sometimes a person may fall into both classes as would be the case if we banned the manufacture and sale of cigarettes and a given manufacturer happened to be a smoker as well.

Thus we may first divide paternalistic interferences into "pure" and "impure" cases. In "pure" paternalism the class of persons whose freedom is restricted is identical with the class of persons whose benefit is intended to be promoted by such restrictions. Examples: the making of suicide a crime, requiring passengers in automobiles to wear seat belts, requiring a Christian Scientist to receive a blood transfusion. In the case of "impure" paternalism in trying to protect the welfare of a class of persons we find that the only way to do so will involve restricting the freedom of other persons besides those who are benefitted. Now it might be thought that there are no cases of "impure" paternalism since any such case could always be justified on nonpaternalistic grounds, i.e. in terms of preventing harm to others. Thus we might ban cigarette manufacturers from continuing to manufacture their product on the grounds that we are preventing them from causing illness to others in the same way that we prevent other manufacturers from releasing pollutants into the atmosphere, thereby causing danger to the members of the community. The difference is, however, that in the former but not the latter case the harm is of such a nature that it could be avoided by those individuals affected if they so chose. The incurring of the harm requires, so to speak, the active cooperation of the victim. It would be mistaken theoretically and hypocritical in practice to assert that our interference in such cases is just like our interference in standard cases of protecting others from harm. At the very least someone interfered with in this way can reply that no one is complaining about his activities. It may be that impure paternalism requires arguments or reasons of a stronger kind in order to be justified since there are persons who are losing a portion of their liberty and they do not even have the solace of having it done "in their own interest." Of course in some sense, if paternalistic justifications are ever correct, when we are protecting others, we are preventing some from injuring others, but it is important to see the differences between this and the standard case.

Paternalism then will always involve limitations on the liberty of some individuals in their own interest but it may also extend to interferences with the liberty of parties whose interests are not in question.

IV

Finally, by way of some more preliminary analysis, I want to distinguish paternalistic interferences with liberty from a related type with which it is often confused. Consider, for example, legislation which forbids employees to work more than, say, forty hours per week. It is sometimes argued that such legislation is paternalistic for if employees desired such a restriction on their hours of work they could agree among themselves to impose it voluntarily. But because they do not the society imposes its own conception of their best interests upon them by the use of coercion. Hence this is paternalism.

Now it may be that some legislation of this nature is, in fact, paternalistically motivated. I am not denying that. All I want to point out is that there is another possible way of justifying such measures which is not paternalistic in nature. It is not paternalistic because as Mill puts it in a similar context such measures are "required not to overrule the judgment of individuals respecting their own interest, but to give effect to that judgment: they being unable to give effect to it except by concert, which concert again cannot be effectual unless it receives validity and sanction from the law."[2]

The line of reasoning here is a familiar one first found in Hobbes and developed with great sophistication by contemporary economists in the last decade or so. There are restrictions which are in the interests of a class of persons taken collectively but are such that the immediate interest of each individual is furthered by his violating the rule when others adhere to it. In such cases the individuals involved may need the use of compulsion to give effect to their collective judgment of their own interest by guaranteeing each individual compliance by the others. In these cases compulsion is not used to achieve some benefit which is not recognized to be a benefit by those concerned, but rather because it is the only feasible means of achieving some benefit which *is* recognized as such by all concerned. This way of viewing matters provides us with another characterization of paternalism in general. Paternalism might be thought of as the use of coercion to achieve a good which is not recognized as such by those persons for whom the good is intended. Again while this formulation captures the heart of the matter—it is surely what Mill is objecting to in *On Liberty*—the matter is not always quite like that. For example when we force motorcyclists to wear helmets we are trying to promote a good—the protection of the person from injury—which is surely recognized by most of the individuals concerned. It is not that a cyclist doesn't value his bodily integrity; rather, as a supporter of such legislation would put it, he either places, perhaps irrationally, another value or good (freedom from wearing a helmet) above that of physical well-being or, perhaps while recognizing the danger in the abstract, he either does not fully appreciate it or he underestimates the likelihood of its occurring. But now we are approaching the question of possible justifications of paternalistic measures and the rest of this essay will be devoted to that question.

V

I shall begin for dialectical purposes by discussing Mill's objections to paternalism and then go on to discuss more positive proposals.

An initial feature that strikes one is the absolute nature of Mill's prohibitions against paternalism. It is so unlike the carefully qualified admonitions of Mill and his fellow Utilitarians on other moral issues. He speaks of self-protection as the *sole* end warranting coercion, of the individual's own goals as *never* being a sufficient warrant. Contrast this with his discussion of the prohibition against lying in *Utilitarianism*.

> Yet that even this rule, sacred as it is, admits of possible exception, is acknowledged by all moralists, the chief of which is where the with-holding of some fact . . . would save an individual . . . from great and unmerited evil.[3]

The same tentativeness is present when he deals with justice.

> It is confessedly unjust to break faith with any one: to violate an engagement, either express or implied, or disappoint expectations raised by our own conduct, at least if we have raised these expectations knowingly and voluntarily. Like all the other obligations of justice already spoken of, this one is not regarded as absolute, but as capable of being overruled by a stronger obligation of justice on the other side.[4]

This anomaly calls for some explanation. The structure of Mill's argument is as follows:

(1) Since restraint is an evil the burden of proof is on those who propose such restraint.

(2) Since the conduct which is being considered is purely self-regarding, the normal appeal to the protection of the interests of others is not available.

(3) Therefore we have to consider whether reasons involving reference to the individual's own good, happiness, welfare, or interests are sufficient to overcome the burden of justification.

(4) We either cannot advance the interests of the individual by compulsion, or the attempt to do so involves evils which outweigh the good done.

(5) Hence the promotion of the individual's own interests does not provide a sufficient warrant for the use of compulsion.

Clearly the operative premise here is (4) and it is bolstered by claims about the status of the individual as judge and appraiser of his welfare, interests, needs, etc.

> With respect to his own feelings and circumstances, the most ordinary man or woman has means of knowledge immeasurably surpassing those that can be possessed by any one else.[5]

> He is the man most interested in his own well-being: the interest which any other person, except in cases of strong personal attachment, can have in it, is trifling, compared to that which he himself has.[6]

These claims are used to support the following generalizations concerning the utility of compulsion for paternalistic purposes.

> The interferences of society to overrule his judgment and purposes in what only regards himself must be grounded on general presumptions; which may be altogether wrong, and even if right, are as likely as not to be misapplied to individual cases.[7]

> But the strongest of all the arguments against the interference of the public with purely personal conduct is that when it does interfere, the odds are that it interferes wrongly and in the wrong place.[8]

> All errors which the individual is likely to commit against advice and warning are far outweighed by the evil of allowing others to constrain him to what they deem his good.[9]

Performing the utilitarian calculation by balancing the advantages and disadvantages we find that:

> Mankind are greater gainers by suffering each other to live as seems good to themselves, than by compelling each other to live as seems good to the rest.[10]

From which follows the operative premise (4).

This classical case of a utilitarian argument with all the premises spelled out is not the only line of reasoning present in Mill's discussion. There are asides, and more than asides, which look quite different and I shall deal with them later. But this is clearly the main channel of Mill's thought and it is one which has been subjected to vigorous attack from the moment it appeared—most often by fellow Utilitarians. The link that they have usually seized on is, as Fitzjames Stephen put it, the absence of proof that the "mass of adults are so well acquainted with their own interests and so much disposed to pursue them that no compulsion or restraint put upon them by any others for the purpose of promoting their interest can really promote them."[11] Even so sympathetic a critic as Hart is forced to the conclusion that:

> In Chapter 5 of his essay Mill carried his protests against paternalism to lengths that may now appear to us as fantastic. . . . No doubt if we no longer sympathise with this criticism this is due, in part, to a general decline in the belief that individuals know their own interest best.[12]

> Mill endows the average individual with "too much of the psychology of a middle-aged man whose desires are relatively fixed, not liable to be artificially stimulated by external influences; who knows what he wants and what gives him satisfaction or happiness; and who pursues these things when he can."[13]

Now it is interesting to note that Mill himself was aware of some of the limitations on the doctrine that the individual is the best judge of his own interests. In his discussion of government intervention in general (even where the intervention does not interfere with liberty but provides alternative institutions to those of the market) after making claims which are parallel to those just discussed, e.g.

> People understand their own business and their own interests better, and care for them more, than the government does, or can be expected to do.[14]

He goes on to an intelligent discussion of the "very large and conspicuous exceptions" to the maxim that:

> Most persons take a juster and more intelligent view of their own interest, and of the means of promoting it than can either be prescribed to them by a general enactment of the legislature, or pointed out in the particular case by a public functionary.[15]

Thus there are things

> of which the utility does not consist in ministering to inclinations, nor in serving the daily uses of life, and the want of which is least felt where the need is greatest. This is peculiarly true of those things which are chiefly useful as tending to raise the character of human beings. The uncultivated cannot be competent judges of cultivation. Those who most need to be made wiser and better, usually desire it least, and, if they desired it, would be incapable of finding the way to it by their own lights.
>
> . . . . A second exception to the doctrine that individuals are the best judges of their own interest, is when an individual attempts to decide irrevocably now what will be best for his interest at some future and distant time. The presumption in favor of individual judgment is only legitimate, where the judgment is grounded on actual, and especially on present, personal experience; not where it is formed antecedently to experience, and not suffered to be reversed even after experience has condemned it.[16]

The upshot of these exceptions is that Mill does not declare that there should never be government interference with the economy but rather that

> . . . in every instance, the burden of making out a strong case should be thrown not on those who resist but on those who recommend government interference. Letting alone, in short, should be the general practice: every departure from it, unless required by some great good, is a certain evil.[17]

In short, we get a presumption not an absolute prohibition. The question is why doesn't the argument against paternalism go the same way?

I suggest that the answer lies in seeing that in addition to a purely utilitarian argument Mill uses another as well. As a Utilitarian Mill has to show, in Fitzjames Stephen's words, that:

> Self-protection apart, no good object can be attained by any compulsion which is not in itself a greater evil than the absence of the object which the compulsion obtains.[18]

To show this is impossible; one reason being that it isn't true. Preventing a man from selling himself into slavery (a paternalistic measure which Mill himself accepts as legitimate), or from taking heroin, or from driving a car without wearing seat belts may constitute a lesser evil than allowing him to do

any of these things. A consistent Utilitarian can only argue against paternalism on the grounds that it (as a matter of fact) does not maximize the
good. It is always a contingent question that may be refuted by the evidence.
But there is also a noncontingent argument which runs through *On Liberty.*
When Mill states that "there is a part of the life of every person who has
come to years of discretion, within which the individuality of that person
ought to reign uncontrolled either by any other person or by the public collectively," he is saying something about what it means to be a person, an
autonomous agent. It is because coercing a person for his own good denies
this status as an independent entity that Mill objects to it so strongly and in
such absolute terms. To be able to choose is a good that is independent of the
wisdom of what is chosen. A man's "mode of laying out his existence is the
best, not because it is the best in itself, but because it is his own mode."[19]

> It is the privilege and proper condition of a human being, arrived at the maturity
> of his faculties, to use and interpret experience in his own way.[20]

As further evidence of this line of reasoning in Mill consider the one exception to his prohibition against paternalism.

> In this and most civilised countries, for example, an engagement by which a per-
> son should sell himself, or allow himself to be sold, as a slave, would be null and
> void; neither enforced by law nor by opinion. The ground for thus limiting his
> power of voluntarily disposing of his own lot in life, is apparent, and is very clear-
> ly seen in this extreme case. The reason for not interfering, unless for the sake of
> others, with a person's voluntary acts, is consideration for his liberty. His volun-
> tary choice is evidence that what he so chooses is desirable, or at least endurable,
> to him, and his good is on the whole best provided for by allowing him to take his
> own means of pursuing it. But by selling himself for a slave, he abdicates his
> liberty; he foregoes any future use of it beyond that single act. He therefore
> defeats, in his own case, the very purpose which is the justification of allowing
> him to dispose of himself. He is no longer free; but is thenceforth in a position
> which has no longer the presumption in its favour, that would be afforded by his
> voluntarily remaining in it. The principle of freedom cannot require that he
> should be free not to be free. It is not freedom to be allowed to alienate his
> freedom.[21]

Now leaving aside the fudging on the meaning of freedom in the last line it is
clear that part of this argument is incorrect. While it is true that *future*
choices of the slave are not reasons for thinking that what he chooses then is
desirable for him, what is at issue is limiting his immediate choice; and since
this choice is made freely, the individual may be correct in thinking that his
interests are best provided for by entering such a contract. But the main consideration for not allowing such a contract is the need to preserve the liberty
of the person to make future choices. This gives us a principle—a very narrow

one—by which to justify some paternalistic interferences. Paternalism is justified only to preserve a wider range of freedom for the individual in question. How far this principle could be extended, whether it can justify all the cases in which we are inclined upon reflection to think paternalistic measures justified remains to be discussed. What I have tried to show so far is that there are two strains of argument in Mill—one a straightforward Utilitarian mode of reasoning and one which relies not on the goods which free choice leads to but on the absolute value of the choice itself. The first cannot establish any absolute prohibition but at most a presumption and indeed a fairly weak one given some fairly plausible assumptions about human psychology; the second while a stronger line of argument seems to me to allow on its own grounds a wider range of paternalism than might be suspected. I turn now to a consideration of these matters.

VI

We might begin looking for principles governing the acceptable use of paternalistic power in cases where it is generally agreed that it is legitimate. Even Mill intends his principles to be applicable only to mature individuals, not those in what he calls "non-age." What is it that justifies us in interfering with children? The fact that they lack some of the emotional and cognitive capacities required in order to make fully rational decisions. It is an empirical question to just what extent children have an adequate conception of their own present and future interests but there is not much doubt that there are many deficiencies. For example it is very difficult for a child to defer gratification for any considerable period of time. Given these deficiencies and given the very real and permanent dangers that may befall the child it becomes not only permissible but even a duty of the parent to restrict the child's freedom in various ways. There is however an important moral limitation on the exercise of such parental power which is provided by the notion of the child eventually coming to see the correctness of his parent's interventions. Parental paternalism may be thought of as a wager by the parent on the child's subsequent recognition of the wisdom of the restrictions. There is an emphasis on what could be called future-oriented consent—on what the child will come to welcome, rather than on what he does welcome.

The essence of this idea has been incorporated by idealist philosophers into various types of "real-will" theory as applied to fully adult persons. Extensions of paternalism are argued for by claiming that in various respects, chronologically mature individuals share the same deficiencies in knowledge, capacity to think rationally, and the ability to carry out decisions that children possess. Hence in interfering with such people we are in effect doing

what they would do if they were fully rational. Hence we are not really opposing their will, hence we are not really interfering with their freedom. The
dangers of this move have been sufficiently exposed by Berlin in his *Two
Concepts of Liberty*. I see no gain in theoretical clarity nor in practical advantage in trying to pass over the real nature of the interferences with liberty
that we impose on others. Still the basic notion of consent is important and
seems to me the only acceptable way of trying to delimit an area of justified
paternalism.

Let me start by considering a case where the consent is not hypothetical
in nature. Under certain conditions it is rational for an individual to agree
that others should force him to act in ways in which, at the time of action, the
individual may not see as desirable. If, for example, a man knows that he is
subject to breaking his resolves when temptation is present, he may ask a
friend to refuse to entertain his requests at some later stage.

A classical example is given in the *Odyssey* when Odysseus commands
his men to tie him to the mast and refuse all future orders to be set free,
because he knows the power of the Sirens to enchant men with their songs.
Here we are on relatively sound ground in later refusing Odysseus' request to
be set free. He may even claim to have changed his mind but since it is just
such changes that he wished to guard against we are entitled to ignore them.

A process analogous to this may take place on a social rather than individual basis. An electorate may mandate its representatives to pass legislation which when it comes time to "pay the price" may be unpalatable. I may
believe that a tax increase is necessary to halt inflation though I may resent
the lower pay check each month. However in both this case and that of
Odysseus the measure to be enforced is specifically requested by the party involved and at some point in time there is genuine consent and agreement on
the part of those persons whose liberty is infringed. Such is not the case for
the paternalistic measures we have been speaking about. What must be involved here is not consent to specific measures but rather consent to a system
of government, run by elected representatives, with an understanding that
they may act to safeguard our interests in certain limited ways.

I suggest that since we are all aware of our irrational propensities,
deficiencies in cognitive and emotional capacities and avoidable and unavoidable ignorance it is rational and prudent for us to in effect take out
"social insurance policies." We may argue for and against proposed paternalistic measures in terms of what fully rational individuals would accept as
forms of protection. Now, clearly since the initial agreement is not about
specific measures, we are dealing with a more-or-less blank check and
therefore there have to be carefully defined limits. What I am looking for are

certain kinds of conditions which make it plausible to suppose that rational men could reach agreement to limit their liberty even when other men's interests are not affected.

Of course as in any kind of agreement schema there are great difficulties in deciding what rational individuals would or would not accept. Particularly in sensitive areas of personal liberty, there is always a danger of the dispute over agreement and rationality being a disguised version of evaluative and normative disagreement.

Let me suggest types of situations in which it seems plausible to suppose that fully rational individuals would agree to having paternalistic restrictions imposed upon them. It is reasonable to suppose that there are "goods" such as health which any person would want to have in order to pursue his own good—no matter how that good is conceived. This is an argument that is used in connection with compulsory education for children but it seems to me that it can be extended to other goods which have this character. Then one could agree that the attainment of such goods should be promoted even when they are not desired at the moment, by the individuals concerned.

An immediate difficulty that arises stems from the fact that men are always faced with competing goods and that there may be reasons why even a value such as health, or indeed life, may be overridden by competing values—thus the problem with the Christian Scientist and blood transfusions. It may be more important for him to reject "impure substances" than to go on living. The difficult problem that must be faced is whether one can give sense to the notion of a person irrationally attaching weights to competing values.

Consider a person who knows the statistical data on the probability of being injured when not wearing seat belts in an automobile and knows the types and gravity of the various injuries. He also insists that the inconvenience attached to fastening the belt every time he gets in and out of the car outweighs for him the possible risks to himself. I am inclined in this case to think that such a weighing is irrational. Given his life-plans which we are assuming are those of the average person, his interests and commitments already undertaken, I think it is safe to predict that we can find inconsistencies in his calculations at some point. I am assuming that this is not a man who for some conscious or unconscious reasons is trying to injure himself nor is he a man who just likes to "live dangerously." I am assuming that he is like us in all the relevant respects but just puts an enormously high negative value on inconvenience—one which does not seem comprehensible or reasonable.

It is always possible, of course, to assimilate this person to creatures like myself. I, also, neglect to fasten my seat belt and I concede such behavior is not rational but not because I weigh the inconvenience differently from those who fasten the belts. It is just that having made (roughly) the same calculation as everybody else I ignore it in my actions. [Note: a much better case of weakness of the will than those usually given in ethics texts.] A plausible explanation for this deplorable habit is that although I know in some intellectual sense what the probabilities and risks are I do not fully appreciate them in an emotionally genuine manner.

We have two distinct types of situations in which a man acts in a nonrational fashion. In one case he attaches incorrect weights to some of his values; in the other he neglects to act in accordance with his actual preferences and desires. Clearly there is a stronger and more persuasive argument for paternalism in the latter situation. Here we are not really not—by assumption—imposing a good on another person. But why may we not extend our interference to what we might call evaluative delusions? After all in the case of cognitive delusions we are prepared, often, to act against the expressed will of the person involved. If a man believes that when he jumps out the window he will float upwards—Robert Nozick's example—would not we detain him, forcibly if necessary? The reply will be that this man doesn't wish to be injured and if we could convince him that he is mistaken as to the consequences of his action he would not wish to perform the action. But part of what is involved in claiming that a man who doesn't fasten his seat belts is attaching an irrational weight to the inconvenience of fastening them is that if he were to be involved in an accident and severely injured he would look back and admit that the inconvenience wasn't as bad as all that. So there is a sense in which if I could convince him of the consequences of his action he also would not wish to continue his present course of action. Now the notion of consequences being used here is covering a lot of ground. In one case it's being used to indicate what will or can happen as a result of a course of action and in the other it's making a prediction about the future evaluation of the consequences—in the first sense—of a course of action. And whatever the difference between facts and values—whether it be hard and fast or soft and slow—we are genuinely more reluctant to consent to interferences where evaluative differences are the issue. Let me now consider another factor which comes into play in some of these situations which may make an important difference in our willingness to consent to paternalistic restrictions.

Some of the decisions we make are of such a character that they produce changes which are in one or another way irreversible. Situations are created in which it is difficult or impossible to return to anything like the initial stage at which the decision was made. In particular some of these changes will make it impossible to continue to make reasoned choices in the future. I am thinking specifically of decisions which involve taking drugs that are physically or psychologically addictive and those which are destructive of one's mental and physical capacities.

I suggest we think of the imposition of paternalistic interferences in situations of this kind as being a kind of insurance policy which we take out against making decisions which are far-reaching, potentially dangerous and irreversible. Each of these factors is important. Clearly there are many decisions we make that are relatively irreversible. In deciding to learn to play chess I could predict in view of my general interest in games that some portion of my free time was going to be preempted and that it would not be easy to give up the game once I acquired a certain competence. But my whole life-style was not going to be jeopardized in an extreme manner. Further it might be argued that even with addictive drugs such as heroin one's normal life plans would not be seriously interfered with if an inexpensive and adequate supply were readily available. So this type of argument might have a much narrower scope than appears to be the case at first.

A second class of cases concerns decisions which are made under extreme psychological and sociological pressures. I am not thinking here of the making of the decision as being something one is pressured into—e.g. a good reason for making duelling illegal is that unless this is done many people might have to manifest their courage and integrity in ways in which they would rather not do so—but rather of decisions such as that to commit suicide which are usually made at a point where the individual is not thinking clearly and calmly about the nature of his decision. In addition, of course, this comes under the previous heading of all-too-irrevocable decisions. Now there are practical steps which a society could take if it wanted to decrease the possibility of suicide—for example not paying social security benefits to the survivors or, as religious institutions do, not allowing such persons to be buried with the same status as natural deaths. I think we may count these as interferences with the liberty of persons to attempt suicide and the question is whether they are justifiable.

Using my argument schema the question is whether rational individuals would consent to such limitations. I see no reason for them to consent to an absolute prohibition but I do think it is reasonable for them to agree to some kind of enforced waiting period. Since we are all aware of the possibility of temporary states, such as great fear or depression, that are inimical to the making of well-informed and rational decisions, it would be prudent for all of us if there were some kind of institutional arrangement whereby we were restrained from making a decision which is (all too) irreversible. What this would be like in practice is difficult to envisage and it may be that if no practical arrangements were feasible then we would have to conclude that there should be no restriction at all on this kind of action. But we might have a "cooling off" period, in much the same way that we now require couples who file for divorce to go through a waiting period. Or, more farfetched, we might imagine a Suicide Board composed of a psychologist and another member picked by the applicant. The Board would be required to meet and talk with the person proposing to take his life, though its approval would not be required.

A third class of decisions—these classes are not supposed to be disjoint—involves dangers which are either not sufficiently understood or appreciated correctly by the persons involved. Let me illustrate, using the example of cigarette smoking, a number of possible cases.

1. A man may not know the facts—e.g. smoking between 1 and 2 packs a day shortens life expectancy 6.2 years, the costs and pain of the illness caused by smoking, etc.
2. A man may know the facts, wish to stop smoking, but not have the requisite willpower.
3. A man may know the facts but not have them play the correct role in his calculation because, say, he discounts the danger psychologically because it is remote in time and/or inflates the attractiveness of other consequences of his decision which he regards as beneficial.

In case 1 what is called for is education, the posting of warnings, etc. In case 2 there is no theoretical problem. We are not imposing a good on someone who rejects it. We are simply using coercion to enable people to carry out their own goals. (Note: There obviously is a difficulty in that only a subclass of the individuals affected wish to be prevented from doing what they are doing.) In case 3 there is a sense in which we are imposing a good on someone since given his current appraisal of the facts he doesn't wish to be restricted. But in another sense we are not imposing a good since what is being claimed—and what must be shown or at least argued for—is that an accurate accounting on his part would lead him to reject his current course of action. Now we all know that such cases exist, that we are prone to disregard dangers that are only possibilities, that immediate pleasures are often magnified and distorted.

If in addition the dangers are severe and far-reaching we could agree to allowing the state a certain degree of power to intervene in such situations. The difficulty is in specifying in advance, even vaguely, the class of cases in which intervention will be legitimate.

A related difficulty is that of drawing a line so that it is not the case that all ultrahazardous activities are ruled out, e.g. mountain climbing, bullfighting, sports car racing, etc. There are some risks—even very great ones—which a person is entitled to take with his life.

A good deal depends on the nature of the deprivation—e.g. does it prevent the person from engaging in the activity completely or merely limit his participation—and how important to the nature of the activity is the absence of restriction when this is weighed against the role that the activity plays in the life of the person. In the case of automobile seat belts, for example, the restriction is trivial in nature, interferes not at all with the use or enjoyment of the activity, and does, I am assuming, considerably reduce a high risk of serious injury. Whereas, for example, making mountain climbing illegal prevents completely a person engaging in an activity which may play an important role in his life and his conception of the person he is.

In general the easiest cases to handle are those which can be argued about in the terms which Mill thought to be so important—a concern not just for the happiness or welfare, in some broad sense, of the individual but rather a concern for the autonomy and freedom of the person. I suggest that we would be most likely to consent to paternalism in those instances in which it preserves and enhances for the individual his ability to rationally consider and carry out his own decisions.

I have suggested in this essay a number of types of situations in which it seems plausible that rational men would agree to granting the legislative powers of a society the right to impose restrictions on what Mill calls "self-regarding" conduct. However, rational men knowing something about the resources of ignorance, ill-will and stupidity available to the lawmakers of a society—a good case in point is the history of drug legislation in the United States—will be concerned to limit such intervention to a minimum. I suggest in closing two principles designed to achieve this end.

In all cases of paternalistic legislation there must be a heavy and clear burden of proof placed on the authorities to demonstrate the exact nature of the harmful effects (or beneficial consequences) to be avoided (or achieved) and the probability of their occurrence. The burden of proof here is twofold—what lawyers distinguish as the burden of going forward and the burden of persuasion. That the authorities have the burden of going forward means that it is up to them to raise the question and bring forward evidence of the evils to be avoided. Unlike the case of new drugs where the manufacturer must produce some evidence that the drug has been tested and found not harmful, no citizen has to show with respect to self-regarding conduct that it is not harmful or promotes his best interests. In addition the nature and cogency of the evidence for the harmfulness of the course of action must be set at a high level. To paraphrase a formulation of the burden of proof for criminal proceedings—better ten men ruin themselves than one man be unjustly deprived of liberty.

Finally I suggest a principle of the least restrictive alternative. If there is an alternative way of accomplishing the desired end without restricting liberty then although it may involve great expense, inconvenience, etc. the society must adopt it.

GERALD DWORKIN

UNIVERSITY OF ILLINOIS, CHICAGO CIRCLE
JULY, 1971

NOTES

[1] J. S. Mill, *Utilitarianism* and *On Liberty*, ed. by Mary Warnock (London: Fontana Library Edition, 1962), p. 135. All further quotes from Mill are from this edition unless otherwise noted.

[2] J. S. Mill, *Principles of Political Economy* (New York: P. F. Collier and Sons, 1900), p. 442.

[3] Mill, *Utilitarianism* and *On Liberty*, p. 174.

[4] Ibid., p. 299.

[5] Ibid., p. 207.

[6] Ibid., p. 206.

[7] Ibid., p. 207.

[8] Ibid., p. 214.

[9] Ibid., p. 207.

[10] Ibid., p. 138.

[11] James F. Stephen, *Liberty, Equality, Fraternity* (New York: Henry Holt & Co., n.d.), p. 24.

[12] H. L. A. Hart, *Law, Liberty and Morality* (Stanford University Press, 1963), p. 32.

[13] Ibid., p. 33.

[14] Mill, *Principles*, **II,** 448.

[15] Ibid., **II,** 458.

[16] Ibid., **II,** 459.

[17] Ibid., **II,** 451.

[18] Stephen, *Liberty, Equality, Fraternity*, p. 49.

[19] Ibid., *Utilitarianism* and *On Liberty*, p. 197.

[20] Ibid., p. 186.

[21] Ibid., pp. 235-36.

RISIERI FRONDIZI

THE PROBLEM OF FREEDOM: FROM PHILOSOPHICAL THEORY TO HUMAN REALITY

From Socrates to the existentialists, many philosophers have been concerned about the public good. I do not mean they were interested in the public good as citizens, but as philosophers.

Unfortunately, this has not always been the case. Why is philosophy kept away from its interest in human affairs? In my opinion there are two main reasons. The obvious one is the case when philosophy consciously becomes a tool to solve technical problems. There is a deliberate decision to keep away from any consideration about good and bad, either individually or socially. This tendency has made very important contributions to the technical development of philosophy but has left the human problems as they were before. In some cases, philosophers that belong to this group have sharpened the tools to solve those problems; in others, they turned their backs to them and even despised those interested in human affairs. Logical positivism and its offsprings are good illustrations of this position. But we can find similar cases in the past.

A psychological interpretation of these philosophers could be misleading. It is not a question that they try, consciously or unconsciously, to avoid being involved in thorny problems, as was the case with Descartes, but they arrived at that position for theoretical reasons. Or, to be more precise, for methodological reasons. As they want to apply the scientific methods, they think they have to avoid value judgments altogether and restrict themselves to a descriptive attitude. But human behavior needs guidance besides description, and philosophy is not able to provide it for methodological reasons. Alfred J. Ayer is a clear case that it is not a psychological reaction. As a human being he is deeply involved in political, social and human problems; and he usually takes the right position, in my estimation. But when it comes to dealing philosophically with the same problems, Ayer gets into a neutral position. The reason is very simple. He follows Hume in believing that there are two and only two classes of propositions; one concerns relations of ideas and the other matters of fact. The former comprises the a priori propositions of logic and mathematics, and these are necessary because they are analytic. Empirical matters of fact propositions are empirical hypotheses. There is no room for genuine statements of value; they can either be reduced to matters of fact propositions or they are mere expressions of emotion and meaningless as propositions, since there is no way to verify them.

Since Ayer is making value judgments all the time, defends them with reasons and fights for them, they cannot be completely meaningless. They are meaningless according to a narrow epistemology which leads to restricted criteria of verification. If value propositions have no place in that type of epistemology, so much the worse for it. We have to change the epistemological and methodological attitude, not drop something that is clearly there, everyday, in every human being.

I am taking Ayer as a mere illustration. My point is that there have been many important philosophers who have kept away from human problems—and particularly the public good—for methodological reasons. This seems rather obvious.

The second case, on which I will elaborate, is less obvious. Philosophers have kept away from human concern because they got involved in abstractions and, more specifically, because of the tendency to *reify* qualities and processes. This is what I may call the substantialist attitude that derives mainly from the Cartesian doctrine of the two substances.

There is, of course, no philosophy without abstraction. The danger lies in the possibility of confusing our own notions, forged to interpret reality, with reality itself. After all, philosophy is an interpretation and not a substitution for reality. A clear case of this type of mistake is Descartes's and the Cartesians' concerns about the relations of the two substances they created and later separated. There are not two independent substances in the world; as a matter of fact, there is no substance at all.

I will try to show that the reifying tendency is responsible for the lack of influence on, and/or concern with, human affairs, taking the problem of freedom as an illustration. For lack of space I give up the possibility of showing my point through an analysis of the different theories about freedom. I have to restrict myself just to the ways the problem has been posed.

There is no doubt about the importance of how the problem is set and the way you phrase it. When you ask a question, you already limit the range of answers because a set of alternatives is implicit. That is why some questions should be not answered but dropped. As a matter of fact, they should never have been formulated.

What is wrong in the formulation of the problem of freedom? First of all that it refers to 'freedom', making it an entity, i.e. reifying a quality. If you concentrate on 'freedom' ignoring the particular situation of the people who are or are not free, you run the risk of detaching yourself from reality. And that is what has happened. I will briefly trace the different steps of the problem of freedom to show how it moved from a very abstract approach to a more concrete one, and how that movement is parallel to a deeper concern of philosophy in human affairs.

As I have pointed out, the first mistake in setting the problem of freedom is to be concerned about 'freedom' and not about free acts, decisions, wishes, persons or institutions. The shift from the adjective to the noun makes a lot of difference. If we concentrate on freedom as an entity or an abstract notion, we are less concerned about what happens around us, what is the situation with concrete individuals, including ourselves. Freedom is too big a word that casts shadows on individual persons. And we take a decision on freedom regardless of what is happening to many individuals.

This treatment of freedom has misled people to pseudoproblems like the divisibility or indivisibility of freedom. Hayek and many others maintain, for instance, that freedom is indivisible and that if there is any restriction to economical freedom, there are also restrictions on the political and social levels too, because, he maintains, "freedom is indivisible". These are pseudoproblems derived from the wrong notion of considering it as an entity. As soon as we realize it is a quality, the whole problem becomes meaningless. We can be free in one respect or situation, and not free in another. It is obvious that a quality has a different type of existence than an entity and 'divisibility' a different meaning in each case.

As freedom is a reification of the quality of being free, in the name of the abstract freedom many concrete individual freedoms are stifled. At least half of the present day dictators have suppressed concrete and specific forms of freedom in the name of Freedom, which they claim to defend.

Freedom is an abstraction from an adjective, as it is the case with sweetness, tallness or fatness. It has no independent existence, because of its very nature of being originally a quality; it has an adjectival nature. If we realize this fact, we can move a step forward to more concrete situations and in such a way our concern increases about what is really going on in the world.

. The next step to concreteness is to move from the problem of the existence of freedom to the question that has been asked many times, namely, is man free? There is here an improvement in the formulation of the problem because of the substitution of the abstract noun by the proper adjective. The trouble now is about the subject: man. 'Man' is a strange creature. He has both sexes and/or none of them; he is at the same time old and young, white and black, short and tall, etc. Berkeley has already shown in his *Principles* the contradictions of such an entity. If we are told that we are speaking about man in general, we must reply that there is not such a thing. Besides, if such an entity may have contradictory qualities, like being male and female, it is clear that he may be free and not free at the same time. And that is actually the case. There are men who may be called 'free'; it is impossible to call others that way, no matter how low your requirements for freedom are.

The ambiguity in the subject carries the difficulties a step forward. Whom are we having in mind when we ask if 'man' is free? Do we include children? Insane people?

Do we mean actually or potentially free? 'Free' is also an ambiguous term. The distinction between free *from* and free *for* is well known. One can be free *from* but not free *for*; the negative freedom is only part of the story. We all feel so much oppressed in the present world that we get into the illusion that once we are free from oppression we are totally free. But that is not the case. The contemporary concern about the proper use of free time shows that there are millions of people who carry their own chains; once they are free "from", they do not know what to do with their freedom. And they usually get back to the routine or get into stupid entertainments because they are unable to exercise their creative freedom.

Even if we distinguish the negative from the positive freedom, we are not sure what is the case when a person states that he is free, meaning free from. He may be free from prison, from a dictator, his wife or his oppressive father. Sometimes the context may help us to understand; at other times, the ambiguity keeps floating in the air.

These ambiguities explain why two opposing persons, political groups or countries may claim, in good faith, to be defending freedom. One group may have in mind a certain type of restriction while the other a different one. For instance, one who defends freedom of enterprise believes that economic activities should be free from State interference. Those who oppose it, are not against freedom; on the contrary, they believe the State should control production, distribution and prices to free the consumers from the exploitation of big business. The American Civil War is also a clear case. The North was fighting to free the slaves and the South to free the states from federal interference.

To all these ambiguities we must add the fact that words like 'freedom' are emotionally loaded; no one wants to be against freedom. The descriptive and emotive meanings are closely interrelated.

These are not the only difficulties. It is not enough to say that 'freedom' does not make much sense; for, by its very nature, it is a quality, an adjective and not a noun. We must also realize that it is a particular type of adjective; it is not like 'odd' and 'even', that exclude each other. By not realizing this fact, people have the tendency to think that we are free or not free. Actually, it is an adjective that admits degrees, like healthy or beautiful. Besides, it is not a permanent quality like being tall, because the quality of being free may change from one day to the next. We are not born free and we cannot become free forever; one cannot graduate as a free man, as one graduates as a Ph. D. We can lose this quality any minute and not only because of our own wishes and decisions, but also as a consequence of events that are not under our control. 'Free' is a quality that admits degrees and is not permanent; it is more fragile than a delicate glass.

The basic difficulty in the second step in the formulation of the problem of freedom, namely, is man free?, was due to the ambiguity of the general abstract notion of the subject. Mainly due to the influence of the existentialists, in recent times the question has been asked in the first person: am I free? There is here no ambiguity in the subject and there is also an approach to real, actual life; each one is supposed to ask this question about himself. There is nothing to hide; each one has to face the problem: am I free or am I not?

Here lies part of the difficulty: you have to give an affirmative or a negative answer. We pointed out before that 'free' is an adjective which admits degrees and the requirement of an affirmative or negative answer is misleading because the correct answer would be between the two extremes. In that case, the proper question should be how free or determined are we? But there are still further difficulties. In the question we consider ourselves as a unit, while we may be free in one type of activity and not free in others. An artist may be free when creating his works of art, but he is not free while driving his car on a highway. The great majority of our activities are not free; they are determined by physical, chemical or physiological conditions, where we have no choice at all.

We should then ask how free are we for each particular type of activity and on each particular occasion. I have pointed out that there are activities which by their very nature are determined by biochemical factors, like digesting; others could be the expression of freedom, like painting, writing poetry or music. But the circumstances have a lot to say. If I am a sick and starving poet, the possibilities of creative writing are reduced to almost zero. From temperature to sociocultural factors, every part of our situation has an influence upon our freedom. There are oppressing political, social and economical structures; while others help the individual to reach his freedom.

The question, therefore, that should be asked is: how free am I on this particular occasion? What are the factors that interfere with my freedom? Do they depend on me or on the environment? What can I do to remove them? How free am I to remove them and become more free? And so on and so forth. As the question gets nearer to human concrete reality, philosophical theory gets more involved in human affairs, including public good.

When we ask this type of question, we realize the vacuum of rhetorical statements like "man is born free" and of any consideration about the existence of freedom in the abstract. We also realize that millions of people are not free, in many cases for the simple reason that they are starving, sick or ignorant. Can we say that a man who is starving is free because the law permits him to express his opinion in the press, to worship and enjoy all the other "individual freedoms"?

As it is the case with many other problems, the question of freedom has been asked having in mind only the ordinary, educated, male adult of the middle class, as if females, children, poor and non-white people were not human beings. This is one of the explanations of the contradiction of the American Declaration of Independence, which states that it is "self-evident, that all men are created equal, that they are endowed by their Creator with certain unalienable rights, that among these are Life, Liberty, and the Pursuit of Happiness"; while at that time there were in the United States hundreds of thousands of slaves and millions in the rest of the world. Many who signed such a statement owned slaves themselves.

Metaphysical considerations on Freedom have the same effect on concrete human situations which rhetorical, political phrases have, namely, none. The same is true when we speak about 'man', because it leaves aside what is happening to the particular individuals. Millions of people are not free, not because "human nature" is not free, but because other human beings have enslaved them, oppressed them for *their* own benefit. Philosophy has to face this fact, analyse the factors that lead to this oppression, show the alternatives and serve as a guidance to a better situation.

We come back again to the relation between theory and praxis. No real progress is obtained by chance. A proper advance needs a lot of good theory, but 'good theory' about human behavior does not only mean to be free from logical contradictions and the other technical requirements; it must also go deep down in actual human life. We must remember that it should be good theory for an actual way of living.

This quick analysis of the development of the problem of freedom shows us that contemporary philosophy is approaching the real problem of men, of men of "flesh and bone", as Unamuno used to say. The possibility of influencing actual behavior becomes greater, since philosophy is not floating up in thin air but trying to consider every relevant and concrete factor in everyday life.

This approach to concreteness keeps philosophers' feet on the ground. There is a philosophy which is an abstract theory, that is involved in its own problems and is able to create a technical jargon, but there is also a philosophy as a theory of a praxis. While it is true that there is no proper praxis without a theory, it is not less true that if philosophy does not take into consideration human reality, it may become a complex intellectual entertainment with no consequence for human life. Philosophy should be both an interpretation and a guidance. The interpretation is not for its own sake; we want to know, to be able to treat our fellow men in a better way. And to know ourselves to behave in a better way.

Fortunately, in its development through the centuries, philosophy is getting nearer to the actual feelings, needs and sufferings of the individual man and his community. Thus it is becoming more and more relevant to human life and to the public good.

RISIERI FRONDIZI

SOUTHERN ILLINOIS UNIVERSITY
CARBONDALE
SEPTEMBER, 1972

HARLAN CLEVELAND
WORDS AND MEANINGS*

I

When Professor Anderson asked me to make tonight a speech which he briefly and fiercely described as "short", I responded I would try to think of something wise and philosophical—or at least philosophical—to say. He replied that you would appreciate hearing some "wisdom rather than philosophy—but if the latter is the best you can do, we will have to rest content."

Inspired by this stirring mandate, I have been asking philosophers of my acquaintance what goes on in your profession these days. My canvass has proved a rewarding experience. I have been rewarded with some of the finest epithets, some of the most genteel profanity, and some of the unkindest cuts of all. (Bear in mind that I was once Dean of a Graduate School, no stranger to the academic *Sturm und Drang* of intradisciplinary strife.)

The impression I have thus derived from my unscientific sampling is that most professional philosophers think that most other professional philosophers are on the wrong track.

* This address by the Honorable Harlan Cleveland, then Assistant (U. S.) Secretary of State for International Organization Affairs, was, by invitation, delivered on December 28, 1963, before the annual meeting of the Eastern Division of the American Philosophical Association in Washington, D. C. The editor of this volume, seeing the direct connection between its title and the intent of Secretary Cleveland's address, asked for the privilege of printing it here, where, from an outsider, it precisely makes the point which has been the major import of Schilpp's philosophical position and commitment. Harlan Cleveland is now President of the University of Hawaii.—EDITOR'S NOTE.

One acquaintance tells me that the philosophers *he* disagrees with are merely "practicing therapy on a disease they catch from each other and pass on to their students." It isn't true, another argues in rebuttal, that philosophers take in only each other's dirty linen; they are quite willing to take in other people's dirty linen too.

These cracks tell me nothing at all about American philosophers, but they do tell me something about the frustrations of my friends among you.

That cliché coiner, Shakespeare, called your trade "adversity's sweet milk, philosophy." There is still plenty of adversity in the world; but what has happened to the sweet milk? Has it soured? And if it has, that is probably a good sign. Professional polemics are the needful noise of a lively profession.

For our purposes this evening, therefore, let us assume that philosophy is not what Ambrose Bierce called it, "A route of many roads leading from nowhere to nothing." I am willing also to posit for purposes of argument that the profession of philosophy is just as useful, and just as much fun, as editing a magazine, managing a university graduate school, or running a government bureau—the three trades which I have hugely enjoyed and at which I, like you, have failed to make a decent living.

II

I am told that the best philosophers prefer questions to answers—a wise preference indeed. And since I am here, flattered by your invitation to speak, warmed by these academic surroundings, confident that if I am not among friends I am at least among strangers, I am emboldened to ask some questions about the meaning of some large, oblong, fuzzy phrases that are the very meat and marrow of modern diplomacy.

The basic question I would ask of you this evening is whether you, who are or should be the experts on meaning, are applying your good minds in a way that is useful and relevant to my work as a practitioner of public affairs. *Are* you writing only to impress each other? *Are* you taking in each other's intellectual linen, or will you take some of mine too?

Is your discourse relevant to a time of crisis—and is it comprehensible to the public officials who must somehow master problems of appalling complexity and somehow decide we shall live rather than die?

It seems to me that our national debate about foreign policy, and much of the international discourse about peace and trade and development, is thoroughly confused by the widespread use of words which have lost their meaning. I appeal to you as students of meaning to get to work on these words—either to bury them or to update them.

Take, as my main example, the principle of nonintervention in the internal affairs of other nations. You can't find anybody who does not agree with the principle of nonintervention—and that is already a suspicious circumstance. It is always the propositions to which everybody agrees that turn out to have been drained of their meaning.

In this world where everybody agrees about nonintervention, the nations are, of course, deeply immersed in each other's affairs. They give each other technical assistance, they beam culture and propaganda at each other, they freely discuss each other's internal politics in matters of race and religion, sex and sin, ethics and economics. Most of the developing countries actively seek to bring foreigners into the very citadels of national sovereignty—the places where decisions are made about the allocation of national resources, the management of foreign trade and exchange, the health and welfare and education of their children, the executive training of their leaders. Many countries even invite outsiders to help with their police and their armies. Nobody admittedly intrudes across national frontiers in matters of "politics". Yet in a developing country the internal security forces and the program of economic and social development are, of course, the ladder to power and the scene of the power struggle we call politics.

Given this state of affairs, given this matrix of mutual involvement across national frontiers, what does the principle of nonintervention mean, judging from the practice of nations?

It isn't intervention, apparently, if you're merely *talking* about the other fellow's internal affairs—even though loud international talk can help stir up a local opposition and change the chemistry of a local power struggle.

It isn't intervention, apparently, if you are invited to come in. This proposition seems nice and simple—but again, it is suspect because everybody agrees with it. In the real world of international politics, is an engraved invitation the key to an ethic of intervention? Or is it just the doorbell to the really interesting questions? For example:

1. How much arm-twisting may permissibly precede the invitation? Remember that when those Russian tanks rumbled onto the streets of Budapest in 1956, they were there by invitation of the Hungarian government.

2. Can the outsider, once invited in for one purpose, stay on to serve other purposes? Apparently so, since most of the activities of most of the outsiders in most countries are not covered by specific letters of invitation. But does the acquiesence of the constituted authorities justify whatever the outsider then wants to do?

3. Who are those "authorities"? From whom does the engraved invita-

tion have to come? In building an ethic of intervention, maybe it is not enough to depend on an indefinite invitation by an undefinable "they". Maybe we ought to examine the *purpose* of the penetration across national frontiers, asking whether the purpose is beneficent or malignant, whether it is helping build free institutions or the institutions of repression, whether the outsider is truly helping to fulfill the aspirations of "the people".

But who are "the people" whose aspirations are to be served? And where a struggle for power is in process (and in what nation is it not in process?) *which* aspirants to leadership are the correct interpreters of the people's aspirations?

There will probably be forty or fifty changes of government in the world during 1964, and some of them will be violent. Even in the North Atlantic community, that supposed island of political stability in a turbulent world, ten of the fifteen NATO countries changed their government leadership during 1963—and that includes four of the five major powers in NATO.

In such a world, diplomacy is not just the art of getting along with the powers that be; diplomacy is the art of getting along with the next government, and the one after that as well.

In this era of rapid change and deep mutual involvement of the nations in each other's internal affairs, my hunch is we will find an ethic for this international involvement, *not* so much in the actions and aspirations of the weaker countries, as in the self-restraints and self-denying ordinances of stronger countries.

Yet the time has passed when we can say that our judgment about what we should do in other people's backyards is the only judgment that means anything to us. That is why we are developing so many international organizations in which weak countries and strong countries can together decide how the mutual involvement (which science and technology has made both possible and necessary) will be organized, and by what restraints the outsiders will be guided while working with the insiders in each country.

That is why an increasing proportion of all the international involvement takes the form of international people—that is, civil servants working for the secretariats of international organizations—travelling across national frontiers and helping sensitive countries to govern their own countries without risking the charge from their own domestic opponents that they have sold out to one or another powerful nation.

III

In this welter of fascinating ethical and political questions, how useful is this much-used-word "intervention"? How relevant a guidepost is something called "the principle of nonintervention"? If you are the experts on meaning, how about dissecting this ancient phrase for us, questioning its usefulness, helping us weave a tapestry of words and concepts that more nearly matches the complexity of international relations in the real world? (And don't ask me what the word "real" means in that sentence! That's *your* kind of question, not mine.)

For a start, why doesn't the American Philosophical Association offer a prize for the best substitute for the word "intervention"? We need a substitute because intervention and all of its usual synonyms carry such a load of pejorative connotations that it is literally quite difficult to discuss with you in public the subject I have been discussing with you in public. The best synonym I have been able to come up with is "mutual involvement". I don't think that's very good, and I am sure that you can do better.

When you have sorted out the concept of intervention, and fuzzed up the principle of nonintervention, I will be glad to suggest some further grist for your semantic mill.

You might practice on "uncommitted"—does it mean uncommitted to parties, or principle, or both? Or neither?

You might then go to work on "self-determination", a phrase which draws universal approbation and is mighty useful to us in Berlin and elsewhere—but which is also widely in use to justify oppressive rule by majorities, wars of subversion and secession, and the creation of new societies too proud to remain dependent, but too small to remain independent. In the largely honorable and remarkably bloodless revolution of independence, we are getting down now to the last fifty-odd dependent territories, mostly islands and enclaves, which are seeking to find a place in a world which understands dependency and understands independence but has not organized the constitutional no-man's land in between.

So, how far down the scale of resources and power and population should the principle of self-determination be applied? Does Pitcairn Island need to find among its 2,800 people a Prime Minister, a Foreign Minister and a delegate to the UN? And if not, how is the lofty principle of self-determination to be applied in support of the inalienable rights of the Pitcairn Islanders?

When you've worked that out, I suggest you go to work on the term "free enterprise", and help us to stop describing our mixed economy (with its fruitful and constructive intervention by government in everything from the aero-space industry to the price of the bread you buy in the corner grocery store) by misconstruing those lovely words inherited from Adam Smith. Or you might take a crack at the word "socialism" which is causing all kinds of grief in countries that still feel they have to describe the imperatives of their modern industrial society, or the case for land reform, with tired and reactionary phrases from a nineteenth-century economics textbook.

IV

Most people seem to think of words as different from reality. But you know—and I suspect—that the words often are the reality. This makes it all the more important that we continuously reinterpret the words, and that we not suffer what Madison called "a blind veneration for antiquity, for custom, or for names." Madison thought it was our glory that we Americans did not allow "the opinions of former times and other nations . . . to overrule the suggestions of [our] own good sense, the knowledge of [our] own situation, and the lessons of [our] own experience." Can we still claim this form of glory?

As a professional doer I do not ask you professional thinkers for instant ideology. There is far too much of that around already, and besides, it would be too easy an assignment. I ask for something more complicated, more interesting, and more relevant: that in addition to reminding us about the wisdom of the past, you insist we stop using and reusing words and phrases for which it is increasingly difficult to find the referents in the real world.

We still have the good sense Madison gave us credit for. We know what our situation is, which is to be both the oldest and most powerful democracy in the history of mankind. If we can just get our vocabulary under control, I think we can come close to doing what the vast majority of men and women, who aspire to freedom and diversity even when they are not allowed to say so without risking arrest, would like to see us do.

In that task, we who manipulate the words and you who manipulate their meaning have work to do together—more work than we have been doing, and more of it together.

HARLAN CLEVELAND

PRESIDENT
UNIVERSITY OF HAWAII
DECEMBER, 1963

W. H. WERKMEISTER

REFLECTIONS ON OUR TIMES

"To be radical," the young Marx wrote, "means to go to the root, and the root—is man himself."[1] It is from this perspective that I should like to take a brief look at the contemporary scene, here and abroad.

I take it to be beyond serious doubt that, in a very real sense, man must and does create himself—both individually and as a species in cultural development.[2] He no longer lives, as animals do, a life confined to the level of instincts. His intellectual capacities, his ability (as Kant would say) to impose laws upon himself and to live in accordance with his insight into laws, have raised him above that level. His creative achievements, his slow rise from Neanderthal to modern man, testify to this liberation from mere animality. But we know also the evil that man is capable of—"the perversion of the heart," to use a Kantian phrase—that despoils man's noblest efforts. Our own century provides more than sufficient proof of this. And, as never before, man's very existence has become a problem for him—a problem which he cannot escape and for which he must find a solution.

Actually, there is only one way open to man and that is making the world a truly human world and, in the process, becoming truly human himself. In his projected ideals and self-images, in his value commitments (no matter what they may be), man always reaches out into the future and, haphazardly or with determined purpose, he charts his course of action. Learning but little from history, he plunges ahead, always hoping that, somehow, he is on the right track. His passions and drives involve his total existence as that existence is conditioned and molded by his interactions with the world around him, with nature and with his fellow men. But man's reason suggests at least that he strive for a harmonious integration of his interests and desires—individually and as a species; and that he create a society, nationally and internationally, which furthers the self-development of the individual in terms of his own creative powers, and sets common goals of cultural achievement in peaceful cooperation.

To be sure, to achieve such a goal—or even to work toward it, consistently and in the long run—requires self-discipline and the constant effort to bring man's desires and passions, individually and collectively, under an increasing degree of rational control. What is needed, however, is not a suppression of emotions and feelings—for such suppression would mean doing violence to an essential part of human nature—but an adjustment of them that is in harmony with rational alternatives to disruptive actions. It is not an easy task, this self-molding of human nature; and a permissive society—a society which thinks little of value norms as basic to its own existence—can hardly be counted on to provide guidance and incentive.

Ever since the days of Hegel and Marx there has been talk of man's alienation; but alienation from what? At one level of the discussion what is meant is the alienation of the worker from his work and from the fruits of his labor; and, surely, we cannot deny that the man on the assembly line who tightens a bolt here or places a screw there—who, in other words, contributes but a small part to the assembly of a motorcar or of some other object of mass production—can never become absorbed in his work or find self-fulfillment in what he is doing. But let us not forget that the situation is the same wherever production is keyed to the assembly line, be the social structure what it may, be the economic order that of capitalism or that of communism. Alienation in the sense here considered is simply intrinsic to mass production and cannot be eliminated short of reverting to the Age of the Craftsman that preceded the Industrial Revolution; and to take such a step is an historical impossibility. Modern technology and mass production require large factories, the assembly line, and automation. Without them, twentieth-century culture is no longer possible. What is currently happening in Russia and mainland China, in India and Africa, is but proof of this fact. All we can hope for—and work for—is that the deadening effect of the assembly line have a compensatory counterpart in the politico-cultural activities and, thus, in the personal life of the individuals.

But more profound even than alienation from work is man's alienation from himself; and this may take two quite different forms. It may mean, on the one hand, that the individual, though convinced of his own worth and dignity as a person, experiences himself as manipulated by others, as being reduced to a mere means, a mere "thing." And it may mean, on the other hand, that the individual abandons himself by sliding off into the anonymity of the impersonal, thus becoming part and parcel of "the herd."

The first of these two types of alienation means that the individual feels himself alienated from a society in which he cannot participate without losing his self-respect, in which he is prevented from sharing in the decision making on issues which affect himself and his very existence as a human being. Members of minority groups feel this perhaps more keenly than do other members of our society, and rightfully resent it. It is beyond dispute, I believe, that alienation in this sense is at least part of the cause of the restlessness and disaffection of minority groups, and is a symptom of our social malaise. The fact that it is the lingering effect of historical events is no justification for its perpetuation in a society that prides itself on standing committed to the principle of equal rights and equal opportunities for all. What is needed here is a new emphasis on the human priorities of social living—a commitment, individually and socially, in action as well as in words, to the values of our common humanity, to a new respect for the person irrespective of color, creed, or racial descent. Granted that much has changed in this respect in recent years. But laws alone cannot make us civilized when the heart remains unaffected—when there is no rebirth of spirit, no willing acceptance of the same value scale for all.

The second type of alienation referred to above means that the individual is intrinsically alienated from himself; that he no longer sees any sense even in his own existence as a distinct person having his own worth and dignity. Existentialist philosophers have made much of this form of alienation; but one need not be an existentialist in philosophy to recognize the facts and the symptoms in the case. Our drug-oriented subcultures are sufficient proof of their reality. What these facts and symptoms disclose is a perversion, if not an abandonment, of those values that give meaning and purpose to personal existence. It is not only a protest against the world and the values of tradition but, quite often, an escape into a world of unreality.

Behind this form of alienation, as a causative factor, there is not only a profound disillusionment with conditions as they are, but a feeling of loneliness and fear and personal frustration in the face of problems and forces that far transcend an individual's best efforts. Religion no longer serves as a dependable guide; and science offers no substitute values. The optimism of earlier ages, the belief in inevitable progress, seems ill-suited for generations to come that must live in the shadow of the mushroom cloud.

To be sure, the twentieth century has been a period of tremendous changes, technologically, sociopolitically, and valuationally. As history goes, it was only yesterday (December 17, 1903) that the Wright brothers made man's first power flight at Kitty Hawk; and now we have landed men on the moon. We of the older generation have lived through two world wars and their disruptive consequences. We have seen empires fall on a worldwide scale and have witnessed revolutions that have transformed the sociopolitical conditions of existence for hundreds of millions of people. There is no place on earth that has remained unaffected by these changes. Moreover, in all of these changes, and as a result of them, values have been lost—irretrievably lost—and not always have higher ones taken their place. And this fact, I submit, is indicative of the dilemma and the tragedy of our times—a dilemma and a tragedy of which alienation in all of its forms is but a symptom.

If this diagnosis is correct—as I think it is—then the real issues of today (as always in human affairs) are value problems which demand theoretical as well as practical solutions; and the contribution which philosophy can make to these solutions is twofold: (1) it can and must attempt to clarify the conception of values and value standards; and (2) it can and must reexamine the sociopolitical means through which those values are to be realized.

As to the first task, little need be said here. In the vast literature dealing with problems of value and value standards[3] there is general agreement that man himself with his needs and desires, his feelings and aspirations is at the center of all valuations, and that his own existence *as a person* provides a standard of evaluation in the light of which each individual can appraise his own actions as well as the sociopolitical conditions of his existence.

But we must realize that man is not only a creature of bodily needs and desires; he has other interests as well. His "immense journey" from the days of *Pithecanthropus erectus* to our own times is evidence of abilities (intellectual and creative) that are intrinsic to his nature, and of a drive toward the full realization of those potentialities. When this drive is thwarted, frustration results and the individual does not truly exist as himself. He may seek escape from his misery in an imaginary world of compensatory future bliss, or he may rebel against conditions that prevent his full self-realization and may try to alter forcefully the inhibitive conditions. In either case, however, it is the individual as a person that strives toward self-fulfillment and, in doing so, sets the standard of all valuation.

But to live truly as a person the individual must also understand himself and his essential interests and needs, and must discipline himself so as to achieve that harmonious integration of his desires and drives which alone makes possible the full realization of his potentialities. In this process of self-creating the worst enemy one can encounter (to paraphrase Nietzsche) is always oneself. Are we "the master of our passions," "the lord of our virtues"? "Or does the animal speak in our wish?"[4]

To be sure, in this process of personal development the sociopolitical environment provides an historically grounded valuational framework of opportunities and/or hindrances. But in forming himself by reacting to the traditional valuations, the individual may also modify or radically transform that tradition—his own needs and potentialities requiring new attitudes and new standards for their full realization.

Lest this view be mistaken for a complete and vicious value relativism, let me add at once that certain fundamental needs are universally human. Their satisfactions are the basic values on which all can agree: food, shelter, security, freedom from pain, acceptance in a group, and happiness rather than frustration—although the mode and the quality of their realization differ widely within a given culture no less than from culture to culture.

But let me repeat: the ultimate value is and remains the human being, the individual person in full realization of his creative potentialities. Society is a conditioning (but not a determinative) circumstance and democracy merely a method of actualizing human ends. Neither is ever an end in itself. And let us face it: rule by majority is still only rule by majority. It does not necessarily reflect man's highest valuations or most enlightened value priorities.

It is true, of course, that democracy as a method for achieving human ends cannot function properly unless its principle of decision making is agreed upon by the vast majority of people affected by the decisions. Even such agreement, however, is no guarantee that the democratic process will result in the realization of man's highest values; for a whole society may be sick, and even democratically agreed upon ends and purposes establish no standard or norm for humanity when the ends pursued reflect sociopathological valuations. Recent history—here and abroad—provides sufficient proof of this fact.

Still, the democratic method of decision making is perhaps the best we have in the sociopolitical sphere; for, in principle at least, it provides opportunities for all sides to be heard. I said "in principle." In actuality, the political power struggle may drastically curtail such opportunities, and majority rule per se can be just as oppressive as any form of dictatorship. A just, fair, and properly functioning democratic process of decision making is possible only within a carefully conceived, constitutionally guaranteed juridico-moral framework under the constant vigilance of all concerned. But the true opposite of collectivism and dictatorship is not democracy. It is the principle of freedom which usually but not always (see the functioning of the Russian soviets) is intrinsic to the democratic process.

But let us remind ourselves of the fact that every freedom has a limit beyond which it becomes a danger to itself and to society—a limit beyond which a permissive society lacks the self-discipline requisite to the realization of the highest human values and thus tends to abandon all standards. It seems to me that, today, we have come dangerously close to this point. The danger is all the greater because large sections of the younger generation have become disillusioned with the established process of decision making. They feel powerless in their efforts to deal with "the establishment" (be that a university administration or the federal government), and are cynically critical of policies in the making of which they had no voice.

Although reforms stressing the need for a participating democracy that builds from the local level up and effectively reduces the dominance of centralized and absentee government may go far in remedying the situation just alluded to, they are not a cure-all for the problems of our times; for the problems are manifold and, in the last analysis, they involve our whole conception of social living. The belief, for example, that the plight of the "disadvantaged" in our culture is essentially one of material needs is at best only a partial truth. I would be the last one to deny that an adequate material basis is an indispensable presupposition for any truly human mode of existence; but I do deny that it is a sufficient condition for it. Taken as absolute, as the alpha and omega of social responsibility, the concern with the material basis only reflects a value blindness that disregards the more profound needs and requirements of human dignity and personal worth. What is at issue is not only material security or independence but the autonomy of total existence as a human being.

A science-based technological culture accepts only too readily the material values as ultimate and minimizes or disregards entirely the values inherent in a humanistic orientation. It is a view of life which, when not counteracted by a reversal of value priorities, tends to dehumanize human existence and to place man at the mercy of inexorable and inhuman forces. It is intrinsically a perversion of the human value scale. I find much in our own culture that exemplifies the humanly disastrous consequences of such an orientation. The far-reaching disillusionment of present-day youth is but one of its manifestations. The frightening emptiness of human existence, the wide-spread cynicism and radical hedonism of our times are others. We call it progress; but it is anything but that—if by progress we mean an elevation of human existence to a truly human level of authentic being. I may be old-fashioned in this respect, but I still believe that life is meaningful for a person only when it is directed toward the realization of the highest conceivable values inherent in a truly humanistic world-view. And society falls short of its purpose and its obligation when it does not provide for, or does not stress, such an orientation; for society is but a means, an instrument. Man himself is the end. There is no higher value than the worth and the dignity of the human individual. Society is simply a cooperative interaction of autonomous persons for the realization of that worth and that dignity. It has no other reason for its existence.

W. H. WERKMEISTER

FLORIDA STATE UNIVERSITY
JUNE, 1972

NOTES

[1] Karl Marx, *Die Frühschriften,* ed. by S. Landshut (Stuttgart: A. Kröner, 1953), p. 247.

[2] W. H. Werkmeister, *Man and His Values* (Lincoln: University of Nebraska Press, 1967), Chaps. I, II.

[3] W. H. Werkmeister, *Historical Spectrum of Value Theories,* Vol. I, *The German-Language Group* (Lincoln: Johnsen Publishing Company, 1970); Vol. II, *The Anglo-American Group* (Lincoln: Johnsen Publishing Company, 1973).

[4] Friedrich Nietzsche, *Thus Spake Zarathustra,* trans. by Thomas Common, from *The Complete Works of Friedrich Nietzsche* (London: G. Allen & Unwin, Ltd., 1923-24), Vol. XI, pp. 73, 79.

FRITZ-JOACHIM VON RINTELEN

THE PUBLIC GOOD AND THE ATTAINMENT AND LOSS OF REALITY IN SCIENCE AND PHILOSOPHY

1. Science and Reality

Can the philosophy and science of our time offer man guidance for his public life? Can it give him spiritual backbone and respond to his deeper needs, bound up as it is with the methodology of the natural sciences? Or must it limit itself to defining the world and reality (*Wirklichkeit*) solely according to mathematical quantities in the sense of a mathematical system (*Mathematizismus*), confining itself to the pure givenness of sense experience, and devoting itself in the narrower philosophical sphere *only* to "linguistics, semantics, symbolistics, grammarians or logistics?"[1]

Professor Paul Arthur Schilpp has called upon us not to limit ourselves to logical "hairsplitting" and a mere "clarification of concepts" or "manipulation of language".[2] Is this adequate, he has asked, for enduring and removing the enormous threat made possible by the "atomic age?" What inner impulses do we still have, then, to state and defend the humanitarian demands which for our public good derive from the wholeness of our being?[3]

This challenge should in no way be construed as an objection to genuine scientific research, which, if it exhibits really indubitable and conclusive results, must be taken into consideration by any philosophy. It is precisely in the natural sciences, especially in atomic physics, that the earlier assumptions of a purely mechanistic interpretation of reality have reached a limit, and a great change has taken place (microphysics, Planck: quantum leaps).[4] We must never bypass the view of reality which has here been opened up.

How, then, did the modern interpretation of the world and life, so widespread today, come to be so confined to the method of physics as the sole method for which exactness is claimed (physicalism)? Surely because of its undreamt of successes in the control and utilization of natural forces, and the resulting technology. But Richard Hönigswald once said that "the method anticipates the object". By so doing the result is already prejudged and delimited by the condition that only what is determinable by the previously assumed method can be admitted as reality. Everything else appears as unreal, devised and subjective. But such onesidedness is scarcely adequate for the profusion of public life.

What then does *reality* mean? The German word *Wirklichkeit*, contains also the idea of functioning, of being active, of the actively dynamic, a kind of perceiving which is quite characteristic of the present day. *Wirklichkeit* is not adequately translated into English as "reality", in French as *réalité*, in Spanish as *realidad* (which link them with the Latin word *res*) since *res* can be translated merely as "thing". *Wirklichkeit* expresses also a set of circumstances of facts that can exert an effect, and reality, in Rothacker's words, "is as it is". This has its particular significance when, further on, we must raise the question concerning active psychic and spiritual reality.

The thus characterized approach to reality was initiated in the late Middle Ages by Nicole Oresme (d. 1382, impetus, mechanics), and gained more and more acceptance in the modern age, that, in the last analysis, measurable forces underlie existence in the world. Aristotle already, it is true, designated the nature of what is, with *energeia on*.[5] From Descartes's conservation of measurable motion, one came to the conservation of mechanical force, clearly introduced by Newton—an approach which has become a matter of course for our contemporary understanding of nature (of fields of force).[6]

If the earlier period focused its attention on the static in the flux of appearances, it is characteristic for us to emphasize activity, change, becoming. However, in all the becoming of being, there is something of the always identical being which remains as, for example, the law of order, just as in all being there is something of becoming. Both are reality. Modern man, critically and realistically oriented, has now the irresistible urge to investigate this, to learn from the facts (cp. Bacon of Verulam) and not to be deceived by illusory suppositions. But, if we are not to be one-sided, it is very important for the social community to see also the wholeness of reality.

How is this possible? We are dependent on our experiences, on our sense experiences, their judgment and interpretation—on sensation and reflection in Locke's sense.[7] If we hold strictly to this, then we say there is exact science. This word "exact", originally used by Pascal for "exact definition", is, in the first instance, intended in a quite limited and specific sense—sense experience, which we are to grasp according to strictly formal principles and in quantitatively and mathematically definable terms. Roger Bacon attempted this already in the thirteenth century. It is interesting to note how all at once an entirely different appraisal of the sciences developed which has prevailed into our times. Originally the status and the significance of the sciences was determined by their content: for instance, theology, metaphysics, and ethics, which stood at the top. Nowadays their status is determined (cp. William of Occam) by the degree of certain, *certa*, we say today, exact knowledge, with the accompanying tendency to reduce qualities to quantitative measurements.

Indeed Plato, in the *Philebus* in his critical period, following the lead of the Pythagoreans, had already taken recourse to number, so that in boundlessness (*apeiron*) he might be able to make assertions about the unlimited, the enduring (*peras*).[8] But there number as quantitative determination was the basis for proportion, for harmony, in order to be able to conceive of the cosmos—i.e., ornament—under qualitative aspects *à la* the aesthetic world-picture of the Pythagoreans. Augustine likewise speaks of the beauty of the forms of creation—*in quantum numerosa sunt*—"to what extent they are determinable by numbers".[9] But for him that was only the beginning of the understanding of "reality" (*Wirklichkeit*).

What happens, then, if we proceed to carry the quantitative point of view, in itself both justified and fruitful, through with absolute consistency, and say, all "reality" is "nothing but" a determinate quantitative relation? Doesn't this lie at the very roots of our time? And yet will not the man of the future be completely hollow if nothing more is recognized as "reality"? Or will his will lead him to be on the lookout for something more essential? It was for this reason that the younger generation in the East-West Philosophers' Conferences (Hawaii, 1969) said: "We ask for new values". Did not Poletajew already say that—seen as the last orientation—the mechanically functioning cybernetic apparatus, the robot, could replace man—with merely the difference of not being able to beget and procreate?[10]

Or, let us be still more *exact* and recognize only what is indisputably and immediately given to us. In that case wasn't the English philosopher Berkeley in the last analysis right when he said that, strictly speaking, we have only our inner-sense complexes of ideas which we order and formally define? We cannot even speak of a demonstrable external world, for it is by no means given exactly and directly but only mediated by the senses. David Hume, without, to be sure, becoming a disciple of Berkeley, says it is an "I know not what".

What, then, is left us? Ultimately—for let us for once be entirely consistent here—we have only sense perceptions which we interpret mathematically as variations of number; processes of experience whose mechanical course we thus record unambiguously. In the face of the immense triumph which modern natural science has achieved, it would be foolish indeed to attack the consideration of this method in its own sphere. And the other sciences adapted themselves to this more or less.

However, the question forces itself upon us, as to whether we thereby also fully comprehend the total "reality" to which belong not only physical processes but also the spontaneous organic life processes (Pascual Jordan) with their rich variety of forms, and, above all, "reality" as the *activity* of spiritual-creative being. Is it not true that only a part of reality is conceived in thought by that quantitative method, and must we not be still *more* realistic? Is not the task, so far from restricting the spirit, to allow it to manifest itself in all the richness of its potentialities? As Schilpp put it: "It is not less thinking we need, but more".[11] What builds up destroys, and what destroys can build up; that is to say, great one-sided achievements may produce a disintegration; and this in turn could produce constructive, enhancing, conquering forces, in short, an integration. Thus in broad outline the movement of the spiritual life has always been. It is striking that even the extreme of the widespread dialectical materialism now firmly rejects the mechanicism of a Plekhanov and a Bucharin, and even speaks of qualitative entities which, in that way, are incomprehensible.[12] At the same time, the results of the natural sciences, where they are definitive, must be acknowledged, they cannot be overlooked because theirs is an exact interpretation of a real level of being. For our public good, however, we shall need a richer answer.

2. *Natural and Human Science as Unity for the Public Good*

Some decades ago this situation already led the neo-Kantian philosopher, Heinrich Rickert, to write a work entitled *The Limits of the Conceptual Structure of Natural Science* (1902, 1929). Rickert means ultimately: if we adhere *solely* to the methods of the natural sciences and utter the "nothing but", then an enormous loss of reality ensues. What is, above all, decisive for our existence? Man, as a spiritual-personal being with the particular quality of his cultural creations and his influence, is completely eliminated from consideration and placed under a point of view essentially foreign to him. According to Scheler and Fridjof Bergmann (U. S. A.), reality itself is much richer and fuller.[13] Otherwise, we become with Scheler a "brain creature which is distinguished from animals only by a greater use of the cerebral cortex". It was in this sense that Heidegger spoke of the modern alienation of human existence (*Daseinsentfremdung*) and of the deterioration of being (*Seinsverfallenheit*) which places man in question, robs him of his inner existence. It is no wonder that man then, as a consequence of the necessary process of being, which in general is everywhere identical, feels himself relieved of the obligation of making any decision and is completely at the mercy of the external processes pressing on him. Under such circumstances an inner ethical relation to the good of public life is very difficult and that is the beginning of social anarchy with the consequences of totalitarianism. This has also had the effect, that so much is heard today about the fundamental inner feeling of anxiety, of *Angst*, in man, especially since a sustaining inner meaning of life is largely lacking.

Perhaps one may in this connection cite Goethe's well-known words:

> By that I know the learned lord you are!
> What you don't touch is lying leagues afar,
> What you don't grasp is wholly lost to you,
> What you don't reckon, think you, can't be true,
> What you don't weigh, it has no weight, alas.
> What you don't coin, you're sure it will not pass!
>
> *Faust* II, 1

Here a view had already been expressed which is beginning to gain ground again today as the new. One need only take note of the tendencies which were expressed at the international philosophical congresses at Vienna (1968, Bertanlanffy-Canada, Gabriel-Vienna, Heitler-Zürich, etc.). What contemporary man is on the lookout for—questions which are more decisive and have far deeper implications for his being—became clear to me some years ago at the East-West Philosophers' Conferences in Honolulu (1959), where Americans as well as Asians had an opportunity to express themselves. There was no real discussion or encounter until the moment when the limitations of what Werkmeister has called "scientism" were overcome and questions were formulated which concerned the intellectual or spiritual public life of peoples and cultures. It was revealed in an astonishing manner how, in spite of all the differences, much was felt to be in common, for instance such questions as responsibility, justice, love, self-realization, etc.[14]

However, at this point we enter a realm which one generally regards as the theme of the *Geisteswissenschaften* or humanities. The striking observation can be made that today the ground is being prepared for relation and cooperation between the natural and the human sciences; we need only to think of the biologist Portmann (Basel), of his pronouncements on the self-representation of nature in its aesthetic tendency; of Meyer-Abich's work on biology and its historical foundations in the human sciences.[15] And yet we may ask whether we are even entitled to speak at all of science (*Wissenschaft*) in the spheres which we have called the human sciences—such as history,

history of art, psychology, sociology, philosophy and so on—in the strict sense of the term science?

It is a matter of how one understands this word. We considered above the meaning of science. The German word *wissen* corresponds to the classic word *oida*, the Gothic *wait*, "*Ich weiss*, I know", *videre*, "to see with the mind". We know of infinitely many real events, which are richer and more many-sided than the characterized limited physical sight is able to convey. If, for example, someone has experienced great shocks in the sense of depressing or elevating moments, we say that he "knows" it, he has experienced it within himself. Doesn't the word "exact" in this context demand precisely that these realms of reality (*Wirklichkeit*) be also drawn into our purview as themes of the human sciences in a responsible, in a more possible, unequivocal, and justifiable manner? There is plainly a limit not only to the possibility in which things can be objectified in a merely formal or in a mathematically determined sense, but also to the abstraction of impersonal it-ness; much may, in the final analysis, not be formal-rationally analyzable, but be the expression of occurrences beyond that kind of interpretation (cp. the physicist Heisenberg).

The very fact that our life has been lived is in some sense only ascertainable but not ultimately explicable. Nevertheless its established "reality" is not on that account to be denied. It is unscientific to deny realities for the sheer reason that they do not clearly fit the presupposed schema. On the contrary, what is given must be recognized and plainly interpreted. This is our concern today in the interpretation of organic life—whether we think we can do so most effectively in terms of a theory of totality or only in terms of isolated emergence. However, if we overlook the self-evident reality which presents itself, this entails a loss of inner reality with the negative consequences following from this.

But these areas of life are often what is most important for us, and we must try to delve into their depths, otherwise we evade the issue of reality for man. In our opinion, Nicolai Hartmann was correct in stating that there are different levels of being (*Daseinsschichten*), something many ancient philosophers saw at least in part long ago, levels of existence which could be defined by only applicable categories, although many categories may be held in common. In this sense he separates purely physical being, organic life, the unconscious-conscious life of the soul and living spirit from each other. Transferring categorial principles from the physical level, as if they were the only valid ones, to the phenomenon of life is no more admissible than is the converse. It will be even less adequate when we come to the conscious level of soul and mind.[16]

Such considerations contributed to the fact that already Wilhelm Dilthey (d. 1911) distinguished, as he says, "the natural and the human sciences". According to him, the latter constitute "an empirical science of spiritual phenomena" whether of the human individual or of historical communities. We must not approach them with alien points of view which only relate to external facts; but must, he insists, view their reality by understanding the value-relations which appear here and at the same time enter into their world-view in order to understand their concern.

Only thus will we be able to give something to other men in our society, to men of other cultures, appeal to their inner needs, while, at the same time, being ready also to accept something from them and to understand their mentality. If we bypass their spiritual life and sensibilities and can offer them only external goods and the scientific-technological achievements on which those are based, we will never be able to arrive at a tolerable community. The danger is then, that a reaction begins a radical emotional behaviour and irrationality, as we see today in the young generation. This "alienation of man" was the theme of the above-mentioned East-West Philosophers' Conferences (Hawaii, 1969) and the young representatives said: "we live in a senseless emptiness".

With Ernst Troeltsch we must be clear about the fact, that any given time, any given culture, indeed any given person always lives in the context of a meaningful totality (*Sinntotalität*).[17] These too are spheres of reality (*Wirklichkeit*). In order to gain access to these, one has today learned to speak not only of outer but also of inner, experiences. Naturally, they too are communicated to us by others and therefore are also given us from outside. However, only an inner understanding will be able to disclose the impulses, the deeper levels, shall we say, for this or that cultural unit. In order to grasp such things we must hold very precisely, that is, exactly and objectively, to the inner reality of the experience which underlies them and to their given manifestations and have our criteria for them; otherwise, any assertions about them cannot be justified.

In this process spiritual forces will certainly be called forth which are able to go beyond the purely discursive, rationally-calculating and quantitative intellect. This holds true also ultimately if we wish to delve into the mythical realm; for every genuine myth has assertive power and is the original, concentrated rendering of a significant symbol (*Sinnbild*) which is qualitative in nature; i.e., it is intelligible only out of itself and not derivable from anything else. But the meaning-content must be brought to light in an objective manner which conforms to the phenomenal content. This is possible only if we approach it with an inner readiness for understanding, with candor and without reservations. That holds true, above all, when it is a matter of understanding another human being.

But if we lose this spiritual capacity, we will have "nothing to communicate" and remain sterile in the sector of public affairs. It is all the more to be insisted that the decisive intellectual demands be subject to the control of systematic accuracy and not to anyone's interpretation "apart from scholarship" (Whitehead), because they are decisive for the public good and for our human community and must be examined for their "normative components" (Schilpp).[18]

3. Total Reality, Total Man

This is as much as to say that total reality can be illuminated only by the total man with all his capacities. To be sure, an intellectual effort and aptitude are indispensable for this. Such is not granted to everyone in any marked degree, and it requires special cultivation. However, when such insights are expressed, anyone willing to make the effort will be able to follow. That is true also of the mathematician, who, like Blaise Pascal, is impressed by the clear mathematical mode of cognition, the *clara et distincta perceptio* of Descartes; otherwise he would not succeed, as he says himself; Pascal places the *ordre de la raison* the *ordre du coeur*, and the *esprit de finesse* side by side which, however, complement one another in an overall view in the fine balance of the spirit.[19] A preservation and repeated revitalization of such views will continue to be essential for future man also. Though physical and technopractical progress may in our day be immense, it will not be of permanent avail if its support, the human foundation, begins to wither in its soil.

We see, therefore, that man is a multidimensional being, and, if he intends to take a stand toward life and existence, none of his distinctive capacities may be stunted. To do so would in fact signify loss of reality and spiritual decay.

Is not this the very thing we find to deplore in our time, and in the most recent past? Were we not more and more openly dominated by a calculating, one-sided, purely formal practical intellect, by a knowledge of work (*Wirkwissen*) which was sceptical toward and treated as relative all other realms of mental capacity? Often we have been hearing the words "there is nothing at all in it". The result was that, out of this extreme (cp. the above-mentioned "inner emptiness") came another extreme; that is insofar as one finally affirmed and valued nothing anymore but the primitive drives, the vital force which is simply there and is undeniable. This is why Scheler decades ago said: "The revolt of nature in man and of all that is dark, compulsive and instinctive—everything unconscious against the conscious, indeed of things themselves against mankind and his reason—it had to come sometime and here it is".[20]

The result was that the vital, irrational, unrestrained lust for power took the calculating intelligence into its hands so as to prevail even more completely; this was then extolled as the highest and the sole thing of worth. Thus the breath of spirit was deprived of its oxygen. This led to those catastrophes (two world wars) which we have lived through, to the inner shocks of our day, in which man is himself disgraced. Now technology has bestowed on us murder weapons, whose effect in the way of destruction and atrocities puts in the shadow anything that has ever occurred in history. The future result could then be self-annihilation, unless reason—a reason which possesses its full resonance in the totality, in the substance of man—banishes the danger. That, to be sure, assumes an ordered ethical will with the idea of "Humanity". An inner desert had already begun to develop in us, however, before the devastation of our time came and covered everything with its leveling shadow. Nietzsche had foreseen this with prophetic vision. "Did not all solace, everything holy and redeeming ultimately have to be sacrificed along with all hope and all faith in hidden harmonies, and in future bliss and justice?"—since they do not, after all, yield to exact proof. "Did we not have to sacrifice God himself, and out of cruelty to ourselves worship rock, stupidity, gravity, fate, nothingness?"[21] We all know something of this already. The burden was too great! Let us avoid such questions, many say today. Let us forget these concerns and adapt ourselves conformably to the attitude of the "every-dayness" (Heidegger). Let us be satisfied with "merely reacting" (Schilpp) to the given situation. "Let us favor spiritual inflation", says the economist Otto Veit (Frankfurt) in a critical assessment of the situation, "for, asking more searching, deeper questions is villainy and is disturbing".

Nevertheless, we shall do it out of a sense of responsibility for the public good and avow in so doing that man himself has become problematic to himself today. With this we implicitly repeat with Goethe Psalm VIII, 5: "What is man that thou art mindful of him?" It appears that to a large extent, we venture to say, man has lost his center, that inner core where sensuality meets spirit with its guidance. Then the sense may not bypass the spirit and spirit may not linger on in pure abstraction and a "misuse of reason" (Schilpp) will not occur, but the spirit has the task of ordering the senses and summoning them to partnership in order that the soul may not become deprived and the mind may not become powerless and lifeless. Even Plato knew this insofar as he speaks in the *Phaedrus* (246, 247) of *thymoeides*, of the noble part of the soul, which is tied to sensibility and by this very fact makes possible spiritual elevation and creative action. Then the total "integral man" is involved (Leo Gabriel), perhaps not in all, but in his overall behavior. Immanuel Kant knew this also, when he placed the "practical (ethical) reason" above his *Critique of Pure Reason* with its orientation to the natural scientific method of his time, both of which with the added interplay of the "aesthetic judgment" in the *Critique of Judgment* afford expression of the whole man.

It would be completely misleading to say here hastily that all this is grounded in the irrational and is therefore not to be justified by reason through proof. No, it would be a disparagement of the human spirit, which encompasses also more than a mere explication based only on sense data in the strict form of a mathematical demonstration. It is a question rather of intellectual insights which are capable of their own justification and reveal their corresponding essential character. Of course their existential adoption, as it is frequently put today, activates a concomitant spiritual impression. Let us consider, for example, the phenomenon of reverence (Goethe), whose essential significance for mankind probably no one will deny. In connection with this attitude we raise the question which man cannot avoid asking in every age, namely, the question of the meaning of our existence. It is in our opinion the prime question of all philosophy, indeed also of our public life. For, who is capable of living meaninglessly? One may perhaps talk oneself into it out of disappointment and in heroic rebellion (cp. Nietzsche) and as a consequence of this the meaning is sought either in the facts or, for a while, in the immediate, shallow happiness of everyday life, whose dubiousness our time has experienced fully.

4. Meaning and the Problem of Value

What is *meaning*? Heyde-Berlin, in the collection *Sinn und Sein*,[22] has exhaustively dealt with the meaning of this word in its many-sidedness. Let us say, meaning includes the idea of inner determination, of significance, and assumes absence of contradiction. Meaning is not comprehensible merely by means of the senses. A word may, Plato says, consist of sense-perceived letters; but only mind can introduce meaning into them. Meaning finds expression in concept, in speech, in gestures, and in pictures. Michelangelo's *Creation of Man* in the Sistine Chapel has, for instance, the meaning that the outstretched finger of God causes the spark of spirit to leap over to man, arousing him to life.

Beyond this, the word "meaning" also involves the direction of something meaningful towards a goal, a purpose, yes, an end in itself. Then thought and action are tied to each other, and, when Goethe said, "In the beginning was the deed", he meant the spiritual activity of "realizing the purpose yielded by its insight".[23] To be sure, many lack such mental courage and many scholars content themselves with "pure description" (Schilpp); but this lacks guidance and challenge for genuinely practical action, something to which philosophy is also obligated. It is obvious that, according to Schilpp, such considerations underlie the "criteria for value judgments".[24] Though in *many details* agreement may here be lacking, yet, in the basic questions of human behavior it does exist, as we can daily observe even across the boundaries of various cultures.

We thus formulate the question of the meaning of life by what fulfills life, which at the same time is the question about truth. We are then not merely dealing with meaning as immediately given as an aim, but, more significantly, with what includes an end in itself. As Kant says: "You should never treat the other man as a means to an end but as an end"; at the same time, we add, as an end in himself, actually a social demand.[25] Taken in this more significant manner, meaning is understood as an end to what one calls a value, *intrinsic value*. Eduard Spranger has expressed the same opinion.[26] It is that which is capable of justifying itself. Again Nietzsche very truly saw the great significance of such value experience for the fulfillment of our existence (*Daseinsvollzug*). "The world revolves ever so inaudibly around the inventors of new values"—we would say discoverers of values—not around our "deathly-silent noise".[27]

But now let us ask what are the underlying reasons for the great antitheses we find in modern societies and cultures? Actually, they are not of a merely technological, economic nature; rather they lie also in the differing judgments concerning man, whether it be now in the sense of a free human person bearing *intrinsic value* in himself, or whether it be insofar as the individual man occupies exclusively a functional place in the greater collective with the resulting suspension of his personal uniqueness and freedom. Was not Hegel somehow right in saying that the ideas, let us say value ideas, acquire a decisively real significance and effective force in concrete events, insofar as the reality of life is essentially determined by them? The meaning content of a value experience can exert a great attractive force, and, like the released energy of an atomic nucleus, produce a tremendous effect. Values are thus decisive dynamic moments in human living. But we have to prove them, by refusing to fall back on an irrational unrealistic ideology.

Therefore give the age one great idea so that it can live from it—such as the idea of freedom in obligation, the social idea for the public good, that of the dignity of man, of peace, of the development of personal existence as well as of the value-centered fullness of life—to use Schilpp's words: "political liberty", "freedom of conscience", "self-enlightenment", and "welfare", whereby it must surely be recognized that the economic standard as a necessary condition of existence worthy of a human being, also must keep pace with the development of the "human personality".[28]

All pedagogues are aware of the import of value insights insofar as they recognize that in a young person the full self-development of his innate tendencies, talents, and potentialities takes place only to the extent that he has awakened to a future-directing life-goal which he can accept as worth living for, and to which he then devotes himself in order to grow. Are we supposed to eliminate completely these facts—for man so essential—and his understanding of existence from scientific and philosophical responsibility? Perhaps just because this cannot so definitely be determined and because in the course of history a multitude of variations of evaluation can be found? However, we ask ourselves, do not certain fundamental values (*Grundwerte, Sinnkern*) always exist in different ages which present themselves again and again, despite their distinctly varied aspects?

I know of no culture, for example, in which, however they may otherwise differ, it is not still basically well known that love stands above hate, honesty above falsehood, service to another above crass egoism, reverence for life and ultimate things above frivolous irreverence. To be sure, some of us seem to be fond of speaking of a "disintegration of value systems" while we still make quite specific demands on our fellow men, demands whose disregard is most severely condemned.

Let us be clear about it, obviously there is such a thing as a change of times and of value-judgments. But, on conscientious inspection it is never an absolute one, for man still has his *oikeion*, what the Greeks insisted is proper to his nature. In our opinion it would be irresponsible to overlook such decisive questions; the more so as man, public life, indeed the times, live on the basis of an answer to them and are determined in their reactions by such answers. Therefore I again agree with Schilpp when he calls for a "back to reason", for an intellectual liberation which, to be sure, is something more than mere formal intellectualizing; and calls for an orientation which can be verified.[29]

Consequently, one would have to speak of an unavoidability of the value question. This is exactly what should be pointed out in conscientious, exact, phenomenological analysis; the literature of intellectual and cultural history offers an immense amount of material here for systematic research, which needs to be investigated for its essential content, its meaning content. We cannot overlook it without bypassing the reality of man simply as it is. It must not be abandoned to a purely arbitrary, subjective feeling or left to mere literary treatment.

It is very striking, moreover, that the distinction between instrumental and relative utility (in Greek: *ophelimon kai hedy*) and intrinsic value (the *agathon auto*) was already formulated in antiquity. By intrinsic value, we would say, one understands an inner content, which, as in the examples mentioned, justifies itself in the very realization of human existence. Or, to say it again with Kant as concerns ethical value, it happens "for its own sake".

It is not possible here to deal with the question of value in detail. I would like to say only in which direction what I understand by value seems to lie. *Value* is what—to repeat with Le Senne (Paris)—is not indifferent. There is present in value (1) an affirmation and a denial such that (2) we note a striving for or against what is being evaluated. (3) It may present itself as intrinsic value, utility value or instrumental value, and presupposes (4) an intellectual subject who assumes an attitude. At the same time there is in it (5) an intention to realize the highest possible increase of its qualitative content so that a vertical dimension of degrees, a scale of values (*Hoehendimension*) is one of its characteristics. This appears to me to be a decisive fact, for an inquiry from the point of view of natural science does not concern itself with anything like that, when, for example, the question concerns the determination of, say, a kind of rock. Still a further element (6) enters in, relating to the extent to which in the *individual* realization it is possible to reach differential depths of penetration and manifestation of the sought-for value content in the subject (*Tiefendimension*); that is to say, how a differential level of fulfillment can be attained. We need here merely to think of the *personal values* of an aesthetic, ethical or religious nature.

Thus what is decisive lies in the *real* actualization, in what I would like to call real value. In order to attain the genuine value experience, we look therefore not primarily to abstract ideality, but direct our questioning toward the concrete reality of the events of our lives in accordance with the public good.

5. Summary

Let us summarize. As a consequence of the scientific and technological successful development which, in modern times, has increasingly prevailed, the contemporary man is fascinated by its technical-mathematical methodology. Much the same thing has always been the case in history whenever a notable success has been registered in a given field. The just named method has simply become the ideal for today's scientific approach.

At the same time we are obviously experiencing an alienation of man from life and existence along with a sinking to a merely calculating rationality and a one-sided limitation of the human-psychic-spiritual powers. This, on the other hand, has brought with it a mighty outburst of unrestrained, irrational, instinctual urges and lust for power. Under such circumstances we cannot help asking ourselves whether the man of the future will be able to marshall the necessary strength to prevent the annihilating catastrophe of a devastating atomic war.

We believe that it will be possible only if the aforesaid loss of reality is overcome and total man is again imbued with and determined in his innermost existence by reality in its totality. We shall then not be able to pledge ourselves to a one-sided method of everything, be it ever so efficacious, but must, rather, through a meeting of the natural and human sciences (cp. the physicists Pascual Jordan, Weizsaecker, Heitler), revive those ways of seeing which convey to man spiritual and normative content through which he may be able to answer concerning the meaning of his existence, instead of speaking of meaninglessness and despair in virtue of which latter anything could then happen.This has an enormous importance for the public good. It is a striking sign of the times that the younger generation wishes to gain an inner foothold for the future in order to endure the besetting dangers and threats of our age. It is therefore all the more the obligation for all intellectually alert men, as well as for philosophy, not to ignore this. If science and philosophy intend to comprehend total reality, they must deal responsibly with all areas of human existence, including man's spiritually creative achievements as they present themselves in real events, investigate their actual qualities and not accept their essential content under viewpoints which are inadequate.

Our know-how must be complemented and surmounted by an intellectual understanding of meaning and value. The very realistic tendency of our time demands that we point the way to the coming generation, and that we ourselves see that such decisive questions are central for the life of the individual as well as for our public good. In the same way that an inner law is something real for nature and its creatures, so too is the inner ordering of his personal existence for man, if he wishes to call "humanity" his own.

FRITZ-JOACHIM VON RINTELEN

PHILOSOPHISCHES SEMINAR
UNIVERSITÄT MAINZ
GERMANY
AUGUST, 1972

NOTES

¹ Cp. Paul A. Schilpp, "The Abdication of Philosophy," *Kant-Studien,* **51,** No. 4 (1959-60), 480. (Presidential address delivered before the 57th annual meeting of the Western Division of the American Philosophical Association at the University of Wisconsin, Madison, Wis., April 30-May 2, 1959.)

² Ibid., 481 f. Also: "Does Philosophy Have Anything to Say to Our (Atomic) Age?" ed. by G. C. Sansoni, *Atti del XII congresso internazionale di Filosofia,* Firenze, **8** (1961), 240.

³ F. von Rintelen, "Positivism, Humanitarianism and Humanity," *Philosophy and Phenomenological Research,* **11,** No. 3 (1951), 413 f.; excerpt from "Positivismus und gefährdete Humanität," *Festschrift für Aloys Wenzl, Natur, Geist, Geschichte* (München: Filser, 1950).

⁴ Cp. Arthur March, *Das neue Denken der modernen Physik* (Hamburg: Rowohlt-Verlag, 1957), pp. 95, 123 f. The physicist Pascual Jordan says: "spontaneity" in *Schöpfung und Geheimnis* (Oldenburg-Hamburg: Gerhard Stalling Verlag, 1970), p. 15.

⁵ *De coelo et mundo,* Chap. 4. Cp. Aristotle, *Physics,* I, 9, 192a, 16-23; *Metaphysics,* VIII, 2, 1043a, 28.

⁶ René Descartes, *Principia Philosophiae,* II, 36 (Amsterdam, 1644). I. Newton, *Philosophia Naturalis. Principia Mathematica,* II, def. 4 (London, 1687). Bernard Bavink, *Ergebnisse und Probleme der Naturwissenschaften,* 5th ed. (Leipzig: Hirzel, 1933), p. 55.

⁷ John Locke, *Essay Concerning Human Understanding* (London, 1690), II, 7.

⁸ Plato, *Philebus* 16, 17 d, 23 c. Cp. Paul Wilpert, "Neues Fragment *aus peri tagathou,*" p. 225 f. Über Plato (*Hermes,* **76** [1941]). *Zwei aristotelische Schriften über die Ideenlehre* (1949), pp. 158 f., 164 f., 169 f.

⁹ Augustine, *De libero arbitrio,* II, 42.

¹⁰ I. A. Poletajew, *Kybernetik,* Übers. aus dem Russischen von G. Klaus (Berlin: Dt. Verlag der Wissl, 1962), pp. 219 f., 328, 377.

¹¹ "The Abdication of Philosophy," p. 484.

¹² Cp. Gustav A. Wetter, *Der dialektische Materialismus. Seine Geschichte und sein System in der Sowjetunion* (Freiburg: i. Br., Herder, 1952), pp. 117, 165.

¹³ S. Radhakrishnan, "Doubts Concerning Fundamental Assumption of Contemporary Ethics," in *Menschliche Existenz und moderne,* ed. by Richard Schwarz, Welt Internationales Symposion (Berlin: de Gruyter, 1967), Vol. II, p. 236.

¹⁴ W. H. Werkmeister, "Scientism and the Problem of Man," in *Philosophy and Culture, East and West,* ed. by Charles A. Moore (Honolulu: University of Hawaii, 1962), pp. 135 f. Cp. F. von Rintelen, "Values as a Foundation for Encounter," ibid., pp. 400 ff.

¹⁵ Adolf Portmann, "Philosophie des Lebendigen," in *Die Philosophie im XX. Jahrhundert,* ed. by Fritz Heinemann (Stuttgart: Klett-Verlag, 1959), p. 342; *Biologie und Geist* (Zürich: Rein-Verlag, 1956), pp. 25, 309 f., 342. Adolf Meyer-Abich, *Geistes-geschichtliche Grundlagen der Biologie* (Stuttgart: Gustav Fischer Verlag, 1963), pp. 118, 296.

¹⁶ Nicolai Hartmann, *Der Aufbau der realen Welt* (Berlin: Walter de Gruyter, 1940), Chaps. 20, 21; *Philosophie der Natur* (Berlin: Walter de Gruyter, 1950), Chaps. 1, 4, 16-18.

¹⁷ Ernst Troeltsch, "Die Krise des Historismus," *Die Neue Rundschau,* **33,** No. 6 (1922), 573.

¹⁸ Schilpp, "The Abdication of Philosophy," pp. 486, 494; with statement from A. N. Whitehead, *Modes of Thought* (1938), pp. 235 f.

[19] Blaise Pascal, *Pensées,* ed. by M. Laros (Kempten: Kösel, 1913), I, 1; IV, 34, 37.

[20] Cp. Max Scheler, *Die Stellung des Menschen im Kosmos* (München: Nymphenburger Verlag, 1947), pp. 74 ff.

[21] Friedrich Nietzsche, *Beyond Good and Evil,* p. 55.

[22] Heyde-Berlin, *Sinn und Sein,* ed. by R. Wisser (Tübingen: Niemeyer, 1960).

[23] Goethe, *Maximen und Reflexionen,* IV, 227; *Wanderjahre,* XX, 25: "Das Tun am Denken, das Denken am Tun prüfen"; Jubiläums-Ausgabe (Stuttgart: Cotta, 1912).

[24] "The Abdication of Philosophy," pp. 485, 490, 492.

[25] Immanuel Kant, *Grundlegung zur Metaphysik der Sitten,* 2. Werke IV, 286, ed. by Ernst Cassirer (Berlin: Bruno Cassirer Verlag, 1922).

[26] Eduard Spranger, *Lebensformen,* 4th ed. (Halle: Niemeyer, 1925), pp. 13, 24.

[27] Friedrich Nietzsche, *Also Sprach Zarathustra,* Kröner ed., I, 144.

[28] Paul A. Schilpp, "Presuppositions of Democracy as a Basis for East-West Rapprochements," *Actes du Xième Congrès International de philosophie,* XIV, Bruxelles (Louvain: Nauvelaerts, 1953), pp. 240 f.

[29] Paul A. Schilpp, "A Challenge to Philosophers in the Atomic Age," *Bibliothèque du Xième Congrès International de Philosophie,* I, Proceedings 1, ed. by F. W. Beth, H. J. Pos, J. H. A. Hollak (Amsterdam: North-Holland Publishers, 1949).

ROBERT M. GORDON

THE ABORTION ISSUE

I

The fact that a human pregnancy can be terminated by deliberate intervention does not in itself raise the moral issues; what does, is rather the fact that such intervention can usually be expected to result in the death of the fetus. This is, of course, the usual purpose of intervention: to secure the death of the fetus. But, whatever its purpose, if intervention is performed in such a way or under such conditions that it can be expected to result in the death of the fetus, I shall refer to it here as abortion.

The possibility of abortion raises two moral issues. One concerns the act of abortion itself. The other, which I shall not treat in this paper, concerns the legal prohibition of abortion. At the heart of either issue is the question of the moral status of the fetus; and at the heart of *that* question is the question of the moral significance of a being's *potentiality*. Until we have made up our minds on these subsidiary questions, no other considerations have force enough to decide the main issues.[1] Many people, no doubt, have had strong opinions on these subsidiary matters, one way or the other, but it has not been obvious how we can adjudicate the clash of such opinions. This is the task I set for myself in Sections V and VI, after several important preliminaries have been gotten out of the way. The former issue (hereafter, the "abortion issue") arises from the following assumption, which (with some qualifications to be introduced shortly) is granted by all sides: that *the reasons for which abortions are usually performed*[2] *would not be adequate to justify the killing of a human being once he is born.* Consider any human being of any age after birth: Suppose that he was born to an unwed mother who wishes, for her own sake or the sake of the child, that he hadn't been born; or suppose that the child is a product of rape; or suppose that he was born to a couple who already had all the children they could afford to raise properly; or suppose that he is a somewhat (but not severely) retarded or malformed human being. These conditions, singly or compounded, would not seem in most eyes to justify killing him. The abortion issue concerns the performance of an abortion for reasons that admittedly would not justify the killing of a "postnatal" human being.

What I have said thus far focuses the issue too sharply, at least for some proabortionists, on the difference between the born and the unborn. Many "proabortionists" would rule out abortion, at least by certain methods, once the fetus has reached a stage where it would have some chance, or a good chance, of surviving *ex utero*—normally somewhere between the twentieth and twenty-eighth week after conception. The usual method of abortion, from about the sixteenth week after conception on, is to induce actual labor by first killing the fetus, usually by introducing into the amniotic sac a quart or so of saline or glucose solution. Obviously, such a method does not discriminate between those fetuses that are capable of surviving *ex utero* and those that are not—it indiscriminately kills them all. For this reason it would be proscribed, at least at later stages, by some people who would otherwise condone abortion.[3]

I do not want to force the proabortionist into a position in which he must defend all abortions or defend none. Since it is at the twentieth week that reservations begin to be sounded, and since most abortions are actually performed well before that time, it seems fair to confine the main issue to abortions performed prior to the twentieth week. Hereafter when I speak of "abortion" without further specification, I shall understand abortion performed prior to the twentieth week after conception.

At the other extreme, some proabortionists might wish to draw the line, not at the twentieth week nor even at birth, but rather at a day or a week or perhaps a month after birth: they would be prepared to condone infanticide. They would therefore not share the assumption that the reasons for which abortions are usually performed would not be adequate to justify killing a human being once he is born; on the contrary, they would hold these same reasons to justify killing a newborn infant, or a "neonate." Unless we are to exclude such people from the debate, we should reformulate the assumption as follows: that the reasons for which abortions are usually performed would not be adequate to justify killing a human being who is (say) one month or more past birth. (I shall designate such a human being by the term *postneonate*, abbreviated PNN.) Although there may not at present be many proabortionists of this persuasion, the view is not so outrageous as to reduce the proabortionist position to obvious absurdity—unlike, e.g., the view that abortion is OK because in general it is OK to murder unwanted people. We must therefore not frame the issue in a way that would rule this position out of court.

The abortion issue is a question of consistency. The question is whether, granting that the reasons for which abortions are usually performed would not be adequate to justify the killing of a postneonate, one can consistently hold them adequate to justify abortion. A person is being inconsistent, in the appropriate sense, if he fails *to treat like cases alike*, whether in his actual conduct, his policies, or his moral or legal judgments. Whether one can consistently judge certain reasons to be adequate to justify abortion but inadequate to justify the killing of a PNN depends on whether abortion and the killing of a PNN are "like" kinds of acts; and this in turn depends on whether fetuses (prior to the twentieth week) and PNN's are "like" kinds of beings. This of course, is a matter of what similarities and differences there are, which of these are relevant to the moral issue, and how great a weight is to be assigned to each of the relevant factors.

II

It is remarkable that the abortion issue does not turn on any dispute over biological or medical matters. Among those informed in these matters there are, of course, differences of opinion; but there is no systematic difference of opinion between those on one side of the abortion issue and those on the other. It is true that many people see the issue as pivoting on such questions as whether the fetus is alive, or whether it is a human being, or whether it is a distinct individual rather than merely a part of the mother's body. But those who see the issue as pivoting on one of these questions would not generally be content to relegate the crucial question to physicians or biologists. For the *criteria* that a biologist might use, for instance, to determine whether something is a distinct organism are intended only to meet the needs of biological theory. (It would surely be an onerous burden if biologists had to go about their business in the knowledge that they were shaping a conceptual system that would be used to determine the boundaries of the moral world.) It remains an open question whether the biologist's criteria are at all relevant to, much less decisive for, the moral question of abortion.

Once the biologist's criteria are opened to question, the abortion debate often degenerates into an unbridled dispute over, e.g., "What is life?" or,

"What makes something a human being?" Sometimes these criterial questions may just be disguises for the original moral question: viz., "What are the features of a postneonate—i.e., a being that is indisputably a live human being—that make it so wrong to kill one?" But when they are *not* so understood, two very serious problems arise. First, it is hard to know how to proceed with such questions unless they are tied down in some way, e.g., to features that are important to biological theory or to features that are important to some particular moral issue. More serious still, any answer that may evolve from such unguided inquiry will be of questionable relevance. Should it be decided, on the basis of the criteria finally agreed upon, that the fetus is (is not) a human being, this finding will not be relevant to the moral issue of abortion, much less decisive for it, *unless the criteria selected are themselves relevant to that issue.* So, having taken a long detour into such questions as, "What is life?" or, "What makes something a human being?"—a detour from which discussions seldom return—the upshot is that we have only postponed the moral question with which we began: viz., "What are the features of the postneonate that make it so great a wrong to kill one, and to what extent are these features also possessed by the fetus?" If we wish to come closer to a resolution of the abortion issue, it would be far more efficient to avoid such detours altogether.

(Not all of these remarks can be applied equally well to the question, "Is the fetus a person?" This question does not, at least, masquerade as a question of biology. And usually when the term *person* plays a crucial role in some moral discussion, the question, "What is relevant to something's being a person?" is openly acknowledged to be a moral question itself. The only danger is that one is apt to get the idea that whatever is to count as a person so far as one moral issue is concerned must also count as a person so far as any other moral issue is concerned. This would be a mistake, since the morally relevant similarities and differences may shift from one moral issue to another. Thus, while some of the "rights of persons" may extend to fetuses—or to "human vegetables," or to robots—others may not.)

III

We misrepresent the abortion issue if we suppose that there is some one feature of postneonates that makes it wrong to kill them—personality, humanity, self-consciousness, or whatever—and that the outstanding question is simply whether fetuses have this feature, too. This is to presuppose that the abortion issue has one of two possible resolutions: if fetuses do have the X-feature, then abortion is wrong, and indeed wrong in precisely the same way and to precisely the same degree as the killing of a PNN; if fetuses do not have the X-feature, then abortion is not wrong, at least under the usual circumstances.

The outstanding questions concern, rather, whether this or that difference between fetuses and PNN's is relevant to the moral issue, and, if so, how important it is. For example, the fetus, unlike the PNN, is unborn: has this any bearing at all on whether the fetus, unlike the PNN, may justifiably be killed? The fetal brain, like that of the PNN, registers electrical activity: is this relevant? At some stage the fetus begins to exhibit what appear to be pleasure and pain responses, thus resembling the PNN (and other members of the animal kingdom): granting, perhaps, that this is relevant, is it an important point of similarity? Again, compared to the fetus, the PNN, because of its visibility and its complex behavioral interactions with others, is in a much better position to be an object of individuated love: this, it might be held, is undeniably a relevant difference, but a difference of little importance, compared to the very important ways in which the fetus resembles the PNN.

But if the abortion issue pivots on many questions rather than one, and on questions of degree rather than of quality, it loses its all-or-nothing cast: we then have no reason to buy the disjunction, "Either abortion is not wrong, or it is wrong in the same way and to the same degree as the killing of a PNN." The reason is simple. The wrongness of a given type of act is mitigated, not only when the act is performed in mitigating circumstances, but also when it is performed in an attenuated form, stripped of some of its wrong-making qualities. If abortion lacks some of the features that, taken together, make the killing of a PNN as great a wrong as it is, then abortion is not as great a wrong as the killing of a PNN. (I assume, of course, that abortion introduces no new wrong-making features of its own. So far as I know, this is a point on which all are agreed.)[4] For example, suppose that the fact that PNN's have engaged in complex behavioral interactions with other human beings is one of the factors which, compounded, make it so great a wrong to kill a PNN. This will then be one of the relevant differences between the PNN and the fetus. Granting this much, abortion must be a lesser wrong than the killing of a PNN—the degree of mitigation depending on how important a difference this is. Thus, even though we were to judge the similarities between the fetus and the PNN to outweigh the differences, it would not be as if we had acknowledged no relevant differences at all. Though we may still judge abortion to be wrong, in virtue of its similarities to the killing of a PNN, we cannot judge it to be as great a wrong as the killing of a PNN. The fact that there is even one relevant difference cannot be wholly discounted.

IV

Now I propose to ask: Is abortion as great a wrong as the killing of a PNN in comparable circumstances?

Those who say Yes face battle on two fronts, for they are committed on each to an extreme position. First, regarding the fetus and the PNN, they must hold that *none* of the features distinguishing us from fetuses, nor *all of these taken together*, have *any* bearing at all on why it is *so great* a wrong to kill one of us: they do not so much as aggravate the wrong. (Their opponents, we should remember, do not have to hold that it is ever *justifiable* to kill a being that lacks one or even all of these features; only that it is not quite as grave or serious a wrong.) Second, when asked what makes it so much more wrong to kill us than to kill members of other vertebrate species, they can only point to features that have already been acquired in the prefetal stages of our existence. They cannot, for example, point to our capacity for rational thought, since human fetuses give no more evidence of such a capacity than do pig fetuses.

It is at this point that they must appeal to the *potentialities* of the fetus.[5] Aristotle distinguished between the capacity to speak Greek and the capacity to acquire the capacity to speak Greek. It might be said that the human fetus, though not yet endowed with the capacity for rational thought, has at least the capacity to acquire the capacity for rational thought; and that in this regard it is, even in its present state of development, significantly different from the pig fetus. More generally, the human fetus has the capacity to acquire the capacities of an adult human being; for it has, we might say, the "master" capacity to *become* an adult human being.

It is clear that to say that the fetus has the potentiality to become an adult is not the same as saying that the fetus *will* become an adult. In one respect, we are saying less: if the right conditions do not prevail, its potentiality will go unfulfilled, and it will die without ever becoming an adult. But the fetus whose potentiality goes unfulfilled nevertheless *would have* become an adult if the right conditions had prevailed; for it was already so definitively formed that it was *impossible for it to fail* to become an adult, provided of course that the right conditions prevailed. So we are saying or at least implying something about the *present state* of the fetus when we say that it has the potentiality to become an adult.

No doubt, many people have had notions of potentiality that are richer in content than the one I have sketched. One's notion might, for instance, take account of the homeostatic processes by which the fetus insures its development under a range of conditions. Or one's notion might include an evaluative element: what something has the "potentiality" to become is what it would become under *optimum* conditions. But I think that the most important element for the present context is the element of immanent necessity, as explained above.

The question to be decided is whether the possession by the human fetus of the potentiality to become a postneonate and ultimately an adult makes it as great a wrong to kill a human fetus as it would be to kill an actual PNN or adult in comparable circumstances. In addressing this question, I shall first retell an old story in such a way as to suggest that there is a crucial difference between the killing of an actual human PNN and a merely potential human PNN.

Consider the prince who, under a witch's curse, became a frog. The frog the prince became squats before us now. If there is a glint in its frog's eye, it is because the frog is destined to become the prince once again, once certain conditions have been satisfied. The glint in our eye is frog's legs.

What stands between this frog and the frying pan? The dignity and rights of a man, even of a prince? Should we have the culinary compunctions due a prince?

The answer is Yes, provided that the prince is presently *in* the frog, in a sense that fairy tales allow but Wittgenstein did not: as a person costumed, as it were, in a body. (" 'You see,' [the Prince] said, 'I wasn't what I seemed to be! A wicked old woman bewitched me. No one but you could break the spell, little Princess, and I waited and waited at the well for you to help me.' ") We may imagine, even, the prince's mind beclouded and constricted to a frog's perceptions and joys, as if by some potent drug. His mind now befits his new body. But if it is *his* mind, *him*, under the cloud, then we must treat this frog as a man, perhaps even as a prince, in bad straits. No frog's legs tonight.

Those who profess to be "the voice of the unborn" sometimes seem to presuppose that there is really a postneonate in every fetus, "bottled up" in it in a way that fairy tales allow—its powers in temporary eclipse, like those of a grown man in a coma, or a prince befrogged. ("How would *you* feel if you saw the knife coming toward you?") Once we allow such magic, anything goes, and no one knows: toddlers embody octogenarians, frogs embody toddlers, spiders are really elephants, the genie is in the bottle, and pebbles squeal silently underfoot. Barring this, it is useful to be reminded that we are not *in* our fetal stages in the way that the prince was in the frog.

Now suppose that when the witch made the prince into a frog she did not *embody* him in it: no prince peered out, now through human eyes, now through frog's eyes. The frog the prince became was *really* a quite ordinary frog, undistinguished except for, and by, its genesis and its potentiality. If it survives until next Halloween, when the witch's spell expires, the frog will be changed back into the prince.

I should still be inclined to say that it would be wrong, perhaps even a great wrong, to kill this frog for frog's legs. Asked for a reason, I should refer to the frog's potentiality—to what it would or at least might become if allowed to live. But if we should spare the frog, it is not because the frog acquires a new dignity, or a new right, in virtue of its potentiality; but only because it acquires a new *usefulness*, as *an instrument for restoring the prince.* Two arguments help to make this clear.

First. The fact that the frog will (or would) *become* the prince is not relevant in itself. It would be no less wrong to kill this frog if frog and prince could live side by side after Halloween, provided only that the prince's return hinges on the frog's surviving till Halloween. It would also be wrong to break the witch's wand, if the prince's return depended on its remaining intact. This is a matter, not of the wand's dignity or right, but of its utility.

Second. Suppose that, if this frog were to die before Halloween, other means of restoring the prince would magically come into play. The frog is no longer necessary; by killing it, we do not prevent the prince's return, for he will return anyway. (We can imagine a second frog, which would become the prince if the first did not survive.) If this were assured, no grounds would remain for sparing this frog in particular, *despite the fact that it would, if spared, become the prince.*

If it is wrong to kill the enchanted frog for frog's legs (or wrong to a greater degree than it would be to kill another frog), it is wrong because our act would have the further consequence of preventing the restoration of the prince. Had the witch's curse attached a different consequence instead, our act might not have been wrong. Were the frog destined by a witch's spell to engender an army of giant people-eating frogs, we should probably be wrong *not* to interfere by killing it. What is most important in the present case is not the fact that the frog will engender a man, but that it will engender a man of whom we can say: "*We owe it to him* not to prevent his restoration." If the witch's purpose were to create *new* human beings, whether newborn infants or older specimens complete with memories, we should certainly be under no similar constraint to let her have her way. (Or else we should have to give carte blanche to biologists of the future who, by cloning or other methods, might vastly expand our reproductive capacity and direct it to their own ends.) When it is a witch's whim to make human beings miserable or to make miserable human beings, it may even be our duty to interfere, though this entail killing a frog.

In abortion we kill a fetus that would have become, not some long-gone PNN, but a new creation—a PNN that would have had no prior history, except as a fetus. The act has two moral components. We *kill* a fetal human being; by killing it, we *prevent the existence of* one more postneonate human being. This further consequence abortion shares with contraception and even sexual abstinence. Whether such a consequence is desirable or not depends, of course, on the circumstances of the particular case. There is a growing consensus that the prevention of childbirth is generally desirable, except where children are wanted and can be brought up in a suitable environment. Surely the fact that abortion accomplishes this end, just as do contraception and abstinence, cannot be said to make the act *wrong*, except in the rarest of circumstances.

To coin a saw: When you meet a caterpillar, treat it as a caterpillar, not as a butterfly. If you kill it, you *kill* a caterpillar; you only *prevent the existence of* a butterfly. And that makes all the difference in the world.

V

Unlike contraception and other methods of child prevention, abortion entails the killing of a fetal human being. Does this make the act wrong, and does it make it wrong in the same degree as the killing of a PNN? Disregard the fact that fetal human beings become postneonate human beings; this fact, if the foregoing argument is right, merely makes abortion a method of child prevention and has no further significance.

Once potentialities are left out of account, only trivial differences remain between the human fetus and fetuses of even the most primitive vertebrate species. In the first few weeks, only the chromosomes differ—hardly a source of dignity or rights. At such a stage, we must conclude, it is no more wrong to kill a human fetus than to kill any vertebrate fetus, given comparable circumstances. Gradually thereafter, the paths diverge: by stages, the human fetus comes to be less and less like other fetuses, and more and more like us.

One could still maintain that the great *moral* gulf between an inchoate vertebrate fetus of four or five weeks and a postneonate human being is crossed quite early, in a single leap; and that all further modifications, beyond, say, the sixth week after conception, are without moral significance. It would be surprising if this were so, given how slowly we develop; given that a newly hatched chick is infinitely more capable of fending for itself than a newborn human infant. I am inclined to think that anyone who maintains this really has his eye on the momentous changes that lie ahead and prejudicially reads them into the first perceptible gropings in the right direction. Any phenomenon that dimly *presages* "rational behavior," for instance, he will see as an early *expression* of rational behavior. Thus, in his very perceptions he presupposes the potentiality argument. It is hard to get over the habit of doing this, even after the potentiality argument has been intellectually discredited and renounced. As an aid to overcoming prejudice, one might try to imagine a distinct species of parasite rather similar to the human fetus, but developing only to the stage attained by a seven-week-old fetus. Crude though the analogy may be, it prepares one to consider the fetus stripped of its potentialities. Few people, once they have succeeded in looking at the fetus in this way, can persist in regarding abortion as "murder"—i.e., as morally "just like" the killing of a PNN in comparable circumstances. Most will have to allow that, because of the differences between the fetus and the PNN, abortion may be justifiable even though, in comparable circumstances, the killing of a PNN would not.

The framework and the arguments provided in this essay do not fully equip us to answer the following questions: Is abortion wrong *at all*, prima facie (i.e., unless justified by overriding moral principles, duties, or obligations)? If so, under what circumstances would it be justifiable? But these questions become less pressing when one is assured that, *at worst*, abortion is not—not nearly, I should say—as *serious* a wrong as the killing of a PNN. We can be sure that, when the dust settles and the clouds are dispelled, mankind will not discover to its horror that it has for years been condoning something that is tantamount to murder.

ROBERT M. GORDON

UNIVERSITY OF MISSOURI
ST. LOUIS
DECEMBER, 1971

NOTES

[1] See, for example, B. A. Brody, "Abortion and the Law," *Journal of Philosophy,* **68,** No. 12 (June 17, 1971), 357-69. Brody argues that the various reasons given for legalizing abortion cannot be decisive until the fetus question has been resolved. The "right to one's body" argument, I might add, will hardly work, once it becomes technically feasible to extract the fetus alive for transfer to another womb; even now, at the most, it permits one to kill the fetus on the nasty technicality that it happens to have gotten lodged, so to speak, in one's bailiwick.

[2] Here I exclude abortions performed in order to save the life of the mother. If what I say in Section VI of this paper is correct, then there is a clear presumption in favor of saving the mother's life.

[3] Unfortunately, the notion of viability *ex utero* must be completed by a specification of the *ex utero* conditions under which the fetus is to be viable. Without incubation, for instance, no fetus would be viable *ex utero;* with a sufficiently advanced form of artificial womb, on the other hand, it is conceivable that even a one-week blastocyst might continue to develop *ex utero.* I suppose most proponents have in mind viability with both incubation and other measures that are commonly available in present-day delivery rooms; although it is not at all clear why abortion should not be extended to fetuses that are viable under such conditions if it is condoned for fetuses that are viable under more sophisticated *ex utero* care.

[4] Unless we consider the doctrine that it is a greater evil to kill the unbaptized. I have heard it denied that this is part of the official Roman Catholic position. But even if it is, I do not know what would prevent a priest from baptizing the abortus: the Code of Canon Law even *enjoins* this, where possible, in case of "spontaneous" abortion, i.e., miscarriage.

[5] I am indebted to Edward Costello, Peter Fuss, and Carl Wellman for correcting my conception of the potentiality argument and for providing overall illumination.

WARREN E. STEINKRAUS

PAUL SCHILPP
AND THE SOCIAL RELEVANCE
OF PHILOSOPHY

The life and thought of Paul Arthur Schilpp have been marked by an abiding and serious interest in the relevance of philosophy for practical and social issues. While never for a moment viewing philosophy as merely a tool for social change, he has always been concerned with philosophizing which had some visible effects. But visible effects need not be as obvious as those of Jean-Paul Sartre who actively engages in the marketplace by helping to distribute far-left newspapers. Nevertheless, there should be some report of philosophic contemplation in the life of human beings and in the social order. The endeavor to determine what that relation should be has been one of Paul Schilpp's dominant interests for the past several decades. And he has been equally interested in the methods whereby one translates contemplation into action. This study will focus on three aspects of Professor Schilpp's consideration of these questions.

1. Schilpp as a Critical Observer of Culture and Civilization

In one of his earliest articles, Schilpp concerned himself with the "American Neglect of a Philosophy of Culture." He pointed out that thinkers in Europe and especially Germany viewed philosophy as either responsible for civilization or for its collapse for they understood philosophy to be "not merely a discipline of theoretical intellectualizing but a practical instrument in the solution of all the most vital human problems."[1] That

emphasis, he noted, was not common or typical in American philosophy in
the first quarter of this century. In spite of the heavy burdens of editing the
renowned "Library of Living Philosophers," much of Professor Schilpp's
philosophical and critical capacities have been employed in just that area
which he found to be neglected by American philosophers. He offers thoughtful and realistic critical evaluations of education, science, politics, religion,
and even of philosophy itself. His perspective is uniformly ethical.

His early views, as one might expect from his family background and
original interests, involve an examination of the role of religion in life. His
first published volume was, *Do We Need a New Religion?*. Though he
perhaps would not now reaffirm *all* that he says in that volume, there is much
that is of relevance today. He discusses the role of institutional religion in
society, especially Christianity, and concludes that "the hide-bound, creed-
encumbered system which has so long gone by the name of 'Christianity'
needs to be replaced by the revitalized religion of Jesus which is life instead of
being 'dead in letter'."[2] Religion must allow more room for freedom and
while not forsaking doctrines must avoid "finality." Furthermore, the essential criterion of judgment of Christianity and any religion must be ethical. If
religion has not fulfilled its ethical role, it has little justification for being.
Here one sees the backlying emphasis of Immanuel Kant in Schilpp's views,
for in Kant's view a religion which did not emphasize duty and inspire the
moral life was worthless. Schilpp remarks, "Only a God conceived essentially
in terms of morality could meet the needs of today."[3] One of his most powerful and searching utterances from this early volume is one he would no doubt
willingly repeat today.

> Materialism, mechanism, industrialism, scientism, provincialism, nationalism
> and the orthodox habit of mind which defends the *status quo* simply because it
> happens to *be*, are the forces which are rapidly transforming the life of the
> modern Western man into that of a mere thoughtless but pleasure-seeking
> automatic machine; a fact which is not only robbing the Western man of his great
> spiritual birthright but is, without doubt, bringing him to the very brink of the
> abyss of self-destruction.[4]

In recent years, he has challenged organized religion even more vigorously as
being other worldly and not helping man discover himself. "Organized Christian religion, instead of stemming the rising tide which with every decade
gained new momentum in sweeping against the citadel of human worth and
dignity, only aided in the common process of dehumanization."[5] Nor has it
seriously or unequivocally opposed war.

Science too comes under Professor Schilpp's scrutiny and it is evaluated
by the criterion of its effect on persons and our understanding of them. It is

not so much pure science that is judged but rather the adulation given it and the tendency of some scientists to have too narrow a perspective. "Science has become the modern substitute for the 'open sesame' of yesterday's fairy tales."[6] It has come to be more of a fetish than the sort of thing it really is because the success of the method and spirit of science have stimulated men to take more interest in things than in themselves. This has led to the "wholesale depreciation of man." Earlier he put it this way: "Science and things are the twin-goddesses of modern America, and a materialistic, scientifically directed philosophy" is more representative of America today than any other.[7]

The sciences which deal with human beings have been too restrictive. Those who take the simplistic view that man is a biological and meaningless accident on this planet have limited their approach to one kind of fact alone, and have ignored, for example, the capacities of man which differentiate him from the animal.[8] Psychology could more appropriately be called "ratology" because of its a priori limitation of data. How can a branch of learning be regarded as scientific when it leaves unstudied "vast areas and aspects of human experience which every human being actually knows in himself, merely because one has—unscientifically—prejudged the field of study in advance?"[9] Similarly, Schilpp charges the combined efforts of the social scientists with falling "far short of giving us as nearly complete a view of man we need if we are to comprehend even ourselves and our fellowmen."[10]

Our philosopher has also been a critic of some facets of education. As early as 1930, he edited a volume entitled, *Higher Education Faces the Future* which contained essays by some leading educators and scientists. The introductory page of the volume has this statement: "Higher Education has ceased to be of interest merely to the professional educator. It has become a practical problem affecting the very existence of contemporary civilization." In his own essay, Schilpp urges that colleges and universities should meet the needs brought about by industrialization, that they educate for democracy to avoid mobocracy, that they prepare persons for a wise use of leisure, that they provide students with a basic fund of facts and that they awaken in them a vital interest. He warns against those programs which diminish the liberalizing influence.[11]

More recently he noted differences in the educational goals of the United States and the USSR, observing pointedly that while the United States has a bias against studying languages, it is far ahead of the Soviet Union in the study of the humanities. He specifically supports John Dewey's general viewpoint of subject-centered education against the latter's misinterpreters, and he argues that the true object of teaching is not a philosophy but persons. Knowledge is a tool of life and learning is motivated by interest.[12] Elsewhere he argued that teachers must be openers of doors instead of being, as sometimes happens in our country, "tools of democracy, capitalism, and free enterprise."[13]

Schilpp discerningly sees that any so-called crisis in education which might have been generated in America by evidence of superior scientific achievement on the part of the USSR, really "turns out to be a crisis of the American life and mind,"[14] which has sold out to materialism, power, and thoughtlessness. The educational systems of both the United States and the Soviet Union are geared to defense and behind that gearing is the uncriticized assumption that one best solves political differences by military power or the threat of military power. He challenges the validity of that assumption and reproves Americans for spending billions of dollars "to increase the number of times we can wipe out mankind" by nuclear weapons.[15]

In many respects, Professor Schilpp's general appraisal of civilization and culture resembles that of Albert Schweitzer, whom he has always held in highest esteem. Both men draw heavily on Immanuel Kant not only for their ethical and social outlook but also for inspiration. Schweitzer's doctoral dissertation was on the "Religious Philosophy of Kant" and one of Schilpp's earliest volumes is his distinguished *Kant's Pre-Critical Ethics*. In each thinker there is an effort to understand the root problems of culture and man ethically. And while both Schweitzer and Schilpp do not overlook the corruption and weakness of Western civilization and man, neither acquiesces in "fashionable pessimism." They are distressed at the denigration of man and the deterioration of society and they offer proposals for improvement. In his *Decay and Restoration of Civilization* of 1923, Schweitzer wrote: "The future of civilization depends on our overcoming the meaninglessness and hopelessness which characterize the thoughts and convictions of men today, and reaching a state of fresh hope and fresh determination."[16] Schilpp, with the broader awareness of problems in a nuclear age, admits that "most of what we think of as civilization is only veneer . . . because not much of it ever touches either the spirit or the mind of man."[17] Yet he affirms that "every human problem is capable of a rational and moral solution." Given the atomic age with the possibility of the destruction of civilization, it is incumbent upon persons to work "towards the end of a democratic federal world government before it is, forever, too late."[18]

While Schweitzer always impresses one with an uncommon earnestness, Schilpp's writings evince an unmistakable sense of urgency along with earnestness. Across a span of over forty years of philosophical activity and writing, one detects a pervasive note of concern and warning over human problems and crises. In 1926, Schilpp warned that philosophy might perish with Western civilization,[19] and wrote an essay entitled "Is Western Civilization Worth Saving?"[20] In 1929, he spoke of the "revolutionary convulsions which are shaking the contemporary world,"[21] and in an article on Max Scheler urged that there has been no time when philosophy could afford less to give up its task "than today."[22] In 1948, he wrote on philosophy's task in an age of crisis;[23] in 1954, that "man's present plight cries aloud for a fundamental re-discovery of man";[24] in 1958, that "just now . . . we Americans find ourselves in the most severe crisis of our entire history."[25] And in 1959, he argued that philosophers need to provide wisdom "in the hour of humanity's most dire need."[26] In 1963, he published *The Crisis in Science and Education*, and in the next year wrote on "Philosophy and the Social Crisis."[27] In 1969, he warned that "men must face the possibility of mankind's annihilation."[28]

Now one might well wonder about Schilpp's persistence in calling attention to crises and future doom. He has done it consistently for over forty years and the critic may well ask why. How can there be so many crises? Is this just a device of a pamphleteer-type philosopher to gain attention? Surely not. The truth is that Schilpp whose boyhood and early college days were spent in the relatively peaceful times preceding World War I, began to notice profound changes in society and the world. A perceptive critic of culture, he called attention to problems as he saw them and it now seems evident that there has in fact been an evolution, or development at least, of critical social situations from the time of World War I to the build-up of crisis situations in our present decade. What Schilpp has observed as he has surveyed man and his civilization for over four decades, is that there has been a gradual increase of difficulties. These are largely caused by man's willingness to try to solve problems by resorting to armed violence—which in turn produces even greater problems so that nowadays the distinct possibility of nuclear annihilation is upon us. What is striking is that through all these discouraging times (and Schilpp by virtue of his earnestness and basically ethical outlook has been especially conscious of them), he has not lost hope and constantly pleads with his contemporaries to seek rational solutions motivated by goodwill.

2. Schilpp and the Rightful Responsibilities of Philosophers

When it comes to the task of trying to decide what the proper task of philosophy is, one thing seems clear. There is considerable disagreement over it. There have been different ways of philosophizing and there have been different ways to state problems all through the history of thought going back to Thales. It does not seem that there will soon be a "breakthrough" in philosophy which will settle once for all what philosophy should be doing, though there may be a breakdown. There is not much reason to believe that philosophic knowledge has the cumulative character of scientific knowledge. The scientist usually begins where the last man left off, but philosophical problems are persistent and they have a perennial character. There will no doubt be vigorous clashes of opinion and judgment even on the definition of these problems for some time to come. Of course it is true that we have had philosophic messiahs at about the rate of one every decade in this century. They have come forward to tell us about the errors of past philosophizing, the wrongheadedness of most of the great thinkers of the past and how they by their new methods will "'revolutionize" philosophy and thus enable us to "begin again" the proper task of philosophy. We will not name any of these messiahs, but we see their followers in the enthusiasm of their immaturity, lining up in camps, developing a peculiar jargon and looking with disfavor on the disciples of some other leader. Indeed, they sometimes refuse to communicate with each other. Happily, some eventually learn that there is something more to philosophy than splash, dazzle and public relations, and they begin to try to comprehend those who have different viewpoints. But the last several decades in the Western world have not been characterized by much mutual respect among philosophers of competing schools. No doubt another innovator will arise in the next ten years and with great flurry and a little arrogance, inveigle and entice some followers to see things in his new and "exciting" way. But the steady trudge of earnest seekers after truth and wisdom will go on in spite of such flourishes. Eventually, the ideas of the "revolutionary" will die of inanation or perchance, if unique enough, be incorporated in the corpus of philosophical literature to be studied by future generations.

Now one of the things that has characterized Paul Schilpp's philosophical approach has been a steadiness of outlook which has evolved and deepened with the years. Uniquely able to gauge and assess so-called "trends" because of his close contact with most of the leading philosophers throughout the world in his role as editor of the "Library of Living Philosophers," he himself has never lost his independence of outlook nor has he been swayed to adopt some new movement which appeared to be in vogue. He has not only corresponded with the leading philosophical figures of this generation, he has also been in personal touch with them. The list is impressive: Dewey, Santayana, Whitehead, Moore, Russell, Cassirer, Einstein, Radhakrishnan, Jaspers, Broad, Carnap, Buber, and C. I. Lewis. In addition, he is now completing editorial tasks in collaboration with Popper, Marcel, Blanshard, von Wright, and Quine.[29] Accordingly, when Professor Schilpp adopts a position and strikes a critical note on certain ideas or viewpoints, it is with a richness of background not found among many of his peers.

For several decades, he has taken the position that any philosophy to be worth doing must eventually justify itself by being able to say something of value to living human beings and must be able to provide some general guidance for problems confronting mankind. This does not make him some sort of a cryptic existentialist nor an uncritical disciple of Dewey. Schilpp has never once upbraided technical philosophical enterprise for its own sake and he has shown high competence in the upper levels of abstract theorizing himself. One evidence of his concern for the practical outreach of philosophy is his very conception of the "Library of Living Philosophers."

The clue to Professor Schilpp's own position, I believe, is found in the Kantian doctrine of the primacy of the practical reason. The doctrine was not developed much by Kant, but it means that theoretical knowledge is always dependent for its function in life on the purposes of the moral will. Or, the speculative activity of philosophy must be justified in some way by including practice. Practice, in turn, is not sound unless grounded in reason and reason is not fully sound unless it involves practice in some sense. Accordingly, one could say that in his own outlook Schilpp tries to overcome the Kantian dualism between the theoretical and practical reason. In an early article he wrote that philosophy is "not merely a discipline of theoretical intellec-tualizing but a practical instrument in the solution of all the most vital human and cultural problems."[30] Later, he maintained that philosophy's "analyzing and criticizing function must also . . . reach over into the actual concrete everyday life of the individual and of society."[31]

But can this view that philosophy has this function be supported philosophically? Citing Socrates on several occasions, Schilpp holds that philosophy was never intended to be separated from life and he notes that the great philosophers of all times "have made all of life in all of its ramifications the appropriate subject of their critical examination."[32] Philosophy's very nature is to deal with live human issues. As early as 1930, he wrote that any philosophy which limits itself in such a way as not to be able to account for meaning and values "to that extent fails to take account of the whole of human life and experience, and to an equal extent fails to be . . . really and truly a philosophy."[33] Nor can it "grow so abstract as to lose contact with the concrete life which flows around it and alone has made it possible."[34] In short, philosophers historically have generally not been able to avoid dealing with live practical issues and philosophy itself grows and feeds on such issues.

This does not mean that there is no room or need for technical work. "A philosophy which would undertake to examine life as it is lived every day in the large, but failed to concern itself seriously with technical and detailed problems, would soon cease to be in the best sense 'critical'."[35] But to take philosophy away from life and its problems and place it on a purely technical level exclusively is to subvert it in such a way as to make it irrelevant on principle and hence irresponsible. At the same time can one expect as much from philosophy as Albert Schweitzer did? He saw it not only as a critic of civilization, but as its watchdog, its intellectual challenge, its moral judge and guide and its source of vision.

Schilpp does not just assert that philosophers have responsibility, he directly, on occasion, has attacked the position of those who would limit it in some way. As early as 1935, he gave attention to the views of Schlick, Wittgenstein, Frank, and Carnap "who insist that philosophy really has no distinct subject matter, nor ever has had such."[36] Especially did he subject to criticism the view of Moritz Schlick who held that it was possible to have "standpointless philosophy" because there are initial insights which precede the formulation of every theory. Schilpp argued that though one may take "final refuge" in the immediately given, "there is no human experience which is not capable of being further intelligibly and meaningfully questioned."[37] He criticized Schlick and others with falling "back on self-evidence whenever they find it impossible to furnish a reliable proof of their contentions."[38] Just as Gellner detected an uncritical metaphysical naturalism at the base of Wittgenstein's thought, so Schilpp earlier charged Schlick with the assumption of pure "physicalism," an assumption "which does not permit him to admit anything non-physical into his philosophy."[39]

When philosophers take such a limited view, they have "abdicated" their rightful function. If they, who are the students "par excellence of human values," do not take it upon themselves to analyze and discuss the larger ethical and political questions, who will do so? They are uniquely able to see things in broad perspective and have the tools to analyze basic concepts. When, instead, they deal with distant abstract questions, their rightful function will be taken over by others. Indirectly they may play into the hands of power groups or become unwitting pawns of the state. When one thinks that such concerns can be given over to the social scientists, one needs to be made aware that social scientists have "limited themselves to pure *description*. And to this extent, the whole realm of values as normative is quite beyond their ken."[40] While value inquiry is not simple, it is a job for philosophers. Though they may not propound precise answers, "is this," Schilpp asks, "a good reason for not pointing out directions and possible consequences to result from different courses of action?"[41] Even natural scientists have shown, collectively, more concern for man's plight since the atomic bomb than most philosophers. In 1954, Schilpp observed that "Einstein has become the conscience of mankind, albeit entirely unintentionally on his part," because he saw the dangers of totalitarianism and recognized that its appeal is "unfortunately not limited to the goosestepping German."[42] Moreover, a decade ago, Schilpp observed that three International Congresses of Philosophy had been held since the end of World War II. "Not one of the three has raised its collective voice on mankind's contemporary crises. Scientists, the Pope, and major church-bodies speak out—but never a peep seems to come from the world's 'lovers of wisdom'!"[43]

An overriding reason why philosophers should address themselves to the larger life issues is because we are in a period of crisis in human affairs. Instead, a high proportion of philosophers in the Western world have been engaging in essentially diversionary activities. Schilpp remarks: "Instead of playing its intended role of being the ethical conscience and rational guide of mankind in the hour of humanity's dire need, philosophy contents itself with linguistic hairsplitting and with the analysis of either ordinary or constructed language."[44] It is important to note, by the way, that Schilpp did not feel this way twenty-five years ago. At that time he expressed satisfaction with what some outstanding philosophers were doing, especially Dewey and Russell. Both raised their voices "in behalf of social, economic, political, and educational reform."[45]

There has never been anything personal in Schilpp's criticism of today's philosophers who seem to deal with irrelevancies. Who could be more unlike Paul Schilpp in personality and outlook than George Santayana? Yet Santayana, as he spent his last years in Italy, eagerly welcomed visits from Schilpp. And the latter remarked that we are far too close to this great man to pass judgment on him. At one of their last meetings, Schilpp did ask the aged thinker for his views on current questions. When queried about the use of atomic bombs, Santayana responded, "I do not judge. I think a nation has a right to do anything it may think necessary." Of their potential destructive effect, he said, "so is the eruption of Vesuvius a disaster."[46] If obligated to live in a totalitarian state, Santayana noted that he would write but not publish. To state such views is to throw Schilpp's own views, which are in direct antithesis, into sharper outline. It is doubtful if a man like Santayana would have ever challenged Schilpp's mode of philosophizing, but there are others who would and do.

Today's analytic philosophers, particularly of the language type, do not have the resilience of a Santayana, nor do they, unfortunately, have his light touch or his sense of humor. In place of maintaining a discreet silence when men like Schilpp prefer to spend their philosophical efforts on the larger questions of mankind, they seem to enjoy deciding what is "philosophically interesting" and who is really "doing" philosophy. Thus, J. L. Austin used to speak of the cackle and muddle of philosophers who sought solutions to difficult value questions. As his biographer Warnock put it, Austin regarded the quest for general conclusions on large issues "as little more than gossipy distractions from the serious business."[47] Doubtless others take that view too, but the thing that Schilpp would stress is that such analysts are also men and they are citizens of some nation. Are they unable to see perhaps that a philosopher ought to say something about naive national allegiances? A philosopher living in these times cannot dodge the larger issues any more than Socrates, Plato, Spinoza and Kant could in their times. "The philosopher cannot escape coming into conflict with the powers that be in almost any age."[48] Yet philosophers flocked to the colors of their respective nations during World War II with scarcely a whimper of criticism. Paul Schilpp, on the other hand, who had long cultivated a deep philosophical concern for the question of international peace saw through some of the machinations of heads of states, recognized the propaganda manipulation of the populace on both sides, and noted that the war was hardly begun or carried out for the sake of high principles.[49] Thus he opposed the war and things did not always go smoothly for him. He noted about war what Austin said one should watch out for in philosophy, namely "the wilder kinds of confusion, myth-mongering, and intellectual trickery." That war, as any modern war, produced far more problems than it ever solved. And the destruction of human lives by both sides was an abomination. That war made possible the annihilation of civilization should any future war occur. Schilpp could never take the view of Austin, who after World War II was over, told a friend that were he to become involved in another war, he would like to be employed in problems of supply.[50] For Schilpp, philosophical investigation should be able to give some guidance on such matters.

In all of his efforts to get philosophers to deal with issues of social significance, Schilpp does not in any way prescribe what their views should be, though from his own activities and writings it is not hard to see where he himself stands. He has trouble understanding what Borden P. Bowne used to call the "closet philosopher," one who lives as if his thought had nothing whatever to do with his life and whose life never drew upon the results of thought. For Schilpp, some of today's analytic philosophers become paradigm cases of philosophers who have denied their true vocation. With Walter Kaufmann, Schilpp would agree that every great philosophic work says that you must change your life, but in the case of some "the challenge to change one's life is not heeded, and a void remains—to be filled, unfortunately, without the benefit of philosophy."[51] Socrates thought differently. Though much intrigued with the clarification of concepts, he did not spend his time talking about sense data or other minds but rather about the meaning and use of important words. He did not refrain from governing his life by what he found to be so as a result of his analysis. Nor could Paul Schilpp ever assent to indulging himself in games of the privileged intellectual elite while the world moves towards chaos. Thus it was that in his vigorous Presidential Address in 1959, before the Western Division of the American Philosophical Association, he charged philosophers with abdicating their responsibility and heartily seconded the criticism of Bertrand Russell that "the new philosophy . . . seems to concern itself, not with the world and our relation to it, but only with the different ways in which silly people say silly things."[52]

But since that speech, things have changed among philosophers in the United States. The Vietnam War, the nonviolent struggles of Blacks for equality, student protests and even the movement of Women's Liberation, have begun to have their effects on philosophical activity. As never before, and only in the last four or five years, attention is being paid to the questions of civil disobedience, the obligations of the citizen to his government, conscientious objection, the validity of nonviolence, and such special problems as abortion and population control. Texts are being adapted to deal with these live issues from philosophical perspectives. And journals which devote themselves to such topics have begun to make their appearance within the last five years, and two in this new decade. One can mention *The Journal of Value Inquiry*, the *Journal of Social Philosophy*, *Telos*, and the quite new *Philosophy and Public Affairs*. Monographs and symposia on socially important themes treated from a philosophical perspective have likewise made their appearance. Professor Schilpp himself has contributed to one which includes essays by philosophers from seven nations, namely, *The Critique of War*, edited by Robert Ginsberg. And at long last philosophical associations in the United States have begun to make collective pronouncements on controversial issues. We are beginning to see that the message of Paul Schilpp to philosophers that they deal with live, socially relevant issues, is being fulfilled. And no one can be more pleased than Schilpp himself who has been virtually a lone voice for so long.

3. Schilpp's Own Contributions to the Discussion of Social Themes

We must now consider what Professor Schilpp has been saying and doing on matters of ethical and social importance to philosophers. We have noted before that he approaches problems and formulates his criticisms in the light of an ethical perspective which stresses the welfare of persons above all. We may here observe that Professor Schilpp is gifted with the ability to detect moral implications in certain political and social phenomena where others might overlook them. We can also note that he is uniquely sensitive to the role of social causality operating in human life, and finally, we can call to mind that he himself has actively participated in socially relevant causes in various ways.

Early in his professional life he evinced his skill at detecting issues of significant social impact. It is doubtful if many philosophers in the late 1920s saw as quickly some of the things that were happening. In 1929, he had the insight to see that the immigration laws of the United States relating to Japan were "inexcusable" and at the same time he warned about the views of the Ku Klux Klan which insisted "upon *Nordic Supremacy*" and a "doctrine and policy of race discrimination and antipathy." Similarly, he pointed out the easy tendency in those years to justify war. It is needless to remind ourselves that two of the factors that brought about World War II were the barriers against Japan and the Hitler doctrine of racial superiority. Schilpp was writing about these things when few were aware of the rise of Nazism and few saw the clouds of war on the horizon. In addition, he pointed out the reality of class distinctions in America, commenting that "our aristocracy of wealth is no less exclusive and proficiently forbidding than any aristocracy of blood or tradition."[53] Later he observed that the United States loses the benefits of skilled people because family finances determine education.[54] In 1944, he raised some serious questions about a proposal of the Chicago Superintendent of Schools to make High Schools move from a twenty percent to an eighty percent emphasis on vocational training. He viewed that as a weakening of the need for education in a democracy.[55]

Professor Schilpp has been an unrelenting critic of war, before, during and after wars. He was one of the few philosophers during World War II who knew indeed what had started the war, some of the political intrigues and manipulation that went on, the difference between the actual causes and the announced ones, and who maintained a persistent opposition to the method of the military in all nations while most intellectual leaders in warring nations silently went along with their governments, or, like Ralph Barton Perry of Harvard, became pamphleteers defending their own country's position. Had Schilpp been teaching in Germany at the time he would have suffered confinement in a concentration camp or something worse.

Like one of his mentors, Albert Schweitzer, he saw and sees the implications of nuclear warfare and nuclear testing and was an early opponent of both. He has persistently urged that constant preparation for war will lead to it. "And since we won the war 'to end all war', we have had nothing but wars! Yet have we learned our lesson. . . .What you prepare for sooner or later you are bound to get." And in a very cutting way he observed a few years ago, "So we have to spend 53 billions next year, in order to increase the number of times we can wipe out mankind."[56]

Through all of his social criticism one needs to be aware that a principle is operating. This becomes the dominant clue to the specific and sometimes disturbing moral judgments he makes. That principle is simply respect for the worth and dignity of the person. Thus he opposes communistic totalitarianism or any type of government "in which the individual is lost sight of" and which is "a violation of the fundamental dignity of man."[57] While this may sound like a commonly accepted policy of Western thinkers, we should bear in mind that Schilpp holds no special brief for any nation, his own included, when, in the name of the ideal of protecting the worth and dignity of persons, war is entered into which destroys persons of other countries. Schilpp is not soothed by the common "patriotic" argument that one can destroy an evil idea by engaging in the destruction of human beings. So-called defensive wars are instances of misplaced altruism. We favor killing some in order to prevent others from being killed. Wars destroy the very values that they allegedly are trying to preserve. If there is to be any kind of world community it cannot be based on violence but must be grounded on common understanding gained through communication and self-understanding, international law and the exercise of reason.

But there are no easy answers. Schilpp realizes that changes for the better come about in complex ways. It is not merely a matter of education or a change of attitude. He recognizes the factor of social causality—that forces of all sorts are at work molding lives and conditioning opinions. Even philosophical differences are affected by environmental pressures. In a recent essay he observed the extent of the grip of nationalism on people, saying: "The entire population in every existing independent state has been indoctrinated from kindergarten . . . with the absolute sacredness of the notion of sovereign nationhood."[58] And he is concerned with how such attitudes can be overcome. Ideas often seem powerless against social forces and are often significantly conditioned by them.

His awareness of social causality is pointedly set forth in his evaluation of the views of Albert Schweitzer. As we have noted, he shares Schweitzer's views on many things, but in the Nobel Peace Prize address in 1954, Schweitzer claims that peace among the nations is possible only as a result of a change of heart on the part of individuals. He said: "Only to the extent in which the peoples of the world foster within themselves the ideal of peace will those institutions whose object is the preservation of peace be able to function."[59] Now Schilpp does not hesitate to criticize this. He argues that it is illusory to think that peace depends on a change of attitude in millions of the world's peoples. A rule of law can be much more quickly established than a change of heart in the world's population. And while he would favor the latter, he admits he is not sanguine enough to believe that it could happen in sufficient time to avoid World War III. He argues that if a structure can be maintained by law *within* nations even though a majority of citizens have not had a change of heart, "it should be possible to achieve an international order in the relationships *among* nations" as well. Indeed, the achievement of world law is not beyond possibility "even in the most immediate future" partly because a rule of law has already been established in most civilized countries. The structure of a society through its laws can promote peace and justice more quickly and efficiently than a mass change in individual attitudes. Moreover, Schweitzer argued that the peoples of the world could do more to stop atomic testing than governments could. But Schilpp counters, asking whether public opinion "has any chance even to *form*, let alone express itself in opposition to governmental policy in a totalitarian regime?"[60]

Schilpp is far too versed in political and social understanding to have an easy optimism. Though not yielding to despair, he is not naive on the larger questions facing humankind. Accordingly, he rejects Teilhard de Chardin's view that some day in the natural course of evolution all mankind will be in harmonious unity. Human progress is neither automatic nor inevitable.[61]

His positive proposals for changing the directions which seem to be leading to chaos are, broadly speaking, twofold. The first is a concern for broad structure and organization and the second is to suggest ways in which individuals may promote such goals through education. In one of his recent articles, Professor Schilpp claims that the belief in national sovereignty is the root cause of disorder and chaos among nations, the primary source of warmaking. Noting that so-called international law is really nonexistent because "no national government will accept any law as being above its own laws" and that national self-interest dominates, Schilpp observes that treaties turn out to be little more than "scraps of paper." The idea of loyalty to the national state is not just the view of formal governments but is rooted in our minds since infancy. "It is the common populace to whom this doctrine is of all sacred cows the most sacred." The international anarchy which results from that view in our nuclear age really "amounts to treason against mankind."[62] Earlier on he wrote: "Internationalism is no longer one of the many alternatives: it is either that or annihilation."[63] To avoid the destruction of mankind by nuclear war and to achieve a world of order and law, it is imperative, just as Kant urged in 1784, that the relations of nations to and among each other "be regulated in orderly fashion by law superior to that of *any* national laws." While millions profess allegiance to the principle of universal brotherhood, when the choice is really presented, the majority prefer the national state even though it leads to anarchy and "the threat of annihilation." Accordingly, Schilpp recognizes that as long as nations maintain that they are laws unto themselves, international law is impossible. Thus he favors the extension of the United Nations and all moves that take mankind in the direction of international government. The impact of Kant on his thinking in these matters is unmistakable.

One reason that suspicion and tension occur among nations is that there are failures in communication. These failures are primarily failures of reason and of not having the proper view of what human beings truly are. While Schilpp surely believes that education will assist in overcoming such failures, that is only one factor. In one of his earliest theoretical articles on ethics, he writes:

> To interpret the other person's conduct from the point of view of my own momentarily governing engrossment makes real comprehension and understanding of the human conduct of one's 'neighbor' impossible and thus shuts men out from each other and from any possibility of ethically fruitful social intercourse.[64]

Communication must be kept open at all costs, not just on the individual level but among nations. It can be kept open because human beings are not mere machines who can be understood by some mathematical formula but have the capacity for "self-transcendence" which enables them to get outside of their own engrossments or their nation's selfish interests. He comments: "It is, moreover, an attitude of absolutism on the part of the non-self-transcending democrat as well as communist which closes each effectively off from the other."[65]

In support for his view that men and nations are capable of self-transcendence, Schilpp urges an elucidation of the doctrine of what a human being is in order to discover that in man which makes him truly human. To hold the view that man is a biological and quite meaningless accident, as some scientists do, is to betray the scientific attitude for it avers that there are no human facts beyond the experimental method. There are unique human traits that can be found by other means. Thus it can be pointed out that man has evolved a capacity for meanings because he is capable of abstract reflection, moral judgments and spiritual self-transcendence. One cannot explain away morality by reducing it to desire or a pleasure-pain principle because there "seems to run through the whole of humanity an almost uncanny and certainly never-ceasing tendency to pass moral judgments quite independent-

ly of one's own individual or momentary likes or dislikes." Furthermore, few
are ever quite satisfied with themselves or their status. Ideals and hopes
motivate and may even determine an actual deed in the present. Such
"aspirational self-transcendence" is one human capacity which makes social
relations among humans possible. "Rationally reflective, morally judging
and choosing, and spiritually self-transcending—man stands, in the unique
and only known union of these three distinctive characteristics, by himself."[66]

Instead, then, of just criticizing inhumanity and corrupt social institutions, Schilpp offers an affirmative outlook saying that human
brotherhood is indeed possible "insofar as men, individually as well as collectively learn to transcend their narrow-minded and provincial particularity by
achieving spiritual community of interest and endeavor." Thus he can conclude:

> I believe that—given today's atomic age and the possibility of completely
> destroying civilization on this planet . . .the application of goodwill *and* of
> rational intelligence to today's world situation requires the creation of world law,
> applicable to all human individuals and societies, under a world government.[67]

Thus the hope that Professor Schilpp offers mankind is a hope based on
the human potential. He never despairs of men for the future but worries
about men in the present. They are neither overwhelmingly bestial nor are
they divine. In his own life and teaching, one finds an energy and ebullience
which betrays any tendency toward melancholy or dejection. Paul Schilpp
has noted crises in human history for well over forty years and yet maintains
an active personal concern for justice and peace in his own country and the
world. The very first time I saw him was in 1939 at a student meeting during
my freshman year at our common alma mater, Baldwin-Wallace College. He
was energetically speaking about the basis for peace and how certain
diplomatic machinations were leading the United States into war. He urged
us to begin a door-to-door campaign to promote peace for he foresaw the
coming war.

While a scholar of a high order who early demonstrated his talents and
capabilities, he has always emphasized that one should live out his views in
the practical arena of society and politics. He has been directly active in the
cause of peace since he joined the Fellowship of Reconciliation in 1939. That
national pacifist organization honored him in its magazine, *Fellowship*, by
placing his portrait on the cover of the June, 1955, issue and citing some of his
peace activities. He has used his talents for broader causes not only in
philosophical discussions and at student gatherings, but has also participated
in formal radio debates and conferences aimed at practical solutions to

serious questions.[68] He has done some pamphleteering and has broadened his appeal by creative efforts at poetic expression. One of his powerful free verse poems is called "Lamentations on Christmas." It appeared in 1945 and was later set to music and performed in Chicago and Evanston. Later he wrote a free verse cantata entitled "Why See Ye the Living among the Dead?" This was performed for the first time in Evanston in April of 1955. And there are other things Professor Schilpp has done to implement in concrete ways the ideals and policies he has worked out philosophically.

William Ernest Hocking used to talk about the principle of alternation, that one should have periods of reflection and periods of action, that there should be some coherence between what one thinks and what one does, that reflection should entail commitment. Surely Paul Schilpp has through all of his professional life sought to practice this ideal. Never forsaking or ridiculing the lofty heights of contemplation and technical investigation, he has nevertheless felt obliged to take part in the world of decision and practical action. He has sought to wed thought and life and has tried to persuade others that this is the vocation of the true philosopher. He stands in the grand tradition. He still maintains a vigor and commitment which inspire those who know and honor him.

WARREN E. STEINKRAUS

STATE UNIVERSITY COLLEGE
OSWEGO, NEW YORK
APRIL, 1972

NOTES

[1] Paul A. Schilpp, "American Neglect of a Philosophy of Culture," *Philosophical Review,* **35** (1926), 434. Unless otherwise indicated all items cited in the following notes are products of Professor Schilpp's pen. When articles or books are referred to a second time or more, only titles will be given.

[2] Paul A. Schilpp, *Do We Need a New Religion?* (New York: Henry Holt, 1929), p. 318.

[3] Ibid., p. 320.

[4] Ibid., p. xiv.

[5] Paul A. Schilpp, *Human Nature and Progress* (Stockton, California: College of the Pacific, 1954), pp. 13 f. See also his more recent article, "Science, Theology and Ethical Religion," *Zygon,* **1** (June 1966), 186-90.

[6] *Human Nature and Progress,* p. 10.

[7] Paul A. Schilpp, "American Philosophy," *Philosophy,* **5** (1930), 277.

[8] *Human Nature and Progress,* pp. 16-19.

[9] Paul A. Schilpp, *The Crisis in Science and Education* (Tempe, Ariz.: College of Education, 1963), p. 33.

[10] Paul A. Schilpp, "Does Philosophy Have Anything to Say to Our Age?" *Bulletin of Atomic Scientists,* **15** (May 1959), 217.

[11] Paul A. Schilpp, "The Most Critical Failure of the American College," *in Higher Education Faces the Future,* ed. by P. A. Schilpp (New York: Liveright, 1930), pp. 207-30.

[12] *The Crisis in Science and Education,* pp. 22-26.

[13] Paul A. Schilpp, "Teaching: The Opening of Doors," *Saturday Review,* **41** (February 15, 1958), 16.

[14] *The Crisis in Science and Education,* p. 40.

[15] Ibid., p. 38.

[16] Albert Schweitzer, *Decay and Restoration of Civilization* (London: A. & C. Black, 1923), p. xi.

[17] "In Defense of Liberalism," *The Philosophical Forum,* **10** (Spring 1952), 4.

[18] Ibid., p. 9.

[19] "America's Neglect of a Philosophy of Culture," p. 444.

[20] Paul A. Schilpp, "Is Western Civilization Worth Saving?" in *Recent Gains in American Civilization,* ed. by Kirby Page (New York: Harcourt Brace & Co., 1928), pp. 305-25.

[21] *Do We Need a New Religion?* p. xiv.

[22] Paul A. Schilpp, "Max Scheler 1874-1928," *Philosophical Review,* **38** (1929), 547.

[23] This appeared in L. Bryson, L. Finklestein and R. Maciver, eds., *Learning and World Peace,* the 8th volume in a series published by the Conference on Science, Philosophy and Religion (New York: Harper & Brothers, 1948), pp. 300-310.

[24] *Human Nature and Progress,* p. 14.

[25] "Teaching: The Opening of Doors," p. 16.

[26] Paul A. Schilpp, "Schweitzer's Practical Moral Judgments and his Ethical Theory," in *In Albert Schweitzer's Realms,* ed. by A. A. Roback (Cambridge, Mass.: Sci-Art Publishers, 1962), pp. 229 f.

[27] Paul A. Schilpp, "Philosophy and the Social Crisis," in *The Anarchists,* ed. by Irving Horowitz (New York: Dell Publishing Co., 1964).

[28] Paul A. Schilpp, "National Sovereignty and International Anarchy," in *The Critique of War,* ed. by Robert Ginsberg (Chicago: Henry Regnery Co., 1969), p. 160.

[29] It is interesting to note that Professor Schilpp tried to arrange for a volume on Heidegger but was not able to get cooperation on it even after a special visit to the philosopher's home in Germany.

[30] "American Neglect of a Philosophy of Culture," p. 434.

[31] Paul A. Schilpp, "Philosophy as Criticism," *Social Science,* **19** (July 1944), 120.

[32] Ibid., p. 119.

[33] "American Philosophy," p. 277.

[34] "America's Neglect of a Philosophy of Culture," p. 444.

[35] "Philosophy as Criticism," p. 119.

[36] Paul A. Schilpp, "An 'Apology' for Philosophy," *Journal of Higher Education,* 6 (May 1935), 232.

[37] Paul A. Schilpp, "Is Standpointless Philosophy Possible?" *Philosophical Review,* 44 (1935), 239. See also Schilpp's related article, "The Nature of the Given," *Philosophy of Science,* 2 (1935).

[38] Ibid., p. 248.

[39] Ibid., p. 248. Nevertheless, Schilpp interestingly notes how Austrian fascists besmirched and assailed Schlick even after his assassination probably because he offered a critical analysis of social conditions ("Philosophy as Criticism," p. 122).

[40] Paul A. Schilpp, "The Abdication of Philosophy," *Proceedings of the American Philosophical Association,* 32 (1958-59), 34.

[41] Ibid., p. 37.

[42] Paul A. Schilpp, "A Great American's Credo," *Saturday Review,* 37 (December 11, 1954), 15.

[43] "The Abdication of Philosophy," p. 23.

[44] "Schweitzer's Practical Moral Judgments," p. 230.

[45] "Philosophy as Criticism," p. 124.

[46] "Roman Brahmin," *Saturday Review,* 35 (November 1, 1952), 36.

[47] G. J. Warnock, "J. L. Austin: A Biographical Sketch," in *Symposium on J. L. Austin,* ed. by K. T. Fann (London: Routledge & Kegan Paul, 1969), p. 17.

[48] *Human Nature and Progress,* p. 82.

[49] If one needs documentation for the correctness of Schilpp's early insight on the causes and intrigues of World War II, he would do well to consult J. M. Swomley's *American Empire* (New York: Macmillan Co., 1970), Chaps. 4-6.

[50] "No doubt," says Warnock, "the unlimited intricacies of the logistics of warfare tempted him as a new field to conquer, a new maze to be mastered," "J. L. Austin: A Biographical Sketch," p. 9.

[51] Walter Kaufmann, *Critique of Religion and Philosophy* (New York: Harper & Bros., 1958), p. 41.

[52] Quoted in "The Abdication of Philosophy," p. 32.

[53] *Do We Need a New Religion?,* p. 59. The quotations just above are from p. 62.

[54] *Crisis in Science and Education,* p. 14.

[55] "Philosophy as Criticism," p. 126 f.

[56] *Crisis in Science and Education,* p. 37 f. On p. 35 he writes: "The means chosen do help determine the end we get."

[57] *Human Nature and Progress,* p. 89.

[58] "Natural Sovereignty and International Anarchy," p. 159.

[59] Albert Schweitzer, *The Problem of Peace in the World Today* (London: A. & C. Black, 1954), p. 19.

[60] "Schweitzer's Practical Moral Judgments," p. 241 f.

[61] Paul A. Schilpp, "Toward a Super-conscious Tomorrow," *Saturday Review,* **47** (December 19, 1964), 32.

[62] All quotations in this paragraph except the next are taken from "National Sovereignty and International Anarchy," pp. 153-61.

[63] *Human Nature and Progress,* p. 80.

[64] Paul A. Schilpp, "On the Nature of the Ethical Problem," reprinted in his *Kant's Pre-Critical Ethics* (Evanston: Northwestern University Press, 1960), p. 181.

[65] *Human Nature and Progress,* p. 68.

[66] Ibid., p. 24. The previous quotations in this and the next paragraph are from this same source.

[67] "In Defense of Liberalism," p. 8.

[68] For example, note his report "Toward a Warless World" based on a conference he participated in chaired by Norman Thomas (*Christian Century,* **81** [February 12, 1964], 212-14).

BIBLIOGRAPHY

THE PUBLISHED WRITINGS OF PAUL ARTHUR SCHILPP

Compiled by
Niki Nimmo Van Ordstrand

DISSERTATION

"A Critical Analysis of Kant's Ethical Thought of the Precritical Period."
Ph. D. dissertation, Stanford University, 1936.

I. PUBLISHED BOOKS

Do We Need a New Religion? New York: Henry Holt, 1929.

Contemporary Morality. Stockton, Calif.: private printing, 1929. A course of
lectures.

Commemorative Essays: 1859-1929. Stockton, Calif.: private printing, 1930.
Evolution, Bergson, Husserl, Dewey. A course of lectures.

Kant's Pre-Critical Ethics. Evanston and Chicago: Northwestern University
Press, 1938, 1960, 1966. Spanish trans., Mexico City: Centro de
Estudios Filosóficos, Universidad Nacional Autónoma de México,
1966.

The Quest for Religious Realism. New York: Harper and Brothers, 1938.
Mendenhall Lectures, DePauw University, 1938.

Lamentations on Christmas. Evanston: private printing, 1945.

Human Nature and Progress. Stockton, Calif.: College of the Pacific
Philosophy Institute Publications, 1954. Tully Cleon Knoles Lectureship at the University of the Pacific.

The Crisis in Science and Education. Tempe, Ariz.: Arizona State University, 1963. Grady Gammage Memorial Lectureship at Arizona State University.

II. BOOKS EDITED AND CONTRIBUTED TO

A. *General*

"The Most Critical Failure of the American College." In *Higher Education Faces the Future*, edited by Paul Arthur Schilpp. New York: Liveright, 1930.

"The Need for a New Ethics." In *College of the Pacific Publications in Philosophy*, edited by Paul Arthur Schilpp. Vol. I. Stockton, Calif.: College of the Pacific, 1932.

"Goethe as Philosopher" and "Why Spinoza Still Speaks to Us." In *College of the Pacific Publications in Philosophy*, edited by Paul Arthur Schilpp. Vol. II. Stockton, Calif.: College of the Pacific, 1933.

"On the Possibilities and Limitations of Natural Science." In *College of the Pacific Publications in Philosophy*, edited by Paul Arthur Schilpp. Vol. III. Stockton, Calif.: College of the Pacific, 1934.

"The Meaning of Rational Faith." In *Theology and Modern Life*, Essays in Honor of Harris Franklin Rall, edited by Paul Arthur Schilpp. Chicago: Willett and Clark, 1940.

"The Nature of the Spiritual." In *A. R. Wadia: Essays in Philosophy Presented in His Honor*, edited by Sarvepalli Radhakrishnan et al. (including Paul Arthur Schilpp). Madras, India: G. S. Press, 1954.

B. *The Library of Living Philosophers*, edited by Paul Arthur Schilpp (since 1961 all volumes published by Open Court Publishing Company, La Salle, Illinois).

Vol. I. *The Philosophy of John Dewey*. Evanston and Chicago: Northwestern University, 1939; 2d ed., 1951. New printing, La Salle, Ill.: Open Court, 1971.

Vol. II. *The Philosophy of George Santayana*. Evanston and Chicago: Northwestern University, 1940; 2d ed., 1951. New printing, La Salle, Ill.: Open Court, 1971. Essay contributed: "Santayana on 'The Realm of Spirit'."

Vol. III. *The Philosophy of Alfred North Whitehead*. Evanston and Chicago: Northwestern University, 1941; 2d ed., 1951. New printing, La Salle, Ill.: Open Court, 1971. Essay contributed: "Whitehead's Moral Philosophy."

Vol. IV. *The Philosophy of G. E. Moore.* Evanston and Chicago: Northwestern University, 1942; 3d rev. ed., La Salle, Ill.: Open Court, 1968.

Vol. V. *The Philosophy of Bertrand Russell.* Evanston and Chicago: Northwestern University, 1944. 4th rev. ed., La Salle, Ill.: Open Court, 1971. Paperback in 2 vols.: Harper Torchbooks, 1963.

Vol. VI. *The Philosophy of Ernst Cassirer.* Evanston: The Library of Living Philosophers, Inc., 1949. German trans., Stuttgart, 1966.

Vol. VII. *Albert Einstein: Philosopher-Scientist.* Evanston: The Library of Living Philosophers, Inc., 1949; 3d rev. ed., La Salle, Ill.: Open Court, 1970. German trans., Stuttgart, 1955; Italian trans., Torino, 1958; Spanish trans., Santiago, Chile, forthcoming; Hungarian trans. (partial), Budapest, 1971. Paperback in 2 vols.: Harper Torchbooks, 1959.

Vol. VIII. *The Philosophy of Sarvepalli Radhakrishnan.* New York: Tudor Publishing Co., 1952.

Vol. IX. *The Philosophy of Karl Jaspers.* New York: Tudor Publishing Co., 1957. German trans., Stuttgart, 1957.

Vol. X. *The Philosophy of C. D. Broad.* New York: Tudor Publishing Co., 1959.

Vol. XI. *The Philosophy of Rudolf Carnap.* La Salle, Ill.: Open Court, 1963. Italian trans., forthcoming. Spanish trans., forthcoming.

Vol. XII. *The Philosophy of Martin Buber.* La Salle, Ill.: Open Court, 1967. German trans., Stuttgart, 1963; Japanese trans. (partial), Tokyo, 1970.

Vol. XIII. *The Philosophy of C. I. Lewis.* La Salle, Ill.: Open Court, 1968.

Vol. XIV. *The Philosophy of Karl Popper.* La Salle, Ill.: Open Court, 2 vols., 1974.

In preparation:

Vol. XV. *The Philosophy of Gabriel Marcel.*
Vol. XVI. *The Philosophy of Brand Blanshard.*
Vol. XVII. *The Philosophy of Georg Henrik von Wright.*
Vol. XVIII. *The Philosophy of W. V. Quine.*
Vol. XIX. *The Philosophy of Jean-Paul Sartre.*

III. INVITED ESSAYS CONTRIBUTED TO BOOKS

"Is Western Civilization Worth Saving?" In *Recent Gains in American Civilization*, edited by Kirby Page. New York: Harcourt, Brace and Co., 1928.

"Philosophy." In *Trends and Equilibria in Nature and Society*, edited by Oliver J. Lee. Private printing, 1944.

Articles on autonomy of the will; ethical formalism; ends; happiness; law; moral law; practical imperative; Scheler, Max; and will, the free elective. In *Dictionary of Philosophy*, edited by Dagobert D. Runes. New York: Philosophical Library, 1948.

"The Task of Philosophy in an Age of Crisis." In *Learning and World Peace*, 8th Symposium of the Conference on Science, Philosophy, and Religion, edited by Lyman Bryson, Louis Finkelstein, and R. M. MacIver. New York: Harper and Brothers, 1948.

"The Dialectic Process in Philosophy." In *Dr. Sarvepalli Radhakrishnan*, edited by Jagonnath Singh. Allahabad, India: The Leader Press, 1953.

Article on Albert Einstein. In *New Century Cyclopedia of Names*, edited by C. L. Barnhart. New York: Appleton-Century-Crofts, 1954.

Untitled essay. In *This is My Faith: The Convictions of Representative Americans Today*, edited by Stewart G. Cole. New York: Harper and Row, 1956.

Article on Albert Einstein. In *World Book Encyclopedia*. Chicago: Field Enterprises Education Corporation, 1958.

"The Place of Pleasure in the Good Life." In *The Student Seeks an Answer: Ingraham Lectures in Philosophy and Religion at Colby College 1951-1959*, edited by John A. Clark. Waterville, Maine: Colby College Press, 1960.

"Schweitzer's Practical Moral Judgments and His Ethical Theory." In *Albert Schweitzer's Realms*, edited by A. A. Roback. Cambridge, Mass.: Sci-Art Publishers, 1962.

"Philosophy." In *New Frontiers in Christianity*, edited by R. C. Raughlev, Jr. New York: Association Press, 1962. July, 1962, selection of the Religious Book Club.

"Radhakrishnan's Message." In *The Radhakrishnan Number*, edited by Ramaswami Aiyar et al. Madras-Hyderabad, India: Vyasa Publications, 1962.

"The Faith of John Dewey." In *Horizons of a Philosopher*, edited by Joseph Frank, Helmut Minkowski and Ernest J. Sternglass. Leiden, Holland: E. J. Brill, 1963. Festschrift in honor of David Baumgardt.

"On a Visit with the President of India." In *Dr. S. Radhakrishnan Souvenir Volume*, edited by J. P. Atreya. Moradabad, India: Darshana International, 1964.

"A Philosopher of Religion Ponders Science." In *Religion Ponders Science*, edited by Edwin P. Booth. New York: Appleton-Century-Crofts, 1964.

"Philosophy and the Social Crisis." In *The Anarchists*, edited by Irving L. Horowitz. New York: Dell, 1965.

"Bertrand Russell: The Philosophical Critic of Religion." In *The World of Philosophy*, edited by C. A. Qadir. Lahore, Pakistan: The Sharif Presentation Volume Committee, 1966. Festschrift in honor of M. M. Sharif.

"Ernst Cassirer." In *International Encyclopedia of the Social Sciences*, edited by David L. Sills. Vol. II. New York: Macmillan Co. and Free Press, 1968.

Article on Charles Sanders Peirce. In *Encyclopaedia Britannica*. Chicago: Encyclopaedia Britannica, Inc., 1966, and future editions.

"National Sovereignty and International Anarchy." In *The Critique of War*, edited by Robert Ginsberg. Chicago: Henry Regnery Co., 1969.

"Kant and the Problem of World Peace." In *Value and Valuation*, edited by John Davis. Knoxville, Tenn.: University of Tennessee Press, 1972. Festschrift in honor of Robert S. Hartman.

The Foreword to *Contemporary Indian Philosophy*, by Rama Shankar Srivastova. Delhi, India: Munshi Ram Monohar Lol, 1965.

"Albert Schweitzer: January 14, 1875-September 4, 1965." Essay contributed to a volume of essays in honor of Nobel Prize winners, submitted on invitation to Fratelli Fabbri Editori: Milano, Italy (1968), to be published in Italian. Forthcoming.

"Bertrand Russell: May 18, 1872-February 3, 1970." Essay contributed to a volume of essays in honor of Nobel Prize winners, submitted on invitation to Fratelli Fabbri Editori: Milano, Italy (1968), to be published in Italian. Forthcoming.

IV. SELECTED ARTICLES

"Give Us Men!" *Pacific Christian Advocate*, Portland, January, 1923.

"Can We Be Optimistic?" *Zion's Herald*, Boston, January 7, 1924.

"Thoughts on the Present Theological Controversy." *California Christian Advocate*, San Francisco, January 17, 1924.

"A Rational Basis Demanded for Faith." *Journal of Philosophy*, New York, April 10, 1924.

"Methodism and Militarism." *Zion's Herald*, Boston, July 30, 1924. Also in *California Christian Advocate*, San Francisco, August 14, 1924.

"Making World Citizens." *Sunday School Journal*, Cincinnati, December, 1924.

"Social Sciences Versus Social Science." Editorial in *Social Science*, Winfield, Kans., February-March-April, 1926.

"Scientists Accept the Moral Universe." *Stockton Daily Independent*, Stockton, Calif., March 7-14, 1926. Also published privately.

"The Revolt of Youth." *Zion's Herald*, Boston, July 21, 1926.

"Certainty in Religion." *The Methodist Review*, New York, July, 1926.

"American Neglect of a Philosophy of Culture." *Philosophical Review*, Ithaca, N. Y., September, 1926.

"Rudolf Eucken—Idealist Thinker and Scholar." *Stockton Daily Independent*, Stockton, Calif., September 20, 1926.

"Do We Need a New Religion?" *Social Science*, Winfield, Kans., February-March-April, 1927.

"The 'Formal Problems' of Scheler's Sociology of Knowledge." *Philosophical Review*, Ithaca, N. Y., March, 1927.

"Why Seek Ye the Living Among the Dead?" *California Christian Advocate*, San Francisco, August, 1927.

"The Philosophic Basis of All Social and Economic Theories." *Social Science*, Winfield, Kans., August, 1927.

"Is the Professor Blameless?" *School and Society*, New York, November 5, 1927.

"The Doctrine of 'Illusion' and 'Error' in Scheler's Phenomenology." *Journal of Philosophy*, New York, November 10, 1927.

"Is Social 'Science' Possible?" *Social Science*, Winfield, Kans., February-March-April, 1928.

"Salvaging Western Civilization." *The World Tomorrow*, New York, September, 1928.

"Zur Amerikanischen Litteratur der Gegenwart." *Die Zeitwende*, Munich, Germany, January, 1929.

"What Price Culture?" *Social Science*, Winfield, Kans., May-June-July, 1929.

"Aspects of Permanent Value in the Coherence View of Truth." *Personalist*, Los Angeles, July, 1929.

"Max Scheler, 1874-1928." *Philosophical Review*, Ithaca, N. Y. November, 1929.

"The Subjectivism of the Neo-Pragmatic Theory of Knowledge." *Monist*, La Salle, Ill., April, 1930.

"American Philosophy." *Journal of Philosophical Studies*, London, April, 1930.

"Einstein on the Relations Between Science, Morality, and Religion." *The Christian Advocate*, New York, August 7, 1930.

"Can America Ever Become Cultured?" *Social Science*, Winfield, Kans., January, 1931.

"Toward Scientific Humanism." *Methodist Review*, New York, March, 1931.

"Guaranty For The Future." *Journal of Higher Education*, Columbus, Ohio, March, 1931.

"Spiritual Religion." *The Christian Century*, Chicago, October 28, 1931.

"The 'Tyranny' of Reason." *The Modern Thinker*, New York, April, 1932.

"The Social Scientist: The Man of the Hour." *Social Science*, Winfield, Kans., January, 1933.

"Present Problems and Mr. Whitehead." *The New Humanist*, Chicago, December, 1934.

"The Nature of the 'Given'." *Philosophy of Science*, Los Angeles, April, 1935.

"An 'Apology' for Philosophy: The Place of Philosophy in the Liberal Arts Curriculum." *Journal of Higher Education*, Columbus, Ohio, May, 1935.

"Is 'Standpointless Philosophy' Possible?" *Philosophical Review*, Ithaca, N. Y., May, 1935.

"Can God Be 'Known'?" *The Personalist*, Los Angeles, Summer, 1935.

"The Paradox of Certainty." *Philosophical Review*, Ithaca, N. Y., September, 1935.

"On the Nature of the Ethical Problem." *International Journal of Ethics*, Chicago, October, 1936.

"Are We Doing Enough?" *Northwestern University Alumni News*, Evanston, Ill., November, 1937.

"John Dewey: America's Citizen Number One." *Educational Trends*, Evanston, Ill., November-December, 1939.

"Parents Look at the New School." *Educational Trends*, Evanston, Ill., March-April, 1940.

"Are There Absolute and Universal Principles on which Education Should Be Founded?" *Educational Trends*, Evanston, Ill., July-August, 1941. Negative part of a public debate with Mortimer Adler.

"The Division of Social Sciences: Closed for the Duration." *Northwestern University Alumni News*, Evanston, Ill., January, 1943.

"Shall We Lose the Peace?" *Motive*, Nashville, Tenn., February, 1943.

"Philosophy as Criticism." *Social Science*, Winfield, Kans., July, 1944.

"In Defense of Socrates' Judges." *Enquiry*, Chicago, Fall, 1944.

"Is Another World War Inevitable?" *March of Progress Magazine*, New York, May, 1946.

"Does World Government Need to Wait for World Community?" *Motive*, Nashville, Tenn., May, 1947.

"Millions Now Living Will Die—Unless. . . ." *Motive*, Nashville, Tenn., March, 1948.

"A Challenge to Philosophers in the Atomic Age." *Proceedings of the Xth International Congress of Philosophy*, Amsterdam, 1948.

"Has the Church a Message for Today's Atomic Age?" *Zion's Herald*, Boston, April 21, 1948.

"How Will the North Atlantic Pact Affect Us?" *Northwestern University Reviewing Stand*, Evanston, Ill., July 17, 1949.

"Goethe as Philosopher." *Al-Hikmat Journal of Philosophy* (a research journal of the Department of Philosophy, University of Panjab, Lahore), J-22 printed at Panjab University Press, 1967; also *The Humanist Way*, Calcutta, India, **4,** No. 3 (1949-50).

"The Fate of Mankind." *The New Lanka: A Review Quarterly*, Colombo, Ceylon, July, 1951.

"In Defense of Liberalism." *The Philosophical Forum*, Boston, Spring, 1952.

"The Distinctive Function of 'Philosophy of Education' as a Discipline." *Educational Theory*, Urbana, Ill., July, 1953.

"Pre-Suppositions of Democracy as a Basis for East-West Rapprochement." *Proceedings of the XIth International Congress of Philosophy*, Brussels, 1953.

"Germany's Experiment in Democracy." *Motive*, Nashville, Tenn., January, 1954.

"The Need for Human Understanding." *Bulletin of the Ramakrishna Mission*, Calcutta, India, September, 1954.

"Are Unitarians Christians?" *Christian Register*, Boston, February, 1956.

"Nature and Purpose." In *Proceedings of the Third Session of the Pakistan Philosophical Congress*, edited by Saadat Alikhan and Bashir Ahamd Dar. Lahore, Pakistan: Pakistan Philosophical Congress, 1956.

"A Non-positivistic Western Philosopher Looks at Logical Positivism." In *Proceedings of the Third Session of the Pakistan Philosophical Congress*, edited by Saadat Alikhan and Bashir Ahamd Dar. Lahore, Pakistan: Pakistan Philosophical Congress, 1956.

"Are 'Neutralists' Against U. S.?" *Headline Series Foreign Policy Association—Decisions . . . 1957*, Foreign Policy Association, New York City. No. 121, 1957.

"Summary." Special supplement of the *Chicago Daily News*, "The Challenge of Russia," November 16, 1957.

On Teaching: ". . . The Opening of Doors." *Saturday Review*, February 15, 1958. Excerpt also printed in *The Wiley Bulletin*, Spring, 1958.

"Is the Teacher a Tool?" Special Education Issue of *Saturday Review*, February 15, 1958.

"Gandhi—Ten Years After." *Chicago Sun Times*, special feature section, February 16, 1958.

"This I Believe." *Unity*, Chicago, March-April, 1958.

"What is Progress?" *Chicago Sun Times*, December 7, 1958.

"Does Philosophy Have Anything to Say to Our (Atomic) Age?" *Bulletin of the Atomic Scientists*, May, 1959; also in *Proceedings of the XIIth International Congress of Philosophy*, Florence, Italy, 1961.

"The Abdication of Philosophy." Presidential Address, The American Philosophical Association (Western Division), published in:
  a. Proceedings and Addresses of the American Philosophical Association, October, 1959.
  b. Kant-Studien, Germany, **51**, No. 4 (1959-60).
  c. Texas Quarterly, Austin, Tex., **3**, No. 2 (Summer, 1960).

"The Impact of John Dewey's Philosophy on American Education." *Chicago Review*, Spring, 1960.

"The Pick of the Paperbacks in Philosophy and Religion." *Chicago Sunday Sun Times* Book Section, September, 1960.

"Alfred North Whitehead: 1861-1947." *Christian Century*, Chicago, February 15, 1961.

"Toynbee is Right!" Reply to Dr. Arnold Toynbee's article in "Dignitaries" section of the *Chicago Sunday Sun Times*, February 12, 1961.

"The Most Profound Question in the World: What is Man?" *Proceedings of the XIIIth International Congress of Philosophy*, Vol. II, Mexico City, 1963.

"The World in Conflict." *Northwestern University Alumni News*, Evanston, Ill., October, 1963.

"Are Colleges Obsolete?" *Daily Egyptian*, Carbondale, Ill., May 25, 1966.

"Science, Theology, and Ethical Religion." *Zygon, Journal of Religion and Science*, Chicago, June, 1966.

"Dewey on Education—Appraisals." A critical review and discussion of Reginald D. Archanbault's book by this title. *Studies in Philosophy and Education*, Edwardsville and Carbondale, Ill., Winter, 1966-67.

"Ethical Implications of the Space Age." Privately published by Wartburg College, Waverly, Iowa, February 16, 1967.

"Is Man Without Moorings?" *Religious Humanism*, Yellow Springs, Ohio,

Part I, Summer, 1967; Part II, Autumn, 1967.

"Bertrand Russell Was Always Searching." *Daily Egyptian*, Carbondale, Ill., March 7, 1970.

"Friend Einstein Remembered." *Daily Egyptian*, Carbondale, Ill., April 25, 1970.

"Are 1 1/2 Children Enough?" *Daily Egyptian*, Carbondale, Ill., October 10, 1970.

"True Respect for the Individual Human Person." *Daily Egyptian*, Carbondale, Ill., March 6, 1971.

"Some Recollections of Bertrand Russell, 1872-1970." *Journal of Thought*, Norman, Okla., April, 1971.

"Albert Einstein: Saintly Scientist." *Mountain-Plains Quarterly*, Wichita, Kans., July, 1972.

"Is Religious Humanism Enough?" *Religious Humanism*, Los Angeles, Autumn, 1972.

"Albert Einstein—Grösse eines Menschen und Denkers," *Universitas*, Stuttgart, Germany, April 1973; also in *Darmstädter Blätter*, Darmstadt, Germany, November, 1973.

"Can We Afford to Give Man Least Priority?" In *Proceedings of the XVth International Congress of Philosophy,* Varna, Bulgaria, 1973; Vol. I, pp. 223-25.

V. SELECTED BOOK REVIEWS

The Social Theory of Georg Simmel by N. J. Spykman. *Social Science*, Winfield, Kans., May, 1926.

The Moral Standards of Democracy by H. W. Wright. *Social Science*, Winfield, Kans., May, 1926.

Problems of Conduct by D. Drake. *Social Science*, Winfield, Kans., May, 1926.

The Making of the Modern Mind by J. H. Randall. *Social Science*, Winfield, Kans., August, 1926.

The New Age of Faith by J. Langdon-Davies. *Social Science*, Winfield, Kans., November, 1926.

What I Believe by Bertrand Russell. *Social Science*, Winfield, Kans., February, 1927.

The Meaning of God by H. F. Rall. *Social Science*, Winfield, Kans., February, 1927.

The Dilemma of the Liberated by Gorham Munson. *Saturday Review*, New York, 1930.

Hegel (Part II of *Die Philosophie des deutschen Idealismus*) by Nikolai Hartmann. *Books Abroad*, Norman, Okla., 1930.

Denkformen by Hans Leisegang. *Books Abroad*, Norman, Okla., April, 1930.

The Philosophy of the Act by George Herbert Mead. *The Christian Century*, Chicago, August 3, 1938.

Rousseau—Kant—Goethe by Ernst Cassirer. *The Christian Century*, Chicago, September 5, 1945.

Let's Talk About the Peace by Henry G. Alsberg. "A World State—Quick!" *The Christian Century*, Chicago, February, 1946.

Einstein: His Life and Times by Philipp Frank. *The Chicago Jewish Forum*, Fall, 1947.

The Works of the Mind by R. B. Heywood. *The Chicago Jewish Forum*, Spring, 1948.

Recovery of Faith by Sarvepalli Radhakrishnan. *Saturday Review*, July 30, 1955.

Albert Schweitzer: The Story of His Life by Jean Pierhal. *Saturday Review*, September 28, 1957.

Man's Western Quest by Denis de Rougemont. *Saturday Review*, April 20, 1957.

A Source Book in Indian Philosophy by Sarvepalli Radhakrishnan and Charles A. Moore. *Saturday Review*, May 11, 1957.

Kants Weltanschauung by Richard Kroner. *Journal of Philosophy*, New York, July 18, 1957.

Jawarharlal Nehru by Frank Moraes. *Chicago Jewish Forum*, Summer, 1957.

Can People Learn to Learn? by Brock Chisholm. "Re-Educate or Perish," *The New York Times Sunday Book Review* section, April 27, 1958.

The Sleepwalkers: A History of Man's Changing Vision of the Universe by Arthur Koestler. Chicago Tribune, May 31, 1959.

Philosophy in a Time of Crisis by A. Koch. *Saturday Review*, February 20, 1960.

Bertrand Russell Speaks His Mind by Bertrand Russell. *New York Times Sunday Book Review* section, May, 1960.

Albert Schweitzer of Lambarene by Norman Cousins. *New York Times Sunday Book Review* section, July 10, 1960.

The Phenomenon of Man by P. Teilhard de Chardin. *Chicago Review*, Spring, 1960.

The Future of Mankind by Karl Jaspers. *Chicago Sunday Tribune Magazine of Books* section, January 29, 1961.

What is Philosophy by Jose Ortega y Gasset. *Chicago Tribune Sunday Magazine of Books*, April 30, 1961.

The Great Philosophers by Karl Jaspers. *Chicago Sunday Tribune Magazine of Books*, April 15, 1962.

The Broken Image by Floyd W. Matson. *Chicago Daily News*, Summer, 1964.

The Future of Man by P. Teilhard de Chardin. *Saturday Review*, December 19, 1964.

The Second Session by Xavier Rynne. *Chicago Daily News*, August, 1964.

The Way of Response: Martin Buber by Nahum N. Glatzer. *St. Louis Post Dispatch*, December 4, 1966.

Gandhi's Emissary by Sudhir Ghosh. *St. Louis Post Dispatch*, September 21, 1967.

Philosophical Correspondence: 1759-1799 by Immanuel Kant, translated by Arnulf Zweig. *Saturday Review*, August 5, 1967.

Philosophical Faith and Revelation by Karl Jaspers. *The Christian Century*, Chicago, November 27, 1967.

Illustrious Immigrants—The Intellectual Migration from Europe 1930-1941 by Laura Fermi. *Daily Egyptian*, Carbondale, Ill., April 6, 1968.

Right and Wrong—A Philosophical Dialogue Between Father and Son by Paul Weiss and J. Weiss. *Daily Egyptian*, Carbondale, Ill., May 4, 1968.

The First Freedom by Bryce W. Rucker. *The Christian Century*, Chicago, December 4, 1968.

Bertrand Russell's Theory of Knowledge by Elizabeth Eames. *Daily Egyptian*, Carbondale, Ill., March 1, 1969.

The General Will by Lotar Zahradka. *Daily Egyptian*, Carbondale, Ill., May 24, 1969.

The Insecurity of Nations by Charles Yost. "Pros and Cons of the United Nations," *Daily Egyptian*, Carbondale, Ill., October 18, 1969.

INDEX